# LEARNING TO LEAD AND MANAGE INFORMATION LITERACY INSTRUCTION

ESTHER S. GRASSIAN AND JOAN R. KAPLOWITZ

NEAL-SCHUMAN PUBLISHERS, INC.
NEW YORK    LONDON

*Information Literary Sourcebooks*
1. Information Literary Instruction: Theory and Practice
2. Learning to Lead and Manage Information Literary Instruction

Published by Neal-Schuman Publishers, Inc.
100 William Street, Suite 2004
New York, NY 10038

Printed and bound in the United States of America.

The paper used in this publication meets the minimum requirements of American National Standard for Information Sciences—Permanence of Paper for Printed Library Materials, ANSI Z39.48–1992. ∞

### Library of Congress Cataloging-in-Publication Data

Grassian, Esther S.
 Learning to lead and manage information literacy instruction / Esther
S. Grassian, Joan R. Kaplowitz.
  p. cm. — (Information literacy sourcebooks ; no. 2)
 Includes bibliographical references and index.
 ISBN 1-55570-515-4 (alk. paper)
  1. Library orientation—Planning.   2. Information literacy—Study and teaching.
3. Communication in library administration.   4. Leadership.   5. Information
literacy—Research.   6. Proposal writing in library science.   7. Libraries—Marketing.
8. Educational technology.   I. Kaplowitz, Joan R.   II. Title.   III. Series.
 Z711.2.G75 2005
 028.7'068—dc22                                                          2005009356

I dedicate my portions of this book to those exceptional leaders and managers who respect, cherish, and humbly give credit to the intelligence, creativity, experience, and knowledge of others, both those above and those below them. As Dwight D. Eisenhower put it, "You do not lead by hitting people over the head—that's assault, not leadership."

E. G.

This book is dedicated to information literacy pioneers everywhere. Because of your vision, your courage, your passion, and your leadership, information literacy continues to grow and prosper as a force in our profession. And as it does people everywhere become more effective, efficient, and responsible consumers of information, and are empowered to develop the skills that make them life-long learners.

J. K.

# Contents

# List of Figures

# Foreword

You can do it! You can make a difference.

This is the perfect time to be an information literacy manager and leader—to forge partnerships across the campus with faculty from various disciplines, to become a strong campus leader, advocating the importance of integrating information literacy principles throughout the curriculum, for exercising vision and creativity in the development and delivery of instructional programs that enhance, enrich, and improve student learning; increase academic achievement; and contribute persistence toward a degree.

You matter. Whatever your title or level in the organization may be, your ideas, knowledge, energy, expertise, and enthusiasm translate into results-oriented action—and *Learning to Lead and Manage Information Literacy Instruction* will empower you to accomplish your goals.

The authors, seasoned professionals, are experts. They help you become an effective leader by translating your vision into tangible, strategic outcomes. They provide examples of effective practices to help you promote, foster, and create integrative learning environments on the campus, while supporting information literacy principles and programs. As Bennis and Townsend tell us, "vision grabs" (Bennis and Townsend 1995, 45), and you'll learn how to make this happen within your own organizational culture.

Leaders and managers can be found at all levels in the organization—they are the listeners, the curious ones, the passionate ones, making "people" connections to carry out their plans, aligning information literacy goals with strategic initiatives of the larger institution, cultivating trust, building support, managing and achieving change, and educating and mentoring others along the way.

Kenneth Shaw states in *The Successful President* that "leaders are the institution's conscience" (Shaw 1999, p. 11). You can be that person in meetings, reminding everyone about your institution's core values related to teaching and learning and the role that information literacy can contribute to the intellectual growth of students. Emphasize and repeat these words often to various constituencies, stakeholders, partners, and potential opponents (who will become allies with time). Sustainable leadership can lead to meaningful results and long-term change.

Effective leaders deliver results by using their skills and abilities to influence others, motivate and build high-performance teams, break down individual and organizational barriers, stimulate and promote innovation, and gain loyalty. Lead through collaboration and show the impact of your work in preparing students to work in an information-rich, globally connected, multicultural society.

Align information literacy goals with institutional strategic initiatives and action agendas. If distance learning is a priority, show faculty how to integrate information literacy Web-based modules and tutorials, electronic resources (e.g., e-books, e-course reserve readings, e-pathfinders, full-text journal articles, quality Internet resources, Webliographies), and self-paced learning materials into course management systems to help students gain necessary skills in search strategy development, critical thinking, problem solving, and information evaluation. Brand your pages so users will know that they come from the library. Set up e-alerts so users can receive tables of contents from journals of their choice and keep current in their field even when they are away from the traditional library. All of this demonstrates how the library anticipates user needs, engages students in their own learning, promotes a positive image, and demonstrates an ethic of service.

If campus computer labs are to be reconfigured and reconceptualized as interactive cross-disciplinary learning commons, provide leadership to the planning process. Help to redesign the physical facilities, the Web pages, and the training programs for staff and student assistants and explain how information literacy plays an important role in collaborative learning outside the classroom. Don't remain library-centric; become learner-centered. Find ways to coordinate the library with other institutional goals and priorities to show how your services can be customized to support and anticipate changing campus information needs.

If your campus emphasizes electronic portfolios, help faculty assess student retention of information literacy skills. Prove how scoring rubrics and other tools can be used to evaluate the portfolios so that students will meet information literacy standards. If service learning and civic education are priorities, illustrate how students benefit from using their research skills within the real world of their communities to solve problems, communicate ideas, and help others.

If your campus promotes residential learning communities, these settings are perfect vehicles for outreach activities to anticipate student research needs. Market "Ask a Librarian" and other research services in advance and collaborate with the residential advisers to get the word out. Exceed expectations and reduce constraints to become more responsive to users. Within this context, provide opportunities for individuals to develop intellectually, personally, and professionally by developing and increasing their information literacy skills and abilities. If outcomes-based assessment is one of the institution's strategic goals, show how you can contribute by integrating information literacy into the general education program, freshman-year activities, courses in the major, graduate, and professional programs, or capstone experiences. Suggest strategies for assessing these skills and show how they fit into an institution's overall assessment plan.

Conduct research studies and contribute to the knowledge base of higher education. Follow the publications of higher education research institutes and think tanks, such as the National Center for Postsecondary Improvement, and show how information literacy can play an important role. Share the work of the Partnership for 21st Century Skills, which suggests that "today's education system faces irrelevance unless we bridge the gap between how students live and how they learn" (*Learning for the 21st Century* 2003, p. 4). Reveal how information literacy bridges that gap.

Don Riggs tells us that "transformational leaders have to be excellent strategists, strong planners, synthesizers, change agents, and visionaries" (Riggs 1997, pp. 3–8). *Learning to Lead and Manage Information Literacy Instruction* helps you to achieve all of these goals and more. It provides detailed guidance and wise counsel. The authors are generous in sharing their insights and experiences with us, and we are all the richer for it.

Ilene F. Rockman, Ph.D.
Manager, Information Competence Initiative
The California State University, Office of the Chancellor
Long Beach, California

## REFERENCES

Bennis, Warren, and Robert Townsend. 1995. *Reinventing Leadership: Strategies to Empower the Organization*. New York: Morrow.

*Learning for the 21st Century*. 2003. Washington, DC: Partnership for 21st Century Skills, p. 4.

National Center for Postsecondary Improvement. October 2002. *Beyond Dead Reckoning: Research Priorities for Redirecting American Higher Education*. Stanford, CA: Stanford University, http://www.stanford.edu/group/ncpi/ [18 July 2005].

Riggs, Donald E. January 1997. "What's in Store for Academic Libraries? Leadership and Management Issues." *The Journal of Academic Librarianship* 23(1): 3–8.

Shaw, Kenneth A. 1999. *The Successful President: "Buzzwords" on Leadership*. Phoenix, AZ: American Council on Education/Oryx Press, p. 11.

# Preface

Leadership is a tricky business. You can be a leader where you work or a leader in an organization like a professional association. Management can be difficult as well. You can manage an organization or manage people or groups in a work environment. Yet, good managers are not necessarily effective leaders, and good leaders may or may not be effective managers. Rarely does one person combine both roles effectively.

Can you learn to be a leader? Can you learn to be a manager?

*Learning to Lead and Manage Information Literacy Instruction* helps answer these questions as they relate to information literacy instruction (ILI). We wrote this book for librarians who already have some experience with ILI but want to enhance and expand their knowledge and skills while also becoming change agents within and outside their own spheres. We hope it will be a source of new ideas and approaches for experienced professionals at various levels as well. *Learning to Lead and Manage Information Literacy Instruction* includes background theory, practical examples, strategies, hints and tips, sample materials, exercises, and checklists as well as a bibliography of further readings.

In Chapter 1, "Developing the Leader within You," we discuss the traits, skills, abilities, beliefs, and characteristics that make an individual stand out. Whenever a person takes a stand, expresses an opinion, and in some way tries to make a difference—regardless of job title—that person takes on a leadership role.

In Chapter 2, "Managing through Communication, Collaboration, and Team Building," we explain what it means to manage and what is necessary to do it effectively in the unique environment of information literacy instruction.

Chapter 3, "Embracing Cooperation and Change," delves into networking and change management and then tackles the often ticklish issues of working with colleagues, teaching faculty, administrators, and computer trainers, within and outside the library. Here we describe creative problem-solving techniques as a means of focusing attention on issues, rather than on individuals. We also discuss research into attitudes toward ILI among these constituencies and practical means of transforming negative attitudes into positive ones.

Chapter 4, "Fostering Growth in Yourself and Others," explores a variety of issues all related to keeping yourself, your colleagues, and your staff fresh and energized. We examine coaching and mentoring, developing yourself through teacher appraisal, and stress, burnout, and renewal.

In Chapter 5, "Adding to the Knowledge Base through Research," we focus on the importance of research in keeping a discipline robust and moving forward. We explain how to get ideas, the steps of the research process, ethical considerations, and other potential pitfalls to watch for as you plan your study.

Tight budgets and short staffing may mean long delays in assessing the effectiveness of existing IL (Information Literacy) programs and in revising them accordingly. In Chapter 6, "Grant Writing and Grants," we describe the history and growing significance of special funding for library-related projects and how this funding can serve to support research, innovation, and risk-taking projects. Just developing a proposal can be quite costly, but it may be the only way to tackle a large and complex problem when existing budgets cannot support the time or additional staff. In this chapter, we describe various types of grants as well as the costs and benefits of acquiring funding. We also provide practical tips and techniques for identifying and applying for ILI-related grants in various environments.

A perfectly planned and developed instructional program is useless without learners. In Chapter 7, "Marketing, Publicity, and Promotion," we cover both theory and practical, proactive strategies for getting attention. We draw from business world models and findings, as well as a rich variety of research studies, to help you learn effective methods for drawing attention to IL and its relating the short- and long-term benefits of ILI in various environments and for a variety of learners.

Where do many people turn first when they need information? The Internet, of course! Google, Yahoo!, and other general search engines make it all seem so easy, and there is little hint of the fact that free public search tools like these do not list all information. Google Scholar muddies the issue further, as news reports about it may provide only partial information and may give the impression that anyone can get free complete copies of all digitized information online. What do technological developments like this mean for ILI and for ILI librarians? Information literacy and information technology (IT) have become so entwined that some degree of proficiency in both is now essential for an information-literate society. So, in addition to keeping on top of traditional research tools and other resources, librarians must now continually learn and make good use of IT-related skills. In Chapter 8, "Learning to Manage Technology," we focus on the fundamentals of this increasingly complex, time-consuming, and critical task. Here we cover issues such as hardware and software for ILI, preparing technology-related upgrade proposals, training staff, instructional partnerships, technostress and technoaddiction, and the learning and teaching aspects of continual training and retraining.

Each chapter lists key points covered and includes exercises, as well as a "Read More about It" section. A complete bibliography follows the last chapter. The companion CD-ROM contains a copy of the entire bibliography, with live links to Web sites for easy searching or browsing. The CD-ROM also includes many other sample materials that will help you apply the information presented in the book chapters. (Please see "What's on the CD-ROM?" page xix, for a complete description.)

Keep up, keep up, get ahead, faster, faster! These are the pressures confronting ILI librarians today and for the foreseeable future. We teach users to be nimble and apply the concepts they learn as they face new research tools and sources. We, as professionals, must be even more nimble and resourceful as we face constant, unending change in interfaces, ever-increasing numbers of research tools, more and newer versions of hardware and their uses, and in teaching and learning.

Stop and take a deep, slow breath. We hope *Learning to Lead and Manage Information Literacy Instruction* helps you feel more confident and informed about your options and more successful in your management and leadership, regardless of your position.

# Acknowledgments

## ESTHER S. GRASSIAN

As I drowned myself in work over yet another book, I have so much appreciated the support and love of my two wonderful sons, David and Daniel, and the man I love, Howard Cowan, that wonderful renaissance man, fabulous cook, incredible gardener, and science lab teacher. How many incredibly great dinners have you invented and cooked for us, and how many countless times have you saved me with a hug and an "I love you"? I am so grateful, too, for the love and support of my dear friends, especially Mimi Dudley, Isabel Stirling, Bob Rose, and Michael Oppenheim, all of whom have helped me in difficult times, with their kind words and good deeds.

I also very much appreciate Trudi Jacobson's very helpful review of our entire manuscript and Michael Oppenheim's close reading and many extremely helpful and detailed suggestions regarding four of our book chapters.

Now, the following will probably seem quaint to you if you read this in five, ten, or more years, but I am also particularly grateful for all sorts of swiftly advancing technology: a cable modem, a fast PowerBook G4, the transitional technology of zip disks, and tiny new flash drives with what seem like huge storage capacity—1 GB! I also continue to be grateful for e-mail and for the wonderful/terrible, terribly exciting Web. Just since our last book was published, we have gone from FedExing paper manuscripts to Neal-Schuman to e-mailing electronic copies of them. And, the Web, the Web—it just continues to grow and impact all of our lives in such amazing ways! I appreciate so much having it at my fingertips, tapping into such rich creativity, worldwide, while trying hard to keep a skeptical, questioning eye on it all. It's been quite a ride, and it is not over yet!

JOAN R. KAPLOWITZ

I would like to thank all the people in my life, both professional and personal, who expressed their belief in my views on leadership and management and who encouraged me to share these ideas through the writing of this book. A special thanks goes out to the members of the American Library Association's (ALA) New Members Round Table (NMRT). I spent ten wonderful years in that group as a young professional. NMRT takes leadership development seriously, and its members model, nurture, and encourage the characteristics, behaviors, and values that make leadership possible. My interest in, and ideas about, leadership and management were planted in those early NMRT years.

I would also like to thank my family (Hillary and Greg), and all my friends and colleagues, who once again listened, commented, critiqued, and generally served as cheerleaders through the long and arduous process of birthing this book. Thanks, too, to Barnabus, Josette, and Zen, whose purring acted as a soothing backdrop to the scratching of my pen and the clicking of the computer keys.

Finally thanks to all the students and colleagues with whom I have interacted and mentored via my experiences both in ALA and at the University of California, Los Angeles (UCLA). As in all the best mentoring experiences, I profited as much by these encounters as hopefully they did. The enthusiasm, excitement, and vision of these students and colleagues guarantee a bright future for information literacy and for librarianship as a profession.

# What's on the CD-ROM?

The following is a list of the contents and brief descriptions of each tool on the CD-ROM.

**Sample Information Literacy-Enhanced Syllabus.** (Chapter 3, page 94.) This UCLA Teaching Fellows syllabus illustrates how to analyze the key elements for a university-level undergraduate course in order to develop and insert suggested information literacy goals, expected learning outcomes, exercises, and assignments.

**Sample Memo to an Administrator.** (Chapter 2, page 60 and Chapter 3, page 103.) This memo is a model for a simple, straightforward description of an instructional problem and a request for approval and support to address it.

**Sample Proposal to Librarians Association of the University of California.** (Chapter 6, page 188.) This successful proposal is an example of a lengthy, detailed grant proposal to support researching and writing *Information Literacy Instruction: Theory and Practice.*

**Sample Proposal to the UCLA Office of Instructional Development, Instructional Improvement Grant: ESL (English as a Second Language) Tutorial.** (Chapter 6, page 188.) This document is another successful example of a detailed grant proposal to support development of a UCLA Library online information literacy tutorial, "Road to Research" (Grassian 2004b).

**IL Help Forms.** (Chapter 7, page 227.) This is a model for a simple, single-page listing of a large variety of forms of instruction. Instructors can choose from a number of forms, ranging from various types of in-person help (individual and group), to online help.

**Book Bibliography (with live links).** Provides easy access to the Web sites cited in *Learning to Lead and Manage Information Literacy Instruction*, as well a means of printing or copying the bibliography and keeping it up to date on one's own.

# Introduction

*Learning to Lead and Manage Information Literacy Instruction* offers a timely and important contribution to librarianship. I think of information literacy instruction as the culmination of a development in academic librarianship initiated many years ago. As far back as the nineteenth century, some college librarians taught students how to make more effective use of their libraries' resources. Libraries were simpler then, but as catalogs, periodical indexes, subject bibliographies, and other keys to resources expanded in number, they also grew in variety and complexity, and so did the need to instruct students about their uses.

Over the twentieth century, as library collections became extensive and as more classroom teaching involved the use of library resources, the practice of library instruction, under a variety of designations (e.g., library education, instruction in use of the library, library orientation, bibliographic instruction), gradually took hold. By the 1980s and 1990s, as electronic information changed, almost every aspect of librarianship and academe acknowledged the role of librarians who provided such instruction. This teaching was almost always provided by reference librarians, and it was not too many years before "reference/instruction librarian" morphed into just "instruction librarian" in many of the "help wanted" ads in the professional journals. The proliferation of online databases necessitated additional change by requiring more and more instruction. Librarians needed to instruct not just students but also faculty, many of whom knew that they needed to learn how to use electronic information for teaching and research. As students increasingly depended on databases, the most accepted designation for teaching use of library resources—the term "bibliographic instruction"—seemed archaic. During the 1990s "information literacy," a more inclusive concept reflecting the incorporation of electronic technology, became the more commonly used term.

At a symposium in 1997, James Wilkinson, Director of Harvard University's Bok Center for Teaching and Learning, suggested that adding to their traditional roles, libraries become the "locus and advocate for electronic teaching." This role will mean creating new partnerships among librarians, faculty, and students and pursuing an ongoing effort to master technologies subject to constant change. His suggestion turned out to be a straw in the wind as on a number of campuses, partnerships of teaching faculty and librarians appeared with increasing frequency. This new role, in turn, has contributed to an enhanced status of librarians on campus. Whereas at best, librarians had been regarded as helpmates in traditional methods of teaching and learning, now they are increasingly looked upon as guides to new ways of applying electronic technology to the teaching/learning process. Librarians have become leaders in a field characterized by continuing and rapid change.

Traditionally, the scope of most articles and books for ILI librarians has been confined to their time-honored role of IL instructors as helpmates. *Learning to Lead and Manage Information Literacy Instruction* moves us beyond that role. Esther Grassian and Joan Kaplowitz suggest that IL instructors and the librarians associated with them take advantage of this rapid change to become leaders on campus, not just to fulfill that role but also to enhance it. This approach presents something new and something needed. Indeed, it is a timely and important contribution to librarianship.

Dr. Evan I. Farber
College Librarian Emeritus
Earlham College
Richmond, Indiana

REFERENCE

"Homesteading on the Electronic Frontier: Technology, Libraries, and Learning." 1997. In *Gateways to Knowledge: The Role of Academic Libraries in Teaching, Learning, and Research*, edited by Lawrence Dowler, p. 195. Cambridge, MA: MIT Press.

# 1

---

# Developing the Leader
within You

*You must be the change you wish to see in the world.*

—Mahatma Gandhi

DO NOT SKIP THIS CHAPTER!

If you are thinking of skipping this chapter, think again. Whether you are a head of a library or a reference department, an ILI coordinator, an experienced reference and instruction librarian, or someone brand new to the profession, leadership is everyone's business and everyone's professional responsibility. Leadership is not something that is bestowed upon a person. It is something you take upon yourself. Each time an individual takes a stand, expresses an opinion (especially if that opinion is not in keeping with the majority thinking), or suggests a new way of doing things, that person is taking a leadership role. Anyone, anywhere in any organization, should be able to do this, and the healthy survival of an organization depends on people taking this leadership role at the appropriate time. It also depends on this situational or grassroots leader being able to persuade others to follow along with the idea. Leadership, therefore, is not dependent on job title or position in the institution. It consists of a conglomeration of traits, skills, abilities, beliefs, and characteristics. A person may take a leadership role in a single situation or in many different areas over time. Leadership can be long-lasting or fleeting. What an individual does, whom he or she inspires, and how these actions affect the institution as a whole make a person a leader, even if those people do not see themselves as leaders.

Administrators and managers may be leaders in their organization. Or they may not exhibit the conglomerate of traits that would truly mark them as leaders. Although they should be leading their organization, they may not always be doing so as effectively as possible. It is important to differentiate those who lead from those who are in charge. People in charge (administrators, managers, and supervisors) have the authority to make things happen. They hold titles that denote their authority. They may be committee chairs or heads of teams charged with the accomplishment of a specific task and thus are responsible for the action of the members of their group.

Leaders, on the other hand, may not have designated titles or the authority to implement change. But they have the dreams, visions, and desires to make a difference. Leadership is not bestowed upon people along with their job title. It consists of a set of values, traits, and characteristics that determine how you behave. The leader is the person who, in the face of sometimes overwhelming odds, speaks out and tries to make a difference. And the most successful organizations nurture and encourage this type of leadership wherever they find it. Those in positions of authority foster leadership in others because they know that those leaders, no matter where they come from, move the organization forward.

## WHY LEADERSHIP NOW?

Leadership, then, is independent of role or position and as such takes courage, vision, perseverance, thick skin, self-confidence, self-reflection, perspective, and frequently a well-developed sense of humor. A more in-depth description of leadership qualities will appear in a later section of this chapter. But before such a discussion can begin, it is necessary to determine why leadership is so very crucial for the library profession in general, and for IL in particular, at this point in the history of the field. Leadership is an extremely hot topic, not just in librarianship, but also in management literature in general.

Perhaps it was only human nature for people in all walks of life to have pondered where new leaders would come from as humanity approached and then entered a new millennium with Y2K and other uncertainties, economic, political, and social. But timing was not the only pressure. This latest turn of the century represented just one more example of the most important and influential aspect of modern life—change. Change is the rule. Change is the only constant. Change is swift and frequent. These are all common aspects of everyday life. The most significant change that has taken place over the last few decades is in the rate of change itself. Change keeps happening at a faster and faster pace, creating a state of turbulence and even chaos that affects everyone. We must be adaptable, agile, and intelligent in order to deal with this incessant barrage of frequent and change, expected and unexpected (Brandon 1998; Wheatley 1999). Leaders are needed who not only can help people deal with this state of affairs but can also try to predict future trends, anticipate change before it happens, create change themselves, and help those around them to deal with the uncertainty of what is to come.

Leaders both create and encourage a sense of nimbleness in themselves and those around them. Nimbleness implies flexibility and anticipation. A nimble organization both delivers what is needed today and predicts what is needed in the future. Those who do best in a nimble environment are resilient in the face of change, resourceful, multiskilled, highly motivated, proactive, have a high tolerance for ambiguity, a desire to experiment, and a willingness to challenge authority appropriately (Connor 1998; Lipman-Bluman 2001; Quinn 2004; Williams 2001). People who succeed in a nimble environment are those who step forward to take on leadership roles, as situations require them to do so.

In the field of library and information studies, the rapid growth in information, the burgeoning numbers of tools that allow access to all this information, and the frequent and often complex developments in information technology create a greater need for nimble organizations than ever before. To be nimble, these organizations must have adaptable, innovative, and creative leaders (Anderson 1997). More new information has been generated in the past thirty years than in the previous 5,000 years. The current estimate of growth is that information will continue to double every four years (Fulmer and Goldsmith 2000), and this rate of change may even increase in the future. Living under conditions of constant change creates great educational and psychological pressure on everyone in the organization, from those who occupy the seats of power to those who work on a daily basis with the public and its information needs. For IL professionals the pressure is doubled. They must not only keep up with all this change; they must develop means of teaching their users how to keep up as well. For many IL instructors, each day feels like a day on a treadmill as they try to stay even one step ahead of the people they are teaching.

So how does all to this relate to leadership in IL? Rapid change requires that everyone, at all levels of an organization, develop a greater capacity for innovation, self-management, and personal responsibility. Each person, no matter what his or her job title, needs not only a greater degree of knowledge and skill but also a higher level of independence, self-reliance, self-trust, and the capacity to exercise initiative. The world is so complex and change is so rapid and persistent that it is no longer possible for those few top administrators to make all the decisions necessary to keep their institutions moving forward (Bergmann, Hurson, and Russ-Eft 1999; Brandon 1998). For libraries to continue to flourish as central components in today's world, the profession must identify and foster appropriate leadership skills and expertise in its members—no matter what their job description (Glendenning and Gordon 1997; Quinn 2004). IL instructors cannot merely wait for someone to tell them to act. They must exhibit the leadership qualities necessary to respond quickly and creatively to the changes that impact them each and every day. They must know when to act, how to act, and where to act. In short, they must know how to be effective leaders in order to continue in their role as mediator, guide, and often advocate for the people they are charged to teach the IL competencies so vital for survival in today's world. Furthermore, they need to develop the good judgment necessary to know when it is appropriate to act on their own and when they need to check with higher-ups or pass a decision on to them.

Want to take a leadership role in getting more active learning components adopted by the library? You can probably try some out in your own classes. But in order to get this idea more widespread, you will need buy-in from your colleagues and your administrators. You can model the new technique, take the risk of trying it out, and even demonstrate your success with it. But to be a real leader, you will have to sell the idea to others. You cannot really be a leader in a vacuum. Leaders have to communicate their ideas and get others on board with those ideas. In other words, you cannot be a leader if you do not have followers. Without followers you are just an oddity marching to the sound of your own drummer. With them you are leading the way down a new road.

Rapid change and information overload, therefore, appear to be driving the current upswing of interest in leadership. Furthermore, leadership is being more broadly defined than ever before. Leadership is not who you are. It is what you do. This trend toward distributed or situational leadership has encouraged libraries to develop a more flattened, decentralized, and bottom-up type of management style. It challenges the way we all look at ourselves and our roles within the organization (Quinn 2004; Riggs 1997). This organizational principle shifts from management by control to leadership through empowerment. The new organization needs to bring out the best in people and enables them to respond quickly and effectively to change (Naisbitt and Abardene 1990). Empowerment implies a move away from the traditional bureaucratic organizational structure so typical in libraries. In order to be flexible, nimble, and adaptable to change, the new library must exhibit a flattened organization, develop empowered cross-functional teams, and maintain a state of constant learning (Martin 1997). In this environment the library staff is encouraged to bring forward new ideas and initiatives and are supported in these creative efforts. They are also involved in any decision making that affects the entire library and its users. An organization cannot be truly responsive to the needs of those it serves unless its frontline people are given authority, autonomy, support, and respect. Top-down organizations, by withholding power from their employees, deprive them of the ability to use their knowledge and expertise to respond to users' needs.

When new resources or changes in policy are being considered, the effective organization invites involvement from those employees most knowledgeable about the topic at hand and both acknowledges and is attentive to the input from these frontline experts before making final decisions. Furthermore, this advance notice allows IL librarians to prepare both themselves and their users for the proposed change.

Power must be derived not from position but from expertise, special knowledge, personal relationships or connections, and creativity. The nimble and adaptable organization takes pride in involving every mind (Bergmann, Hurson, and Russ-Eft 1999; Helgesen 1996; Roitberg 2000; Schein 1996; Wheatley 1999). Everyone has a degree of expertise in his or her own work arena. In today's complex society, the individual frequently knows more about many aspects of the job being done than his or her supervisor does. The wise organization relies on that expertise.

For example, if the library is considering the purchase of a new tool for locating information in the sciences, science librarians should be invited to preview this resource to see if it seems worthwhile for their users. With costs escalating at an extraordinary rate, it makes sense that only those with expertise have a prominent place in the decision making. Plus, having had this sneak peak at the new resource, librarians can make both marketing and instructional plans that will prepare their users for the change.

The bottom line is that effective organizations point their best minds at a problem, provide guidance in the form of overall context, history, and guidelines, and then get out of the way and lets those minds solve the problem (Brandon 1998). Warren Bennis puts it this way.

> Today's laurel will go to the leader who encourages healthy dissent and values those followers brave enough to say no. The successful leader will not have the loudest voice, but the readiest ear. His or her genius may well lie not in personal achievement, but in unleashing other people's talent. (Bennis 2000, p. 30)

## YES, YOU ARE A LEADER

In the new dynamic organization, leadership is not a position. It is a process and one in which everyone should be participating (Depree 1993; Janov 1994; Kouzes and Posner 2001; Wheatley 1999; Youngblood 1997). It is not based on rank, privileges, titles, or wealth. It is a responsibility and as such must be earned (Drucker 1996).

This new view of leadership has implications for everyone. It requires a shift in perception for both those with positional power and authority and for their followers. Those in official leadership roles (administrators, managers, and supervisors) must encourage their followers to take responsibility for their jobs and to make sure that these followers let their superiors hear what they need to know, when they need to know it. Effective followers are courageous, self-confident, and outspoken. They are not afraid to take an unpopular stand if they think it furthers the mission of the organization (Kelley 1998). Robert

E. Quinn refers to them as "positive deviants" (Quinn 2004). These followers feel it is a major part of their job to bring issues and potential solutions to the attention of those who need to know, wherever those people might be in the organization. To be successful in this type of environment, people must be willing to go outside their departments and their comfort zones (Bergmann, Hurson, and Russ-Eft 1999). In short, they must exercise leadership characteristics, regardless of who they are or what they do. At the same time, those in positions of authority must be open to, and even encourage, those who exhibit the characteristics of responsible leadership.

New and creative ideas can occur to anyone in the organization. They often bubble up from below rather than filter down from above (Plas and Lewis 2001). But only those who are willing to swallow their fears and forge ahead will actually take the steps to make their ideas a reality. They must persevere in the face of potential opposition, setbacks, and apparent failures (Baron 1999). True leaders regardless of their job titles are willing to challenge the status quo. They develop new ways of looking at things and reconceptualize what we do. They seek out responsibility rather than avoid it (Bennis 2000; Lester 1988; Plas and Lewis 2001; Quinn 2004). These are the people who, when they see a problem, do not just complain about it or wait for someone else to do something. They actively try to solve that problem and are not reluctant to put themselves on the line in order to push their ideas forward.

The nimble, healthy, and forward-thinking organization is led by administrators who not only encourage this type of behavior but also support it through words and deeds (Chappell 1999). Innovative ideas are welcome. People are allowed to take risks and even to fail on occasion without fear of repercussions. Occasional failure is recognized as a likely element of risk. Failure is not viewed as a step back, but rather as an opportunity to learn and to grow (Kets de Vries 2001). The organization that perceives failure in this light encourages future risk-taking at all levels. Furthermore, everyone in this type of organization is respected for his or her opinions. They are not only allowed to disagree but encouraged to do so (Bennis 2000). The organization that is made up of followers who are willing to speak the truth and administrators and managers who listen to that truth will be one that grows and thrives. It is an organization that not only is responsive to change but also anticipates and creates it. As Max Dupree puts it, "It helps to remember that a group that is dominated by a leader will never exceed the talents of the leader" (Depree 1993).

Crucial to this healthy relationship is that both administrators and followers keep their eyes on the prize—that is, the goals and mission of the organization. Effective followers know how to work collaboratively with everyone in the organization, both horizontally and vertically. They are experts at forging relationships with the appropriate parties who can help them implement their ideas (Kelley 1998). Peter Senge refers to these types of followers as internal networkers or community builders. He views them as the "seed carriers" of the new culture who actively look for others in the organization who are willing and eager to effect change (Senge 1996). They are also referred to by many as grass-roots leaders (Bergmann, Hurson, and Russ-Eft 1999; Helgesen 1996). These are Max Dupree's roving leaders—"The indispensable people in our lives who are there when we need them" (Depree 1992, p. 193).

Roving or grassroots leaders are also gracious losers. Not every idea or initiative is destined for success. Sometimes the time is not right. Sometimes the people necessary to support the idea are unwilling to do so. Sometimes the initiative has unexpected and unfavorable ramifications. Grassroots leaders know when to abandon ship on the idea and move on. This calls for a high level of self-esteem on the part of the grassroots leader who understands that it is the idea that has failed, not the person who promoted the idea (Brandon 1998). Managers can assist in the process by encouraging grassroots leadership in those they manage and by making sure people are rewarded for making the effort even if it fails. Managers can coach their staff on specific leadership traits and encourage employees to seek out mentors who can act as a sounding board for their ideas. Mentors can offer advice on ways to get ideas implemented and can point out potential pitfalls based on their own personal history and experience. They can serve as cheerleaders for the grassroots leader and can help get the kinks out of the idea before it is presented for formal review. For more on developing your staff through coaching and mentoring, see Chapter 4, "Fostering Growth in Yourself and Others."

This notion of a more flattened, participatory management style that relies on grassroots leadership has led to an increase in the use of self-directed teams, often ad hoc in nature, that are formed to solve specific problems. In IL instruction this is often the way in which new courses, programs, and overall instructional efforts are developed. Effective teams require distributed leadership. When everyone has a certain level of leadership skills, he or she can assume a leadership role when the situation requires it. In the best of teams, everyone leads at times and follows at others, and everyone knows when to do each (Janov 1994). This situational or just-in-time leadership creates flexibility in thinking and a more responsive approach to problem solving (Anderson 1997). To achieve this potential for situational leadership requires each of us to look for, develop, and encourage the leader within.

The benefit to the organization is widespread and powerful. Once instructors have taken this journey, the organization becomes stronger and more democratic and one in which the many, not just the few, share the burdens, responsibilities, and the rewards of leadership (Lipman-Bluman 2001).

## WHAT QUALITIES MAKE A LEADER?

If IL librarians are to take this journey to find the leader within, they first must be acquainted with the characteristics of leadership in general. A great deal has been written about what makes a leader, but it all seems to boil down to the following qualities:

- Vision
- Passion
- Courage
- Integrity

These categories hold true whether one reads the classic management works (Bennis 1989, 1994, 1997, 2000; Bennis and Nanus 1985, 1997; Bennis, Spreitzer, and Cummings 2001; Brandon 1998; Covey 1966, 1990b, 1991, 1996; Depree 1989, 1993; Drucker 1996; Greenleaf 1977; Senge 1990a, 1990b, 1996; Quinn 2004) or those dealing directly with leadership in librarianship (Alire 2001; Greenleaf 1977; Heron, Powell, and Young 2001, 2002; Leslie 2001; Martin 1997; Schreiber and Shannon 2001; Sheldon 1991, 1992; Turock 2001; Williams 2001; Williams 2001; Wilson 1996).

### Vision

A leader needs to know where he or she wants the organization to go and must be able to articulate that vision clearly and persuasively to others (Alire 2001; Anderson 1997; Covey 1990a; Kouzes and Posner 1996; Sheldon 1991, 1992; Spears 1995). A clearly stated, compelling, moving, and unifying vision gives everyone in the organization direction and motivation. Once everyone knows where to go and why, these people have a better understanding of where their individual tasks fit into the big picture. They can make effective decisions in their day-to-day work and can look for, and create, opportunities for change that align with that overall vision (Bennis 2000; Youngblood 1997).

A clear vision lets people know what is expected of them. It evokes a positive picture of the future and creates pride in, and energy for, that future. Effective vision statements are memorable, motivating, and idealistic and offer a view of the future that is worth aiming for. They inspire enthusiasm and encourage commitment and are in line with the overall culture and values of the parent organization (Boyett and Boyett 1998). Although the organization as a whole should have an overriding vision, every new idea, project, or initiative starts out as someone's vision. This smaller, more focused vision should, of course, fit into the global organizational vision. But it is a vision nonetheless.

For example, say you know through personal contact, research, and reading that plagiarism is of great concern to educators at all levels from elementary to graduate school. You talk to colleagues about the problem and brainstorm possible solutions. Your collective vision is to create an online tutorial that would help teachers and librarians help their students understand the concepts involved and cite sources correctly. In order to gain the necessary support (financial, technological, staffing) to make this dream a reality, you must communicate your vision to others who can make it happen. You will probably need to talk to your supervisor to see if he or she will give you the time to pursue this dream. You will want to talk to colleagues (those who were in on the brainstorming and others who were not) to see if anyone would be interested in joining you on this project. And you might wish to explore partnerships with instructional and graphic designers in other departments in your institution or community who might have the skills needed to help you accomplish your goal. This is grassroots leadership at its best. You identify the problem (plagiarism) and bring it to your colleagues. You and your colleagues come up with a solution (the tutorial). And you sell your vision to whoever can make it happen, create the necessary team, and oversee the action until your vision has been realized.

A vision or mission statement, whether it is directed at the whole organization or a specific, focused project, that is buried in a drawer, where no one can find it, and no one remembers it, is worthless. It can neither motivate the group nor guide its day-to-day operations. The best mission statements like the best advertising slogans must capture the attention of, and be understood and accepted by, everyone who sees it. When the mission statement clearly articulates a leader's vision for the future, everyone should be able to relate to it and want to work toward attaining the goals embodied by it. In this way the leader inspires and empowers everyone to do his or her best to contribute to the fulfillment of that vision (Brandon 1998; Howe 2001). So what would be the mission statement for our plagiarism tutorial vision? It might be something like "Knowing what's right when you write." It is memorable, catchy, and conveys what you are trying to do. And everyone on the project will understand it and buy into it as a goal.

According to Joyce Kaser and her colleagues, "A true vision is never imposed" (Kaser et al. 2002, p. 99). Leaders act as bridges that connect people to the future. They listen to, and understand, everyone's hopes and dreams and build alliances and partnerships based on those shared desires (Alire 2001; Anderson 1997; Farren and Kaye 1996; Kouzes and Posner 1996; Leithwood, Jantzi, and Steinbach 1999; Turock 2001). The wise leader involves everyone in the development of the vision. Everybody feels a part of the process. The vision is theirs. It belongs to all since everyone has a stake in its development. The resultant shared vision provides focus and energy for learning. It fosters risk taking, experimentation, flexibility, and an openness to change. It is a developmental process based on an intensive dialogue between everyone involved and affected by the vision (Flood 1999). Creating the vision is sometimes dependent upon asking the right question. Even if the question, on the surface, appears foolish or unanswerable, posing the question can change the way people think about the process. It challenges them and fosters an atmosphere in which a new vision can emerge along with the creativity to achieve that vision (Quinn 2004). The result is a sense of pride, enthusiasm, and shared ownership. A vision created in this manner belongs to each and every person involved in, and affected by, it. How was this done for the plagiarism tutorial project? The grassroots leader gathered his or her colleagues together and asked them to brainstorm the problem. The group, as a whole, suggested possible solutions and then picked one, the tutorial, as a means to solve the problem.

Clearly, ILI programs need visionary leaders and a well-developed and memorable mission statements—both for the overall program and for specific initiatives such as the plagiarism tutorial described above—if they are to succeed. An IL instructor who has developed a vision, especially one that was created with input from everyone concerned, and can articulate that vision clearly, passionately, and persuasively both to colleagues within the library and to those in the larger community, will provide both leadership and direction for the larger program and the individual initiatives that support the program.

*Passion*

Closely related to vision is the idea of passion. A vision is useless unless those with that vision believes wholeheartedly in it. No one can turn vision into reality alone. The visionary leader needs others to believe in the cause and help make it happen (Anderson 1997). Passionate belief in the vision creates an atmosphere in which others get caught up in the idea. Passion is contagious and like an infectious disease spreads quickly (Kets de Vries 2001; Quinn 2004). The more people who catch the vision infection, the more likely they will work diligently toward its fulfillment. Passionate leaders motivate those around them and enroll them in the cause (Baron 1999; Bennis 1994, 1989, 2000; Goleman 1998; Kamp 1999; Kets de Vries 2001). Instruction librarians who truly believe in the value of their IL programs will be able to sell them to their colleagues and to those the programs are trying to reach. These IL leaders will also be adept at getting support from wherever it is needed within the organization.

*Courage*

"Every leader and every life that makes a difference develops the ability to evaluate ideas and the courage to seize the opportunities associated with them" (Bethel 1995, p. 135). Being a leader sometimes means taking an unpopular stand. But having a passionate belief in a vision makes that easy. The need to make the vision a reality is so strong that it is unthinkable not to champion the cause. Yes, you acknowledge that developing that online tutorial is going to add more work to everyone's overburdened plate. But your vision is so strong and your passionate belief in the worth of this project so great that you find it unthinkable not to follow through with the idea. And you inspire others to feel the same.

Passionate leaders not only motivate those around them but are self-motivators as well and instill in themselves a burning desire to see the idea through—no matter the cost. Effective leaders must not only believe in their vision. They must also believe in themselves. Courageous leaders must possess a degree of self-confidence that enables them to see the idea through in spite of criticism, setbacks, and even failures (Bergmann, Hurson, and Russ-Eft 1999; Brandon 1998). They must also be self-reflective and self-aware—recognizing and acknowledging both their strengths and weaknesses (Brandon 1998; Quinn 2004). As self-reflective people, they know how to play to their strengths and how to compensate for their weaknesses. They are open to other ideas and are willing to seek aid from others, especially those who can provide the skills they lack. Courageous leaders know themselves, what they believe in, and what they value (Bennis 1994). They can fall back on this knowledge as they shepherd their vision and champion their cause.

Leaders take action. They do not wait for permission. Their passion imbues them with a sense of urgency, and their courage allows them to act and to inspire others to join them in that action (Kouzes and Posner 1996; Quinn 2004; Schreiber and Shannon 2001). Much like effective teachers, leaders know what they want to accomplish, care about accomplishing that end, and take the steps to get there. True change takes time. So the effective leader must temper his or her passion with a healthy dose of patience. Leaders have the courage to take their idea to anyone and everyone who needs to know and who is in a position to help push the idea forward. They are willing and eager to discuss their plans with anyone who will listen. And they gather supporters as they go. It is always wise to make sure that everyone who will be affected by your idea is notified of your plans and approves of your ideas. The lone ranger, who tries to implement change without getting everyone on board, runs the risk of alienating the very people needed to make the dream a reality. IL initiatives are being implemented across the country and around the world because librarians have taken the idea to their colleagues, administrators, and communities. While these initiatives would not have taken root without the support of people in authority, those very people needed to have the idea brought to their attention. That is the role of the grassroots leader—to make sure that those in authority have the information they need to respond to the times and to move the organization in new directions.

IL instructors with their strong commitment to the empowerment of their learners exhibit the vision, passion, and courage necessary for leadership every time they teach. It is only a small step from leading instruction to becoming a leader on a broader scale. Teaching provides the IL librarian with grounding in leadership skills. But the IL librarian must then build on those skills if he or she wishes to have an impact on a larger community. The trick is to realize that IL librarians possess what it takes to lead and to get them to do so in order to make IL a reality in society at large.

*Integrity*

The final component in the leadership mix is integrity. Leaders must practice what they preach in order to get people to trust in their vision and buy into their dreams. Vision, passion, and courage may get the ideas aired. But if leaders do not "walk the walk," they will not get people to join them in their campaign. Leaders must be viewed as trustworthy and credible (Anderson 1997; Bergmann, Hurson, and Russ-Eft 1999; Goleman 1998). Creating trust takes time. It is built on telling the truth, keeping promises, honoring commitments, treating people fairly and equitably, and admitting to, and apologizing for, mistakes (Bergmann, Hurson, and Russ-Eft 1999; Brandon 1998; Depree 1993; Pollard 1996; Quinn 2004; Wilson 1996). Leaders who say one thing but do another quickly lose the respect and trust of those around them.

And a leader no one trusts is a leader no one follows. Since no one can accomplish their vision alone, an untrustworthy leader will find it difficult to move his or her ideas forward. But the trusted leader enlists support because people believe both in the ideas and in the integrity of the person behind them (Kaser et al. 2002).

Leaders have a core set of values, and they behave consistently based on these values. They articulate these values to others so that everyone knows what the leader believes in and can predict how he or she will behave in a given situation. Behaving inconsistently is the fastest road to losing credibility. People are more likely to follow a person they can count on than someone who is frequently seen to shift positions based on external circumstances and opportunities (Bennis 2000; Kamp 1999; Sheldon 1991).

One way to build trust is to model the behavior expected from one's colleagues. Modeling is based on a combination of character (what you value as a person) and competence (what you can do). If action matches values, modeling occurs, and trust is built (Covey 1996; Quinn 2004). Leaders should take every opportunity to set an example. Their behavior exemplifies how committed they are to the values they embrace. Leading by example makes visions and values tangible (Kouzes and Posner 1996). The instruction librarian should find this easy to do since modeling is a major part of the teacher's arsenal.

## WHAT CHARACTERISTICS DEFINE A LEADER?

While the individual instruction librarian may not have any formal, positional authority, it should not stop him or her from trying to take a leadership role when that role is needed. If the librarian has a vision of a better way to do something, feels passionately about that vision, has the courage to articulate the idea to others, and is seen as a credible and trustworthy person, he or she should be able to enlist others in the cause. He or she can then present their case to those in authority. Instruction librarians have a long and impressive history of leading in this manner. They are uniquely qualified to fill the role since the very skills that make for a good teacher have been identified as necessary to being an effective leader.

If leaders should have vision, passion, courage, and integrity, how do they exhibit these attributes in their everyday behavior? Again there is agreement in the literature. A leader

- Communicates persuasively
- Encourages diversity
- Takes risks

- Builds relationships
- Seeks learning opportunities

*Communicates Persuasively*

The greatest of visions languish in the mind of its creator unless that vision can be articulated to others. But merely passing on the message is not enough. To move a vision forward, the leader must be able to persuade others of the idea's worth (Bennis 2000; Covey 1966, 1991; Hersey, Blanchard, and Johnson 2001; Kamp 1999; Sheldon 1991). Who better to sell an idea, to articulate a vision passionately and persuasively than an instruction librarian? The best teachers are articulate, passionate about the subject, and persuasive in their delivery. They wish to share their knowledge and their love for the material and persuade their learners that what is being taught is worthwhile, valuable, and relevant to them. In short, they are natural leaders and exhibit leadership every time they teach.

However, communication is a two-way street. Effective leaders must be accomplished listeners who respect everyone's opinion and make that respect known. They must be able to sense, understand, and appreciate multiple viewpoints and perspectives when articulating their vision to others (Goleman 1998; Kamp 1999; Kaser et al. 2002; Spears 1995). Again the art of listening is part of both the instruction and the reference librarian's everyday arsenal.

Effective communication is intimately tied to effective presentation skills. Whether it is true or not, people think good speakers make good leaders (Bergmann, Hurson, and Russ-Eft 1999; Corcoran and Jones 1997). The most effective leaders tend to be articulate and persuasive speakers and presenters. The accomplished presenter must be well organized, clear, and understandable. He or she must know how to get ideas across through the use of body language, vocal cues, eye contact, and appropriate support material (Kelley 1998). The parallels to teaching are clear. Whether the IL librarian is trying to reach a classroom of learners, a conference room full of colleagues, or a boardroom full of administrators, the skills needed are the same. Effective communication in the teaching or reference environment can clearly translate to that of the leadership arena.

*Empowers Others*

As mentioned previously in this chapter, leaders do not accomplish their visions alone. Leaders who think they do not need the help and support of those around them are doomed to failure. The most effective leaders, whether they are positional leaders or grassroots ones, know that it is only through gaining followers that a vision can be moved forward. But that brings us back to the idea that everyone can and should take a leadership role whenever the situation requires it. Leadership, as it is being defined in this chapter, is not based on job title, but on action proposed and taken.

A nimble organization, one that is proactive about its changing environment, needs people who are willing to take that leadership action no matter where they work in that organization. But people will not take this initiative unless they are encouraged to do so. That means that everyone in the organization must feel empowered to speak up, make suggestions, and within reason have the authority to make decisions that impact on their immediate work environment.

Perhaps nothing has a bigger impact on libraries and their users than the selection of a new Online Public Access Computer (OPAC). Offering the staff the opportunity to be truly engaged in the selection and implementation process not only empowers everyone, but also creates an atmosphere of shared ownership and decision making. Libraries that are engaged in this process can hold open town meetings in which the different possible vendors demonstrate their products. The staff that attended these presentations can offer feedback on the various options. This feedback is taken into consideration when the final selection is made, thus creating an environment in which the entire staff becomes part of the decision-making body.

People who are involved in this manner feel that their action makes a difference and that their work has meaning and significance (Bennis 2000; Bethel 1995). Taking responsibility is expected, and people are given opportunities to do so. Everyone is given the space to take the initiative, volunteer ideas, challenge assumptions, and expand their range (Brandon 1998; Lopez 1995; Sheldon 1991). Each employee in this type of organization is viewed as having some measure of expertise in his or her particular job role and is treated accordingly. Employees' judgment and decisions, therefore, are not second-guessed by their supervisors but are incorporated into the decision-making process (Plas and Lewis 2001). The advent of e-mail and electronic discussion boards has greatly enhanced this process as these electronic communication modes promote a broader base of exchange and discussion. People can be involved from their own offices and work spaces and no longer have to participate in open meetings in order to make their opinions known.

This sort of empowerment leads to a flattened organizational structure—one that encourages the formation of ad hoc project-oriented cross-functional teams. It requires an atmosphere where people know they can take the risks associated with leadership without fear of the consequences impacting negatively on their careers (Chappell 1999; Schreiber and Shannon 2001). Those in authority, positional leaders and managers, must set the tone for this type of flattened organization by modeling the type of risk-taking leadership they are expecting from everyone in the organization. Taking risks and learning from mistakes are all viewed as part of the natural work environment (Bennis 2000). When those in authority are open-minded, reward initiative taking at all levels of the organization, and exhibit the trustworthy behavior that empowers everyone around them, they encourage leaders to spring up whenever and wherever they are needed (Bergmann, Hurson, and Russ-Eft 1999; Brandon 1998; Depree 1993; Kamp 1999; Kaser et al. 2002; Kets de Vries 2001; Orenstein 1999; Quinn 2004). They expect and encourage people to take leadership roles.

Empowering others means having an "abundance mentality" (Covey 1991): the idea that there is plenty of success to go around. It is a commitment to the growth of others and requires a distribution of power throughout the organization rather than the investment of power in a very few high-ranking individuals (Bethel 1995; Hill, Gabarro, and Kotter 1998; Pollard 1996; Sweeney 1997; Wilson 1996). The effective organization believes in the unseen potential of everyone within the organization and encourages each individual to try to reach that potential (Covey 1990b). People are encouraged to take leadership roles as needed. Teams are created, and different people lead those teams depending upon the circumstances. During the selection stage of looking for a new OPAC, the technical folks may be taking the lead. But once the choice is made and implemented, the instruction librarians may take over as they work on ways to teach the community how to use this new resource.

Leadership becomes fluid in this type of nimble environment. Although there are definitely people "in charge," other members of the organization become team or project leaders as needed and are therefore "in charge" of that particular endeavor. When the project is over, so is their leadership role—until the next time their leadership is required. Everyone has the potential of being a leader but is also aware that he or she is not always going to be the one to be in charge. True leaders build communities of leaders and unify those who work within the organization with a common set of goals, values, and beliefs (Quinn 2004; Wheatley 1999). Leaders who empower others do so by exhibiting both courage and integrity in their words and their actions.

While not all organizations may follow this exact model, the grassroots leader looks for places to contribute to change and takes every opportunity to comment on the process. Much like in elections, if you do not vote, you cannot really complain about the outcome. If you believe that you have something to contribute but no formal opportunities present themselves, seek out appropriate groups and volunteer your services. Be gracious and not overbearing. You do not want to sound like a know-it-all. Just indicate why you think your input and perspective might be helpful. And do not become disgruntled or discouraged if you are turned down at that point. Your initiative and enthusiasm may still have made an impression. So do not be surprised if you are called into the process at a later date or are invited to become part of a different project in the future.

*Encourages Diversity*

Empowering others also implies a respect for everyone's opinions, especially those that might be creative, off-beat, and challenging to the status quo (Brandon 1998; Chappell 1999; Drucker 1996; Youngblood 1997). People in nimble organizations recognize the need to have others around them who think differently from the way they do. They encourage creativity and respect expertise, seeking out and welcoming the "committed skeptic" who wants to take on responsibility and demands a share of the risk (Depree 1993). An organization made up of people with differing points of view and skills is an organization that is open to new ideas and can respond to anything that the environment throws at it. Furthermore, those in charge of nimble organizations protect unusual thinkers from the rules and regulations so endemic to many bureaucratic systems (Depree 1993). With a wide range of expertise available to it, this nimble organization has the wherewithal to move in any direction necessary. Those in positions of authority in nimble organizations make a place for the unconventional thinker and are open-minded and flexible in their approach to organizational structure. They recognize the leadership potential in everyone. An organization that adheres to the idea of shared responsibility and distributed leadership and that encourages people, no matter what their job title, to take appropriate leadership roles as needed will stand ready to respond to whatever the world throws at it.

*Takes Risks*

A large part of empowering others and encouraging diversity relates to the role of risk in the organization. Are people willing to put their ideas to the test? Are they encouraged to do so? Is everyone in the organization, from mailroom to boardroom, not only encouraged to take risks but also protected from the consequences of failure? In an organization where individual responsibility and creativity are prized, people feel free to be innovative and resourceful (Bergmann, Hurson, and Russ-Eft 1999; Chappell 1999; Williams 2001). Not every new idea is a good one. And not every good idea succeeds. New ideas should be subjected to cost/benefit/risk analysis. This analysis includes asking not only what will happen if a new idea is implemented, but also what could happen if it is not (Bethel 1995). Risks are not taken lightly. The implications are weighed carefully. But people are willing to take the chance—to risk failure because they realize that the cost of not trying is often greater than the risk itself. Furthermore, the organization views innovative risk taking as part of everyone's job, thus creating an environment that encourages leadership at every level.

*Builds Relationships*

Nobody does it alone. Those who exhibit leadership know that very well. A leader is someone who not only has the vision and passion to pursue a dream but also enlists the people in his or her cause who can make it happen. Building relationships takes time and effort. The best relationships are those that have developed naturally—through a sense of mutual interest and a shared commitment to the goals and mission of the organization or the community at large. These relationships may have formed years before the current new idea was hatched. Or they may be sought for the express purpose of getting this new idea developed and implemented. The key to building the relationship is getting people to buy into the idea. Thus, the initiative leader must call upon his or her ability to communicate persuasively. Leaders must be passionate and effective storytellers who can get others to see their vision and to adopt that vision as their own (Kelley 1998). No matter how great the idea, it must be sold to those who can make it happen. People in positions of authority (administrators, supervisors, and managers) must be convinced that the idea is one to be supported. After all, they control the necessary resources (time, money, and personnel) that will be needed to implement the idea. They are also the ones to set priorities. People can feel overwhelmed by the barrage of projects, tasks, and daily chores that fill their days.

If you want your idea to be taken seriously and to be included as an important task in people's already overcrowded agenda, it needs to be supported at all levels of the organization. Colleagues, coworkers, and collaborators are the ones who will do the work. Administrators, supervisors, and managers are the ones who will say it is worth doing. As the passionate communicator sells his or her grand idea, the stage is set for building the necessary relationships that will bring the idea to fruition.

Relationships are built through trust and open, honest communication. They depend on empathy and the ability to see other people's perspective. The leader who understands varying perspectives and points of view will be able to illustrate the benefits of the relationship under discussion. Effective leaders look for, and find, common ground and build rapport based on it (Goleman 1998). By being nonjudgmental, these leaders can gain the cooperation of other groups more easily (Bergmann, Hurson, and Russ-Eft 1999). Successful leaders are masters of interdependence. They inspire others to share ideas, to trust one another, and to seek collaborative solutions to problems (Nanus 1989). These are individuals who know how to identify the appropriate parties needed to implement an idea and can form those diverse groups into a coherent team.

Leaders are always alert for ways to help people and groups connect with each other (Youngblood 1997). To accomplish this, they spend a lot of their time making contact with others, by talking to people, e-mailing and calling them. Through these contacts they discover pockets of expertise, and when there is a need, they can draw on this expertise (Anderson 1997). Since the contact has previously been made, the foundation for a working relationship already exists. Effective leaders show a genuine concern and interest in others and treat everyone with dignity and respect (Heron, Powell, and Young 2002; Quinn 2004). People come to know and trust this type of leader and are willing to cooperate when asked. Getting to know people at this level paves the way for building necessary relationships and successful partnerships. It is far easier to ask for help from someone you know than from a complete stranger.

Here is one approach for developing these types of contacts and potential partners. See if there is an information technology group on your campus, in your community, in your institution/organization, or at your place of business that you can join. Groups like this offer you the chance to learn how information technology is applied and used in various situations in your particular environment. Plus, you can get to know and form relationships with the people who work on Web pages used in your institution, business, or community. And you can keep these technologists apprised of any new resources the library may be acquiring or any new approaches being adopted in information literacy instruction.

Knowing who the key players are in an organization and building relationships with them is key in ILI because we must partner with stakeholders in our environment (our colleagues, community leaders, school boards, teachers, faculty, administrators, IT departments, student services offices, and others). Without knowing who the players are and how they all fit together, ILI instructors could jump in too quickly with a new and potentially unworkable plan. It is important to remember that in every environment ILI is a shared responsibility. The more we know about what people do, what they value, and how they view IL, the better we can form a collaborative coalition that can develop workable plans specifically geared to our particular environment.

*Seeks Learning Opportunities*

Last, but certainly not least, effective leaders are perpetual learners. They know there is always more to learn and are constantly on the lookout for new ideas and ways to grow and learn. Successful people are self-reflective enough to know when they do not know what they are doing and embrace the experience as an invitation for growth. In addition they model that behavior for others (Kaser et al. 2002; Kouzes and Posner 2001). In the spirit of distributed leadership, everyone in an organization should be encouraged to be perpetual learners. Those who are open to new ideas and who are looking for opportunities to learn and bring out the best in themselves and others will thrive in today's ever-changing world (Kamp 1999).

Attending workshops, going to professional meetings, and reading relevant literature are all obvious ways to keep learning. Working in teams with people who have expertise different from your own is also a way to stimulate your growth and development. If you work in a truly diverse organization that depends on people with differing backgrounds and expertise, take advantage of the opportunity to learn from your colleagues and coworkers at every level of the organization. Seeking the advice of others helps to empower them and indicates a respect for their expertise (Depree 1993). The more you know about what other people do, the better you can see the opportunities for forming the relationships referred to in the previous section. Discussing issues with others is a great way to get a new perspective on the problem. And you can never tell when one of these conversations may spark an idea that can lead to a possible solution or new and exciting project.

Leaders also use their experiences as learning opportunities. They do not see setbacks as failures but instead use these experiences as ways to determine what their next steps should be (Bennis 2000). Leading is a journey of discovery. Experience can be the best teacher. Each new dilemma or magnificent failure can point the way to new learning opportunities (Quinn 2004; Schreiber and Shannon 2001). Failure points out what works and what does not work at a given time. It points out possible new directions, presents new information, and provides new experiences (Bethel 1995).

Being a perpetual learner, always being open to ideas, and having an inquiring mind enable the effective leader to see connections between what is known and what is new. They create an atmosphere in which new ideas and approaches can bubble to the surface, sometimes at the most unexpected moments and from the most unanticipated situations. And they bring out the leader in every person.

In the words of James M. Kouzes and Barry Z. Posner: "That's why leadership has to be everyone's business. Why leadership will always be relationship. How action brings forth the leader within, how leadership is about developing oneself to be an instrument for making a difference" (Kouzes and Posner 2001, p. 90).

## LEADING WITHIN YOUR ORGANIZATIONAL CULTURE

To be effective, leaders must have an in-depth knowledge of the context in which they are operating. Every organization has its own rules, regulations, and culture. And every organization operates within a larger context that has a culture of its own. It is crucial for leaders to become familiar with the culture of their own organization as well as any broader institution in which they are operating. It is critical to be aware of who is in charge, who has power, and how things get done in the larger community or environment (Todaro 2001). Finding out who the stakeholders are and understanding the culture in which those stakeholders function will go a long way not only to successfully communicate new ideas to them but to getting those all-important stakeholders to support the idea as well.

Culture tells people which activities are acceptable and which are not. It establishes ground rules for people and sets expectations and priorities. Culture determines the nature and use of power within the organization—top-down or distributed or a combination of both. It defines reporting structure and status. Culture sets patterns about how people interact and how they resolve conflict. It also establishes management practices. According to William E. Schneider, any organization that has been functioning in a reasonably healthy manner exhibits one of the following core cultures (Schneider 1994):

- Control
- Collaboration
- Competence
- Cultivation

The control culture has its roots in the military and is based on power and status. Collaborating uses sports as its model and is built on teamwork. The competence culture is exemplified by the university and is centered on expertise. The cultivation culture is based on religious organizations and is dedicated to furthering the human spirit, inculcating ethics and values and uplifting humankind to higher plans (Schneider 1994).

So how does this research on cultures relate to leadership in general and leading IL programs in particular? For one thing it helps to understand where the authority to make change lies in your organization. The culture in which you operate will determine what kind of ideas will be viewed favorably, who needs to be sold on the idea, and the approach in which you need to present the idea. Are you a chief with no teeth? That is, have you been charged with implementing a new program but have no real authority over those with whom you need to work in order to complete this implementation? Will an analysis of the culture in which you are operating give you some help in determining how to get your ideas implemented? An examination of the organizational culture, the rules under which you and your colleagues operate, should help you decide the best approach.

Organizational culture sets the stage for how things get done. In many ways the culture frames the values, goals, and missions of the organization. Each of these cultures views innovation and change differently. Knowing what is considered important in your organization can help you get your ideas heard and accepted.

Control and competence are fairly impersonal cultures. Control emphasizes precedents and requires order, objectivity, and rules. It formulates policies and procedures for people to follow. There is very little improvisation in this type of culture. The competence culture establishes achievement goals and deploys people to reach them. The scientific method is often used in decision making. This culture relies on logic and emphasizes empirical data collection (Schneider 1994).

In the control culture being the best or the biggest game in town is a central philosophy. This culture wants to win. So framing your idea so that its implementation will give the organization a competitive edge should help make that idea appealing. Libraries in this type of culture might be persuaded to take on a new and possibly risky project if it offered the opportunity of being the first to do it. Being on the bleeding edge of new technology can be full of pitfalls. But being among the first to conquer that technology can make you and your library famous. Those who were on the forefront of developing instructional Web pages or online tutorials received acclaim and awards. They were looked to as being leaders in the field. So emphasizing how your idea will establish your organization as being innovative and at the cutting edge of the field should be the best way to get that idea implemented.

The pursuit of excellence is prized by the competence culture. Being an expert in the field is a big selling point here (Schneider 1994). So promoting your project needs to be based on the idea that if the project succeeds, you will be doing something better than the rest of the pack. In this case your library does not have to be the first to do something. But it needs to take the task to a higher level. While it is no longer possible to be the first to develop online tutorials, you can develop an approach that combines existing technologies to create a more user-centric approach. Your expertise will raise the standard, and your organization will be touted as one where excellence is valued and rewarded.

Collaboration and cultivation are more people-centered in their approaches. In both cultures people working either individually or in teams determine decisions and actions. Status and rank are not of a great deal of importance in these two cultures. Power is personal in nature and derives from people's experiences with each other. Collaboration and cultivation place people's capability, spirit, and motivation first (Schneider 1994).

Projects that offer the opportunity to work across library environments would be appealing to the collaboration culture since partnering is highly valued. This is a culture of teamwork, empowered teams, and positive relationships (Schneider 1994). So emphasizing building relationships and outreach to other groups should be a plus for any idea presented in this culture. For example, the librarians at the University of California Santa Barbara worked with librarians and teachers in the community to develop IL instruction at local high schools (Martorana et al. 2001). The authors indicated that the key to success was the involvement in, and support of, the project by the high school librarians themselves—a true collaborative effort across library environments.

Finally, in the cultivation culture, which emphasizes the greater good for all, showing how your idea will benefit the people within the organization and society as a whole is the approach that should get your idea accepted (Schneider 1994). Identifying at-risk populations and developing instructional support directed at helping members of those populations succeed should be especially appealing. Developing Web pages and tutorials in a variety of languages should also be supported in the cultivation culture.

Understanding the cultural milieu is the first step toward becoming a leader in your environment. Being a leader means recognizing what is valued in that organization, determining the rules for interacting with everyone in the organization, identifying those who need to be involved, and selecting the correct approach for bringing your idea forward. You need to consider how much autonomy you have to broach new ideas and develop good judgment about when you need to seek out permission for developing your project. You must be able to identify the stakeholders (anyone who might be affected if the project is implemented) and make sure they are apprised of any possible future action on your part. Be alert and sensitive to how things work in your environment.

Knowing the type of culture within which you are operating can help give you clues as to the approach you need to take in order to increase the possibility of success. Although each type of culture may view innovation and change differently, all have a way to allow for that change to happen. It may be slower in some than in others. Ideas may flourish, but implementation lags due to the heavy reliance on teamwork and group problem solving in your culture. Or new ideas may be approached with extreme caution, as they seem to threaten the accepted rules and regulations of the culture. But in each type of culture there is a way to make things happen, though you may need large doses of patience and perseverance. Nothing happens overnight, but developing the right approach for your environment will increase the chances that your idea will succeed. So before you step up into that leadership role, make sure you have done your homework and thoroughly understand how things work in your world. Do not let a good idea be squelched because you did not know how or to whom to present it. Operating in a way that is in conflict with the rules under which your organization works is a sure way to get your ideas dismissed. But by working within your culture, you can make things happen, become a grassroots leader, and enjoy the thrill of seeing your ideas come to fruition.

## LEADING CHANGE

One of the biggest challenges a leader has in any organization is leading change. Moving people from the old, tried-and-true, familiar ways of doing things to a new, different, and sometimes scary approach takes skill, tact, and all the leadership characteristics described above. It does not matter if you are a leader by title or a leader by choice, leading a change initiative requires vision, passion, courage, and integrity. Communication skills are also crucial, as the leader must be able to appreciate where people are and help them see where he or she wishes them to go and why it is important for them to get there. If leaders do not have the skills to be empathic and effective in this way, the change effort will likely be perceived as undesirable, and resistance often occurs. Before people are willing to embrace change, they have to be convinced it is truly necessary. Invite people to ask questions about the change and articulate their misgivings. Effective leaders respect those fears and try to help people deal with them. They address concerns clearly, patiently, and respectfully (Anderson 1997; Brandon 1998; Kets de Vries 2001).

As mentioned earlier in this chapter, nothing is more disruptive for staff and users alike than the change from one OPAC to another. Since the OPAC is the primary tool for finding your way around the library's collections, a change in this fundamental tool can be devastating as everyone must cope with being unable to locate materials that they could easily find with the old system. The wise leader is sensitive to these fears and provides means for dealing with them by involving the staff in the selection and implementation process. This can be done in a variety of ways. The idea of holding open town meetings to discuss options was already referred to in a previous section. Offering e-mail listservs where staff members can air their concerns, ask questions, and receive assistance as they learn the ropes on the new system is another approach. Mounting Web pages that track the implementation process and provide timely and relevant information can also be useful and can act as a way to allay fears. Inviting vendors to present "train the trainers" workshops in which librarians can develop the expertise needed to help their users learn the new system is yet another possibility.

Everyone involved must feel that he or she has some ownership of the change. Significant change cannot be imposed from above (Bennis 2000). The more input people have in the decisions being made, the more likely they will support it. The chances of success are tremendously increased when those who are affected are involved in the planning. Nothing makes people resist new ideas or approaches more adamantly than when they feel that change is being forced upon them (Bennis 1989; Boyett and Boyett 1998; Janov 1994). But if people feel that they have helped to create the change, they will work hard and long to bring that change into being. The best way to create ownership is to have those who will be implementing the change develop the plan of action themselves. No one is successful if he or she merely presents a plan in finished form to others, no matter how brilliant that plan might be. People support what they create (Wheatley 1999).

Get people to discuss what might be wrong with how things currently are. Brainstorm on how you all think things could be better and then figure out how you can aim for that better future. Having a shared goal that has been mutually agreed upon gives people a stake in the outcome. It creates an atmosphere in which people will work hard, in spite of the inevitable setbacks, failures, and delays, to accomplish the envisioned change (Bergmann, Hurson, and Russ-Eft 1999; Boyett and Boyett 1998; Covey 1990a; Diaz and Pintozzi 1999; Kaser et al. 2002; Rooks 1988).

If input is requested, it is imperative that people believe that the leader is really listening to them. Past history between the person leading the change effort and those he or she is trying to lead is very important. Does the leader have a reputation for taking other people's opinions seriously, or does he or she ask for input and then go ahead and do whatever was originally planned regardless of that input? Nothing is more demoralizing to people than to find out that their input was ignored. Clearly, a leader may not be able to implement everything that is being suggested. But he or she has a responsibility to explain the decisions being made and make it clear that although everyone's opinions had been listened to and taken into account, there were compelling reasons to choose the path being taken. And those reasons should be elucidated so that everyone understands what went into the final decision. Leaders who tell the truth and give reasons for the change, who help people understand not only the what of the new direction but the whys that drive it, have a far better chance of getting the necessary support needed to make the proposed change (Bergmann, Hurson, and Russ-Eft 1999; Holland 2000; Kaser et al. 2002).

More than anything, people want to understand how the change will affect them. Naturally, they want to know what's in it for them. They also want to know how their daily lives will be different, what they will have to learn, what sacrifices they may be asked to make during the transition from old to new, and what the ultimate payoff will be. Leaders pave the way and prepare the organization for change.

One of the most important aspects of this preparation is lavish communication. The more people know about what to expect, the better they will deal with what is to come (Bergmann, Hurson, and Russ-Eft 1999; Boyett and Boyett 1998; Depree 1993; Diaz and Pintozzi 1999; Hersey, Blanchard, and Johnson 2001). When the University of California decided to transition every one of their journal article databases to new vendors, Web pages were developed to keep staff apprised. Staff were given the opportunity to discuss the various options and communicate their choices. Basic training materials were mounted on the staff Web pages to help librarians on individual campuses begin to develop instructional materials for their users. Dates for the transition to each new interface were announced well in advance, and publicity was developed to inform users of the impending change. Workshops were offered to help staff make the transition and prepare their users for it.

Remember that people learn in a variety of ways. Some will need to see the message in writing. Others may need to hear it, while still others might need to handle physical models or test out new systems themselves. Honor those differences and make sure that you provide a variety of modes for getting the idea across. Plan to communicate with everyone frequently. Most people need to be presented with a new idea several times before it begins to make sense to them and they can figure out what the impact might be (Holland 2000; Kotter 1996). It is important to remember that one cannot talk people into some new version of reality. Nothing is real to people unless they experience it firsthand, by interacting with it and evoking the possibilities through their personal process of observation (Wheatley 1999). These interactions and direct experiences let people to see how they will fit into the new reality. It also allows them to develop some sense of personal meaning for the proposed change. In order to accept change, each person must in some way change his or her own view of how things are and how things should be. This is frequently a difficult and time-consuming task. But the more that people are allowed to examine the impact of the proposed change on themselves, the better they will be able to incorporate it into their view of the world and of themselves.

Proposed change is almost always met with some kind of resistance. People resist change for several reasons. They may feel that change will increase their workload and therefore, negatively affect their day-to-day well-being. Or they may feel that they lack the necessary skills or abilities for the new environment. Try to predict why and how strongly various groups may resist the change. Think about ways to address these concerns in advance. Deal with the issues of workload honestly. Will it be temporary or long-term? Can staff be deployed differently in the future to compensate for changes in workload? Offer training for those who may feel they need it to get up to speed on the new procedures. Dealing openly with resistance not only helps to sell the idea but increases a leader's credibility. It shows that you as leader have taken the time to think about the impact of change on everyone and are trying to minimize that impact as much as possible. If the degree or extent of resistance seems greater than was anticipated, the initiative itself should be examined. Perhaps it is not the appropriate initiative at the present time. Maybe there is a better solution waiting. Knowing people's specific objectives can help you determine if you need to reconsider what you are proposing (Connor 1993; Kaser et al. 2002; Plenert and Hibino 1997).

It is also important for a leader to understand that people deal with change at different speeds and in different ways. Some jump right into it, while others need more reflection time in order to deal with the idea. All people's style and needs, as they work through the process of thinking about the coming change and figuring out what it means to them, must be acknowledged, respected, and accounted for. Different people perceive change in different ways, and the same change can affect people differently. Factors such as prior experience with change, level of knowledge and skill, individual resiliency, and the degree of influence a person has can affect how he or she experiences the proposed change (Holland 2000; Kaser et al. 2002; Orenstein 1999). Again, dealing with these issues in advance and allowing sufficient time for everyone to get on board will build support and will show that you as a leader really care about the needs and feelings of everyone concerned.

Leaders or change agents can keep people motivated by identifying and celebrating milestones in the implementation process. This helps people know where they are and keeps attention and energy focused on the success of the change effort. It also gives people a sense of accomplishment and a feeling that they have some control over the changing environment (Kaser et al. 2002).

Before a leader decides to propose some new initiative, he or she should carefully examine the consequences of taking that action and consult with colleagues. Does everyone involved have the time and energy to move the idea forward? It is important to factor in the time it will take to get all the affected people to become willing participants in the effort. What would be the impact on others in the organization if the idea is developed, or if it is not? What happens if it succeeds or if it fails? It is always a good idea to try out a new idea in some small way first. Any initial success can be used to gain support from others. Leaders also know when to cut their losses. Not every idea succeeds. Sometimes an idea turns out badly when fully explored, for a variety of reasons, including timing, technological constraints, finances, or lack of a receptive audience. Effective leaders do not hold on to an idea when it proves unworkable. They let it go as gracefully as they can and move on to something else that may have a higher probability of success (Kelley 1998). For more on working with colleagues see Chapter 3, "Embracing Cooperation and Change."

## LEADING IN INFORMATION LITERACY

If leaders are defined not by their job title but by their actions, then the history of ILI is full of examples of this type of grassroots leadership. During the 1970s groups of librarians banded together to form regional groups dedicated to sharing ideas and approaches to teaching and learning. This grassroots movement soon spawned national groups also devoted to the idea of instruction. Examples are:

- ALA's ACRL Bibliographic Instruction Section (now known as the Instruction Section) geared to the needs of academic librarians

- ALA's Library Instruction Roundtable, which serves librarians interested in instruction regardless of environment
- Library Orientation and Exchange (LOEX), which acts as a national library instruction clearinghouse or central depository for all formats of library instruction materials and sponsors yearly conferences on all aspects of ILI (Grassian and Kaplowitz 2001).

None of these organizations, plus numerous others throughout the world, would ever have come into being without the vision, courage, passion, and integrity of individuals who believed in the need for ILI. And these groups continue to flourish, providing new leadership opportunities for their members and inspiring each successive generation of librarians to look for ways to promote the cause of ILI.

On the more local level, new ILI initiatives frequently begin with a single librarian or group of librarians who identify a need for instruction and work long and hard not only to develop that instruction but also to sell it to the parties who would most benefit from it. Reference and instruction librarians in every type of environment (academic, public, school, and special libraries) monitor the questions being asked by their users and develop classes, handouts, tutorials, Web pages, and so on to meet those needs. And they work diligently to promote these developments to their users. They not only build it. They make sure people come.

Leaders are very much like inventors. Both are looking for that better mousetrap. And once they find it, both must get their ideas adopted. All it takes to be a leader is to identify a need; care enough to develop a response to that need; and work long and hard to see that the idea becomes a reality. IL librarians provide this type of leadership every day of their lives. Each new information resource that is developed and every change in information technology provides new leadership opportunities. On an even broader level, the move toward developing IL competency standards spearheaded by both ALA and the American Association of School Libraries (AASL) has opened the door for local groups to do the same. Librarians everywhere are coming together on their campuses, in their schools and businesses, and in their communities to develop both a local definition of IL and a list of competencies that would describe an information-literate person (Grassian and Kaplowitz 2001).

Leadership is everyone's business. And ILI leadership is the responsibility of every librarian who struggles on a daily basis to help his or her users locate, evaluate, and use information effectively and ethically. Are you such a leader? What is the impact on yourself and your users if you abdicate that role? If you have the desire but feel you do not have the requisite skills, look for opportunities to get those skills. Seek out leadership development opportunities. Take classes and attend seminars and workshops offered at your own institution and at local, state, and national conferences. For example, ALA's Leadership, Management and Administration (LAMA) division publishes an excellent journal as well as offering programs at the ALA Annual Conference. See the LAMA Web site for more information—http://www.ala.org/ala/lama/lama.htm. The Association of College and Research Libraries' (ACRL) Institute for Information Literacy offers an annual Immersion Program that among other things emphasizes the development of leadership and management skills. For more information on the ACRL's Immersion Programs see http://www.acrl.org/ala/acrl/acrlissues/acrlinfolit/professactivity/iil/immersion/immersionprograms.htm.

Read the leadership literature in management and psychology as well as in librarianship. Be sure to look at ALA's *A Library Advocate's Guide to Building Information Literate Communities* for tips about promoting your ideas in your community (ALA 2001; Barron 1999). Study people whom you believe have the characteristics you feel you need to develop and ask them to mentor you. Most people will be both flattered and happy to help. Part of being a leader is to provide this type of training for future generations, and leaders will be delighted to know that someone else is interested in taking their passion forward into the future. (For more on leadership development and mentoring see Chapter 4, "Fostering Growth in Yourself and Others.")

IL librarians must continue to be the advocates for their users. They must hone their leadership skills in order to get support from their administrators and their community leaders for the initiatives, programs, and projects being developed. Remember that it is up to the IL librarian to keep these administrators and leaders informed about what is happening in the field. Send them copies of important IL documents or point them to relevant Web pages. Invite them into your classes so they can see IL in action. Share your goals and objectives documents with important stakeholders in the community and ask for comment and suggestions about how best to reach those goals (Beasley 1996a, 1996b). In advocating the integration of IL into the curriculum IL librarians must learn to exercise their political know-how. IL programs must compete with any number of very worthwhile programs for a portion of the available funding. For more on this topic see Chapter 3, "Embracing Cooperation and Change."

The success of our advocacy efforts will depend on how well we show how IL assists others in achieving their goals. IL librarians need to be plugged into the right communication networks in their environment. They must keep constant vigil so they can identify new programs and initiatives with which to partner their IL agenda (Loomis 1995). The trick is to keep all the key players informed and involved. Remember that you are a representative of the library and its IL programs wherever you go. Use every opportunity to promote the idea of IL in general and your own programs and initiatives in particular (Heron, Powell, and Young 2001; Loomis 1995). The success of these IL leadership efforts will ensure that people in every walk of life will indeed become information-literate. The future of IL lies in the hands of each and every one of us. If we do not take a stand, then who else will?

EXERCISES

1.  Identify the type of culture represented by your organization (Control, Collaboration, Competence, or Cultivation).
2.  In what manner and to whom would you need to present your ideas if you wanted to initiate change?
3.  What is the mission of your organization and your library? How does your idea fit in with these missions?
4.  Do an environmental scan of your organization to identify trends, new initiatives, or programs of importance. How does your idea fit in with these organization-wide ideas?
5.  Develop short presentations to "sell" your idea to different audiences including your own staff and colleagues. What would you say if you had two minutes, five minutes, twenty minutes? Prepare presentation to fit these different time frames.

READ MORE ABOUT IT

Bennis, Warren. 2000. *Managing the Dream*. Cambridge, MA: Perseus Publishing.
Bergmann, Horst, Kathleen Hurson, and Darlene Russ-Eft. 1999. *Everyone a Leader: A Grassroots Model for the New Workplace*. New York: John Wiley and Sons.
Brandon, Nathaniel. 1998. *Self Esteem at Work: How Confident People Make Powerful Companies*. San Francisco: Jossey-Bass.
Covey, Stephen R. 1991. *Principle-Centered Leadership*. New York: Summit.
Depree, Max. 1989. *Leadership Is an Art*. New York: Doubleday.
Drucker, Peter F. 1996. "Not Enough Generals Were Killed." In *The Leader of the Future*, edited by F. Hesselbein, M. Goldsmith, and R. Beckhard. San Francisco: Jossey-Bass.

Quinn, Robert E. 2004. *Building the Bridge While You Walk on It: A Guide for Leading Change.* San Francisco: Jossey-Bass.

Schneider, William E. 1994. *The Reengineering Alternative.* Burt Ridge, IL: Irwin Professional Publishing.

Schreiber, Becky, and John Shannon. 2001. "Developing Library Leaders for the 21st Century." *Journal of Library Administration* 32(3/4): 35–57.

2

---

# Managing through Communication, Collaboration, and Team Building

*Our plans miscarry because they have no aim. When a man does not know what harbor he is making for, no wind is the right wind.*

—Seneca

## WHAT'S THE DIFFERENCE BETWEEN LEADERSHIP AND MANAGEMENT?

The previous chapter discussed leadership as a shared responsibility. Leadership was defined by action, not job description. People who exhibit leadership characteristics, who take a stand, who try to make a difference are leaders. So leadership becomes everyone's business. If leadership is indeed everyone's business, then is management everyone's business as well? Leadership and management are often confused in people's minds. Managers can and often do exhibit leadership qualities. And the official leaders of the organization, that is, those in administrative positions, can also be viewed as managers. After all, heads of libraries still have to supervise those who report to them.

Leaders as well as managers are often thought of in terms of being in-charge. But when viewing leadership from the situational angle, there is a clear distinction between leading and being in-charge. Leadership is defined in this sense by what a person does in a given situation or series of situations. In contrast to leadership, management is more tied to the position a person holds—in other words, to his or her job title and responsibility rather than the characteristics the person possesses. Leaders are described in terms of personality traits. Managers are depicted as having particular abilities. An effective leader has certain qualities that define him or her as a person. An effective manager has specific skills. Managers are the people throughout an organization who have the resources (both materials and personnel) to help the leader's vision become a reality. Leaders can be anyone in the organization who envisions a new and exciting future. Managers implement the changes visualized by these leaders, and managers are the ones who move the organization into that future. Leaders are the idea people. Managers put the ideas into practice.

Regardless of where these new ideas arise, it is often up to managers at various levels in the organization to help turn new ideas into reality. As a result, managers are often called upon to exhibit some of the characteristics previously described in relation to leadership. Whether the new vision is coming from the top administrators or is motivated by a grassroots effort, it is often up to the manager to communicate this vision to his or her staff and to help them accept the new approach being proposed (Holland 2000). Since change is often viewed as frightening or disruptive, this can often be a hard sell. Managers, who have credibility with their staff, communicate well, listen to and respect their staff's points of view, and are seen as supportive by those who work for them, are more likely to get their employees to adapt to the change being proposed. But managers must also have the practical skills and knowledge of the day-to-day operations to make things happen. Without strong management behind it, leadership might never follow through enough to get the results needed for the ultimate implementation of those great ideas (Anderson 1997).

In the library world where many new projects are implemented through committee work and teams, being a manager can be a temporary assignment. Those charged with running a team or a project must act in a managerial capacity but only for a given period of time. So being a manager can be permanent position, or it can be a position you acquire either voluntarily or by appointment that you hold for a defined period of time. However, regardless of the duration of the managerial assignment, effective managers have much in common. Effective managers are task-oriented. They are the decision makers and problem solvers in the organization. Managers focus on day-to-day operations, implement technology, specify procedures, and administer policy. Leaders, on the other hand, concentrate on inspiring creativity and innovation, anticipating problems, building relationships, and developing and empowering individuals and teams. They are future-focused and maintain a long-term perspective.

Leaders know where they want their organizations to go. Managers get the organization to that goal. Leadership deals with direction while management deals with speed. Leaders keep the mission in view. Managers establish the structure and systems to get those results and focus on efficiency, cost-benefit analysis, logistics, methods, procedures, and policies (Covey 1990a). Leaders ask what and why. Managers ask how and when. Leadership is getting people to want to do what needs to be done. Management identifies the tasks needed to get the job done and gets people to take on those tasks (Anderson 1997; Bennis 2000; Bethel 1995; Boyett and Boyett 1998; Hiebert and Klatt 2001; Manske 1987; Plas and Lewis 2001). Furthermore, management organizes the project and the tasks that need to be done into a logical sequence, tracks progress, and reports on results.

Information literacy librarians are often called upon to be both leaders and managers and must be able to exercise the traits and characteristics of each as circumstances indicate. They must be both the visionary innovators, the effective and efficient implementers. How managers accomplish their tasks is discussed more fully later in this chapter. However, no matter what role the IL librarian occupies within an organization, when he or she is developing or helping to develop new IL goals and initiatives, then leadership is being demonstrated. On the other hand, when that person is implementing these IL vision, plans, and goals, management is taking place (Plas and Lewis 2001; Yukl 1998).

## WHAT MAKES AN EFFECTIVE MANAGER?

So how do managers make things happen? Managers, just like leaders, work through other people. The leader must gain support for his or her vision. Managers implement that vision through the actions of those who either work for them or, as frequently is the case for IL managers, with them. They do this by explaining clearly and succinctly what needs to be done, by helping people understand how to do their work, and by training people so they can do that work effectively and efficiently.

Managerial functions include planning, organizing, overseeing progress, and motivating people. Planning involves setting goals and objectives, and developing "work maps" showing how those goals and objectives can be accomplished. Organizing involves the efficient deployment of resources both material and people. The oversight function includes tracking progress, and providing feedback and resources as needed.

Management is also very much about motivation. It is concerned with finding ways for people to want to work to meet expectations, to be competent, and to perform at their full potential (Boyett and Boyett 1998; Brandon 1998). Motivation plays a large part in determining employees' levels of performance, which in turn influences how well the goals and objectives are met. Finding ways to motivate colleagues to take on a teaching role and to develop themselves and improve their teaching skills is a large part of the job of the IL manager. For more on helping your colleagues develop themselves see Chapter 4, "Fostering Growth in Yourself and Others."

Oversight involves feedback and follow-up. Effective managers give timely and constructive feedback on the quality of the work and provide rewards for a job well done. They review what has been accomplished and make appropriate recommendations and reports to higher-up administrators, whether or not outcomes have deviated from expectations (Boyett and Boyett 1998; Brandon 1998; Hersey, Blanchard, and Johnson 2001). Effective managers support their staff, make sure that everyone receives appropriate training as needed, acknowledges efforts and results, and rewards successes both large and small (Bethel 1995) or suggests rewards to higher-ups.

Effective managers make people feel that they matter and are important and that they contribute to the overall success of the organization. Motivating others often means paying attention to what makes a difference to people and rewarding them accordingly. If people are to be motivated, they need to feel that their potential is being recognized. Effective managers tell people what they want and then let them do it without constant supervision.

People respond to being asked to take on special tasks. The request indicates belief in their abilities to accomplish that task. It is important to link these added responsibilities or new job duties either to an existing strength in such persons or to their development plan. IL managers do this by alerting their colleagues to growth and development opportunities and by helping them gain the skills to succeed at them. However, managers can only open the door. It is up to their colleagues to step through. In some ways, successful management is like successful teaching and learning; 50 percent of the responsibility for success is yours as the manager (or teacher), and 50 percent is the responsibility of the employees or members of the groups that you manage (or those you are teaching). In practical terms motivation is ultimately self-directed (Rooks 1988). Managers must continue to encourage and motivate their colleagues to take on new responsibilities, to change, and to grow. A library staffed by motivated people becomes an exciting and dynamic work environment in which continuous improvement, quality, innovation, and initiative are the norm (Kamp 1999).

Take the time to recognize achievement and praise improvement. When you acknowledge good work, your acknowledgment will have a strong motivating influence on people that encourages them to continue to perform at high levels and to strive for even higher ones. Recognition of accomplishments contributes to high levels of job satisfaction. People need to feel that what they are doing is useful and worthwhile and that they will receive credit for a job well done. Positive recognition makes people feel like doing more and keeps them going during difficult times (Bergmann, Hurson, and Russ-Eft 1999). Keep in mind that to be valid, recognition needs to be warranted or earned, given seriously, be appropriate to the situation (too much or too little negates the positive effect of the recognition), and be timed correctly. Recognition given too late may as well not be given at all. Recognition given too often and too easily will lose its value (Boyett and Boyett 1998; Rooks 1988; Egan 1985). Although IL managers may not be in a direct supervisory relationship with their colleagues, they can still perform this important motivating task by offering positive feedback and recognition for jobs well done.

On the other hand, managers must not avoid dealing with negative behavior or performance. If people are not meeting expectations that have been established and communicated to employees, managers must act to correct the situation before the unacceptable level of performance becomes the norm. If managers do not accept their responsibility to correct poor performance in some, everyone will experience a loss of motivation as standards decline (Rooks 1988; Wilson 1996). This can be a very tricky and difficult situation for IL managers. Since they frequently have no authority over their fellow IL librarians, constructive criticism can often be ignored or taken in a negative fashion. Modeling different approaches, offering to team-teach with a colleague, and working collaboratively in a team situation with other IL librarians are all ways to help improve everyone's performances. In general IL managers should remember to offer corrective suggestions in private and provide positive feedback and recognition both in public and in writing. See more about developing IL librarians in Chapter 4, "Fostering Growth in Yourself and Others."

IL managers who show an honest interest in their coworkers, both on and off the job, who are supportive to all, and who work to see that people are given the opportunity to achieve their highest potential will have a much easier time coordinating their library's IL programs. Their colleagues will be motivated to work hard and to meet the mission of the library, overcoming incredible obstacles by focusing efforts on that mission. A caring IL manager helps make colleagues look good, and when they look good, so does the manager (Wilson 1996). Involving people in decision making and the operation of IL programs and sharing authority and responsibility with others empower everyone and increase the likelihood of accomplishing the program's goals. Sharing authority and responsibility results in a collective effect and creates a team or family atmosphere. Most people will meet a higher standard of performance when there is a feeling of kinship or team spirit in the workplace. All people are energized when they feel they are an integral part of the organization (Wilson 1996). When people are allowed to analyze an issue in depth, carefully think through the implications and the alternatives, and responsibly make their recommendations, everyone is more committed to the solution selected and is more willing to work toward that goal (Covey 1990a).

Implicit in this approach is the acknowledgment that everybody's opinions are valid and should be listened to with respect. The emphasis, however, is on solving the problem, not defending a particular position. Conflict, when it inevitably arises, is seen as part of the natural progression leading to creative solutions. The IL manager must make sure that discussions stay focused on issues, not personalities. Everyone is allowed to state his or her opinion and possible solution without criticism and is given an equal opportunity to speak. No one is allowed to monopolize the discussion. The IL manager who can facilitate meetings, brainstorming sessions, and discussions in this manner can successfully lead the group toward a solution that is acceptable to all (Wilson 1996).

Managing IL programs can often be tricky and complicated. Librarians who are designated IL coordinators or program directors often do not have actual authority over their colleagues. They must work through and with other librarians to accomplish program goals but are often not in a position to set policy, determine expectations of quality, or give orders. IL managers must develop the skills to work horizontally even when they do not have authority or control over the resources they need (Bergmann, Hurson, and Russ-Eft 1999). For more on working with colleagues see Chapter 3, "Embracing Cooperation and Change."

IL managers must be able to sell their ideas to others and motivate them to participate. The IL manager then must be able to oversee the day-to-day operations and make sure that his or her colleagues are keeping the program objectives moving forward. If new courses, classes, and programs are being developed, it is up to the manager to make sure that deadlines are being met, that resources are being deployed properly to support new endeavors, that positive steps forward are praised, and that setbacks are addressed and remedied. IL managers walk a very delicate line, as they must perform these managerial tasks without appearing to micromanage while at the same time modeling creativity and encouraging the creative efforts of their colleagues. Librarians who find themselves in the role of IL managers do well to view themselves not as bosses in the traditional, hierarchical sense of the term, but as coaches, facilitators, and mentors. They lead teams through discussions that result in mutually agreed-upon decisions. They help their colleagues to develop their skills through modeling new techniques and by alerting other librarians to continuing education opportunities. Peer appraisal of teaching, which is discussed in a later chapter, is one way not only to reinforce excellent performance but to help instruction librarians develop their skills. Since peers rather than supervisors do it, peer appraisal provides a nonthreatening way for managers to encourage the continued growth and development of the instruction librarians with whom they work. See Chapter 4 for more on this and other development approaches as well as Chapter 3 for a further discussion on working with colleagues.

IL managers have many and varied responsibilities. Admittedly, a large portion of the IL manager's day is taken up with the never-ending round of logistics and administrative tasks that are required to keep a program running. What are these logistical and administrative responsibilities?

- Identifying needs by developing and conducting needs assessments.
- Coming up with tentative expected learning outcomes to meet identified needs.

- Working with IL librarians to list and develop means of helping students meet expected learning outcomes.
- Developing policies regarding instruction programs and efforts.
- Developing outreach and marketing plans and policies, including outreach to faculty, to teachers, to learners, to the community, and to other groups outside the library and outside the institution or organization.
- Developing partnerships for sequencing instruction with groups and institutions within and outside the library and the institution or organization.
- Developing continuing education and internal training for new and continuing ILI librarians.
- Developing assessments for programs, for ILI instructors, and for ILI materials.
- Handling and tracking ILI statistics.
- Reporting to, and making long-range plans with, higher-up administrators.
- Planning for change in research tools and materials and helping ILI instructors be prepared for constant change.
- Considering various grant and other opportunities to keep the instructional program up to date and moving forward with changing circumstances.

ILI managers must also keep the following questions in mind as they deal with individual instructional requests:

- Who has requested ILI?
- What sort of learning outcomes do they expect?
- Is there an information/research-related assignment?
- If so, what is it and what are its expected learning outcomes?
- If not, what sort of menu of ILI options would you offer the person requesting instruction?
- What would be an optimum time for an in-person session—for example, for academic and school libraries, at what point during the term?
- How many learners are expected?
- How much time would you have for a synchronous in-person group instruction session?
- Is there enough advance notice to develop the instruction properly?
- Which rooms are available for the requested day and time?
- Who is teaching which class?

- Has a room been booked for the session?
- Are there any scheduling conflicts, and if so, how can they be resolved?
- Are handouts or supporting Web pages being developed and completed in a timely manner?
- Are the supporting materials being reviewed and updated regularly?

This last point is extremely important when dealing with instructional Web sites, which seem to need constant care and maintenance to keep them relevant, attractive, and user-friendly. But a major job for the IL manager is also to take a step back from these day-to-day operations and examine the library's IL program as a whole, looking for both gaps and opportunities. Are all the users' needs being taken into account? What changes in information technology or in the library's information infrastructure offer new instructional challenges or opportunities? It is very easy to get caught up in, or even overwhelmed by, the day-to-day operations. The IL manager has the responsibility to stay focused on these details while never losing sight of the bigger picture.

Furthermore, the manager should be responsible for seeing that the components of a library's ILI program are being assessed. Are we able to determine what students know prior to instruction? Have they already had ILI? Has the ILI librarian worked with appropriate partners in their organization, institution, or environment such as campus leaders or faculty; school boards and teachers in their local schools; library boards, civic leaders, town council members; community leaders; representatives of local businesses, potential employers or managers and supervisors within their companies; and so on to set expected learning outcomes? Are goals and objectives being reached? Are students' learning outcomes being met? Managers should both encourage individual IL librarians to include assessment of each of their endeavors and also try to develop assessment techniques that measure the overall success of the program as a whole. For more information on both program planning and assessment see Chapters 7 and 12 in *Information Literacy Instruction: Theory and Practice* (Grassian and Kaplowitz 2001).

Since no one can do everything alone, all managers delegate tasks to some degree. But the IL manager works primarily through delegation. He or she sets the stage by performing needs assessments, analyzing program and course assessments, and facilitating planning meetings. The IL manager is also often the first contact for instructional requests, interviewing faculty, teachers, and others to determine need, and making tentative scheduling arrangements. Having helped his or her colleagues to identify what needs to be done, the effective manager lets people solve the problems on their own (Brandon 1998). This does not mean that the IL manager abdicates all responsibility. The IL manager needs to work with his or her colleagues in order to make sure that reasonable timelines, milestones, and deadlines are established. Effective managers will also check in at regular intervals to be sure matters are progressing as expected. This type of IL manager acknowledges that people learn and grow at a far better rate if they are allowed to struggle and come up with solutions themselves. He or she gives people real responsibility and avoids micromanaging at all costs (Baron 1999).

Maintaining your oversight role, without micromanaging, calls for walking a very fine line. Frequently, you must go against your own nature in order to create the right balance. If you tend toward overdelegation, where you give a lot of responsibility to members of the teams to set their own agendas and timetables, or have a laid-back attitude in which you let teams function with very little oversight from you, make sure you design a regular reporting schedule for the project. It is useful not only to set a schedule for these reports but also to indicate what everyone involved is expected to accomplish during the time between the reports. This really helps keep the project or task moving along and on track. It also allows for troubleshooting if events are not going as well or as quickly as planned. Perhaps additional training is needed, or resources or staff need to be reallocated in order to complete the project. It is better to discover these things sooner rather than later and regular checkup reports enable you as a manager to offer assistance as needed. If, on the other hand, you are the type of person who likes to be in complete control and would rather do everything by yourself, lighten up and let go a bit. Remember, giving people responsibility is a way of helping them grow and develop. The effective manager believes in the potential of the people with whom he or she works. Effective managers see the best in people and by doing so, inspire them to be the best that they can be (Covey 1990a).

The best managers build a network of relationships with people throughout the organization. It is wise to begin building these relationships before they are needed. IL managers should focus their energies on cultivating relationships with the key people on whom they are dependent to get their ideas implemented. They should pay particular attention to critical gaps, people who are crucial to their success but with whom they do not as yet have a relationship (Hill, Gabarro, and Kotter 1998). This could include people in administration, information technology departments, marketing and public relations, student services, and so on. Many management theorists recommend the practice of "management by walking around" (Covey 1990b; Hill, Gabarro, and

Kotter 1998; Plas and Lewis 2001). Get out and meet people. Talk to people in other departments and ask questions. Find out what their goals and objectives are and see if there is some common ground between what they are trying to do and the initiatives you are trying to promote.

IL librarians need to spend more time talking to nonlibrarian groups who share their concerns. They must build coalitions within their organizations and with the larger community in which their organization operates. Speaking at nonlibrarian forums and inviting nonlibrarians to speak at ours help build these connections, as does publishing in nonlibrarian professional literature. Coauthoring with faculty, administrators, or community leaders also helps to bridge the gap between librarians and those with whom they need to be partnering (Loomis 1995). Networking, making connections, and maintaining those relationships can prove to be the difference between success and failure when you are trying to move your IL program into new and previously untried territories.

Since IL librarians have rarely been in a "power" position, they have always had to operate through influence, consensus building, partnerships, and modeling. They have had to become experts in team building and collaboration and have used their skills as persuasive communicators to develop these collaborations among their colleagues. The move toward a more flattened organization in which collaboration is the norm rather than the exception offers the IL librarian a unique opportunity to use these team-building skills on a broader playing field. As they move out into the community to market their IL programs, IL librarians can feel confident that they have the requisite skills to build the partnerships needed to create and implement IL programs of benefit to all. Let's take a closer look at these three important skills— communication, collaboration, and creating teams.

## HOW DO MANAGERS MAKE THINGS HAPPEN?

*Communicate*

In the previous chapter, persuasive communication was listed as one of the earmarks of an effective leader. Managers, too, must be effective communicators not so much to see their ideas or the ideas of their leaders accepted, but to forge the partnerships and coalitions needed to get the job done.

Strange as it may seem, a large part of communication is listening. Management texts indicate that as much as 80 percent of work time can be spent in talking to others. The more managerial responsibility one has, the higher the percentage of time is spent in communication. Communicating and listening skills, therefore, are essential to effective management (Sheldon 1991). The effective manager pays attention to both the spoken and the unspoken message. Body language, eye contact, gestures, and posture convey as much or possibly more information than the words themselves. Tone, intonation, conversational pauses are all clues to what is going on inside a person's head. What is left unspoken can frequently be extremely meaningful and important. It is estimated that humans are capable of producing 650,000 nonverbal messages. According to some social anthropologists over 50 percent of all human communication is nonverbal in nature. Furthermore, whenever the verbal and the nonverbal messages are inconsistent, it is the nonverbal ones that the listener pays attention to (Lewis 2000). The effective manager is skilled in interpreting these cues in order to get to the real message behind the words. Knowledge of this unspoken language can also help the manager make sure that his or her spoken and unspoken communications are consistent and therefore better understood and trusted (Anderson 1997; Bergmann, Hurson, and Russ-Eft 1999; Charvet 1997; Lewis 2000; Wilson 1996).

Facial expressions are a vital part of nonverbal communication. People who are enthusiastic and lively in their expressions tend to be listened to. They maintain the listener's attention. Nonverbal communication telegraphs interest or the lack of it in the conversation at hand. Eye contact or the lack of it can be extremely important. In many cultures, especially Western ones, looking away can indicate disinterest in the speaker (Lewis 2000). Looking someone in the eye in this type of cultural setting indicates attention to the issues and honesty in responding.

Gestures, postures, and expressions can also communicate particular attitudes or feelings. Again, these may vary from culture to culture. For example in Western cultures, the person who walks with his or her head down, eyes downcast, shoulders hunched, chin jutted forward is perceived as depressed or with low self-esteem. But the person who walks with head high and arms swinging freely radiates the appearance of poise and self-confidence. The person who is deliberate in his or her steps will be perceived as a focused and friendly individual (Lewis 2000). People make these assumptions because they know how they feel when they walk like that. Effective managers can use this knowledge to change how others perceive them. By standing up straight, walking with head held high, and making consistent eye contact, managers can communicate a positive self-image and will look like someone who should be listened to. And as people respond positively to that behavior, the manager's self-confidence increases. Acting the part can often lead to becoming the part. Practicing positive body language can go a long way toward developing the type of managerial affect needed to gain people's trust, loyalty, and cooperation. See Chapter 14 in *Information Literacy Instruction: Theory and Practice* for more on nonverbal communication and cultural differences (Grassian and Kaplowitz 2001).

Effective communication is not so much a matter of intellect as it is of trust and acceptance of others, of their ideas and feelings. It rests on the belief that people have differing opinions and that from their point of view, they are right (Covey 1990b). Effective communicators listen to and hear others completely and without judgment. They wait before speaking, re-create in their own mind what was just said, and check to make sure that they truly understand what has been spoken. Effective communicators restate what they think the speaker said and allow the speaker to clarify the message if there is any misunderstanding (Raspa and Ward 2000). A person who listens well actively checks for the intended meaning from the sender's point of view and allows the sender to finish what he or she has to say. This not only increases the likelihood of everyone's being understood but also conveys empathy for each person's point of view. This form of communication or active listening shows interest in, and respect for, the other person's perspective (Anderson 1997; Wilson 1996) and should be very familiar to anyone who has worked successfully with the public during a reference interview.

Active listening means paying attention to the situation and the attitudes and feelings of the speaker. Effective listening must be open-minded and nonjudgmental. Nothing will destroy communication faster than a premature judgment or criticism. Critical assessment of an embryonic idea can shut down communication and kill the idea before it is even fully developed (Raspa and Ward 2000; Rooks 1988). Managers must hear the speaker out and not start formulating their response even before the speaker has concluded. It is a common reaction to get a sense of what is being said and then to stop listening and start thinking about what to say in return. This often leads to missing some vital bit of information, a misinterpretation of the entire message, and therefore an inappropriate response. A large part of what people hear is misunderstood, forgotten, or ignored because they do not listen to the complete message. Not talking while others are speaking shows respect and gives them a chance to completely express themselves (Rooks 1988; Wilson 1996). Listening to only part of the message is not only rude; it is dangerous. It can effectively shut down the current conversation and can detrimentally affect future communications as well.

Part of active listening is attending. Attending means giving undivided attention to the speaker. This is indicated through body language and gestures such as facing the other person, squaring the shoulders, maintaining eye contact, leaning in, and standing an appropriate distance from the speaker (Anderson 1997). Remember that some of these attending postures are culture-bound. For example, the distance between speaker and listener varies from culture to culture. When two people from different cultures are engaged in conversation, you might notice one trying to back away in order to maintain his or her comfort zone, while the other person, who is from a culture where the critical distance is closer, keeps trying to close the gap. The result can be the pair slowly moving across the room as each tries to maintain what is the optimal distance for conversation in his or her culture. So watch for any signs of discomfort on the part of the speaker and adjust these attending postures appropriately. Above all, do not invade someone's personal space (Grassian and Kaplowitz 2001; Lewis 2000; Richmond, McCrosky, and Payne 1991; Wilson 1996). Attending forms the basis for observing another person accurately and perceiving his or her message without distortion (Anderson 1997). See Chapter 14 in *Information Literacy Instruction: Theory and Practice* for more on nonverbal communication and cultural differences (Grassian and Kaplowitz 2001).

Effective communicators use vocal sounds that indicate they are listening and to communicate both attention and empathy. These sounds (yes, uh huh, hmm) keep the focus on the message and imply a nonjudgmental attitude. Remember not to overdo it, though. Saying "uh huh" too often can be distracting and even annoying. Good listeners also encourage people through phrases, words, and sentences that urge the speaker to elaborate on the message. Phrases such as "Go on," "Tell me more," and "Explain how you felt," can be extremely useful. Another useful approach is to stop concentrating on problems and start asking for solutions. For example, ask the speaker, "What would you do to solve this situation?" (Wilson 1996).

All of us have a set of communication filters shaped by our history, sense of identity, cultural upbringing, mannerisms and taboos, beliefs about what is true, and values about what is right, as well as our own perceptions and interpretations about what is going on. As we listen, we squeeze what is being said through our own personal filtering system. People from the same ethnic, cultural, gender, national, or geographical grouping share common histories and beliefs. That makes communication within groups easier and less prone to misunderstanding than communication between people from different backgrounds.

Furthermore, people process information differently based in part on their preferred learning style. Do they like to hear, see, or interact with the information? Do they require many examples before reaching a conclusion, or do they jump in after only a few? Do they analyze, consider, and wait to react? Are they big-picture or detail-oriented types?

Are they attracted to the new and different or the tried-and-true? Some grounding in the learning styles research can help managers become more aware of these differences and adjust the way they present their views accordingly (Charvet 1997; Grassian and Kaplowitz 2001). See Chapter 4 in *Information Literacy Instruction: Theory and Practice* for more on learning styles (Grassian and Kaplowitz 2001).

Effective managers are effective communicators. They know when to speak and when to listen. They are skilled at interpreting both the spoken and the unspoken message. And they know how to present their own message in a way that will be understood and accepted. Many characteristics of effective communication may seem very familiar to the classroom teacher and the reference librarian. Interpersonal communication skills are vital to both tasks. IL librarians need only transplant these skills from the classroom or the reference desk to the arena of IL program management. In doing so, they find they can use these abilities to effectively build the collaborations, coalitions, and teams needed to create and implement their IL programs.

*Collaborate*

Collaborations are based on shared goals and mutual needs. New initiatives, be they large-scale or small-scale, often require resources, skills, and information not immediately available to the IL librarian. In order to get these initiatives implemented, relationships must be forged with others in the organization, those who have the necessary resources. Collaborative interactions enable people with diverse expertise to generate creative solutions to mutually defined problems (Muronaga and Harada 1999).

IL managers must be skilled not only at identifying potential partners, but also at communicating what they, as information professionals, can bring to the table. They must also help foster these skills in their colleagues. Pressures to economize are resulting in major cost-cutting strategies in all walks of life. At the same time, advances in information technologies are changing the way people work and study. As the amount of information available escalates and new ways to access that information evolve, knowledge of how information is organized and published and the capacity to teach the skills needed to gain efficient access to it will increase in value. This increasingly complex and expansive information universe makes it impossible for any one person to master all the relevant skills necessary to function in today's society (Caspers and Lenn 2000; Raspa and Ward 2000). IL librarians should promote their expertise in these areas as the basis of forming collaborations. The key is to show what IL librarians can bring to any proposed collaboration that will help all concerned reach their particular goals.

Successful collaborations are based on mutual needs and common concerns. IL librarians need to understand the issues that are important to those with whom they wish to form a coalition. It is essential that librarians make their case for IL within the context of their potential partners' issues, needs, concerns, and goals. IL librarians need to show how IL can help these future collaborators solve their problems and achieve their aims (Loomis 1995). Building a successful collaboration requires having working insights into the institutional contexts that shape partners' interests and perspectives and requires developing a sensitivity to the culture, ethos, and points of view that have contributed to those perspectives (Raspa and Ward 2000).

It is important to find creative ways to be in close touch with how the organization operates and to identify the key players in the enterprise (Sheldon 1991). This is especially crucial in the IL arena, as IL librarians frequently must partner with these stakeholders in their environment (community leaders, school boards, administrators, teachers, faculty, information technology experts, student services offices, etc.), in order to implement their IL programs. Without knowing who the players are and what is important to each one, IL librarians could move too fast, reach out to potential partners in ways that are not fruitful or are counterproductive, and develop unworkable plans.

It is important to remember that in every environment IL is a shared responsibility. The more IL librarians know about what people do, what they value, and how they view IL, the better they can form collaborative coalitions that can develop viable plans specifically geared for the environment in which the IL librarian must operate. How do IL librarians gain this much-needed knowledge? They do so by looking beyond the library and making contact with many different constituencies within and outside an organization or institution. They read relevant institutional and other documents, learn the historical context and the jargon of other groups, attend meetings, presentations, and conferences sponsored by a variety of organizational groups, volunteer to work on committees that put them in touch with a diverse cross-section of those in the organization, apply for presentations and poster sessions for library and nonlibrary conferences, jointly with partners within and outside the library, and take every opportunity to talk to people in their community. The most casual conversation can spark ideas, highlight connections between projects, point out common goals, and form the basis for future collaborations.

IL librarians should think in terms of building long-term relationships. They should be interested not only in the immediate success of the collaboration but in the development of a relationship that can be counted on in the future (Hill, Gabarro, and Kotter 1998). The key to success in any collaborative enterprise is the ability to listen patiently, without making assumptions into what the other person may be thinking or saying. Working collaboratively means becoming nonjudgmental listeners. In the end, building relationships results in building bridges (Raspa and Ward 2000).

In any collaboration, it is crucial to develop a goal or mission that clearly, meaningfully, and simply connects the self-interest of each partner to the overall purpose of the collaboration (Rubin 1998). The net result is a goal everyone is fully committed to and is willing to work hard toward accomplishing. Of equal importance is the idea of interdependence. Although each party in a collaboration joins it with some particular and possibly self-serving goal in mind, everyone in the group recognizes and invests in the agendas of all its members (Hill, Gabarro, and Kotter 1998). The outcome of the collaboration should be beneficial to all concerned. Successful collaborations are built on a sense of shared responsibility for the end result and the understanding that each member of the collaboration is expected to contribute or generate the resources needed to ensure the success of the project (Rubin 1998).

Successful collaborations are based on open, honest, and clear communication. Partners must understand and respect each other's perspectives. The heart of collaboration is the development of a climate of trust and mutual respect in which these different perspectives are identified and honored. There is a sense of parity in which everyone's contribution is valued (Muronaga and Harada 1999). Nothing bonds people together better than the belief that their comments, suggestions, viewpoints, and recommendations are being acknowledged and taken seriously (Rubin 1998). Collaborative partners must be willing to listen and learn and to take the time and effort to formulate solutions in which every member of the coalition can move closer to accomplishing his or her personal goals. A successful collaboration results in a situation in which everyone feels he or she has come out a winner and that together they have accomplished something that none of them could have done alone. The best collaboration begins with mutually agreed upon goals and a shared vision and ends with that vision and those goals becoming a reality. For more on developing and fostering collaborations within your particular political environment, see Chapter 3, "Embracing Cooperation and Change."

*Create Teams*

By definition, collaboration means working with other people—people with different attitudes, beliefs, behaviors, and ideas. For any collaboration to succeed, these diverse elements must be formed into a team that has a common purpose and a mutually agreed-upon goal. This is true whether the collaboration is between the library and other stakeholders in the organization or among colleagues within the library itself. As discussed in the previous section, the ability to forge collaborative coalitions with those outside the library is important for the development of many IL initiatives. Of equal importance is the ability to develop collaborative teams among those involved in IL instruction within the library.

For IL managers the ability to work effectively in a team environment can mean the difference between success and failure for their IL programs. IL managers rarely have the authority to assign tasks or direct their colleagues. They must ask for help and rely on the cooperation of their colleagues to keep their IL programs alive and well. While the IL manager may be the one to whom instruction requests are initially directed, he or she rarely is in the position to designate the one among the other IL librarians in the library who will actually take responsibility for the instruction. A strong belief in teamwork and the abilities of the IL manager to promote, develop, and nurture a team mentality among his or her colleagues is imperative to keeping an IL program afloat.

The IL manager may be the head of a team or a member of it. The team may be entirely library-centric, or it may consist of people from many different segments of the organization or the community at large. In any case knowing what makes for successful team behavior will help that team reach its goals. Therefore, one of the most vital skills that any manager needs to develop is the ability to lead and/or function on synergistic teams, teams in which people work cooperatively together to reach a common goal.

Knowing how people perform effectively on teams means paying attention not only to the team task but also to the team process, that is, how the team gets its work done. IL managers with a firm grounding in team process can provide guidance into, and act as a model for, effective team behavior regardless of their position in the team—head or member. The more the IL manager understands how people coalesce into a functional and productive team, the better he or she can assist the team to reach a high level of productivity. The IL manager does this not so much by dictating how the team members should go about their collective work. Rather, the IL manager works from whatever position he or she holds on the team to help increase the team's effectiveness and efficiency.

Developing a successful team takes work. And it takes agreed-upon rules for behavior. In other words, successful teams share a team culture. This culture defines the assumptions and beliefs that shape the team norms involving distribution of power, communication patterns, conflict management, and the selection of legitimate topics for discussion (Hill, Gabarro, and Kotter 1998). It is important to remember that all teams go through four stages of development: Forming, Storming, Norming, and Performing (Boyett and Boyett 1998; Orenstein 1999; Palmer 1988). Each of these stages is necessary and important to the team process.

Team culture evolves during the first or "Forming" stage. During Forming, ground rules for discussion, negotiation, and decision making are developed and agreed upon by all team members (Anderson 1997). "Storming," the second stage in the process, is probably the most difficult one and the point at which many teams fall apart. It is only natural that when a number of diverse people with differing viewpoints are brought together, differences of opinions will surface. The way a group handles this very delicate stage can make or break the team. It helps if the team leader views his or her role as "coach" rather than "conductor" at this point (Hill, Gabarro, and Kotter 1998) and makes sure that all team members are abiding by the ground rules set in the Informing stage. But all members of the team can assist in navigating this tricky stage by making sure that they themselves are abiding by the ground rules and calling deviations from the ground rules by others to the attention of the team and its leader.

The Storming stage should be viewed as a place for all team members to air their opinions without fear of criticism. The more the ground rules are respected, the easier it is to work through this very vital stage. During Storming everyone's cards should be put on the table so that all points of view are accounted for. Each team member must understand the needs and the perspectives of the others on the team. The extent to which team members practice open and honest communication and then make a sincere effort to understand each other's point of view is how a successful team is formed (Chamberlain 1995).

It is during the next stage, "Norming," when these varying opinions are discussed and coalesced into a coherent group focus. Once the team has agreed upon a focus and direction, it can enter the fourth and final stage, Performing, in which solutions are proposed, possible actions are discussed, tasks are assigned, and deadlines are set.

Successful team performing depends on a balance of dialogue and discussion. People engaged in a dialogue suspend their views and enter into deep listening as they attempt to see through the eyes of other team members. Dialogue requires paying close attention to everything being said and the suspension of assumptions. For dialogue to be truly successful, time must be set aside for silence, giving team members the chance to reflect upon their own and other people's thoughts. Successful dialogue results in people's making a genuine attempt to appreciate matters of concern from the viewpoint of those raising the concerns. Dialogue implies a desire to learn and discover shared meaning, to integrate multiple perspectives, and to uncover and examine underlying perspectives. The basic essential skill in dialogue is the suspension of judgment that allows for the surfacing of assumptions and beliefs that influence everyone's perceptions of reality. The value of dialogue and the resultant greater mutual understanding among team members is that it is the basis for conflict resolution, consensus, and community building. Dialogue ensures that each person is heard and ideally understood. It often opens up the possibility of a better solution since the goal is finding common ground (Flood 1999; Kaser et al. 2002).

Discussion, on the other hand, is undertaken to make decisions. During discussion different views are presented in an attempt to search for the one to support the issue in question. Discussion comprises telling, selling, persuading, gaining agreement, evaluating choices, and selecting the best of these choices (Flood 1999; Kaser et al. 2002). If discussion follows successful dialogue, the decisions made will be acceptable to all parties, as all perspectives not only are on the table but are understood and appreciated by all. When discussion precedes or preempts dialogue, only the most dominant people in the group may be heard. This puts power in the hands of the few rather than in the hands of the team as a whole. If power is hoarded in this fashion, others may feel their participation is futile. They can withhold their opinions and just go along with the decisions being made. Agreements may be realized prematurely without considering the outcome from all perspectives. Mediocre compromises may be reached, and action plans not acceptable to all may be chosen. Team members who do not feel committed to the resulting action, because they did not contribute to the solution or because their contributions were ignored, may not actively support it or may even act to undermine the decision (Kets de Vries 2001). To avoid this potentially detrimental situation, team leaders and team members should insist that productive dialogue, where all parties are given an equal chance to express themselves, occurs before any discussion with the goal of reaching a decision is undertaken.

Managing change through teams has become a widely accepted practice in the library world. At UCLA, we created a team or interest group model in order to develop our Information Literacy Initiative (ILI), the goals of which are:

- To assess information literacy skills at UCLA
- To improve information literacy skills at UCLA

- To increase awareness of information literacy concepts among members of the UCLA community, within the context of changing information needs and environments.

Five activities were identified as being important to reaching these goals, and five interest groups or functional teams were set up. The Informing team was assigned the tasks of promotion, publicity, and marketing. The Instructional Development team worked on ways of helping UCLA librarians develop their instructional skills. The Measuring group task was to come up with appropriate ways to assess IL at UCLA and to help librarians incorporate assessment techniques into their instructional endeavors. The Collaborating group explored ways of working with faculty and other interested parties on campus on joint IL projects, and the Reaching team examined the various modes of delivering IL to our community—both virtually and in person. A Steering Committee (comprising primarily the heads of each of these groups and the ILI director, who acted as liaison to library administration) was also formed to maintain communication between the teams and act in a general oversight function. Working within this team environment allowed the ILI to move forward on a number of fronts simultaneously and distributed ownership of the project throughout the library. For more information about the ILI at UCLA, see http://www.library.ucla.edu/infolit/index.html.

Powerful teamwork generates synergy. Synergy exists when the sum of something exceeds the whole of its parts. In an organizational setting, synergy increases effectiveness through cooperation or combined action. People come together who have complementary skills and resources, and in combination, they can achieve far more than they could alone (Kaser et al. 2002). Individuals on such synergistic teams acknowledge that they are working toward the same goal. They understand that they cannot reach that goal unless they work cooperatively with others on the team. They not only share a common cause but recognize the interdependency of their actions. People on synergistic teams demonstrate the ability to function in a value-added manner. Each person believes he or she has something of value to contribute and that these contributions are important to, and appreciated by, the organization as a whole (Connor 1993). Working synergistically is more likely to produce win-win rather than win-lose solutions because people negotiate what they will contribute and work toward, until all are invested in a common goal. Working synergistically, then, requires greater involvement that empowers people and increases commitment to agreed-upon solutions, outcomes, and actions (Kaser et al. 2002).

Creating and coordinating effective teams take diplomacy, tact, and excellent interpersonal and communication skills. Teams do not always run smoothly. There is great potential for problems and pitfalls along the way. Creating the ideal team environment takes diligence and effort. Team problems can include members who do not contribute to the team or make just minimal efforts. On the other extreme are those who try to "hijack" the team with their own agendas or are so dominating that they do not allow all members to participate fully. The head or coordinator of a team should always remember that his or her role is not to force a decision upon the team, but to facilitate discussion that leads to a mutually agreed-upon solution to the problem at hand. It is the coordinator's role to keep discussions on target, to help the team resolve conflict by referring back to the team's ground rules, to ensure that all parties are heard from and that all opinions are treated with nonjudgmental respect. The head of the team encourages everyone to express his or her opinions and frequently reviews, rephrases statements, and synthesizes the discussion for the group to ensure that everyone is on the same page. Effective team coordinators play to people's strengths and involve each member of the team in ways that highlight his or her skills and expertise. Idle, unmotivated, and uninvolved team members become bored and lose interest in the process (Zemon 1996). The team leader also must be the liaison to administration, keeping administration informed about progress and problems. The team leader makes sure that both the members of the team and the administration are on the same page—that is, that the goals for the team coincide with the expectations of the people who appointed the team.

Are you trying to develop a new online tutorial aimed at helping undergraduates gain basic information literacy competencies? The IL manager can use the team approach to help make this project a reality. First, the manager defines the tasks to be done and identifies the skills, knowledge, and expertise needed for the project. In this case, the team probably needs someone with Web design skills, instructional design experience, someone perhaps with some technical expertise in developing online tutorials, and of course, someone knowledgeable about the content. The IL manager can then form the team either by asking for volunteers or by approaching individuals that he or she feels would most effectively fit the required roles. The IL manager then works with the team to make sure everyone understands the tasks to be accomplished; knows what his or her role is in the team; ensures that the team gets the necessary training and resources needed to accomplish the task; and helps the team set reasonable milestones and timelines.

The specifics of effective team management go beyond the scope of this book. However, much has been written on this topic. One example is *Team Building. Blueprints for Productivity and Satisfaction*, edited by W. Brendan Reddy and Kaleel Jamison. Pay special attention to the chapter by Judith D. Palmer entitled "For the Manager Who Must Build a Team" (Palmer 1988).

Many team leaders have come to understand that they can be more effective if they share responsibility and authority for managing the team with the team itself. Effective team performance is more likely if all team members assume responsibility for making it a success. Some team leaders even rotate the person who acts as facilitator at different team meetings. The team leader, however, must remember that he or she is ultimately responsible for getting the task at hand accomplished. Teams count on the leader to provide timely and specific feedback on their progress and to keep everyone on the team accountable for his or her actions (Hill, Gabarro, and Kotter 1998).

IL managers, whether they are part of the team itself or merely have nurtured its creation, should monitor the team's progress toward the desired goal. Someone needs to do this, or the team will lose its focus and direction. Reading meeting minutes and asking for regular progress reports is not a sign of micromanaging. It indicates interest in the team's progress and a desire for the team to reach its goals in a timely manner. Managers should make sure the team has set some kind of timetable, with clearly designated deadlines, and must be alert to slippage in this timetable. IL librarians have many demands on their time, and team projects may receive less attention than the many other tasks that fill their days. The IL manager can ensure that team projects do not die of neglect by keeping a friendly eye on the team's progress. If a project seems to be going off course or is not being moved along in a timely manner, it may be time to call the team together to find out if the project is still a viable one. Perhaps the project needs revising or updating or even abandoning. If the project is still felt to be worthwhile, the manager should help the team brainstorm how to get the project back on track. Does the team need additional resources, either personnel or materials? Would additional training help them reach their goal? Does the team need to develop partnerships or collaborations with other teams either within the library or outside its doors? In short, how can the project get moving again, and what, if anything, can the manager do to assist in creating this forward momentum? Back to our tutorial example, has the team hit a roadblock because they do not know how to use the desired Web authoring software? This might be a good time to bring someone with these skills into the team. Alternatively, someone on the team could be offered the opportunity to take classes in order to learn the necessary programming to accomplish the task. In either case, an adjustment in the timeline of the project might need to be made in order to allow for either of these options to take place.

Bringing good people together who are all committed to some mutual goal is only the first step in building successful teams. The IL manager must support the team effort in any way necessary so that the team can succeed in its task. People who have succeeded in a team effort will be more willing to participate in others in the future. Developing effective, efficient, synergistic teams empowers everyone in the organization. It allows more widespread input into decision making and demonstrates a belief in shared responsibility in the running of the organization.

IL managers can create an environment in which teamwork is the norm. Rather than trying to do everything by themselves, IL managers should ask for assistance from their colleagues. They should identify strengths, special skills, and specific interests among their coworkers and should appeal to those with these special talents to join them on particular projects; for example, a cataloger might be a good addition to a project when the team is trying to organize a variety of tutorials or instructional modules into a user-accessible database. Or the team might wish to confer with a subject specialist in order to make sure they have included all the most pertinent resources on a particular topic.

IL managers who model a team mentality will soon find that teams begin to pop up spontaneously among their colleagues. As problems or issues arise, people stop trying to think about how they can solve the problem themselves but look for people with whom they should partner—people who can help them develop possible solutions. Learning to work in teams within the library also provides the right mind-set to help IL librarians look for, and build, collaborative coalitions outside the library. So all in all, the IL manager who works through and within library-based teams sets the tone for moving IL courses, programs, and initiatives forward beyond the library itself.

## MANAGE YOUR IL PROGRAM EFFECTIVELY

The individual charged with managing IL programs in today's fast-paced, ever-changing environment needs to be able to keep his or her eye on both the small details and the big picture. It is generally the role of the IL manager to ensure that the everyday details of the program are running smoothly. At the same time the IL manager is responsible for determining that the overall program itself is meeting the needs of the library's constituencies. Communication, collaboration, and team-building skills are invaluable to both these endeavors. Let's look at some of the tasks that make up the typical IL manager's job and see how these three essential abilities contribute to the accomplishment of those tasks.

*Review the Program*

IL managers keep an eye on the big picture by engaging in regular pro-grammatic review. This would include an analysis of what current in-struction (both virtual and live) is in place and the resources available to support instruction (budget, equipment, personnel, and space—the who, what, why, when, and where). It is just as important to know where you are starting as to know where you want to go. Program-matic reviews should also include some kind of needs assessment to determine if changes in the current program are warranted. Needs as-sessments help the IL manager discover gaps in instruction and also identify potential partners outside the library who might be called upon to assist in developing and implementing programs that could fill these gaps.

For example, is there a large undergraduate course that is taught every semester and requires a research paper but has no IL component built in? Do hordes of students descend on the library with questions about how to accomplish this task? The IL manager can identify this problem, discuss possible solutions with colleagues, and help to de-velop a way to work with the department to implement these solutions. One approach could be for the IL manager to survey current students in order to pinpoint places in which they are having difficulties doing their library research, present the results to the appropriate faculty or teaching assistants, and coordinate a collaborative effort between the li-brary and the department that can address the problem.

It is imperative that the IL manager be attuned to the goals and ob-jectives of the parent organization as well as those of the library itself. Be sure to check with administrators every so often to be sure your IL goals still match the institution's and the library's goals. New major or-ganizational initiatives may offer opportunities to promote the library's current IL program and identify possibilities for growth (Grassian 1993; Grassian and Kaplowitz 2001). Excellent communication skills help the IL manager gather the needed information, forge the collaborative part-nerships, and build the effective teams that can move the library's IL programs into new and needed directions.

Written as well as oral communication skills are of equal impor-tance. While IL managers may be given the opportunity to "sell" their ideas in person, the sharing of written material offering background and justifications for the proposed new idea frequently precedes these in-person meetings. The ability to write a clear, succinct, and persua-sive memo is invaluable. Include just enough to get the recipient's attention—no more than one or two pages at most. Whet their appetite for more information. Refer them to sources for additional material and even more importantly offer to meet with them in order to expand on the proposed ideas. Practice the "less is more" philosophy for memo writing. Use the same techniques for trimming the fat that IL instructors use for selecting what to fit into a given instructional section. Identify what are the main facts that need to be highlighted. Explain only as much as is needed to get the idea across. Give a few illustrative examples and then offer to address any questions or concerns. Hopefully, this will lead to potential collaborative partners or potential team members asking to meet with you to discuss the matter further.

Instructions for how to write a "Memo to an Administrator" can be found on the CD accompanying this book. You might use this as a model. Your memo could include sections such as Problem Statement, Significance of Problem, a History of Attempts to Address the Problem, Proposed Solution, Resources Needed, Draft TimeLine, and so on.

*Plan and Develop Instruction*

Once instructional needs have been identified, the IL manager must oversee the planning and development of an instructional response that meets that need such as developing an IL online tutorial to address the needs of a specific population like International Students or English as a Second Language Students. Depending upon the nature of the instruction, the IL manager will be working with "outside the library" collaborators, in-house library teams, or both to plan and develop this response. The IL manager may need to identify sources for additional funding and secure that funding from institutional partners or outside funding agencies. See Chapter 6 for more information on grants and grant writing.

Although the IL manager may work in conjunction with collaborative partners to identify an instructional need, it is usually up to the library staff either to develop the appropriate response or to partner with others to address it jointly. Of course any joint venture should be cleared with library administration before it is proposed to others outside the library. The library staff generally will be the ones to figure out ways to respond to the problem, while IL managers tend to be assigned the task of working out the means to develop and foster joint efforts. As discussed above, the team approach to instructional development offers the advantages of both tapping into a variety of expertise and getting more buy-in from the IL librarians who may be called upon to implement the plan. The IL manager who encourages problem solving via the formation of synergistic teams creates an environment where new ideas are both welcome and enthusiastically pursued.

TRAIN

Although IL managers may be only nominally in-charge of their IL colleagues, it is up to them to make sure that all people involved in the IL program receive the necessary training to do their jobs. The IL manager, therefore, should keep attuned to any training opportunities being offered locally, regionally, nationally, and worldwide and should share this information among everyone involved in the library's IL program. Of special interest are the many virtual instruction opportunities now available, as well as the IL Listserv and other listservs. Teleconferences, Web casts, online tutorials, and courses are all excellent ways to keep everyone up-to-date on IL issues and offer the advantage of coming directly to each person's workstation. Furthermore, in most cases these virtual events can be viewed at the learner's convenience and so can fit into even the busiest of schedules. Live Web casts are frequently archived and can be viewed after the fact. The Teaching, Learning and Technology (TLT) group is an example of a group outside the library setting who hosts IL-related Web casts that can be viewed at the time of presentation or from their archive at a later and more convenient time. For more information on TLT see: http://www.tltgroup.org/Events/WebcastsDemos/Archives.htm.

Training can also occur in a more informal, collegial manner if IL librarians are encouraged to team-teach, work collaboratively together on instructional Web pages or handouts, or engage in observation and mutual peer appraisal of their teaching. IL managers can encourage this behavior best by modeling it. The IL manager who asks his or her colleagues to observe an instructional session in order to receive constructive feedback from these colleagues creates an atmosphere of trust and cooperation that should encourage others to do the same. For more on developing IL librarians, see Chapter 4.

ASSESS

Clearly, it is not enough to identify instructional needs, develop an instructional response, and make sure that IL librarians are trained to provide that response. It is also important to determine if users' needs are being met by the library's instructional program. IL managers should encourage instructors to begin by setting expected learning outcomes, figure out how to test for what students already know, and then continually assess their own sessions and materials. Furthermore, the IL manager should work together with his or her instructional colleagues to determine whether or not those learning outcomes have been achieved and then the best way to assess the overall effectiveness

of the program. Perhaps one or more librarians are interested in assessment and would like to form an ad hoc team to deal with that issue.
However assessment is handled, it is the responsibility of the IL manager to make sure that the goals and objectives of individual endeavors
and the broader program are being met and to identify places where
improvement can be made. Assessment often leads to revising some
programs, eliminating others, and developing new instructional endeavors that better enable the library to fulfill its IL instruction mission
(Grassian and Kaplowitz 2001). For more on assessment see Chapter 12
in *Information Literacy Instruction: Theory and Practice* (Grassian and
Kaplowitz 2001).

## Market

The best IL program in the world does no one any good if it languishes
unseen and unheard within the library's walls or on the library's Web
site. Today's IL manager must become adept at calling attention to what
the library has to offer and to sell the value of its IL programs to the
people these programs are designed to help. But first the concept of IL
itself needs to be promoted to the larger organization, and potential collaborative partners must be identified. Marketing at this level requires
identifying common goals and effectively communicating how the library and its programs can support those goals. To be successful, marketing must show people what they will gain by partaking of the
product. In other words, what is in it for them? No matter who the
audience is or what medium is used to promote IL and the library's
programs—Web sites, flyers, written reports and memos, or bookmarks
and other promotional materials—the important point to highlight is
how IL can help get people where they want to go. Although IL librarians may not have had much marketing training, they are experts at persuasive communication as exhibited by their teaching expertise and
should be able to translate this expertise into the marketing arena. See
Chapter 7 for more on this issue.

## Schedule

Last but certainly not least comes scheduling. The more successful
the IL manager is at promoting the library's IL programs, the more
demands will be placed on the library and its staff to deliver those programs. The IL manager must not only juggle rooms, personnel, equipment, and materials, but also make sure that the demand does not
exceed the supply. The IL manager must be adept at negotiating with

both the requesters and his or her own colleagues to ensure that appropriately sized programs are developed that can be supported by the library's current resources without causing undue stress and burnout. You can read more about the issues of stress and burnout in Chapter 4. Demands that exceed supply can offer opportunities to request additional funding for staff and materials from higher-ups in the organization as well as opportunities to offer a menu of alternative approaches, not to mention creative thinking about new ways to leverage what you have. For instance, do you have online help guides? Consider turning them into exercises that can be completed and turned in to either you or the course instructor for feedback in lieu of face-to-face instruction. This method will help to reduce the workload on your staff and may be very appealing to the course instructor, who may not wish to give up class time for ILI.

Above all, the IL manager must become adept at saying no—or at least trying to scale down the request to something the library can handle. Can the IL manager identify alternatives to classroom instruction that could address the need of large groups without overburdening the library staff? In many settings, developing a "train the trainer" program, where supervisors, teachers, faculty, or teaching assistants can be shown how to teach the IL strategies and skills needed by their population, works well. These IL trainers not only can share the strategies and skills they have learned but serve as goodwill ambassadors for the library and its programs. Developing training materials, lecture outlines, and demonstration scripts and allowing these trainers to use them in their subsequent sessions with others go a long way to make this kind of program a success.

Other possibilities include the use of technology such as Web pages or other computer-based tutorials to provide the instruction. Although there may be a big up-front investment in such a project, the long-term benefits are obvious as this material can reach large numbers of people and is available whenever and wherever a person needs it. If librarian-led, in-person instruction still seems to be the preferred approach, teleconferencing or Web casts of the sessions may allow a single instructor to reach large numbers of learners. The IL manager in conjunction with his or her IL colleagues can generate many more innovative instructional ideas. But it may be up to the IL manager to negotiate the use of these solutions and possibly work collaboratively with others in the organization to implement these alternatives to traditional instruction methodology.

It is clear that today's IL manager cannot afford to operate alone or in a vacuum. IL managers succeed through the development of excellent communication and interpersonal skills. They look for, and promote, appropriate collaborations and are excellent team leaders and team players. Most of all, these devoted IL managers never lose sight of the overall goals of IL and work tirelessly to implement the initiatives and programs that make IL a reality in their environment.

EXERCISES

1. Working in teams is the general way we do business in libraries these days. Teams function best when they share group norms for how to behave and interact as a group. The following is a team building exercise that could be done at an early team meeting, preferably the first one, in order to create a positive team working environment.
    a. Think back to an experience that you had working within a team environment. Was it a successful experience? Did you enjoy working in that team situation? Why or why not?
    b. Based on your experiences working in teams, come up with a list of ground rules under which you would like any team that you would be involved in to operate.
    c. If you were the head of the team, how would you get the team to develop and abide by ground rules under which the team would operate?
2. You are a manager who has to oversee a major new initiative in your library. Your colleagues have mixed feelings about whether or not this change is a good idea. Some are enthusiastically in favor of it, others are strongly opposed, while still others are adopting a wait-and-see attitude. Your job is to get everyone on board and working together collaboratively to implement the change. Describe three different approaches you might use in order to get group buy-in for the change.
3. You and your colleagues have an idea for a new "blended" instruction program combining both in-person and virtual modes of delivery to expand your reach with limited staff.
    a. Identify all the "key players" in your environment (both within and outside the library) that you need to collaborate with in order to implement such a project.
    b. Develop a presentation geared to each of the above-identified groups to enlist their assistance. Make sure you emphasize how your project will benefit the goals of these other groups.

4. Make a list of the various groups that constitute your environment (cultural, ethnic, age, gender, disabilities, educational backgrounds, etc.).
   a. Do some research on interpersonal communication preferences in each group. Pay special attention to the use of gestures and body language and to issues involving personal space. You may wish to contact appropriate agencies in your community such as offices for international students, reentry students, people with disabilities; senior citizen centers; agencies offering English as a second language instruction, and so on.
   b. Enlist the aid of a colleague to do some role-playing with you. Simulate conversations with your colleague while he or she takes on various interpersonal preference roles. See how well you can adjust to these styles during your conversation.
   c. Have your colleague debrief you to identify your strong points and to suggest ways to improve your responsiveness to different communication styles and preferences.
5. You and your colleagues are trying to decide whether or not to take on a new project by engaging in the following brainstorming exercise:
   a. First, give everyone one minute to list all the reasons that the new project would be a bad idea.
   b. Then give them one minute to list all the reasons the new project would be a good idea.
   c. Review the list of "good" ideas first. Then move on to the bad ideas. For each bad idea, ask the group to come up with a solution for the problems indicated if the new project was implemented.
   d. Finally, ask the group, "What risks do we run if we implement this plan?" and "What are the risks we run if we do not?"
   e. Use all the discussion generated by these exercises to decide if the project is worth pursuing.

## READ MORE ABOUT IT

Bennis, Warren. 2000. *Managing the Dream*. Cambridge MA: Perseus Publishing.
Curzon, Susan Carol. 1989. *Managing Change: A How-to-Do-It Manual for Planning, Implementing, and Evaluating Change in Libraries*. New York: Neal-Schuman Publishers.
Kamp, Di. 1999. *The 21st Century Manager*. London: Kogan Page.

Orenstein, David. 1999. "Developing Quality Managers and Quality Management." *Library Administration and Management* 13(1): 44–51.

Raspa, Dick, and Dane Ward. 2000. "Listening for Collaboration: Faculty and Librarians Working Together." In *The Collaborative Imperative: Librarians and Faculty Working Together in the Information Universe*, edited by Dick Raspa and Dane Ward. Chicago: Association of College and Research Libraries—American Library Association.

Reddy, Brendan W., and Kaleel Jamison, eds. 1988. *Team Building: Blueprints for Productivity and Satisfaction*. Alexandria, VA: NTL Institute for Applied Behavioral Sciences.

Wilson, Leslie. 1996. *People Skills for Library Managers*. Englewood, CO: Libraries Unlimited.

3
_____

# Embracing Cooperation and Change

*We must learn to live together as brothers or perish together as fools.*
—Martin Luther King, Jr. (1929–1968),
Speech at St. Louis, March 22, 1964

## COOPERATE, NETWORK, AND MANAGE CHANGE

Socrates was poisoned for religious heresies and for corrupting the morals of the young. The Inquisition tried Galileo for contradicting Scripture by supporting the Copernican theory that the earth moved around the sun. Humans often fear change and do not always take well to new ideas or the people who come up with them. Yet little or nothing in our world stands still. Egyptian pyramids erode, and giant redwoods many hundreds of years old topple. Libraries, too, are no longer quiet, seemingly unchanging institutions.

The same is true for technological changes that have mutated libraries into new entities. For some time, the process was painful and frightening to many, thrilling to some, and stressful to all. Some, staff and users alike, have tried to ignore or resist technological change, while others have lambasted those they deem responsible for it. In 1994, Nicholson Baker loudly lamented the passing of the card catalog in one of the most prestigious U.S. literary magazines, *The New Yorker* (1994). In 2001, he published *Double Fold*, expanding his attack on libraries by accusing them of discarding paper newspapers and other items he considered irreplaceable, because they were available online. He even started his own American Newspaper Repository in 1999 to hold paper copies discarded by libraries; in 2004, he donated it to Duke University (Galloway 2004). Even in the integrated technological and print library, however, we constantly replace the online catalogs and e-mail systems we are used to with new systems. Database vendors often alter interfaces during the third business quarter of each year, (July–September), sometimes just at the beginning of the fall term for K–12 schools and higher education. Administrators increasingly expect librarians not only to teach evolving online information resources but also to use technology like live chat for virtual reference, software like Dreamweaver to create and revise Web pages, and other software to create interactive Web tutorials, as well as other digital learning objects (DLOs) of various kinds, sizes, and complexities.

What is a DLO? In 2001, Wiley defined a DLO broadly as "any digital resource that can be reused to support learning" (Wiley 2000). That did not end the matter, though, as technology experts are still debating its definition (Metros 2004; Polsani 2003). New technologies seem so amorphous that even their defining characteristics may be hard to pin down. Why? It is often difficult to define almost anything new—technology, products, diseases, movements—because the very process of questioning and developing definitions is part of the way we learn about, and come to understand what a new item really is, how it relates to our previous experiences, and what it may mean for the future (LaDuke 2004). This is true for new technology of all sorts, as well as new approaches. Both are difficult enough for many people to handle. To complicate matters, IL librarians and other library staff have varying levels and types of technological skills and means of coping with rapidly mutating tools and environments, just as users do. So, what are the keys to comfort, if not success, for IL librarians in these anxiety-provoking circumstances? How can IL program coordinators and managers help each other and their colleagues as we all struggle to stay on top of new developments and maintain warm, friendly, and humane relations with our user groups and colleagues? If you focus too much on the politics in your environment—who knows what, when they know it, who is your friend, what are your "enemies" cooking up, what are other people after—you may come across as being insincere and Machiavellian. Your reward could be some cold cash for your endeavors, along with resentful colleagues and other staff who have little trust in your aims. How can IL managers build trust and help support their colleagues, while they also work with administrators to make them aware of IL needs and developments? The answers are to be positive, to be honest and diplomatic, to build on each small success, to share freely, to form supportive networks and to mentor others.

*Learn How to Network*

Do you enjoy meeting new people, making small talk, connecting friends and acquaintances with each other? Do you leap on every opening to promote ILI? Or, are you shy? Do you find it difficult to reach out to others? If so, you may wonder how you could possibly build a network of friends and acquaintances, much less find the courage and will to approach strangers, faculty, community leaders, heads of organizations, politicians, library trustees, businesspeople, administrators, and other user groups. Sometimes it is hard to know what networking really is. Is it politicking, supporting, communicating, sharing, partying? When it works well, it can be all of the above. Networks form when like-minded people band together or communicate with each other for a shared purpose or benefit, and the benefits can be enormous. Have a problem understanding how chat or Web casts work? Need to know about CGI scripts for forms, or Flash (Macromedia, Inc. 2004), or Camtasia (TechSmith Corporation 2004) for Web-based tutorials? Want help locating a shareware (low-cost) discussion board for a class or freeware screen capture software? Need to know how credit IL courses actually work, including course structure, readings, grading, and assignments? Want to turn your in-person course into an effective "blended instruction" approach, where you meet in-person only occasionally and "virtually" for most of the course? If you are at a loss for answers to these and other similar questions, it really helps to be able to tap into the expertise of others within and outside the library profession.

Networking at its most basic level simply means locating and getting to know others, often those with similar interests. If you are really good at networking, after you have done it for a while, you may even become a human "gatekeeper" like Lois Weisberg, the subject of a *New Yorker* article on the importance of gatekeeping and how it works. Lois seemed to know every single person in the city of Chicago as well as many people elsewhere, in an astonishing array of fields. She had an extraordinary knack for bringing together people in diverse fields who never would have met otherwise, to advance projects that interested her. The cross-fertilization of ideas and approaches benefited both Lois' pet projects and the people she brought together (Gladwell 1999). How does one find or establish networks and hook up with a "Lois," an experienced person who may already be working within or at the nexus of one or more huge networks?

Effective networking can start with you, whether you are a leader, a manager, a beginning librarian, or beginning a new career track. Each of us can create our own opportunities. To paraphrase Mimi Dudley's adage about teaching—When do we need to network? Where? The answers are always and everywhere. With whom? With everyone, particularly with library and higher-up administrators and colleagues, as well as faculty, but also with students, friends-of-the-library groups, trustees, computing center staff, businesses, and organizations, in all sorts of environments, within and outside your own institution or organization (Dudley 1983, p. 63).

Reach out to offer your skills and knowledge from all areas of your life or, at the very least, offer your time, your effort, and your goodwill. Attend some conferences, workshops, and programs and get to know the organizers. Offer to help or serve on a committee, write a newsletter article, or help out with a Web site. Newsgroups, listservs, and chat rooms are electronic networks of people with similar interests. You can send a query out on a listserv like ILI-L (n.d.), the Information Literacy Instruction List, or on a newsgroup, or respond to calls for help posted by others. *Sparingly,* forward the most interesting and newsworthy e-mail or listserv messages to networking partners. Use caution here, though. Be selective. Do not overwhelm people, or they will begin to delete your messages without ever reading them. Closer to home, pick a small IL problem and ask an instructional technology specialist for advice on it. For instance, you might ask her or him which one piece of new technology she or he would most recommend to support your instructional goals. Look for education- or technology-related groups that meet in or near your physical library and offer to take minutes for them, make room arrangements, or even offer them ILI.

Another word of warning is in order here, however. It is important to proceed slowly at first when reaching out as a beginning networker in a new area. You must remember that if you are a new librarian or in a new position, as much as you may have learned in courses or through experience in other areas, this is a new area for you, so a little humility is warranted. Also, if you want to establish credibility as a worthy networking partner, you must meet all commitments you make regarding deadlines and completing work. Enthusiasm alone will take you only a short way. If you remember to make reasonable commitments, and keep them, your opportunities to contribute will mushroom, and your networking opportunities will expand. It may happen slowly or quickly, but once networking begins, it can snowball quickly. Over time, even the novice IL librarian can metamorphose into a change agent, as well as a contributor, by offering reasoned opinions and advice and by offering time and effort to accomplish mutually beneficial goals. How can you be an effective change agent within an institution or an organization, particularly, to promote and advance an IL initiative or program?

*Collaborate for Decision Making*

To be an IL change agent, you need to be proactive, to collaborate with others, and to think broadly about collaborative endeavors. Learn all you can about how your institution operates, how the library operates, and how any IL programs (past or present) operate. Be friendly, helpful, positive, and enthusiastic and listen well. Try to put out some informal feelers. Get to know the people who work in, or are enrolled in, various departments, administrative units, businesses, or other libraries in your area and see if there is any interest in working together on a project, a single IL session, a workshop, or a program. Attend some programs or classes sponsored by other groups, departments, or organizations. Offer to work with them informally and share instructional materials. Jump on any opportunity that seems even tangentially related to ILI, for instance, calls for ideas regarding "blended instruction" or other proposals, internal and external (see Chapter 6). IL is everybody's business, so ask for administrative support to reach out to other administrative or academic units within the institution or in the community. Check with human resources departments in large businesses in your area. Offer to teach an IL Extension course or to work with a learning resources center or the media or film department of a business.

If you work in a large institution or organization, your immediate or higher-up administrator may be able to identify or make first contact with groups within your institution or organization who are prime potential IL audiences or who could help an IL program become established.

Whether or not you work directly with your administrators during the first contact process, keep them informed as you progress. When you are ready to request funding for ILI projects, consider proposing a pilot project or two that would include assessment of individual learning as well as evaluation of program effectiveness. Whether they succeed or fail, small trials and pilot projects teach us a lot. They help us build our own expertise, interest others in new and different ways to help people learn, and serve as building blocks for the next new endeavor. In other words, they can build a climate of openness to experimentation and risk-taking, as long as there is acceptance of possible failure as well as solid administrative support, whether or not each developing project is successful.

*Working with Colleagues*

Almost anyone interested in the same types of instructional problems as you are can also be a wonderful supporter, a peer mentor, or a collaborator—a colleague, a coworker, a teammate within an institution or organization, or even another IL librarian in a distant location. E-mail and other technologies, like Microsoft's "Sharepoint" collaborative software (2004), have erased time and distance, allowing people to work together fruitfully and creatively without in-person meetings. For example, Susan Clark and Esther Grassian researched, drafted, and finalized a column for the February 1999 issue of *College & Research Libraries News* entirely via e-mail and telephone calls (Grassian and Clark 1999).

We can also learn lessons about collaboration from a much larger example outside the library world—the completely voluntary Open Source movement that began with Linus Torvalds' development of the

LINUX system software in 1991. Seventy-eight developers from twelve countries were working on the code in 1994, and, by 2000, Linux was used on about a third of Web servers (Weber 2004). How was this accomplished, especially in the face of the powerful Microsoft Corporation? Weber describes this amazing process as follows:

> . . . groups of computer programmers (sometimes very large groups) made up of individuals separated by geography, corporate boundaries, culture, language and other characteristics, and connected mainly via telecommunications bandwidth, manage[d] to work together over time and build complex, sophisticated software systems outside the boundaries of a corporate structure, and for no direct monetary compensation. (Weber 2004, p. 2)

This process continues, as individual programmers or groups work to improve bits and pieces of the software, argue, and debate changes, while a loose hierarchy of Linux programmers makes recommendations about changes to the person at the top—Linus Torvalds. Why does this work? As Weber puts it, Open Source really is "anti-rivalness" (2004, p. 154).

In a sense, the Information Literacy Instruction Listserv (ILI-L) serves IL librarians as a sounding board and a community of individuals with similar interests and widely varying experience. We learn from each other remotely through listservs, through newsgroups, and through blogs (weblogs), and we can work together remotely on various projects, often with great success.

Important differences exist, however, between remote work with distant colleagues and continuous in-person work with those who share a physical work space or who work with each other in person just occasionally. Coworkers within the same institution or organization often have a profound influence on one another, for better or worse. Personality, work style, and territorial and political conflicts can lead to time and energy wasted on anger, resentment, and ill will. How can we use this wasted time and energy in productive ways to further our IL goals and those of our institutions and organizations? It is human nature to focus on people and personalities and on the negative rather than the positive. News stories about crime and other problems get our attention more than upbeat and positive stories, or at least local television stations seem to think so, as negative stories tend to dominate news coverage (Budiansky 1996). However, as Bob Dylan put it, "negativity won't pull you through" (1965). We need to make great efforts to reconfigure our personal tendencies toward criticism and negativity, so we can focus on problem solving. We need to acknowledge that whether they realize it or not, and whether they exhibit it or not on a regular basis, everyone has creative ideas that can help solve instructional problems, including you. Some ideas are good and workable; some are not. The first step is accepting the fact that there is an instructional problem. The next step is defining the problem. The third step is using creative problem-solving (CPS) techniques to get to the root of the problem and to bubble all sorts of possible solutions to the surface.

*Define the Problem*

Are you and the other IL librarians you work with floundering in your own success? Is there too much demand for your in-person instruction? Are you exhausted and unable to complete projects? Have you declined invitations to join important committees? Have you failed to meet deadlines of various kinds? Do you notice in yourself or others a growing tendency toward "last-minute-itis," disorganization and insensitivity to learners, colleagues, and others? Situations like these can creep up on you unnoticed, until you start to get poor learner evaluations or until you are reviewed negatively or until you need to review others and can focus only on the negative.

Do not wait for this to happen to you! Monitor your surroundings and yourself for people problems and situation problems. Ask librarians to let you know, for instance, if 150 students in a single class come to the reference desk one by one asking for help with the same assignment, or if large numbers of high school students come to your college or university library singly or in groups, completely unprepared for researching. Ask others to do the same and to report these incidents to you so you can address them before staff become burned out. Isolated incidents may or may not need to be addressed, but if you see consistent logjams, unusual demands on time from the same sources, or similar incidents repeated, you should identify them as problems and define them, using tools like work flowcharts and "critical incident" lists (Andersen and Fagerhaug 2000). Then seek out the root causes in order to prevent the problems from happening again or in order to improve responses to them and continue to monitor for the recurrence of problem symptoms (Andersen and Fagerhaug 2000). Creative problem-solving (CPS) techniques can help you identify concerns, large and small, and target them through a systematic problem-solving process.

*Use Creative Problem Solving (CPS)*

You can help create a culture of creativity and mutual respect by focusing on, defining, and solving problems that we all face by using CPS

---

**Figure 3–1**
**Potential IL-Related Problems**

---

**POTENTIAL IL-RELATED PROBLEMS** (See also Figure 4–1)

Watch for IL librarians exhibiting these behaviors in teaching:

- Disorganized presentations
- Militant adherence to completing what they planned to cover
- Conviction that there is *a right way* to teach
- Lack of sensitivity to learners' feelings
- Poor communication skills with instructors, colleagues, and administrators
- Lack of advance planning
- Unwillingness to be observed
- Inability to accept constructive criticism
- Inability or unwillingness to work with others on team efforts
- Team members ganging up on others to get their way
- Lateness in meeting deadlines or in meeting in-person groups

Watch for administrators exhibiting these attitudes toward ILI:

- Fervent pressure to use "active learning" techniques constantly and in all circumstances
- Lack of trust in IL librarians' individual teaching styles
- Playing the numbers game by pressing for more and more in-person instructions to boost statistics, without adding staff or other resources
- ADD (attention deficit disorder)-like behaviors—always striving for the next new thing before the last has taken hold or has been assessed for impact and effectiveness
- Disinterest in, or inability to focus on and fully examine, the consequences of continually adding new responsibilities to heavily burdened staff
- Lack of communication and leadership in helping staff prioritize responsibilities
- Professional jealousy at successes of lower-level staff

---

techniques. Beware of "lone-ranger-itis," though (Wilson 2000). Before undertaking any sort of creative problem-solving method, approach higher-up administrators with your proposals to examine or reexamine instructional plans and programs. Explain why it is important to do this now, how they will be kept informed, and how follow-up might take place. If you are new to an institution or organization, you should do some legwork first. Find out more about the institution or organization, its mission, goals, and institutional politics, as well as the library's goals. Get a historical perspective on past and existing IL instructional programs, materials, marketing and publicity, staffing, in-house training, budget, evaluation, and revision (Grassian 1993; Grassian and Kaplowitz 2001, Chapter 2). If you expand this self-examination so that it is institution- or organization-wide, you can search for a variety of instructional formats that may address IL elements but may not be labeled as IL (Schoen 2003). You may be surprised to discover in how many ways IL competencies are already being addressed in various higher education academic departments or disciplines, in K–12 schools and elsewhere, though perhaps not as systematically or thoroughly as one would hope regarding information research.

ILI librarian Lynn Lampert's experience is a case in point. In 2003, she prepared to work on IL integration into the curriculum with the California State University, Northridge (CSUN) Department of Educational Psychology and Counseling and CSUN's Center for Management and Organizational Development in Los Angeles County. Her research revealed that in the 1980s, the professional organizations of both of these groups had come up with competency statements/standards very close to what we would now label IL competencies. She drew the faculty's attention to the standards developed by their own organizations. The faculty took it from there, enthusiastically incorporating the equivalent of many IL competencies into their own departmental curricula (ALA. ACRL. CARL. sCIL 2003). This is a good lesson. We need to look for, and acknowledge, efforts like these and bring them to the attention of professional organization members in various disciplines and areas of employment. We can also offer to work with individuals or groups in order to help build upon them whenever possible, utilizing their own organization's language and standards.

Once IL competencies have been identified, successful problem solving can begin by identifying and prioritizing current instructional problems, analyzing them, gathering data, if necessary, coming to consensus on goals, methodologies, and techniques that will help solve them, and presenting these proposed solutions to higher-up administrators (Robson 1993, p. 19). If approved, solutions then need to be implemented, monitored, continually evaluated, and revised as necessary (Grassian and Kaplowitz 2001, Chapter 7).

What makes this process political? Personalities, instructional philosophies, alliances, personal and administrative goals, and organizational dynamics may all play a part in politicizing a problem-solving endeavor.

Idealistic people often find it hard to focus on the political aspects of their efforts, and you should certainly not make all of your decisions based on expected political consequences or undertake efforts that are strictly designed to help you politically. On the other hand, you do need to take into account the fact that you may need to bow to certain political pressures in order to achieve a greater good. Whenever new employees join an existing group, the dynamics change, sometimes unexpectedly, as interviews and recommendations do not always reveal all. Has that new librarian with several years of experience in a different library environment taken the time to understand how things work in your environment? Does she respect the knowledge and teaching experience of those who have been in your environment for a long time? Does she have her own rather rigid approach to teaching, insisting that everyone use her approach to "active learning," that all instructional materials be designed using a particular style or format, that all synchronous group instruction follow the same methodology and content? Or, do the experienced librarians feel that they do not need to change in any way, that if they allow or encourage learners to participate actively, they will not be able to cover all of the important points they need to make? Do they think they will not be able to teach all of the databases and other resources the learners should know about, and as a result, they will "waste" precious teaching time? Do experienced ILI librarians already use a variety of perhaps more subtle active learning techniques and teaching styles? Do they vary their techniques depending on the audience, the time allotted for teaching/learning, and the expected learning outcomes? A successful teaching style for one person may be deadly for another, yet many are the misunderstandings and conflicts we all face as we try to work with others in helping our users learn to learn.

How can you cope with this situation? Try to focus on the problems, rather than the people. Be open to a variety of problem-solving approaches that may become solutions, and you will de-politicize and lower the levels of emotional engagement and defensiveness. Use an instructional needs assessment approach, but be sensitive to the political situation. Work with your colleagues rather than against or around them. Interview them, ask for their advice, and record the ILI history of your library, organization, or institution. Ask what has worked, what has not, and why. Make no assumptions and do your best to be non-judgmental, rather than dismissive. Be interested and respectful and listen well. If you do, you will be amazed at what a difference it will make in your work environment and your relationships with your colleagues.

When you have the ILI history firmly in mind, draw up a chart of current instructional problems based on your own observations and on the interviews you have conducted with others. List the learners, goals, and objectives of the solution(s), programs, and instructional modes currently in use to solve the problem, supplementary materials and techniques, the evaluation/revision process, and the staff responsible for each. Remember to look outside the library, too, to see how other individuals, departments, and groups may be addressing these kinds of problems. Bounce ideas off people who are not normally part of your own work or social network, and you may be surprised at the creative ideas that can result (Erard 2004). Add information to the chart, highlighting areas of potential collaboration. Distribute the chart to colleagues and administrators as a draft and request comment. When consensus has been reached on the current state of instructional affairs, work with your colleagues to plan a CPS meeting to come up with questions related to the needs assessment.

Once you and your colleagues have decided which questions to work on, you will be ready for the next step, selecting one or more team-building CPS techniques to help answer them. Many different active participation methods are quite popular and can help, but how effective are they? If you want to use these techniques to generate a lot of useful ideas, you should keep in mind some important general guidelines (Paulus 2000; Robson 1993).

First, enlist the help of an experienced facilitator who will play a key role. The facilitator needs to make it clear that each and every CPS activity will take place in a fair and open environment, in which everyone has a chance to contribute. She or he needs to be in control, while at the same time maintaining a diplomatic and objective manner. The facilitator should encourage participants to listen carefully, respect the ideas and expertise of others, consider all ideas, vote on them, and submit their own thoughtful individual comments following group CPS and discussion (Paulus 2000).

How do facilitators handle dominant, as well as quiet and shy people, and thereby increase the number of useful ideas generated? A number of CPS techniques compensate for social problems like these by requiring individual contributions in writing or by setting ground rules. For example, a facilitator might say, "Let's hear from each person. We've only got five minutes, and there are five of us, so let's each talk for no more than one minute. I'll keep track of the time, since I'm the facilitator." Another approach is to require a period of silent thinking and individual writing, with each participant jotting down some notes before anyone speaks. This is called "brainwriting" or a "parallel technique," in contrast to an "interactive technique" like brainstorming. Parallel techniques can be partly anonymous, while interactive techniques are not (Zemke 1993). Conducting interactive sessions electronically can be more democratic, generate more ideas, and be less susceptible to dominance by one individual, though body language clues will be lost.

Second, consider whether or not to include administrators in the CPS process. Many people are intimidated by administrators and may not feel free to propose ideas that may challenge existing or accepted practice if an administrator participates in their CPS session. Confidentiality is crucial if people are to feel free to express their ideas and opinions—they are taking a risk in doing so. If you can help your colleagues feel comfortable in taking this sort of risk, you will go a long way toward building good team relations. In order to encourage creative thinking of all kinds and maintain confidentiality, it is probably best not to include administrators in the CPS process until you are close to the end.

Does effective team building take years? Not necessarily. You can use a variety of CPS techniques to build trust and establish good working relations fairly quickly within a physical environment. What do you do, though, if you run a library on your own, or if you are the only librarian in your workplace? ILI-L is an excellent online community of ILI librarians who respond very generously with creative ideas regarding ILI problems (n.d.). Those in one-person libraries may also want to consider joining a local, regional, or national professional organization, where they can use CPS techniques like brainstorming to solve common ILI problems, formally and informally at conferences, programs, or workshops.

## Brainstorm

A modified form of brainstorming provides a good example of a CPS technique that can work well within a relatively short meeting time (one and one-half to two hours), as long as the session focuses on a limited number of well-defined problems with a set of targeted questions to discuss. When properly prepared and conducted, a brainstorming session can also focus attention on instructional problems, rather than personality issues, and generate a respectful atmosphere for all ideas, large and small, good and bad. True or formal brainstorming takes place in an ordered sequence of steps (generate ideas in response to a question; critique; prioritize) and follows some strict rules at each step. For instance, no one is allowed to make critical comments during the idea generation phase. As the process unfolds, and people begin to talk and share experiences and ideas, concerns needing attention are likely to surface, though shy people tend not to speak up in groups as much as more dominant individuals do. Throughout, it is important for everyone to listen carefully and objectively to all suggestions for improvement and ideas no matter how radically different or off-the-wall they may sound. In these situations, it helps a lot to maintain objectivity, to express understanding of, and appreciation for, the voice of experience and caution, and to be thick-skinned.

Generally, a small group takes ownership of, and supports, its own ideas if a member of the group writes those ideas down for all group members to see and correct orally. The same is true for individuals. You will feel much more an owner of your ideas and comments if you write them down yourself. Avoid rewriting what others have written, whether on cards, on a blackboard/whiteboard, or on a flip chart. This warning applies in particular to those leading CPS sessions. If you do, you will be taking subtle control and may unintentionally smother ideas contrary to your own. CPS techniques like brainstorming can help staff feel that they have been part of the planning and development process, by unleashing and encouraging creative thinking about instructional solutions. Always remember that the buy-in necessary for successful problem solving can occur only in a nonjudgmental environment.

Many books and articles describe the popular technique of group brainstorming and the facilitator's role in controlling dominant people and encouraging shy or reticent people to participate actively (Andersen and Fagerhaug 2000; Prather and Gundry 1995; Rawlinson 1981; Van-Gundy 1992). Many of the same publications describe other individual and group CPS techniques, as well as blended approaches that will appeal to different people. You may even recognize some of these techniques as cooperative or active learning methods you have used in synchronous in-person or remote teaching. (See Figure 3–2 for examples.)

---

**Figure 3–2**
**Sample Creative Problem-Solving Techniques**

---

**SAMPLE CREATIVE PROBLEM-SOLVING TECHNIQUES**

1. **"Brainwriting Pool" (VanGundy 2003, p.153)**
   a. 5–8 people sit at a table and individually write down a list of up to four ideas.
   b. All ideas are placed in the middle of the table.
   c. Each person takes someone else's sheet of ideas, adds to it, and puts it back in the middle of the table.
   d. Participants keep exchanging sheets of paper and adding ideas for 10 to 15 minutes.
2. **"The Outrageous Idea" (Prather and Gundry 1995, p.38)**
   a. Identify a problem.
   b. Get a group of staff together and ask them to come up with some outrageous suggestions to solve the problem.

*(continued)*

c. The first few suggestions may be unthinkable, but they will generate new and interesting ideas that you might want to consider.

**3. "Gallery Method" (VanGundy 1992, pp.154–155)**

a. Flip chart pages are posted around a room, one for each person in
the group.

b. Each person silently writes her or his ideas on a page, all at the
same time, for a specified period of time.

c. Group members walk around, silently review other people's flip
chart pages, and take notes.

d. Participants add new ideas, comments, and improvements to
others' flip chart pages.

**4. "Force Field Analysis" (Robson 1993, Chapter 9)**

a. The facilitator states the problem and points out that there are op-
posing forces, some working to improve it, others working to
worsen it.

b. Participants identify both types of forces and rank them in
importance.

c. Participants then rank these forces in terms of how easily they can
be influenced and by whom—"us" or "others."

**5. "Nominal Group Technique (NGT)" (Andersen and Fagerhaug
2000, pp. 49–53)**

a. Individually, group participants write down ideas, one per card.

b. The facilitator assigns a letter to each idea and writes the ideas on
a flip chart.

c. Group members ask for clarification and combine duplicate ideas.

d. Each person individually ranks the ideas on cards, assigning
points (up to 5) for each idea.

e. The facilitator totals the points and lists the ideas in prioritized
order by number of points.

**6. "Brutethink" (Michalko 1991, pp.159–171)**

a. Identify a challenge.

b. Select a random concept or word.

c. Write down a list of related actions, concepts, and words.

d. Force yourself to make some connections between the challenge
and any of the other actions, concepts, or words.

**Note:** See also the Web page, "Creativity Techniques," for a very long list of links
to descriptions of many different CPS approaches for individuals and groups, including references to sources of many of these techniques (Mycoted 2003).

It is easy to get excited and carried away by the energy and participatory nature of these techniques, but remember that when people participate in any public creative-thinking exercise, they are taking risks.
They are exposing themselves to possible criticism, ridicule, and retri-
bution. Therefore, it is extremely important for the leader to remind

participants to listen well, to be nonjudgmental, to focus on ideas they like, and afterward, on what needs improvement in the ideas offered, or how they would do it differently.

Regardless of which CPS technique you use, you must follow up by sharing the results with the participants and checking with them as to consensus regarding where to go from there. When consensus, if not full agreement, has been reached, consider proposing a pilot project to test out the agreed-upon solutions, to be funded internally or externally. Prepare internal pilot proposals for higher-up administrators including pros, cons, and costs and benefits and offer to present your ideas in person or to answer questions in writing. (See Chapter 6 for directions and tips on selecting grants and preparing grant proposals.) Be prepared to explain how a new or newly organized program will benefit learners and the library and ask for volunteers to help out with the pilot project, if it is approved by your higher-up administrators.

Creative CPS techniques are extremely popular these days. Some people throw them at problems, hoping that just going through a CPS process will solve them magically. Unfortunately, there is no magic CPS wand. If you want CPS to work, you must establish an atmosphere of trust and mutual respect. In such an atmosphere, groups are truly expected to consider issues creatively, rather than rubber-stamping a predetermined solution. Administrators must also follow up by considering all suggestions seriously and by providing reasoned explanations for decisions.

## UNDERSTAND THE ADMINISTRATOR'S ROLE

Follow-up and good two-way communication are equally significant factors in successful use of CPS techniques—but prepare yourself. Like it or not, some of your ideas may be rejected or drastically modified by higher-up administrators, in spite of all of your best efforts to engage everyone involved and to make a proposal truly participatory and cost-effective. When administrators reject or greatly modify a jointly proposed pilot, staff who contributed their energy and ideas need to know how and why this has happened. This is both common courtesy and good management practice. Openness and good communication are important indicators of trust and confidence in decision making and in the staff's ability to understand decisions, if not always agree with them. This, in turn, encourages people to focus on the next problem or any of a series of perennial concerns, such as how best to work with faculty in a school or academic setting, rather than wasting energy on anger or resentment about a decision that seems to have been handed down from on high.

Administrators need to remember too that change can be threatening and very difficult for some to accept, especially when "newbies" or inexperienced staff propose the change. So, you can expect some inertia, some negative responses, and fear of being overloaded by the addition of new responsibilities. Understanding, patience, and respect can help. It is best to try to uncover and address all of these thoughts and feelings during problem-solving sessions, interviews, and other meetings so that all involved feel a part of the proposal and the solution. Certainly, there will be points where decisions will need to be made, with administrative approval, and some may disagree. However, if they have a chance to be heard and if their ideas have been considered seriously and fairly, staff at all levels will feel less resentment and offer more support for trying out a new plan. After these discussions have taken place, sometimes, a higher-up administrator who has not participated in the CPS process will need to make decisions about changes, and those resistant will need to learn different behaviors and work patterns.

Of course, administrators have other important responsibilities as well. They should be responsible and mature people who are willing to take chances on untested ideas, who focus on problem solving and do not play "blame games," who engage their employees in open dialogue about proposed changes, who listen well, avoid abrupt change, and do not treat employees like chess pieces. After implementation of a pilot project, staff and administrators need to continue the discussion with colleagues within and outside the library and analyze the benefits and drawbacks of new endeavors or alterations to existing programs. In the end, a fresh new program or revision may fail or may not succeed as expected, but we all need to keep in mind that experimentation and risk are part of the process of improving learning and advancing IL goals, initiatives, and programs, sometimes by working with others outside the library.

## WORKING WITH VARIOUS POLITICAL GROUPS

Many of the following sections focus on faculty in higher education, with a lengthy section on working with public library boards and trustees, as well as other types of libraries. However, in most cases, examples, discussion, problems, and suggestions can be applied to IL instructors in almost any environment.

### Avoid Stereotyping "Faculty"

Is there a single "animal" we can call "teaching faculty"? Can we make generalizations about K–12 or higher education instructors that will be useful in planning, developing, and implementing IL programs and sessions? Instructors at any level can be difficult, wonderful, or just OK, as anyone who has worked with them can attest. No one of these characterizations will fit each and every instructor in your institution, regardless of her or his educational background or the institution's educational level. After all, instructors are people with different personalities, life experiences, and outlooks on what it means to be an instructor at any level, what constitutes significant and effective teaching/learning experiences, and what role IL librarians should play in this process.

ILI librarians can be ignored, tolerated, looked on as support staff, resented, or considered full partners in the teaching/learning experience from K–12 through higher education. In the U.S. K–12 school environment, there is often a special category for a library media teacher, sometimes called a School Library Media Specialist (SLMS). The SLMS usually reports directly to the principal, which means she or he has quite a bit of autonomy. She or he controls the budget for the school library, supervises other school library employees, and may seek grants as well. The SLMS works closely with instructors, especially in secondary schools, to help students learn how to do information research and become information-literate. The SLMS may be a credentialed teacher as well. Do K–12 classroom teachers consult with the library media teacher or SLMS about assignments? Do they work together to develop expected IL learning outcomes? *Information Power* provides some guidance (1998), as do other publications (Cogdell 2003; Fitzgerald 2004), though, of course, there is no guarantee that K–12 teachers and librarians will work together on ILI in school libraries or in public libraries. Is there more cooperation in higher education?

Some higher education teaching faculty, particularly in the humanities, have worked closely with librarians for decades to enhance, enrich, and ease the information research learning process for their students, but many have not. Lest we forget, under one name or another, ILI has been taking place in educational institutions for the past thirty years or more, though perhaps in more limited form than today's ubiquitous electronic world allows. Why, then, was it so difficult for so long to get teaching faculty to collaborate with librarians in integrating IL into the curriculum?

Careful studies from the 1990s, as well as anecdotal evidence, provide some clues. At least for higher education, Hardesty (1995) and Leckie (1996) argued that we needed to understand and work within the "faculty culture" and be attuned to faculty assumptions if we were to succeed in our ILI efforts. According to Hardesty's thorough analysis and literature review, for many years, librarians have had problems trying to work with higher education faculty to establish IL programs under any name—library skills, library instruction, bibliographic instruction, information literacy, and so on. At least in this country, he attributed these problems to a number of factors including the faculty's

> emphasis on research and content and de-emphasis on teaching and process. The result is a highly autonomous, often isolated faculty faced with considerable pressures, including lack of time, to perform in areas in which its members are not particularly well-trained (teaching) or well-supported either by their institutions or the members of the profession. (Hardesty 1995, p. 354)

As Hardesty further points out, for higher education faculty, we need to understand how they go about doing research. In research institutions, they focus primarily on research in their particular niche, rather than on teaching. They are extremely busy people, and most are used to teaching autonomously. In higher education, they decide on specific course content, design their own syllabi and assignments, select readings, teach classes, do research, write articles and books, work with graduate students and doctoral candidates, attend and participate in all sorts of faculty and other committee meetings, and prepare and present papers at conferences. All of this takes a huge amount of time (Hardesty 1995). It takes so much time that some are too busy to come to the library themselves, sending their secretaries, their administrative assistants, teaching assistants, research assistants, and other support staff to do their research legwork. They keep up in their fields by scanning tables of contents of the major journals in their areas, picking and choosing articles to read from those journals. Others feel overwhelmed by the vast numbers of information resources now available in and through libraries, especially electronic tools and materials. Some are computer-phobic; others avidly use the Internet and e-mail and feel no need to use the physical library—they are interested only in fieldwork, in electronic resources available from their offices or homes, and in research in progress in their own fields of study.

What can we do to make faculty at all levels aware of the benefits of information literacy instruction and to find out which forms of ILI will appeal to them? In 1995, Hardesty recommended that we recognize many of these constraints of faculty culture, and he placed the burden on the librarian to keep trying, especially through informal one-on-one contact. In 1996, Leckie presented us with some further insight into "faculty-think." Most are so immersed in the "expert researcher" or scholar's research modus operandi and in their own fields, of course, that they really do not remember what it was like to be a novice, to know nothing at all about a field. The major scholars, researchers, and theorists in faculty members' areas are so familiar to them that they may have great difficulty getting down to the level of the undergraduate encountering those fundamentals for the first time.

So, we need to remind faculty of the differences between novice and expert researchers and the value of ILI in helping students become more expert researchers. We also need to work toward supporting faculty in integrating IL into their own course curricula, rather than teaching all the basics ourselves (Leckie 1996). This approach is quite different from what we have typically resigned ourselves to—offering what are essentially encapsulated mini-instruction sessions within courses or completely stand-alone instruction outside of courses—what some may think of as "IL vaccinations." In fact, Leckie claims that it may be difficult, if not impossible, to develop wide-scale, full-course-integrated ILI but that this should remain our goal nevertheless. Hardesty, too, says that fairly or not, librarians bear the burden of reaching out to faculty to try to educate and involve them in ILI efforts, while at the same time adopting a sensitive attitude toward the constraints of faculty culture and toward our own values (1995).

Those who have worked with faculty in higher education could certainly support these findings with anecdotal evidence of their own. However, in order to be a successful partner in reforming curricula to incorporate IL, we need to have a deep understanding of members of other campus groups as well (Kempcke 2002). Some suggest offering faculty outreach workshops on a regular basis, to keep them up-to-date with new online materials, and offer tips for successful workshops (Braham 2004; Chapman and White 2001). Others offer a variety of alternative approaches to persuade faculty of the value of IL. These include a "Learning Outcomes Model" and a "College Readiness Model" (Curzon 2004), as well as broad strategies for changing institutional culture, particularly at large institutions, so that any successes we have will not disappear if a particular partner leaves an institution (Kempcke 2002). Of course, higher education institutions are so political that many initiatives and programs, even curricular reforms, are highly dependent upon politically powerful individuals who support and promote them. So, it may be difficult to maintain a particular program at an institution or within an organization in any case if its chief promoters are no longer around, but you do need to start somewhere, and you can always build on small successes.

*Progress toward Full-Course Integration*

How can you work toward full-IL-course integration where you work, whether you are one of many librarians involved in IL or a single librarian? For that matter, how does a single IL librarian in any sort of institution or organization stretch herself or himself thin enough to integrate ILI into a course curriculum thoroughly or raise consciousness among her or his various user groups, even when presented with opportunities to do so?

For one, you can try to break through the shell of your encapsulated, one-shot sessions by including in each a comparison of how novice and expert researchers in a particular discipline go about looking for information. You can do this by using a sample topic in a condensed version of Leckie's analysis in a large group oral exercise, on a linear paper handout, or even on the Web. For instance, in a synchronous (simultaneous, real-time) group instruction session, you might start by having a hands-on simple search of the library's online catalog. Then have the students follow along as you limit a search, using Boolean operators, adjacency, or other more advanced techniques, and explain that this is how experienced users make databases work for them.

Again, the Web, the problems of which have brought IL librarians much recognition and respect, may itself offer some solutions, especially when accompanied by options in other formats. Web-based games or exercises such as "The Boolean Machine" (Schrock 2000), "The Mystery of Is It Mine or Ours" (National Council on Economic Education n.d.), and others could help both faculty/teachers (indirectly) and students (directly) understand the differences between these two approaches. Search the "Read, Write, Think" site for more examples (2002–2004).

This Web-based game approach may be adapted for lower academic levels as well, or students themselves might be enlisted to develop a game for their classmates, like "Volcanoes Online" (n.d.). Public or school library librarians may be able to work with K–12 teachers to develop a library-based project or WebQuest that would result in helpful and fun Web pages for those age groups (Dodge 1995; Dodge n.d.).

Success in expanding encapsulated one-shot sessions in these ways may depend in large part on how well you get across to grassroots decision makers, like faculty, the benefits of an information-literate populace.

Stand-alone programs, such as library-initiated workshops, on the other hand, do not necessarily depend upon faculty support for success, though they may get more business if faculty recommend them or require their students to enroll. Often, course-integrated programs depend upon the cooperation of one or more faculty members or the chair of a department or division. If these sessions are arranged with individual faculty, as you can imagine, they are completely dependent upon the faculty member's cooperation and desire to have such sessions take place.

*Improve Faculty/Teacher Attitudes toward IL Instruction*

Hardesty (1995), Leckie (1996), and Kempcke (2002) certainly offer major and helpful insights into the complex challenge of working with faculty, and IL librarians have heeded their admonitions. Has anything changed since they published their articles? Are we succeeding now? In many cases, the answer is resoundingly, "Yes! Finally!" But why?

Today, students rely heavily on Google and Yahoo! for research, so much so that some faculty have banned use of the Internet altogether for research papers. Web-based paper mills abound, and students' uncritical use and outright plagiarism of Web pages have made many teaching faculty sit up and take notice. The plagiarism crisis has even reached national consciousness in the form of an ABC Primetime news report, "Cheaters Amok: A Crisis in America's Schools—How It's Done and Why It's Happening" (ABCNEWS.com 2004). Because of this pervasive problem, some faculty simply preselect readings and require students to use only those readings when writing research papers. How do these students learn about literature searching and how to weigh and select evidence to support an argument? Faculty are beginning to realize that this approach means that most students have no clue about peer review, the differences between magazines and journals, and the existence of information tools librarians take for granted, like periodical indexes. As a result of this rising awareness and some recent publications outside of librarianship per se, their attitudes toward information literacy and librarians have been changing (Barbour 2004; Grassian 2004a).

After decades of effort and struggle, IL librarians with and without faculty status seem to be making a lot of progress, gaining increased recognition and respect as information experts in an unfiltered, Web-centered world. Librarians without official faculty status are talking more with faculty, and they have both anecdotal and solid research-based evidence to support their arguments for IL integration into the curriculum (Caravello, et al. 2001). More and more IL librarians seem to be teaming up with faculty to integrate IL into the curriculum, as Winner proposed in 1998.

Results of an informal survey on the Information Literacy Instruction Listserv in April 2004 support the view that college and university faculty are now turning more to librarians to help them teach information research and general critical thinking skills to undergraduates, as well as the concepts of intellectual property and plagiarism avoidance (Grassian 2004b). Survey respondents suggested a variety of reasons for this development, including the following:

- A joint compulsory series of classes called "eTools for Success" offered by the Libraries, Academic Computing and the Student Advocacy/Writing Assistance Centre (Braaksma 2004)
- A trend in the health sciences due to the Evidence Based Medicine/Health care movement (Graves 2004)
- Librarians reaching out to collaborate with faculty as a result of doing less business at the Reference Desk (Wentz 2004)
- Increased need to teach plagiarism/copyright-related topics (Bratton 2004)
- Grants received specifically for librarians and faculty to work together to "embed research into their courses" (Fister 2004)
- Requirements to include critical thinking components in course curricula (Wurtzel 2004)

There are many ways we can help this trend along, both within and outside the classroom. We can develop or draw faculty attention to ways to improve the effectiveness of their own assignments (California Clearinghouse on Library Instruction, South 2004). We can develop or suggest exercises, workbooks, and lists of assignments that do not require class time (Brasley 2003; Joseph 1992; Memorial University of Newfoundland Libraries 2000; Ricigliano 1999), as well as Web pages of information resources for specific classes, and interactive online tutorials. We can also keep lobbying to get IL integrated into course curricula as standard features of all courses, and we can support full-credit courses by collaborating with faculty to develop and teach one- or two-credit adjunct IL courses or other full-credit courses. This is a rare moment and a great opportunity to build partnerships and faculty support.

How do you get faculty to work with you? It takes lots of time and much patience to develop the kind of long-term, mutually beneficial relationship that can lead to successful collaboration for ILI. Raspa and Ward state that this is the kind of relationship "in which participants recognize common goals and objectives, share more tasks, and participate in extensive planning and implementation" (2000, p. 5). It is true that ILI collaboration must include recognition and acceptance of common goals and objectives, as Raspa and Ward stress (2000). It is also true that full partnership can be the kind of "symbiotic, mutually beneficial relationship" that Gilbert describes (2001, p. 76). However, we need to appreciate the fact that full partnership generally does not happen all at once. Like lasting personal relationships, instructional relationships take time to develop. They can start almost anywhere and any time with just a simple conversation about the changing landscape of information research, the worrisome tendency among learners to think that all information is free and available through Google, and the lack of critical thinking about information, regardless of the format.

Consciousness-raising questions like the following can help jump-start a conversation about the importance of information literacy competency, even without using the phrase "information literacy":

- What do faculty expect students to know and be able to do at various levels in terms of information research?
- What sorts of researching skills should a student have upon entering high school, upon becoming an undergraduate, or upon entering graduate school?
- What sorts of information tools should an employee be able to use effectively in the workplace to answer questions, get background, and weigh alternative approaches or methods?
- Which approaches have been tried before and with what success?
- Which methods work best within particular environments and circumstances?
- How can the use of technology enhance and support the teaching/learning process?
- Who is able to keep up with research tools?
- Who is best able to teach research methods to help people identify the questions first and then some possible answers based on evidence?

Does this sound overwhelming? It does not need to be. You can start small with one-on-one "mini–collaborations." Reach out to faculty or teachers gently and diplomatically, asking them one or two of the questions above. See if you can get them to give you a chance, just a bit of their time and their students' time. See if you can persuade them to give you a ten-to-fifteen-minute chunk of synchronous class time or ask if you may suggest some IL enhancements to an assignment. Then try to discuss and come to agreement on expected learning outcomes, teaching methodologies, and an assessment technique for whichever form of course-integrated instruction you are able to implement.

When you discuss the content of course-integrated ILI, do not be surprised if faculty make assumptions about their students' grasp of the basics and about the nature of what you, the IL librarian, has to offer. A pretest is one way to check on assumptions about students' knowledge. However, sometimes there is not enough time to do a pretest, analyze the results, discuss goals and objectives for a session with faculty, and still allow enough advance time to prepare. Instead, you may need to negotiate with faculty delicately and diplomatically, suggesting perhaps rather generic coverage of the basics with time allotted for students to work on researching their own topics. Or, you may be able to negotiate two or more shorter in-person sessions targeted to helping students achieve different learning outcomes. In a fifteen-minute session, you can introduce the concepts of "your physical library" and "your virtual library" with a building tour, a paper map handout showing campus libraries, and just a few words about the benefits of using electronic resources. Another fifteen-minute session could introduce the concepts of the "visible" versus the "invisible" Web through discussion, questions, and hands-on exploration of the library's Web site and licensed databases. You could extend this type of session outside the classroom by asking students to complete exercises on their own. Other fifteen-minute sessions could consist of exercises on topic selection, topic narrowing and broadening, or evaluating Web sites.

If in-person approaches are not possible or are rejected, you may want to try asynchronous (anytime, anyplace), interactive, Web-based exercises or online tutorials instead, many of which are linked from the LOEX Web site (n.d.). They can be required in place of synchronous in-person IL instruction held during the normal class meeting time. Or you might try scheduling a live chat session with students participating remotely. Students really appreciate customized instruction that addresses their assignments and topics as directly as possible. You can do that by focusing on relevant databases and by using some of their topics as examples. You may also want to be available to answer questions on the class discussion board or listserv or hold instruction "office hours" in person or virtually.

Examples of other types of out-of-class ILI include IL-enhanced exercises or assignments or a Web page of information resources tailored to a particular course, with links to locally mounted databases or systems categorized into "Basic Research Tools" and "Expert Users' Tools." The labels you use for these categories should not offend or be condescending, of course, and such a web page would require quite some rethinking and extra work, but it could be well worth the investment of time and effort, particularly if you can persuade instructors to provide feedback and ideas for links to important sites. Engage them by asking for help in distinguishing between basic and expert users' tools, for instance. This is just one of many interim approaches that may help move faculty along the continuum from total lack of awareness of IL and its value, to full-course integration of one or more formats of ILI.

Start this process by listening well (Raspa and Ward 2000). As you listen, focus on the faculty member's interests and concerns, repeat them to check your understanding, find something of interest to you, and express your enthusiasm honestly. Call on your knowledge of new or updated reference tools and suggest their use to enhance assignments for ILI. Are the students required to do service learning with a community-based organization? Suggest enhancing the assignment by having the students do some research about the type of organization with which they will be volunteering. Then ask the students to document their research in a brief essay and/or an annotated bibliography. Your personal interest can help change attitudes, and faculty/teacher attitudes and influence may make or break an IL program in an academic or school library. These days, they are making them. At UCLA, a 1999 study concluded that the only significant factor in improving information literacy skills was increased use of the library and library resources (Caravello et al. 2001). UCLA librarians have used this study in discussions with the Sociology Department, as the department has restructured its curriculum, helping faculty see the value of information literacy integrated throughout in a sequenced fashion. As of winter 2004, there were IL requirements at the lower division level and plans to develop a required adjunct one-unit IL course for sociology majors (Mizrachi and Brasley 2004).

Of course, you may encounter very warm and friendly faculty who, nevertheless, are territorial about their courses and assignments (Christiansen, Stombler, and Thaxton 2004). Quite aside from the Web-plagiarism issue, some may not see the value of IL for courses in which they expect students to read assigned materials, think about them, attend lectures, and write creative essays expressing their own thoughts, all without reference to any outside sources. In this common situation, you face serious challenges in advocating incorporation of IL into expected learning outcomes.

You may be able to head off this sort of problem before it occurs by providing faculty with a list or menu of the various kinds of ILI they may want to consider, like one-shot guest sessions for classes, one- or two-credit adjunct IL courses that can support full-credit courses, Web pages of information resources, point-of-use guides, exercises, interactive tutorials, and so on. Some faculty may want to take ministeps on their own. You could create a Web page of brief information literacy assignment ideas, written from the instructor's perspective. These could include assignments such as the following:

- If they need to find overview information on a topic: Use a print and a Web-based encyclopedia (general or subject-specialized) to gather background information on your topic (e.g., the print and licensed online versions of *Encyclopaedia Britannica* (http://search.eb.com/) and the freely available Web-only *Stanford Encyclopedia of Philosophy* (http://plato.stanford.edu/contents.html). Compare and contrast the information you find in each (Brasley 2003).

- Compare a primary and a secondary source: Have students choose a historic event and read a primary source/eyewitness account (letter, diary, newspaper story) and a secondary source (history book or textbook account) and make comparisons. This can also be effective with a literary work, with students reading a piece of literature as the primary source and literary criticism as the secondary source (Ryer 2002).
- Finding supporting information: Give the students an article to critique. Have them locate two sources (other articles, Web sites) that support (or not) the points made in the original article. *Purpose:* Gives the students an opportunity to understand the importance of using more than one source when gathering information (Fitzwater 2003).
- Assemble background information on a company or organization in preparation for a hypothetical interview: For those continuing in academia, research prospective colleagues' and professors' backgrounds, publications, current research, and so on (Ricigliano 1999).

Or you may want to set up a Web page where instructors can review a list of in-class one-shot session ILI modules and request any combination of these modules to build the kind of ILI session they want. Or they may choose to collaborate with a librarian to design a different group instruction module (UCLA College Library 2005). Again, this is not necessarily the only approach, as many teaching faculty are reluctant to give up in-class teaching time for ILI, and it may not be necessary for the IL librarian to spend much time in person with a class. At large institutions it would be impossible to do so for each and every course.

The joint Indiana University-Purdue University Indianapolis (IUPUI) enrolled 7,171 graduate/professional school students and 20,416 undergraduates in 1999/2000 (Indiana University 1999). That year, IUPUI librarians collaborated with faculty in developing learning objectives, the syllabus, and assignments for classes for first-year students. Though the librarian appeared only infrequently in the classroom throughout the semester, she or he influenced course activities and projects, had her or his name on the syllabus, and "is acknowledged as a member of the faculty for that course" (Orme 1999). In 2002 a partnership of University of California, Berkeley groups, including the University Library and Educational Technology Services, among others, went further by establishing Mellon-funded summer institutes. These institutes are designed to help faculty "redesign undergraduate courses and curricula that emphasize undergraduate research as a critical component of independent and self-directed learning. The Project strengthens the connections between undergraduate research, information literacy, and library collections" (University of California, Berkeley 2004). Faculty learn various means of altering their course curricula to incorporate IL and use information technology effectively and then move ahead to do so on their own (Edelstein 2004).

New faculty, new teachers, and new courses offer numerous IL advocacy opportunities, and technology is on our side. Why? Although librarians at all levels have learned to use technology, and use it daily, older faculty may not. So, reaching out to offer help with new technology-based information tools can be an effective means of establishing trusting relationships with older, more established faculty. Anyone's new or revised syllabi and assignments can be wonderful pockets of opportunity for enterprising librarians at any level, particularly if they are included at the planning stage.

What do you do if you get some draft syllabi for college-level courses or draft lesson plans for lower grade levels? Read them over and insert suggested IL enhancements throughout, along with some expected IL learning outcomes. Be sure to include suggested IL enhancements for the course goals as well as assignments. (See a sample draft syllabus for a UCLA course, with suggested IL enhancements, on the CD that accompanies this book.) Then meet with instructors to discuss your suggestions and answer their questions about them. End with the ILI menu and an offer to collaborate for improved ILI in whatever ways best suit their needs.

*Talk with Instructors*

Are you nervous about talking to faculty and other professionals? Did that teacher brush you off? Did that professor say she absolutely could not give up one minute of in-person class time for ILI? Do not despair or try to convince her to let you have some of her limited class time. It is easy to fall into the trap of focusing on synchronous (simultaneous) in-person group instruction and insist on taking class time in order to help students become information-literate. Try to avoid this and, instead, offer a variety of ILI approaches. If one instructor does not seem interested, try someone else. If you are at a large institution, ask teaching assistants and lecturers if they are developing new courses. Look for special programs or institutes. If you are in a public library, check for new areas of interest in the community or new community groups. Are you in a school library media center? See if there are new curricular requirements in your school district. If you are in a special library, is your corporate employer interested in beefing up employee skills and planning to institute a new training program? Ask your administrators to be on the lookout for you, too, for new opportunities of all kinds. Once you have some names, take a deep breath and come up with an outline of what you want to say. Contact the new course developers, the new community group organizers, the employer with a new employee training program, and tell them about some new (or newly revised/enhanced) information resources in their fields. Briefly, tell them about the benefits of ILI and give a quick list of your ILI menu—synchronous and asynchronous, in-person and remote. If they stop listening, send them the menu by e-mail, fax, or snail mail, and invite them to contact you at their convenience. If they are still listening, ask if they would like some ILI assignment ideas for their syllabi, for in-class and out-of-class assignments. Remember to keep your conversation brief and to the point and to jump on every possible opportunity to spread the good word about the many benefits and formats of ILI.

When you get a positive response, be sensitive to the political situation and decide when and how you will leverage this success. Would it be better to go back to the resistor and say, "Look, Susan and I are working on an ILI assignment to help her students learn how to distinguish among various types of citations so they can locate those materials more easily. Would you be interested in this sort of assignment for your students, too?" Or, it might be better to wait and return to the resistor after the students have completed the assignment or even the entire term, and the instructor has had a chance to evaluate the effectiveness of this form of instruction. You will need to make this judgment call yourself or in consultation with your colleagues (both on site and virtually) or your administrators. It may help to check tips on collaborating (Jeffries 2000). Look for examples of collaborative ILI projects you may want to use as models or just review for ideas you can adapt to your own environment and circumstances, like Earlham College's librarian/faculty collaborative model, dating back to 1965 (Farber 1993; Raspa and Ward 2000; Ver Steeg 2000).

This "prospecting" takes time, and lots of it, of course, but it is time so well spent. The keys to ILI librarian success in these endeavors are flexibility, administrative support, and the ability to decrease the level of certain responsibilities, even on a temporary basis, in order to put time and effort into opportunities like these as they arise. When working with faculty and computer center staff or Web designers on an interactive Web tutorial, or a one- or two-credit adjunct IL course, or on planning for integration of IL into the curriculum of one or more courses, try negotiating with administrators for temporarily reduced reference desk hours or less collection development or committee work, so that you can give these efforts the quality attention and time they deserve. If your negotiations are unsuccessful, you will probably need much more time to achieve full collaboration and complete your IL projects successfully. Administrators need to know this, so include estimated timelines and milestones for alternative levels of support or even for no support. See a sample draft syllabus for a UCLA CUTF course with suggested IL enhancements on the CD ROM that accompanies this book.

## WORKING WITH LIBRARY BOARDS/TRUSTEES AND OTHER TYPES OF LIBRARIES

You may wonder why anyone would object to your helping people become information-literate. This may seem particularly odd in public libraries because librarians there seem to be on their own turf, as the public library is its own entity. But is it? Remember, public libraries face many political issues in almost everything they do. They are supported by tax dollars and, as a result, they must balance the community's wishes with the library's mission, both as determined by elected officials and in keeping with the *Library Bill of Rights* (ALA 1996), and the ALA *Principles for the Networked World* (ALA 2003c). They must respond to frequent inquiries and challenges from their many constituencies, from parents of young children to trustees, local government officials and organizations of all kinds, with an enormous range of political and social views. Should the public library serve *in loco parentis* complete with Internet filtering software to protect young minds, for example? Or should it abide by the code of intellectual freedom that is ingrained in librarians? Is all information freely accessible to everyone, and if not, should it be? What sorts of examples can and should public library librarians use in ILI for various age groups? Will all public library users be able to gain access, without restriction, to Web sites used as examples in ILI, in person, and remotely?

Because public libraries exist in a sometimes volatile political goldfish bowl, how much should they bend to the political will of individuals, government officials, and organizations? The answer to this question may be an important factor, particularly when it comes to critical thinking and representation of diverse viewpoints and information research tools, as well as funding priorities for teaching and learning information literacy skills and information resources.

Public library trustees generally select the library director and set library policies (Young 1995). They also serve as a bridge between the library director and the governing body of the library (Biggs and Kramer 1994). The trustees may not have thought much about the library's teaching role, however, as this function is newer to public libraries than to academic and school libraries. Anticipate some of the questions they may have when asked to support ILI. These questions may include:

- How does ILI fit in with the library's mission and help the library achieve its goals?
- How much attention, funding, and staffing should ILI get?
- What kinds of ILI should the library offer to different age groups?
- Which research tools can and should you teach to which groups?
- What sorts of examples can you use for various constituencies when teaching?
- What will an active ILI program mean for the library in terms of public relations?
- What will need to happen in order to start and maintain an ILI program?
- How much will be needed in terms of start-up and ongoing resources, including staff training and equipment?
- In what ways will IL help advance other projects in which the library is involved, including homework centers and reading literacy programs?

All of these questions and more are bound to come up, so prepare your answers in advance. If you are unfamiliar with the politics that usually surround public libraries, do some reading, interview more experienced staff in your library, observe them at work, and consider doing some needs assessments for different user populations. (See Beckerman 1996; Biggs and Kramer 1994; CalTac 1998; Mediavilla 2001, 2003; Reed 1992; Young 1992, 1995.)

Once you have an idea of the types of questions, objections, and problems that can crop up regarding ILI, you may be able to inoculate your library against ILI-related problems by helping all of your constituency groups understand first what "information illiteracy" is and then the benefits of an information-literate populace. Offer to provide some background on your library's IL goals, activities, and achievements to new trustees as part of their orientation. You may even want to develop a special annual or semiannual IL workshop, designed just for trustees, whether they fill advisory or administrative functions. If you label the workshop an "update" session, you will help the trustees avoid embarrassment if they lack up-to-date knowledge of information resources. At the same time you can introduce them to new electronic tools and services for their own research or to use as they work with governing bodies, Friends of the Library, and other user groups. You could also make presentations to the City Council and to local organizations, as well as local businesses. In order to get support for ILI, in addition to presenting its benefits, outline both the external and internal policies and activities needed to support ILI. Then enlist the help of these groups in coming up with lists of expected learning outcomes for each learner group. Finally, develop a variety of means of helping each learner group to achieve expected learning outcomes and to become information-literate. Ideally, learners would then select the methodology that appeals most to them, as marketed on printed posters, Web sites, flyers, and/or bookmarks.

Special library librarians must confront political issues, too, as some businesses restrict their employees to their own Intranets, for legal, security or economic (trade secret) reasons, and/or to prevent personal use of the Web on company time. What and how do you teach under these circumstances? How does it help the "bottom line"? How can you help your employer see that having more sophisticated information-literate employees helps save money and supports creativity, not to mention goodwill. These are questions that special libraries need to address, and IL librarians should take the lead in bringing them to the forefront.

In which arenas can you become this kind of leader within your organization or institution? The answer may depend on your own position and role, which you can enhance through collaboration and networking.

If you work in a public library, you may want to collaborate and network with school librarians regarding IL for K–12 students, to help them learn how to help themselves with immediate homework needs and to prepare them for higher-level research, as a number of public libraries are doing by establishing separate and distinct "Homework Centers" within their physical space (Mediavilla 2003). You may also want to collaborate with librarians in special libraries, like businesses, to see what their users' needs are and whether or not you can help by educating them about public libraries' business materials. Do college students use your public library? If so, you may want to collaborate with the colleges and universities in the area to offer some basic instruction in the use of your library's databases. Do senior citizen groups meet in your public library's meeting rooms? If so, they may be ideal collaborators. They can survey their members to find out what their ILI needs and interests may be. Then you can design and offer instruction together that would be of interest to them, pointing out sites such as the *Librarians' Index to the Internet* (2004) for carefully selected and reviewed "visible" (i.e., freely available) Web sites.

As the following examples illustrate, you can adapt and apply to a variety of environments, each networking/collaborating example mentioned in the preceding paragraph. If you are in a school library, reach out to public library librarians. If you are in a business, reach out to school libraries and public libraries. The award-winning Dr. Martin Luther King, Jr., Library, in San Jose, California, is an example of the ultimate in collaboration between different types of libraries (Berry 2004). It is a public library and state university library in the same eight-story building, sharing a space, collaborating, and consulting closely, with a single online system a single Web site. Yet each library continues to maintain its own identity, with its own staffing patterns and fulfilling typical types of functions for public and academic libraries, with SJSU librarians serving as liaisons to academic departments, and SJPL's librarians investigating and moving toward more personal and intuitive customer service. In fact, directors of both libraries call it a "marriage" rather than a "merger" (Berry 2004). If it is a marriage, it seems to be a good one. The directors had to overcome a lot of difficulties, criticism from librarians and user groups, and what seemed to be insurmountable problems, including differing city and university purchasing regulations, as well as other groups competing for the same funds as the library. Collections of both libraries now get much more attention and broader use. The success of this collaborative effort is serving as a catalyst for further discussion between the city and SJSU on other possible collaborative efforts (Berry 2004). The government documents collections of both libraries were merged, for instance, as SJSU was a federal depository, while SJPL did not have a federal documents collection. Then librarians from both SJSU and SJPL leaped on this new merger to join forces and make a presentation to city planners (Kendall 2004).

This is an excellent example of how public library and academic library librarians can work together for the benefit of all of their users. Even if they are physically joined and work together administratively, each can maintain IL-related Web sites and offer classes to particular user populations, as SJPL does with their "Beginning Internet for Adults" class. Their "Paths to Learning" site also shows IL progression and connections among various user groups, from "KidsPlace" to "Adults & Seniors," with separate information resources pages geared to the needs of each group (San Jose Library n.d.).

However, it is important to note that librarians at California State University campuses, like San Jose State University, have faculty status. Librarians at school libraries may or may not have teaching credentials. Does faculty status make a difference in networking and relations with administrators and other staff or colleagues within the academic library, as well as others outside the library? Does it have an impact on IL program planning, development, and implementation? What does "faculty status" actually mean at your institution?

## CONSIDER THE PROS AND CONS OF FACULTY STATUS FOR LIBRARIANS

Many would argue that faculty status does make a difference in academic libraries. If you are a librarian and have full faculty status, you may participate in your institution's academic senate or faculty/teacher committees. You may even be a member of the committee that reviews and approves new courses, new curricula, and new majors. You may be able to participate in discussions and decision making regarding revisions to various academic requirements, such as required general education courses at colleges and universities. You will have greater networking opportunities with teaching faculty, teachers, and administrators, and you will have many opportunities to raise consciousness about the need for IL, as well as various means of integrating it into course goals and curricula (Young and Harmony 1999). In addition, at colleges and universities where librarians have faculty status, the library is often an academic department and may offer courses for credit, taught by librarians. All of this is very positive. It means that as a faculty member, you are more or less on an equal footing with teaching faculty or other teachers.

What are the negatives? Teaching faculty at colleges and universities may resent librarians who have faculty status and may not consider them to be peers. Why? Teaching faculty may perceive that librarians are not held to the same review and promotion standards as faculty are, yet they are paid on the same salary scale. Other drawbacks to faculty status for librarians include the need (and pressure) to "publish or perish," as well as peer review by nonlibrarians who are at a loss to evaluate the librarian's professional activity, research, and creativity.

What is it like for librarians who do not have faculty status? You may or may not be permitted to participate in the academic senate and on faculty committees. Interactions between librarians and faculty at such institutions may be much more limited. Interactions that do occur may be at a different level, as faculty may view librarians as just another class of service employees, whose role is to support the faculty's academic endeavor, rather than work with her or him as a collegial partner. However, you can still lobby to serve as a consultant to curriculum-related faculty committees, so that you are "at the table" when curriculum decisions are made (Kempcke 2002, p. 531). If this tactic fails, you can always contact one or more departments directly. Ask if anyone is developing new courses and if they might be interested in learning about new information resources to support their curricula or their research.

If you do not have faculty status, you may or may not be permitted to teach courses for credit. Are these librarians appointed as affiliate or adjunct members of academic departments when they teach collaboratively? Do librarians who teach separate courses receive a stipend for doing so? Is their library-related workload prioritized and decreased to compensate, as Winner (1998) suggested? Librarians at University of California campuses do not have faculty status. Yet, since the 1980s, many have taught one- to four-credit IL undergraduate and graduate courses as adjunct lecturers within different departments. Often, they teach as lecturers part-time, are partially released from their responsibilities and paid work time as librarians, and are paid separately as instructors, on a pro-rated basis. When there are salary savings from this arrangement, and when replacement staff can be hired temporarily, there is little or no additional burden on remaining staff. Unfortunately, this is not always the case, and when other staff must pick up the slack left by someone off teaching as a lecturer, resentment can build quickly. This can be a serious morale problem.

How much can the library contribute to collaborative teaching efforts in terms of staff time and other resources, while still maintaining its traditional role and keeping up with reference staffing, cataloging, acquisitions, electronic licensing, reserves, and more? Administrators need to realize the key role IL plays and put more dollars into the enterprise or encourage librarians to apply for grants to support these critical efforts, like the University of California, Berkeley Library's 2002/2003 partnership application for a Mellon grant mentioned previously.

This sort of grant support does not occur on its own, however. You must work with administrators to help them see IL and its benefits as the common denominator, a major link between the library, its communities of users, and its partners, both current and potential. And administrators must follow up on words of commitment with action and funding.

## WORK WITH ADMINISTRATORS (WITHIN AND OUTSIDE THE LIBRARY)

### Connect with Library Administrators and Provide Statistical Support

Administrators' attitudes toward faculty can make an enormous difference both in relationships with faculty and in morale among ILI librarians. In some institutions, when a faculty member says, "Jump!" an administrator says, "How high?" In other institutions, teaching faculty and librarians are peers and work in partnership (Farber 1993; ALA. ACRL. CARL. sCIL. 2003). As already noted, the tone set by the library administration in dealing with faculty can definitely make or break an IL program.

Administrators can help organize and implement political approaches to developing and funding IL programs or pilot projects. Library administrators, trustees, and supervisors seem to be much more committed to IL at this time, but how far does that commitment extend in practice? Do they readily provide release time, staff support, training, and funding for new IL projects and programs? Do they need to be convinced of the need for new instructional programs? How willingly do they agree that existing programs need to be revised or even dropped? Do they recognize and reward IL achievements publicly? Solid empirical evidence, particularly instructional statistics, can bolster your efforts considerably.

How do you count instructional statistics? Do you count input (e.g., number of hours of preparation time), output (e.g., number of instructional sessions), new initiatives (including outreach efforts and grant proposals, whether or not they were successful), learning outcomes changes based on pretests and posttests, attitude changes (affective) based on informal assessments, and so on? You could use any of these statistics to support a request to review, add, or delete programs, materials, or specific forms of instruction—to convince administrators of the value of IL programs. What do the instructional statistics indicate for course-integrated and stand-alone IL sessions? Have the numbers increased, decreased, or stayed the same for the past year or two? How many visitors have used the instructional portion of your Web site? What proportion of total Web site visitors use the instructional portions? How many paper handouts have had to be reordered, and which ones have been most popular? Which questions keep recurring at the reference and information desks? What do needs assessments, focus groups, program evaluations, individual learning outcomes assessments, and surveys tell you? Do any new information sources or new interfaces need publicizing and require instruction regarding usage?

Are there any new programs or new learner groups—for instance, have you reached out recently to senior citizens, to K–12 teachers or students, or to businesses? What do your colleagues think? Which faculty and departments have asked for ILI? Whom have you targeted for ILI outreach? What sorts of ILI materials have you developed and in what formats? Your answers to these questions, with statistics to back you up, will get administrators' attention. Much depends on administrators' time constraints, though, so be concise and to the point.

Pick out the most significant statistics and other data, condense all of it, make comparisons to previous years, and incorporate your findings into a one- or two-page descriptive memo to your administrator(s), supporting some proposed solutions to an instructional problem. It is a good idea to include alternative approaches, but if you recommend a particular approach, be sure to include your rationale for recommending it. When you develop a list of pros and cons, remember to include expected attitudinal (affective), as well as learning or skills (cognitive) impacts on primary and other user groups and on staff. Focus on how the solution will enhance library services and use. Discuss its cost-effectiveness in terms of improved public relations and library image. Remember to be realistic about timelines, though, and the need for help to put the solution in place and, later, to evaluate it. You may have a better chance of approval if you propose a small pilot program, carefully designed to test your solutions, with specific milestones and built-in assessment. (See memo instructions on the CD that accompanies this book.)

Strangely enough, expensive problems may be solved before the cheap ones are. Why does this happen? Often, there are sources of outside funding for more expensive, more "showily" visible solutions. Library donors may prefer to pay for some piece of state-of-the-art technology, while public agencies, like a state library, may be interested in funding projects that include multitype library cooperation. An expensive solution to a problem can also generate quite a bit of free publicity.

As for the "cheap" solution—if it is a very cheap solution, you may find yourself working with your colleagues to implement it with little or no additional funding (assuming you have administrative approval, of course). For instance, you may want to develop a walkaround audio tour for use with headphones and a CD player or iPod. Pathfinders and brief guides or point-of-use guides may be funded more easily than lengthy handbooks. Some IL programs can also be designed to be self-supporting. For example, the sale of printed workbooks can support their development, printing, binding, and correction, as Miriam Dudley's *Library Skills Workbook* did in the 1970s at UCLA and in many other parts of the country and the world, where it was copied and adapted (Dudley 1978).

---

**Figure 3–3**
**Tips to Smooth Your Path with Administrators**

---

1. Keep them informed of costs, problem situations, and new developments as they arise.
2. Keep activities visible and follow the chain of command.
3. Routinely write reports and route to higher-ups. Include evaluation summaries and products, even if they are still drafts.
4. Invite members of the administration to observe or participate in new programs and projects.
5. Ask for their help when you need it in involving teaching faculty and in reaching out to partner with others.
6. When administrators lay the groundwork by identifying and making first contact with potential audiences, be sure to follow up with practical application and report back to them in full on any progress you may have made.

---

In what ways do IL administrators show their appreciation for major IL achievements? A very few receive national recognition through formal awards, like the ACRL Instruction Section (IS) Miriam Dudley Librarian of the Year Award, Publication Awards, and Innovation Award (ALA. ACRL. Instruction Section 2004b). More are recognized through the PRIMO Web database, run by an IS committee "to promote and share peer-reviewed instructional materials created by librarians to teach people about discovering, accessing and evaluating information in networked environments" (ALA. ACRL. Instruction Section 2004c), or through LIRT's top twenty IL-related publications of the year (ALA. LIRT 2004). Library school alumni associations and other professional groups recognize librarians' achievements. Even the *New York Times* recognizes outstanding public library librarians through its annual Librarian Awards, with twenty-seven librarians receiving $2,500 each in 2003 (New York Times. Community Affairs Department 2004; "New York Times Honors . . ." 2003). The Indiana University Bloomington Library offers the William Evans Jenkins Librarian Award, "[I]n recognition of truly outstanding contributions to the Indiana University Libraries or to the library profession in general by a present or former librarian" (IUB Libraries 2003). The Librarians Association of the University of California, Berkeley Division offers a Distinguished Librarian Award annually (LAUC-B 2004), while the UCLA Division of this organization offers a Librarian of the Year Award (LAUC-LA 2004). If your institution does not yet recognize librarian achievement in information literacy and other areas, consider broaching the subject with administrators. Awards like these can have an impact, as they do much to bring positive attention to individual librarians, to the library, and to information literacy, both within and outside a single library or even an institution, an organization, or other place of employment.

*Engage Other Administrators and Address Accreditation Issues*

In what other ways can we establish positive and productive relationships with other administrators outside the library and make an impact on an institution? Institutional size may be a critical factor. Many people tend to be tribal, interacting most often with those on the same level and within the same unit or with those in similar units. Computer center staff, for instance, tend to interact most with their immediate colleagues and then with staff in other computer centers. They share jargon, background, work experiences, and challenges. The same is true for librarians. Reaching out to other "tribes" can seem daunting. You can overcome these difficulties by finding common ground and establishing trust. If opportunities do not fall in your lap, you can make them happen, but first you must learn at least some of the jargon and priorities of your potential partner groups and the administrators to whom they report. Oddly enough, the larger the institution, the more easily you may be able to make this happen, as the more potential compatible partners you may find.

Start with colleagues who are approximately at your level in the political hierarchy. The political environment may be tricky at higher levels and best left to one's own higher-level administrators. Direct outreach to high-level administrators outside the library for program planning may or may not be a good idea, depending partly on the attitudes and styles of your own library administrators. Contact and information sharing are important, but often, individual librarians do not have the authority to make program commitments, especially if staff time and money are involved. On the other hand, information sharing can be taken to a higher plane in two ways.

First, you can work from the bottom up, by helping colleagues, faculty, and other nonlibrary staff learn about the benefits of ILI. In fact, ILI librarians have been doing this for twenty-five to thirty years, and they continue to do so, though, until fairly recently, with mixed results.

Second, you can take a highly political approach and work from the top down with standards that really mean business for top-level school and higher education administrators—accrediting agencies that set standards for schools and higher education institutions. The Middle States Accrediting Agency first focused on information literacy as a major issue in 1994 (Simmons 1994). Rader reports that this group's Commission on Higher Education, along with ACRL and the National Forum on Information Literacy, conducted a survey of 830 U.S. institutions to "explore the status of initiatives regarding information literacy" (Rader 2004, p. 75). In fact, many accrediting agencies have reexamined their standards (Marchese 1995; Orlans 1995; Olsen 1999; Healy 1999), and all six U.S. regional higher education accrediting agencies now include some form of IL competency along with other accreditation standards, though they may use different words to describe what we would call "information literacy" or "information competency" (ALA. ACRL, CARL 1997; ALA. ACRL 2003). Thanks to the efforts of numerous hardworking librarians, many levels of the educational system in the United States have a growing awareness of the importance of IL. AASL's IL standards, first published in 1998 in *Information Power*, describe IL competencies for the schools K–12 (ALA. AASL and AECT 1998). ACRL's information literacy competency standards for higher education are intended to "provide a framework for assessing the information literate student" (2000). These developments help everyone see that the need for IL competency cuts across all levels of society, and they strengthen support for incorporating IL competency standards into higher education accreditation standards.

The importance of this effort cannot be overemphasized. Jones International University (JIU), a strictly online, for-profit university, was accredited in 1999 by the North Central Association of Colleges and Schools, with no physical library holdings (AFT 1999), though JIU currently has ebooks available (Heilig 2004). What does this mean for students in these sorts of "virtual" schools? Are they able to identify, locate, evaluate, and use information effectively? To its credit, JIU offers one-on-one appointments with its librarians, as well as live chat reference, phone and e-mail reference, and many online research guides and tutorials. However, it is difficult to work with instructors to integrate IL into curricula and assignments, as all staff and students work online, and also because courses/curricula are developed by some and taught by others (Heilig 2004).

The JIU librarian, Jean Heilig, has also developed a list of information research questions for students. Students must use library resources to answer the questions and then e-mail back their answers. The librarian returns them, corrected, along with instructions on how to find correct answers (Heilig 2004). What happens, though, when online sources are insufficient for their needs? Heilig reports that JIU does a limited number of interlibrary loans for students at no cost to the students, at this time—"up to 5 articles, 2 books (gently used), and 2 dissertations per course" (Heilig 2004). She is aware of the fact that JIU may need to rework this model as the student body grows, if it is to remain profitable (Heilig 2004b). How to do this is a conundrum, however.

Accreditation means federal dollars for schools, colleges, and universities. As IL standards are incorporated into accreditation standards, administrators at the campuswide level in higher education, as well as K–12, may begin to take these standards into consideration in accreditation self-studies, a significant consciousness-raising activity. As they do, they will be paying attention to research resources and whether or not IL standards are being met.

Academic and school libraries do not stand alone in this effort. Public libraries and special libraries can bring businesses and other employers into the picture by getting their support for including IL standards in accreditation standards, in order to help meet the need for a better educated workforce. Why not capitalize on the urgent need for computer literacy by using it to educate both employers and other technical support staff about the need for information literacy, as well?

Contact with separate computing centers or with those who provide computing support in almost any environment can be quite fruitful. Such outreach can lead to significant partnerships and other sorts of interactions, which can then support the achievement of IL competency standards. Librarians could learn about new technology and get training help as well as advice on how to incorporate new technology into the learning/teaching process. In turn, the librarian can introduce IL concepts into the conversation to raise awareness of the broader information competency picture. Computing support personnel deserve our respect and appreciation (U.S. National Institute for Literacy 1999). Our relationships with them can be significant and highly symbiotic. In fact, in some institutions the relationship is so symbiotic that the library and the computing center have merged into a single entity (Frand and Bellanti 2000). What does this mean for librarians? What in fact is the role of the librarian regarding computer training?

## PARTNER WITH COLLEAGUES

*Can Librarians Partner with Computer Trainers?*

Clearly, library staff should be teaching people how to use the library's online catalog. However, who should teach the mechanics of using Web browsers like Netscape or Internet Explorer, how to construct Web pages using HTML, or how to use e-mail, word processing, or chat software? Teaching and training lines are blurry in many libraries. In some institutions, librarians have taught users e-mail and listservs when their use related to course content (at instructor request), as well as how to use HTML to write Web pages (Dupuis 1999). Librarians have also taught applications such as Microsoft Word or Excel, if computer literacy is part of the library's mission (Schwartz 2000). In others, librarians teach only library- or research-related tools offered by the library, including the mechanics of using Web browsers, but excluding e-mail software and Web page creation. This has been the policy at the UCLA College (undergraduate) Library, for example, since the 1990s. In 1994 Web browsers were new and presented an excellent opportunity for collaboration between librarians and computer center staff. At that time, UCLA librarians were teaching Gopher and the most popular Web browser, Netscape. When the campus decided to introduce a suite of software for students, staff, and faculty, including Netscape, the library was invited to participate in training campus trainers in its use and in critical thinking about Web resources. This was a wonderful opportunity to get to know and work with highly skilled computer center staff. The UCLA Library still enjoys the positive effects of this sort of interaction ten years later, in the form of a collaborative effort to create a basic IL tutorial, "The Road to Research" (Grassian 2004b).

In some libraries, lower-level staff may be able to teach the mechanics of using various pieces of software, which may be one way to relieve the instruction librarian's heavy burden—but who can best teach users how to evaluate information and think critically about it? And who can advise on the range of information sources on a topic, in all sorts of formats?

Almost any computer trainer who knows how to teach the mechanics of using EndNote bibliographic software or Web browsers like Internet Explorer or Safari can teach just that—the mechanics. They may have Web sites that are personal favorites and that can be useful for technical questions, or they may prefer one search tool over another for a variety of reasons. However, unless they are subject matter experts, they cannot recommend one Web site over another based on content or authority. Nor can they recommend Web sites as opposed to print reference sources, or vice versa. In other words, computer trainers can tell you only how to get to the mall, where and how to park, and how to go from one store to another and from one mall to another. The librarian, your personal shopper, can tell you which store in the mall would be best for which products and which store will be most likely to have the products you want, reliably stocked, in the size and color you want them (Guyonneau 1996). It seems clear that the unique teaching and training role of librarians lies in the areas of objective evaluation and advice, based on the scope of their knowledge of information resources. However, teaching and training partnerships, both human and electronic, can combine the best of both of these worlds. These sorts of partnerships are growing in importance, particularly as learning management systems (LMS) grow and evolve and as LMS developers and librarians move simultaneously toward unified theories and development of learning objects and digital repositories. Great opportunities lie ahead for all of us in joint definition and development of these items and means for accessing, using, and storing them (McLean and Lynch 2004). How do we develop and maintain these sorts of partnerships, though?

Partnerships can be exhilarating and mutually beneficial, at the very least through an exchange of ideas and at best through truly collaborative endeavors. However, like all relationships, partnerships require time, attention, and conscious sharing of efforts and planning to maintain them. As you build goals and objectives for IL programs and initiatives, think about how you might be able to incorporate pieces "donated" by other experts, or whether you might be able to persuade them to team-teach. Try to find out what they are attempting to achieve and see if you can identify some common ground where IL, IT (information technology), and curriculum-specific pedagogical objectives meet.

Reach out to educational technology and computer support staff at your institution, in your organization, or in your community and share information about computer-related plans and new developments on the library's end, such as new licensed databases and interfaces, plans for a new or improved OPAC, or even policies on use of public computers in the library for various age groups. Take advantage of new developments in technology to discuss how instruction in the basics will be handled and the benefits of an information-literate and information technology-literate society. Librarians are adept at developing point-of-use guides and tutorials. If nothing else, these products could be shared with computer support staff within and outside the library environment. Raise their awareness about the value of the librarian—our knowledge of the range of information sources, our ability to weigh the value and uses of each, objectively, and our ability to help users wend their way through the maze of information sources now available.

Web site developers have already created intelligent software agents, like "Ask Jeeves" (2003), which attempt to replicate the interaction that takes place between a reference librarian and a person with a question or research need. As Zick (2000) suggests, librarians would do well to embrace this sort of new technology and collaborate with the developers, with the intention of helping programmers develop the best of both worlds—a technological approach that may help users with basic queries and instruction, and a human default. Librarians have been working with programmers to create Web-based IL tutorials, and we are continuing to enlarge our instructional world as we explore and expand upon (or segment and decontexualize) our existing online materials to create both new and reusable digital learning objects.

IL is larger than the library and larger than librarians, and this sort of positive partnership outreach has great potential for instilling an atmosphere of goodwill and cooperation for the benefit of all user groups. If we wanted to take this partnering a big step further, we could offer to work with the most popular Internet tools, like Google and Yahoo! Library catalogs are already freely available databases. Why not ask Google, Yahoo!, or even Amazon.com to add a search option for library books and periodicals available freely to everyone through library catalogs? OCLC has taken the first admirable step in joining, rather than fighting this trend, by allowing free searching of a subset of its World-Cat catalog through Google (Quint 2003), and California State University, Los Angeles offers an Amazon.com link on its library catalog records for many items (2004). In an ideal world, the reverse would also be true—any Web search for a book for sale through Amazon.com would also pull up all listings of library books for your region or for any designated region.

There is really little point in trying to fight the human instinct to take the easiest path when there is a choice—that is, to use a general Web search tool to find what appears to be everything or a bookseller site like "bookfinder.com" (2004) to find books. If we can free our thinking, then openness, flexibility, and cooperation can become a cultural mind-set within the organization, and good words about IL and the library may very well drift upward to other administrators and outward to community groups and the rest of the world as a result. How can we let go? We need to listen to our users and the staff.

*Bring IL to Advisory Boards*

One useful way to find out what our users and staff want and need is to develop other kinds of fruitful partnerships. You can do this by expanding the scope of an existing library advisory board to include IL or by establishing a separate IL advisory board, with representatives from both staff and user groups. Some colleges and universities have IL committees or library committees that may vary in nature and membership. However, all address IL-related issues, such as identifying which courses qualify to satisfy IL requirements (Gebb 2003). Special focus on IL can be extremely useful in "bubbling up" staff and user concerns and suggestions for improvement. The group may help you identify user populations and develop and conduct IL needs assessments. Advisory boards can also serve as sounding boards for new programs, and members can even serve as test subjects for new instructional materials, for new Web pages, or even for new workshops for faculty or others. If you can establish a separate IL advisory board, see if your library director or some high-level representative can chair it and request user group representatives and participation. It is important to make it clear that the board will be providing advice to the library director, with a primary focus on ILI for lifelong learning.

IL AND LIFELONG LEARNING

In the long run, it is essential to draw attention to the IL/lifelong learning link, to incorporate IL standards into accreditation standards, to support them by developing sequential learning at all levels, in all types of libraries, to test for knowledge and skills first (pretest), and then test for learning outcomes at major transition points. This may mean more lobbying to incorporate IL into standardized tests, such as the Scholastic Aptitude Test (SAT) and the Graduate Record Examination (GRE). As we know and as others are learning, success in researching can mean true success in lifelong learning, and the Educational Testing Service (ETS) has taken notice. It has established a group to develop an Information and Communications Technology (ICT) assessment instrument for both IL and Information Technology (IT), based on the recommendations of its International ICT Literacy Panel. Those recommendations include development of large-scale assessments, diagnostic assessments, and an IT curriculum that integrates cognitive and technical skills and learning. At least one of the sample assessment tasks includes segments that clearly represent information literacy skills:

**Access:** Using a search engine, locate sites that have articles about holes in the heart, or atrial septal defects.
**Evaluate:** Evaluate the sites and identify three that you would expect to provide reliable medical information.
**Manage:** Identify the treatment information in each article.
**Integrate:** Compare and contrast the treatment options suggested in the articles.
**Create:** Develop a Word document with treatments listed (citing sources) to share with physician (ETS, Appendix C 2002).

The ETS project is a major breakthrough with enormous implications. It extends and expands upon the National Research Council's "Being Fluent in Information Technology" report (U.S. National Research Council 1999), by merging IL and IT and putting them on an equal footing. It illustrates quite clearly that IL's overriding goal of helping people become self-sufficient learners has risen to a very high level. Will it succeed?

ILI librarians know that helping people learn how to learn for a lifetime is an enormous and increasingly complex endeavor. We need to recognize that it is an endeavor we cannot and should not try to achieve on our own. We also need to acknowledge that our joint undertaking will not be finished soon but that the effort will be well worth our time and trouble.

## EXERCISES

1. Through informal discussion with colleagues and administrators, try to identify and describe in writing the three top instructional problems that may face your library in the next two years. Select a creative problem-solving technique and use it to come up with sub–issues to address and possible solutions.

2. Instructors and administrators at your institution know little or nothing about the benefits of an information-literate society. Identify three to five IL "talking points" for a fifteen-minute meeting to help raise consciousness about IL. Then develop an attractive one-page menu of ILI options to distribute at the meeting. Add some internal notes about how you will assess the success of your IL outreach efforts.

3. You have just started your first job as a library director. You want to establish a separate IL Advisory Board composed of representatives from the library's various constituencies. Describe the steps you would go through to identify these groups and then how you would work with them to establish a mission, goals, objectives, and operational procedures for the IL Advisory Board.

4. Use a group creative problem-solving technique to come up with a prioritized list of three possible new IL projects. Work with group members to describe the top project and its importance in one or two brief paragraphs. Write one goal and one objective for this project. Add a means of testing, implementing, evaluating, and revising the project.

## READ MORE ABOUT IT

ALA. AASL and AECT. 1998. *Information Power: Building Partnerships for Learning.* Chicago: American Library Association.

California State University. n.d. "CSU Information Competence Project." www.lib .calpoly.edu/infocomp/. Last update: n.d. [26 August 2004].

Dudley, Mimi. 1983. "A Philosophy of Library Instruction." *Research Strategies* 1(2): 58–63.

Educational Testing Service. 2002. *Digital Transformations.* http://www.ets.org/research/ictliteracy/index.html [17 April 2004].

Fitzgerald, Mary Ann. 2004. "Making the Leap from High School to College: Three New Studies about Information Literacy Skills of First-Year College Students." *Knowledge Quest* 32(4): 19–24.

Hardesty, Larry. 1995. "Faculty Culture and Bibliographic Instruction: An Exploratory Analysis." *Library Trends* 44(2): 339–367.

Healy, Patrick. 1999. "Education Department Proposes Rules to Increase Flexibility in Accreditation." *Chronicle of Higher Education* 45(44): A34.

ILI-L ILI-L@ala.org n.d.

Kempcke, Ken. 2002. "The Art of War for Librarians: Academic Culture, Curriculum Reform, and Wisdom from Sun Tzu." *Portal—Libraries and the Academy* 2(4): 529–551.

Leckie, Gloria J. May 1996. "Desperately Seeking Citations: Uncovering Faculty Assumptions about the Undergraduate Research Process." *Journal of Academic Librarianship,* 201–208.

Mycoted. 2003. "Creative Techniques." http://www.mycoted.com/creativity/techniques/index.php [5 May 2004].

Raspa, Dick, and Dane Ward, eds. 2000. *The Collaborative Imperative: Librarians and Faculty Working Together in the Information Universe.* Chicago: ALA, ACRL.

Winner, Marian C. 1998. "Librarians as Partners in the Classroom: An Increasing Imperative." *RSR: Reference Services Review* 26(1): 25–30.

Young, Rosemary M., and Stephena Harmony. 1999. *Working with Faculty to Design Undergraduate Information Literacy Programs.* New York: Neal-Schuman Publishers.

# 4

## Fostering Growth in Yourself and Others

*If you plan for a year—sow rice. If you plan for a decade—plant trees. If you plan for a lifetime—train and educate people.*

—Kuan-Tzo, Third century B.C.

## GROW AND CHANGE

If you could go back in time—say, fifteen years—what would your current job look like? What would be the same, and what would be different? Even if your present job existed, you would probably see many differences between the way you accomplish your daily tasks now and the way you accomplished them fifteen years ago. Certainly, your access to technology is different now, and looking back, this is not really surprising. But how about thinking about what you were doing just a year ago? Chances are that what occupies your time today is also different in a number of ways from what filled your days just last year. Certainly, some projects have been completed, and new ones have taken their place. New resources have appeared, and old familiar ones have gotten a facelift and no longer seem to function quite like before. New technologies have appeared to change the way you interact with your colleagues and your public. You are probably still teaching but may have shifted more of your efforts and your own learning to online resources and tools, which, in and of themselves, seem to multiply and become fruitful in an almost biblical sense, quarterly, monthly, weekly and even daily. And your days are filled with having to learn how to cope with it all. Do you feel stressed and burned out by all of this? Or do you worry that you may "lose it" because of all this pressure? It is no wonder stress and burnout are major concerns among information professionals, especially those engaged in ILI. Keeping ahead of this ever-changing curve has become a major part of our daily existence.

It might help to consider this: Nothing stands still. No one's job remains exactly the same year after year. No matter what your job title or area of responsibility, if you do not move with the times, you risk being left behind. Whether you welcome it or resent it, change is inevitable. How we react to change to a great degree determines our fate and the fate of our institution. Effective leaders seek out change, welcome it, and are excited by its possibilities. Successful managers embrace it and encourage their staff to embrace it as well. And everyone benefits from working in a dynamic and stimulating environment where learning and growing as a professional are not only expected, but encouraged and rewarded as well.

## FOSTER GROWTH AND DEVELOPMENT

How can we create such a positive learning environment? First and foremost, leaders and managers alike can and should serve as role models. They, themselves, should be actively engaged in continual learning. They should not be afraid to admit that they need training, coaching, and mentoring and that they should seek out people to help them in those roles. Leaders and managers set the tone by being eager to grow and develop themselves and by encouraging others to do the same.

Managers in their supervisory role have an even more direct influence on their staff. They can alert staff to appropriate, stimulating learning opportunities, including in-house training, classes, local, state, and national conferences, workshops, Web casts, and other online instructional opportunities. They can offer financial support to staff members who wish to improve their skills in relevant arenas. And managers can foster a learning mentality by helping individuals set goals that encourage them to stretch and grow in new ways.

Managers can also help individuals stretch through the act of coaching. In coaching, the manager is trying to help someone reach a specific performance goal. This can consist of actual training on specific tasks such as learning a new database or incorporating more student-centered approaches into teaching. Managers can also offer advice on how to achieve particular goals by suggesting attendance at particular workshops or programs or by encouraging participation in peer appraisal or mentoring opportunities (see below for more on these two activities).

Effective coaching is constructive (helpful) criticism, not negative criticism. There is a big difference between the two. The goal of coaching is to help the individual understand what needs to be done and his or her part in accomplishing the task. While negative criticism focuses on what the individual does wrong, coaching is constructive in its approach and emphasizes success. The goal of coaching is to help develop the individual's capability. When coaching is successful, performance improves because individuals understand what is expected of them and why it is expected and because they can visualize successfully accomplishing their goals. Crucial to this process is regular, specific feedback (informally during individual meetings or formally documented in writing) that acknowledges accomplishments and offers advice about how to deal with setbacks (Metz 2001).

Managers as coaches also help others to understand that change is an opportunity for individual self-development and a way to improve the way things are done in the organization. They support appropriate training opportunities, and they allow the time necessary for everyone to get up to speed on the necessary skills and behaviors needed to incorporate the new tasks into their daily routines. The focus of training and development activities is on enabling people to respond positively to changes and to take responsibility for ongoing and personal learning (Dawson 2002). Progress may be slow while everyone gets up to speed. But this time is well spent as everyone is given the chance to adjust to the new game plan at his or her own pace (Metz 2001). Allowing everyone to learn at his or her own pace and in his or her own way creates an atmosphere where everyone feels more comfortable about what is happening and confident that he or she will be able to succeed in the new environment. Stress and anxiety are diminished as a result, and the new tasks, skills, and programs are smoothly incorporated into the way things are done.

The coaching role is directly related to what someone does on the job. Mentoring, on the other hand, is usually directed more toward helping an individual achieve a specific career goal. Mentors are assumed to have firsthand knowledge and experience in a career path that a person wishes to follow. The mentor offers advice on how to accomplish that career objective (Metz 2001). Mentors can be direct supervisors, but more often than not, managers tend to mentor those outside their own departments to avoid any conflict of interest that might arise from the relationship. Since the mentor is trying to help advance the individual's career, it would be awkward for the mentor to have the authority to actually do so (Fiegen 2002; Kaplowitz 1992). Let's take a closer look at the mentoring process and its benefits.

THE MANY FLAVORS OF MENTORING

Most information professionals will engage in some kind of professional development during their careers. These may include attending conferences, classes, or workshops. Or they may seek out coworkers or colleagues with special skills and ask for training on those skills. Having or being a mentor, however, is not as common an occurrence. While some institutions have put formal mentoring programs in place, the majority of information professionals will become involved in mentoring at a more informal level. Regardless of the approach, a mentoring relationship offers many benefits both to the mentor and to the mentee (person being mentored).

Mentoring is generally thought of as being a partnership between someone with experience and someone who is new. However, it can be beneficial anytime we are changing career paths or are taking on new and different responsibilities (Regan 2003). But how does one find a mentor? According to a survey done by the Association of Research Libraries in 1999, only 26 percent of reporting libraries had formal mentoring programs in place (Fiegen 2002). Many professional organizations such as ALA' s New Members Round Table and the Spectrum Scholarship Initiative, ACRL, the Australian Libraries and Information Association, and SLA have mentor programs for new members (ALA 2004a, 2004; Fiegen 2002; Regan 2003; Ritchie and Genomi 2002). UCLA's Department of Information Studies has had a mentor program in place since 1984. This program, which is currently still active, pairs up new information studies students with information professionals not only from UCLA campus libraries but also from all types of libraries throughout the Southern California community. The goals of the program are to help students learn more about what it is like to work in the field and to help them make the transition from student to working professional (Kaplowitz 1992). Individual institutions such as Louisiana State University have also adopted formal mentoring programs to help tenure-track librarians succeed in the process (Kuyper-Rushing 2001). But these programs constitute just a handful of opportunities.

With formal mentoring programs few and far between, today's information professionals must be proactive in finding mentors who fit in with their personal career goals. These mentoring relationships are self-initiated, with individuals seeking out mentors who can assist them at different stages of their professional lives. By creating their own mentoring opportunities, these individuals are taking personal responsibility for their own growth and development. And these mentoring relationships can in turn form one of the essential elements of a successful career (Fiegen 2002).

What makes a successful mentoring relationship? In creating your own mentoring program, you must first determine what it is you want from the relationship. Are you new to your institution? You might wish to seek out someone more experienced in the institutional culture to help you learn the ropes. Look for someone who has experience within the system or organization or who has subject or technical expertise related to your new job. Pay special attention to those who seem to have developed strong collaborative relationships with faculty, teachers, departmental or community leaders, and others outside your library. You want someone who understands the political nuances in your organization and someone who has a positive approach to his or her work and the profession. This is not the time to turn to the disaffected in your organization (Fiegen 2002). Often the most enthusiastic mentors are people who have had mentors themselves in their past. Having been in a successful mentor–mentee relationship not only seems to help them understand the benefits of such a relationship but also encourages them to want to pass on this type of experience to others (Wickman and Sjodin 1997).

Unfortunately, many people think being a mentor is too time-consuming. But mentoring does not need to entail endless hours of handholding and tons of extra work. Mentors should encourage their mentees to engage in creative thinking by asking them leading questions in order to guide them, rather than trying to hand them all the answers (Appleton 1999). Mentors should spend some time at the beginning of the relationship orienting the mentee to organizations, institutions, people, and politics. Mentors serve as sounding boards and supporters. The mentorship relationship is the place for the mentee to try out new ideas safely and discuss projects and plans and for the mentor to offer feedback and advice about them.

The effective mentor models excellent listening skills and asks hard and challenging questions. He or she can offer insights into the profession that would otherwise be unavailable to the mentee. The relationship offers opportunities to both mentor and mentee as it is based on mutual respect and a shared commitment to the values of the profession (Lary 1998; Long 2002; Slattery and Walker 1999). The most successful mentoring relationship results in the mentees taking on the mentoring role for someone else. There can be no greater reward for a mentor than to see a former mentee become a mentor in turn and thus perpetuating the process for another generation of professionals.

It is important to note that you can have more than one mentor, and they do not all need to be IL librarians, or librarians at all. Staff in teaching and learning technology centers in higher education institutions focus on pedagogy and technology and often have both technical and instructional expertise to share with us. We can learn a lot from them, and in turn, we can share the librarian's unique expertise in objective resource evaluation and knowledge of the range of information sources available in all formats. So we can mentor them at the same time they are mentoring us, for as Will Rogers aptly put it, "Everyone is ignorant, only on different subjects" (Rogers 1974, p. 36).

Are you changing job duties or taking on new responsibilities? Look for someone with expertise in that area to mentor you. This may be the time to look outside your own department or institution. Be on the lookout for potential mentors as you go to conferences, workshops, and other meetings. Ask your colleagues and coworkers for suggestions. Watch other people teach and identify areas, approaches, and techniques you would like to incorporate into your own instructional arsenal. Look at instructional Web sites and tutorials. Identify people who have the instructional design or technical expertise you lack.

Approach potential mentors with your questions and concerns. Do not be shy or think that you are bothering people. Most professionals are passionate about their interests and are more than willing to discuss them with anyone who will listen. They are usually delighted to learn that someone else is interested in their personal passion. Mentoring newer professionals can be their way of making sure that their passions, dreams, and ideas live on and are taken into the future.

However, be sensitive to the fact that some of your potential mentors may be very busy people. So precede any requests for help by asking if they have a few minutes to spare or try to set up an appointment to talk to them at their convenience. You will have a better chance of getting some help and attention if you respect their needs and time constraints.

No matter how you select your potential mentor, make sure he or she knows what you want from the relationship. Make lists of what you are interested in learning, ideas you would like to discuss with your mentor, and any concerns you might have about the process. Prioritize your list and share these with your mentor as time permits, so that he or she has a clear picture of your expectations and your career goals. Listen carefully and ask questions if you do not understand. Be considerate of your mentor's time. Remember that a mentor offers you the gifts of his or her experience, time, and expertise. Some mentoring relationships last a lifetime. Others come and go as you move along your career path. Be ready to move on, but remember that as you say goodbye and thank you to one mentor, you will probably be seeking out and saying hello to new mentors as you change and grow in your professional life (Fiegen 2002; Long 2002; Wickman and Sjodin 1997).

The mentee is not the only one to benefit from the relationship. Just as good teachers learn from their students, a good mentor is challenged and can grow from the act of mentoring (Lary 1998; Long 2002; Slattery and Walker 1999; Wickman and Sjodin 1997). Newer professionals tend to ask questions. Why do we do it that way? What is the reasoning behind particular choices? These questions force the mentor to reexamine procedures, policies, and decisions in order to explain them to the mentee. The mentee brings new perspectives, new approaches, and new ideas to the relationship. This questioning is very healthy, rewarding, and stimulating for the mentor and for the organization or institution. The key to a successful mentoring relationship is that both mentor and mentee feel they have something to gain from the process (Kuyper-Rushing 2001; Long 2002).

Furthermore, in these days of ever-evolving new technology, the mentee frequently has skills that the seasoned professional lacks, thereby offering added value to the relationship. Finally, mentoring newer professionals is a good way to see your legacy carried into the future. It allows you to extend your life experiences so that your approach and what you have created can continue in some fashion, even after you are no longer active in the profession. As professionals we have a responsibility to impart knowledge to future generations (Wickman and Sjodin 1997). Mentoring is an excellent way to do this.

So venture forth and observe at conferences, workshops, and programs within and outside your institution or organization for mentoring opportunities. If you are seeking a mentor, look for someone who seems compatible and who has some experience and ask him or her for advice and help. If you are a seasoned professional, be open to these mentoring requests. View them as opportunities for you to help foster the future of the profession.

Establishing a formal mentoring relationship may never really come up, but even the briefest of encounters can be enlightening for both parties. The seasoned professional may learn about new developments and approaches and will see the world through fresh eyes. And the younger professional can acquire a broader context, bounce ideas off an experienced person, and learn about successful and not so successful approaches. It can be rejuvenating for the mentor and a life-altering experience for the mentee.

The "re-minted" mentee may, in turn, have a significant impact on institutions and organizations. Along with offering advice about instructional matters, the mentor can advise the mentee about how to be an advocate for IL. Once mentees have gained some IL experience and credibility within an organization or institution, they can take on a leadership role and help move an institution or organization toward acceptance and full integration of IL into its mission and goals. These transformed mentees may then serve as mentors themselves. A mentor can help advise a mentee about his or her readiness to step up to this role, can suggest some political contacts, and can alert the mentee to potential pitfalls and roadblocks along the way. Managers, leaders, or just about anyone with IL experience can serve as mentors for "new to IL" librarians. Remember, a single person can have a significant impact on an institution, an organization, a library or department, and the people within it.

IMPROVE YOURSELF THROUGH TEACHER APPRAISAL

Being coached by your colleagues or looking for a mentor to assist you as you move through your career are two methods for self-improvement. However, being self-reflective and identifying the places you need coaching or mentoring are the first and perhaps most important step toward continued growth and development. Keeping your instructional endeavors fresh, engaging, and relevant to your learners requires constant attention. The best teachers are those who are always learning, growing, and changing with the times. And they actively seek out opportunities that keep this continued development process going. A commitment to teacher appraisal is a formidable tool in this effort.

Teaching is a very personal endeavor. Being a teacher places you in a very vulnerable position. Risk-taking and a willingness to expose your feelings, enthusiasms, and expertise to your students are all part of effective teaching. You are the focus of all eyes and ears. So it is not surprising that having your teaching appraised can sometimes feel very threatening indeed. However, the wish to improve must translate into a willingness to be appraised.

How do you know if you are a good teacher? Can you identify your strengths and areas that could benefit by improvement? How do you assess your personal growth as a teacher? What can you do to improve yourself? And how do you keep from losing your enthusiasm for, and joy in, the craft of teaching? Knowing what makes a good teacher is, of course, the first step. Being willing to find out how well you fit the profile and having a strong desire to continue to grow and improve is the next. A continued interest in developing yourself as a teacher will also prevent you from falling victim to the stress and burnout that are sometimes experienced by teachers in general and IL instructors in particular. A commitment to revisiting and renewing your skills will keep your teaching fresh, energized, and engaging for yourself and your students.

Furthermore, only a small portion of ILI librarians have had the benefit of any formal teacher training. Data compiled by the ACRL's Education for Library Instruction committee indicated that only 62 percent of all library and information studies students had an opportunity to take a formal class in pedagogy while in school. In addition, courses that were available tended to be electives. So an even smaller number of students actually took the courses offered (Patterson and Edwards 1999). Moreover one course in teaching does not make a master teacher. So whether you had this training or learned your skills on the job, engaging in regular teacher appraisal activities can only enhance your skills and build your confidence.

Teacher appraisal can be viewed as either summative or formative (Bollington, Hopkins, and West 1990; Chisom and Stanley 1999; Scriven 1973). While the methods used for the appraisal can be identical in either the summative or formative situation, the reasons behind the appraisal and the use to which the results will be put vary. Summative appraisal relates to accountability and is closely associated with personnel issues. Generally, this type of appraisal is done by or for a supervisor who is reviewing teaching quality as part of making personnel decisions. These types of appraisals can be very anxiety-provoking to the person being reviewed and have contributed to the reluctance of many teachers to participate in any kind of appraisal process.

Formative appraisals, on the other hand, are for the benefit of the teacher. The results of these types of appraisals are confidential and are not included in personnel files. Formative teacher appraisal focuses on developing teaching skills. It is used as a means of identifying teaching strengths and areas that would benefit from improvement. Formative appraisals help the teacher develop a plan of action that will address areas that need work and can contribute to the growth and development of the individual teacher being appraised. If done correctly, with tact and discretion, formative teacher appraisals not only can result in personal teaching improvement but can contribute to the teacher's confidence and self-esteem and can act as a means for refreshing, renewing, and rejuvenating the teacher's outlook on the act of teaching itself.

## HOW TO APPRAISE YOUR TEACHING

Student evaluations, classroom observations, peer appraisal or peer coaching, and portfolios are the most common types of teacher appraisals (Mayo 1997). Each can be done for summative or formative reasons. However, since the focus in this chapter is on personal growth, the emphasis is on using these techniques for formative purposes. Any one of these methods can be turned into a summative appraisal if the results of the appraisals are placed into personnel records and/or used by a supervisor for personnel decisions.

### Student Feedback Surveys

Feedback from the learners themselves is probably the most widespread and commonly used teacher appraisal method. It has been used for many years, especially in the higher education arena, as a means both to make personnel decisions and to offer constructive feedback to the teacher. In many cases this information is made public and is used by students for course selection (Lowman 1995). While frequently criticized as being too simplistic to offer a complete picture of the teacher's effectiveness, these surveys and questionnaires, if well designed, seem reliable and accurate measures of teacher behavior (Drews, Burroughs, and Nokovich 1987). They are especially useful if they include a mix of quantitative rating scales and a few open-ended qualitative questions. See Chapter 5 for a discussion of quantitative versus qualitative measurement instruments. Reviewing the results of these feedback forms with a colleague who can help interpret the results and make suggestions for improvement can be extremely beneficial. When used for formative, developmental-type appraisal, student/learner feedback surveys can be extremely informative and helpful to the teacher (Lowman 1995). One thing to keep in mind when designing feedback surveys is to make sure you are asking the types of questions that will get you the information you seek. In addition to asking the learners if they thought the class was well organized, ask what about the organization of the material helped (or hindered) their ability to learn the material. The answer to the second question will provide hints about where you need to improve your presentation or your teaching materials.

*Classroom Assessment Techniques*

A second way to collect feedback information is through the use of Classroom Assessment Techniques or CATs (Angelo and Cross 1993). In contrast to learner surveys, which are usually done at the end of a class or course, these CATs are interspersed throughout the actual instruction sessions themselves. They offer more immediate feedback to the instructor about whether or not learning is taking place and can also serve as a means of increasing student involvement and motivation. Watching students working their way through a guided exercise that is reviewing what has just been taught can be very informative. Teachers can immediately see whether or not their methods worked by watching how students perform and by paying attention to the types of questions that they ask. The Minute Paper is a very popular CAT and is widely used in both general education and IL instruction situations (Grassian and Kaplowitz 2001).

*Student Interviews*

Another way to collect student feedback is through interviews. The teacher can ask a colleague to talk to students either one-on-one or in small groups and ask for feedback about what was helpful in the presentation, what types of teacher behavior seemed most conducive to learning, and which they felt could be improved (Lowman 1995). While this method might seem more applicable to full-term course situations, sometimes it is possible to ask a few learners if they would be willing to remain behind after a one-shot session to provide this type of feedback. In an IL instructional situation, the teacher might plan to end the session a bit early in order to leave time for a colleague to come in and conduct a student feedback discussion. While this would probably not be something you would want to do for every session you taught, it might be interesting to do it for a small subset of your instructional sessions. You and your colleague could then analyze the student feedback comments for trends and discuss possible approaches for improvement.

*Peer Appraisal*

Your colleagues can help you appraise and improve your teaching in other ways as well. One very popular approach is called peer appraisal, peer observation, or peer coaching. In this method a pair of teachers form a collaborative and reciprocal relationship the goal of which is better teaching. Peer appraisal is not a mentor/mentee relationship. It does not imply that one person is the expert and the other is the novice. The relationship between the colleagues involved in reciprocal peer appraisal is one of equality, encouragement, discussion, and reflection (Bollington, Hopkins, and West 1990; Chisom and Stanley 1999; Cosh 1999; Fiegen 2002). Reciprocal peer appraisal is often perceived as less threatening than other kinds of review. Those involved feel some sense of ownership for the process and view the outcomes as useful for personal growth and development (Lonsdale et al. 1988).

An atmosphere of trust and confidentiality must be established in order for peer appraisal to be successful. Although individual pairs should develop their own ways of working together, it is useful for some ground rules or guiding principles to be established by anyone undertaking this kind of appraisal. First and foremost is the understanding that this is a formative, not a summative, appraisal and that discussion between pair members remains confidential. The commitment is to improvement and focuses on the behavior, not on the person. The appraiser looks for strengths as well as areas that need further development. Working together, the peer pair develop a plan for how to achieve that development. There should be no surprises in the process as both appraiser and the person being appraised should agree in advance what areas of teaching will be reviewed (Bollington, Hopkins, and West 1990; Chisom and Stanley 1999; Isabell and Kammerlocher 1994). In the library world peer appraisal is often a reciprocal arrangement in which members of the pair switch roles in a mutually supportive environment. In fact, peer appraisal seems to work best when it is reciprocal. Successful peer appraisal relies in great measure on building trust between the participants. It can be very hard to open yourself up to this kind of scrutiny. One of the best ways to develop confidence in this approach and mutual trust between both members of the pair is for the appraiser to be appraised as well during the same appraisal period. If you schedule reciprocal appraisals too far apart, they do not seem reciprocal anymore. Finally, research indicates that voluntary participation in the process is crucial (Isabell and Kammerlocher 1994; Levene and Frank 1992/1993).

Peer appraisal must be carefully planned and requires training for all involved. Both members of the pair must trust each other, be dedicated to the process, and understand their roles and responsibilities in it. The development of an appropriate and useful peer appraisal process for any individual institution or environment can take time, effort, and resources. Therefore, a strong commitment from both those being appraised and their administrators is crucial (Bollington, Hopkins, and West 1990; Chisom and Stanley 1999). Workshops may need to be held in order to train all participants on the appropriate roles and behaviors of the appraiser and the person being appraised. Interview questions for the preappraisal meeting, observation checklists, surveys and other data collection instruments, and postappraisal feedback forms all need to be developed.

Once this planning and training are completed, the actual appraisal process can begin. Successful peer appraisal involves a sequence of steps. Obviously, the first step is the creation of the pair. Peer partners must feel comfortable with each other. They must trust each other and must both be committed to the goal of improvement. Similarities in teaching style have also been shown to enhance the experience as each member of the pair shares common values and beliefs about teaching (Levene and Frank 1992/1993).

After the pair is established, a planning meeting is scheduled that delineates what will be appraised for each of the partners. This planning meeting sets the tone for the entire process. A climate of mutual support, openness, and trust must be established. Reciprocal peer appraisal should be seen as an opportunity for growth for both partners, not one in which the appraiser is passing judgment on the person being appraised. It is during this meeting that areas to be appraised are identified and methods for the appraisal are determined. Although classroom observation may play a large role in the process, it is important to note that support material as well as other modes of delivery such as Web-based instruction can also be appraised. So another topic for this meeting is to determine what will actually be reviewed. Since the goal of peer appraisal is formative and developmental, the person being appraised determines which aspects of teaching should be analyzed and requests that only specific sessions, materials, or modes of instruction are included in the appraisal. The pair should agree on methods of collecting data as well as modes for feedback. The schedule for the process will be finalized, and times should be set for postobservation/analysis meetings. The decision about whether to include narrative as well as rating forms will also be made. The person being appraised will also indicate if he or she would like to prepare a self-assessment as part of the process (Bollington, Hopkins, and West 1990; Chisom and Stanley 1999; Grassian 1993; Jarzobkowski and Bone 1998; Levene and Frank 1992/1993). For examples of forms, checklists, and surveys useful for peer appraisal, see Chisom 1999 and Jarzabowski and Bone 1998. See also Esther Grassian's excellent "Checklist of Evaluating Lecture Presentations" (Grassian 1993).

Once the observations and materials review have taken place, the members of the pair meet again for a debriefing session. This is the time for the appraiser to offer feedback to the person being appraised and to offer constructive suggestions for future development. If the person being appraised has decided to prepare a written self-appraisal, it will be reviewed at this time. These self-appraisals can be a valuable way to focus the debriefing and to promote self-reflection. Persons being appraised should discuss how they feel about the presentation and/or material under review. What do they feel was particularly successful? Where do they see areas that need improvement (Jarzobkowski and Bone 1998)? The appraiser and the person being appraised use both the self-appraisal and the appraiser's comments to determine a plan of action. This plan should be specific and concrete. Goals for development should be set, and ways for attaining those goals should be identified. It is very important to include target dates for achieving these goals and to set future meetings to determine if these target dates have been met (Bollington, Hopkins, and West 1990). Once the process is completed for one member of the pair, the positions are reversed, and the process begins again. However, this time the person who had been appraised on the first round now becomes the appraiser. An alternative approach is to have each member of the appraisal pair be observed by his or her partner before any feedback is given, thus emphasizing that neither member of the peer is more expert than the other.

Reciprocal peer appraisal can be beneficial to both the person being appraised and the person doing the appraising. When acting as appraisers, librarians state that they become aware of new or different techniques and technologies and have incorporated some of these into their own teaching approaches. When being the one appraised, librarians learn what works well and become more confident in those aspects of teaching that are deemed successful by the appraiser (Burnam 1993; Chisom and Stanley 1999; Martin and Double 1998).

Reciprocal peer appraisal seems particularly suited to the collegial atmosphere in which most IL instructors operate. Its emphasis on nonevaluative feedback and mutual support makes it an ideal technique for adding to the growth and development of IL instructors. Because reciprocal peer appraisal is based on discussion between two librarians who work together in the same environment, it can be tailored to the particular requirements of any type of institution or setting. The questions asked, the materials and techniques reviewed, and the format of the appraisal will be relevant to that environment or setting because the people involved in the appraisal have developed the process for themselves. For examples of peer appraisal or peer coaching in IL settings see Isabell and Kammerlocher 1994; Levene and Frank 1992/1993.

*Teaching Portfolios*

While peer appraisal could and should be a continual process, it frequently is undertaken only sporadically due to the time and effort involved. Another approach that can be used as a means to monitor your growth and development as a teacher is the teaching portfolio. A portfolio consists of a variety of materials that reflect a person's teaching style, techniques, and abilities. It is an organized collection of performance-based evidence indicating a person's growth, his or her goals, and level of current knowledge and skills as they relate to a particular area of expertise (Campbell et al. 2000). It can include videos, self-reflective journals, lecture notes, examples of support material, and so on. Portfolios should be updated and reviewed on a regular basis. It is important for the teacher compiling a portfolio to include narrative about why each item is being added. How does each addition reflect growth and development? Why does the teacher feel it is important and representative? Goals for improvement, methods of attaining those goals, and success in reaching them should also be discussed. Including a section that discusses what will be done next carries reflection into the future. It is a critical part of our self-reflection as it indicates how we will use what we have learned in the past to create new opportunities to grow and develop (Bartell, Kaye, and Morin 1998; Chisom and Stanley 1999; Heath 2002; Lowman 1995; Oakley 1998; Wolf and Dietz 1998).

Portfolios can be maintained in paper or electronic format or in a combination of both. Since so much of what we do today is already in electronic format (word-processed documents, Web sites, PowerPoint presentations, etc.), maintaining an electronic portfolio makes a lot of sense. Electronic portfolios are easier to maintain, edit, and update and can be distributed in a variety of ways. They can be burned into CDs or saved to floppies. They can also be made into Web sites for more widespread distribution (Heath 2002).

Portfolios can be shared with a trusted colleague in much the same way as in the reciprocal peer appraisal process. Or they can be kept entirely private. However, discussing the contents with a colleague can be helpful and serve as a further way to reflect on your growth as a teacher. Portfolios can also be used in summative appraisals. In this case, the teacher under review would select portions of the portfolio to be included in a personnel action review. Feedback from those who have already gone through the process can be extremely helpful when you are selecting items to be included in a personnel action portfolio. Portfolios are also useful when you are interviewing for a new job. They can be taken to the interview as a means of exhibiting samples of your work and to promote your successes. In any case, developing the habit of creating a teaching portfolio, compiling evidence of good practice and growth in it, and regularly updating and reviewing the package is a good one to cultivate. The portfolio can contribute to your personal growth and can enhance your self-esteem and confidence as you reflect upon your progress. Furthermore, it can provide excellent examples of your work for inclusion in any formal, summative personnel actions that you may undergo.

## APPLYING TEACHER APPRAISAL TECHNIQUES TO ILI

No matter what appraisal technique is selected, the qualities or characteristics to be examined must be determined in advance. In other words, what should the appraiser be looking for? What are the behaviors, characteristics, or qualities exhibited by the effective ILI instructor? Attempts to identify the characteristics of effective teaching have been the subject of several research projects in both education and IL (Arnold 1998; Botts and Emmons 2002; Dwyer 1998; Lowman 1995; Shonrock and Mulder 1993). These can be used to determine which behaviors, characteristics, or qualities should be under review during the teacher appraisal process. These studies and others like them can be used as a starting point in the discussions between appraiser and person being appraised. Which of the identified behaviors or qualities should be emphasized? What is the best way to determine if the person under review is exhibiting those behaviors or qualities? While it is unlikely that any one appraisal will cover all the aspects described in these studies, they can serve as a starting point from which to select those of most interest to the person being appraised. However, the list should not be viewed as proscriptive. Both appraiser and the person being appraised should feel free to suggest additional behaviors, qualities, or characteristics that seem relevant.

Teacher appraisal in both education and the IL environment contributes to continual growth and development. It allows IL instructors to highlight their strengths, and it can provide suggestions for improving and refreshing their teaching. Teacher appraisal encourages change and creates an atmosphere of forward momentum. As a result it helps to keep teachers fresh and excited. But even the most dedicated of teachers can become overwhelmed by the demands of their jobs. This brings us to the topics of stress, burnout, and renewal.

## STRESS, BURNOUT, AND RENEWAL

Most new ILI instructors begin their careers full of energy and excitement (and maybe a bit of trepidation), but how can this glow be maintained as years go by? Faced with so much to do and so little time to do it, will IL librarians become distressed by the prospect of yet one more IL session? Worse still, will they end up being a bored, disinterested, and unmotivated teacher who cannot be expected to create an ILI environment that encourages learning? Being aware that this can happen, watching for signs of potential problems in yourself as a manager and among your colleagues, and knowing how to deal with these signs are all part of how you can help workers keep their enthusiasm for their jobs. Taking care of yourself, monitoring your own well-being, and encouraging the same in your colleagues, are all instrumental ways to ensure the success of your library's instructional program. Recognizing the symptoms of stress when they occur allows the IL librarian to look for ways to modify his or her behavior and/or environment to reduce that stress. Stress, if not addressed in this fashion, can escalate into the more extreme behavior called burnout. Managers in particular should be ever vigilant to signs of stress and burnout personally and in their staff and be willing to take appropriate measures to alleviate the conditions causing it.

### Stress and Its Symptoms

So what is stress, and how do we recognize its symptoms? Stress has physical, cognitive, affective, and behavioral components (Caputo 1991;

Doctor and Doctor 1994; Hackett and Lonberg 1993; Kuppersmith 1998; Meany 2000; Schooler, Dougall, and Baum 2000). Physical symptoms include shortness of breath, rapid heartbeat, dryness of mouth, muscle tension, headache, stomach problems, and fatigue. Cognitive symptoms can be exhibited as an inability to concentrate, poor judgment, and problem-solving/thinking difficulties. Affective symptoms might include irritability, anxiety, and depression. On the behavioral front, stress might be seen as impulsiveness, avoidance, withdrawal, drug and alcohol abuse, violence, loss of appetite, and insomnia.

Early research on stress indicates it is the body's way of preparing us for danger. It sets the stage for a response of either fight or flight and consists of three stages—alarm, resistance, and exhaustion. Taken together, these stages are referred to as the General Adaptation Syndrome or GAS (Selye 1936). In the first stage, alarm, the body recognizes a stressor and undergoes a series of physiological changes that prepares it for either fight or flight. Various endocrine glands are stimulated to release hormones that cause changes in respiration, heart rate, blood sugar levels, and so forth to prepare for the burst of energy needed to fight the stressor or flee from it. Once the stressor has been removed (either by defeating it or by escaping from it), the body returns to its normal resting state. This is the second or resistance stage of the GAS. However, if the body cannot deal with the stressor and remains in the alarm stage for too long, without time for the repair and recovery of the resistance stage, the body enters the final GAS stage known as exhaustion. It is during the exhaustion stage that stress-related diseases such as headache, ulcers, and hypertension appear. If this final stage continues for too long, death can occur (Caputo 1991; Meany 2000; Sapolsky 1998; Schooler, Dougall, and Baum 2000).

Although a rampaging elephant or a snarling tiger or lion rarely threatens the IL instructor, the demands of the day-to-day work environment can create their own pitfalls and perils. Faced with budget cuts, information overload, staff shortages, heavy workloads, and long hours, the IL instructor can begin to exhibit the same symptoms as someone facing a physical threat. Rapidly changing technology and the resultant demands placed on the IL instructor both to learn it and then to teach it certainly are a major contributing factor (Grassian and Kaplowitz 2001). Lack of managerial support, shifting priorities, lack of private work space, and difficult and demanding clients are all stressors in the library world. Furthermore, a feeling of not being invited to participate in goal setting or decision making, and few opportunities for advancement can also contribute to the problem. The result is a situation in which the IL instructor feels overwhelmed, overloaded, and stressed to exhaustion. He or she is then vulnerable to burnout (Becker 1993; Caputo 1991; Kuppersmith 1998).

*The Burnout Syndrome*

Although stress and burnout share many of the same symptoms, burnout is characterized by an exacerbation of these stress-related characteristics. Psychological characteristics of burnout include both cognitive (disorientation, lapses of memory and attention) and affective (anger, boredom, severe depression, discouragement, disillusionment, despair, dissatisfaction, fear, frustration, guilt, helplessness, hopelessness, pessimism, resentment, self-doubt, lowered self-esteem, and suspicion). Burned-out professionals frequently exhibit behaviors such as cynicism, indifference, apathy, moodiness, irritability, and eating and sleep disorders. As discussed above as related to stress in general, drug and alcohol abuse can also result, often leading to addiction. Burnout victims suffer from a multitude of physical disorders such as backache, frequent colds, migraines, weight gain or loss, hypertension, cardiovascular disease, asthma, and ulcers (Caputo 1991).

Burnout is caused by overdedication, overcommitment, overwork, and the establishment of unrealistic goals. It can result whenever expectation levels are dramatically opposed to reality, making goal achievement impossible (Freudenberger and Richelson 1980). The burnout syndrome is common among people in the helping professions and is a response to the continual emotional strain of dealing extensively with people who have problems (Maslach 1982). Teachers, nurses and social workers, who are chronically overworked, are particularly susceptible to this syndrome. Librarians and information professionals in their instructional roles either at a reference desk or in a more formal instructional setting are no exception.

People suffering from burnout exhibit fatigue, emotional exhaustion, cynicism, impatience, irritability, physical ailments, depression, feelings of detachment (that may escalate into anger), a perception of reduced personal achievement, and a sense of being underappreciated (Freudenberger and Richelson 1980; Maslach 1982). When people work under stressful conditions, when their self-esteem seems threatened, and when it appears that their best efforts are constantly thwarted by circumstances outside their control, they begin to withdraw psychologically from their professional duties (Cherniss 1995). Burnout can almost be viewed as a last, desperate attempt for self-preservation. Overly stressed professionals stop caring in order to protect themselves from these feelings of failure.

**Figure 4–1**
**Signs of Stress and Burnout**

| Types of Signs | Stress | Burnout |
|---|---|---|
| Physical | Shortness of Breath<br>Rapid Heartbeat<br>Dryness of Mouth<br>Muscle Tension<br>Headache<br>Stomach Problems<br>Fatigue | Backache<br>Frequent Colds<br>Migraines<br>Weight Gain or Loss<br>Hypertension<br>Cardiovascular<br>Disease<br>Asthma<br>Ulcers |
| Cognitive | Inability to Concentrate<br>Poor Judgment<br>Problem Solving<br>Difficulties<br>Thinking Difficulties | Lapses of Memory<br>Attention Difficulties<br>Disorientation |
| Affective | Irritability<br>Anxiety<br>Depression | Anger<br>Boredom<br>Severe Depression<br>Pessimism<br>Resentment<br>Despair<br>Discouragement<br>Disillusionment<br>Dissatisfaction<br>Fear<br>Resignation<br>Lowered Self-Esteem<br>Frustration<br>Guilt<br>Feelings of<br>Helplessness and<br>Hopelessness<br>Self-Doubt<br>Suspicion |

(*continued*)

| Figure 4–1, *Continued* Signs of Stress and Burnout | | |
| --- | --- | --- |
| Types of Signs | Stress | Burnout |
| Behavioral | Impulsiveness<br>Avoidance<br>Withdrawal<br>Drug and Alcohol<br>Abuse<br>Violence<br>Loss of Appetite<br>Insomnia | Cynicism<br>Indifference<br>Apathy<br>Moodiness<br>Irritability<br>Eating Disorders<br>Sleep Disorders<br>Drug and Alcohol<br>Addiction |

*Burnout and ILI*

The very nature of ILI contributes to the creation of burnout in those who teach it. Very often IL sessions are scheduled before students actually have their assignments or so early that the nature of the assignment has not really sunk in. At the other extreme are the students who come to us when the pressure is really on, that is, when coping with the very real deadlines of the "dreaded" library research assignment. Regardless of whether our students are blasé about the instruction because it does not seem relevant, or frantic about it because they need to produce something very quickly, we may or may not see if our instructional intervention has had any positive effect. This is especially true if we are involved in a one-shot session or Web-based instruction. Despite the frequent votes of thanks we get from our learners and the occasional round of applause, we receive little or no tangible evidence of our impact on those we teach, and as a result we are denied one of the greatest rewards of teaching, the chance to see the product of our efforts. So we remain unsure about whether or not our learners actually put into practice what we have preached (Becker 1993; Cherniss 1995).

Information professionals choose this type of work because they expect a degree of autonomy. However, many professionals end up working in a highly structured bureaucratic environment. This mismatch between their professional expectations and the practical reality under which they must operate is also a contributing factor to stress and burnout. Administrators who are not involved in direct client service may be perceived as making decisions without realizing how those decisions affect client and professional alike. Bureaucratic red tape, endless meetings, piles of paperwork, lack of positive feedback and administrative support, and communication failures can all create an atmosphere in which burnout thrives (Becker 1993; Cherniss 1995; Grosser 1987).

In IL instruction the continuous expansion of the world of knowledge and the rapid development of increasingly complex technology remain a constant challenge to the competency of the individual (Caputo 1991; Kuppersmith 1998). How can we teach others strategies for coping with all that when we can barely keep ahead of the curve ourselves? IL instructors become frustrated, fearful, and anxious wondering if our instruction is adequately preparing our learners for the information age in which they live. Furthermore, there is the overwhelming threat of becoming outdated and unable to function at professional levels (Grassian and Kaplowitz 2001).

## DEALING WITH STRESS AND BURNOUT

So what can be done about it? Be on the alert for signs of stress and burnout in yourself and your colleagues. One way to do this is to make use of standard measurement tools and instruments that examine stress and burnout levels, some of which may be public domain instruments freely available on the Web. While public domain tests such as these may be useful as a preliminary assessment of your stress levels, keep in mind that these tests may not have been thoroughly reviewed for validity and reliability. Therefore they may not be entirely accurate as stress predictors. See Chapter 5 for a discussion of reliability, validity, and other measurement attributes. However, if the results of any of these stress tests show higher than average stress levels, you or your colleagues may be candidates for burnout and should undertake some action to avoid it.

One approach is to try to maintain a positive attitude toward conflict, problems, and change and to develop effective interpersonal and negotiation strategies. People who have learned to develop organizational negotiation skills seem to be more likely to avoid or overcome symptoms of burnout. They have learned effective ways to approach organizational conflicts. These people have excellent interpersonal skills and are adept at avoiding or resolving interpersonal conflicts, overcoming bureaucratic constraints, and securing support for innovative and meaningful projects. Organizational negotiation skill is a way of thinking about organizational barriers and conflicts that encourages a certain degree of analytical detachment and thoughtful reflection (Cherniss 1995).

When faced with a problem, you have two choices. You can let the problem stand in the way of accomplishing your goals. Or you can begin to look for ways to get around that barrier. So, for example, let's say you have observed that your fellow IL instructors have become reluctant to teach a particular class. When you discuss this with them, they all indicate that the class no longer feels relevant to the participants, and as a result the learners do not seem to be engaged. So your instructors are burning out on the class, and the learners are probably not learning. What to do? Clearly, this calls for a reexamination of this class and a possible overhaul of its structure, methodology, and/or conceptual framework. You will probably need to do this work via some kind of team approach, which includes most if not all the IL instructors involved and also enlists the help of community partners and perhaps some kind of feedback from the population you are trying to teach.

Do not forget to check with your supervisor before you embark on this project. Explain the reasons behind wishing to try something new in terms of both improving the IL program and preventing librarian burnout. If there is support for your ideas, your supervisor may have some advice about who in your environment might be useful to include in the analysis and the revision of the class and may be able to open some doors for you and assist in enlisting some help for the project. How to do all this has been touched upon in a variety of other chapters in this book. However, the point here is that IL managers who are alert to signs of burnout in themselves and their colleagues do not ignore these signs. They take action to alleviate the cause of the burnout and, as a result, may actually improve their instructional programs overall.

Instead of just complaining about the problem, you have taken some positive action to solve it. You are assuming a leadership role. Taking a problem-solving approach to organizational difficulties is not only a way to avoid burnout. It can also provide opportunities for you to effect positive change in your environment. So learn how your organization works and to whom you can appeal in particular situations. Develop your interpersonal skills and negotiating skills. Be assertive but not obnoxious and try to view problems and conflicts from all perspectives. Seek out and nurture appropriate collaborations. Offer solutions or suggestions for new initiatives and make sure you show how those solutions fit into the global mission of the institution.

Burnout comes from frustration, from the perception that we cannot accomplish what we feel is our professional responsibility. However, sometimes we must accept the fact that these self-imposed goals cannot be reached or that the goals imposed upon us by others are unreachable under certain circumstances. The problem is that we feel responsible. We entered the profession to provide service and to hopefully make a difference in people's lives. But if we do not have the authority to actually create a situation where our goals can be realistically accomplished, we must reconsider our options. We frequently suffer burnout because we have allowed ourselves to be saddled with impossible tasks without the resources to accomplish those tasks. We may feel that our best professional efforts continually fall short, and the situation seems hopeless. Keep in mind that although responsibility can be delegated, it cannot be abdicated (White 1990). Although an administrator or supervisor may assign a project to you, they are still ultimately responsible for its completion, especially if the authority to implement the project is not yours. Try to do the best you can to complete the task. However, be sure to alert your supervisor to any circumstances that could interfere with the completion of the task. Point out why the task may not be able to be accomplished within the given time frame or with the available resources or given your other responsibilities. Ask your supervisor to help you prioritize your responsibilities and develop reasonable milestones for achieving them. Make recommendations about alternative means of solving the problem, if necessary. If all else fails, return the task to whoever imposed it on you in the first place if it is feasible to do so. In the end, the person who assigned you the impossible, undoable task is ultimately responsible.

Though you may try, you cannot offset lack of support by working harder, faster, or longer hours. But you can try to work politically smarter. You may decide to call the problems to the attention of those who have the authority and the responsibility to implement change. In doing so, you are taking on a leadership role, and the result may be a new perspective on the situation or a change in the deployment of resources. Try talking to others in your organization to see if you can locate people who might be willing to assist you in your task. Keep in mind that going outside the chain of command can be risky. The person to whom you directly report might not approve. However, sometimes the risk is worth taking. Just be sure to pick your battles carefully. It helps if you have a good handle on your supervisor's management style. This can help you predict what might happen if you take this approach. Understanding the politics and culture of your organization can also be helpful in knowing when stepping outside the chain of command is appropriate and acceptable. See Chapters 1 and 3 for more on these two topics.

If the situation persists, consider changing jobs. If that is not possible, shift your priorities to concentrate on doable aspects of your job or try to vary what you do during the day. You may even have to shift your focus away from your job entirely for periods of time and concentrate on more rewarding outside activities (White 1990).

Another way to offset burnout is to develop some special on-the-job interest and pursue it. Cultivating a special interest will allow you to carve out one area of the job that can be characterized by high levels of autonomy, challenge, responsibility, and meaning. If you are interested in graphic design, offer your services for signs, exhibits, or promotional flyers. Develop handouts or Web pages about subject areas that interest you.

Offer to develop instructional support (either in-person/synchronous sessions or more virtual approaches including blended instruction) for new resources being added to your environment. Special areas of interest provide a way of making an impact and offer the positive feedback that is so important to countering burnout (Cherniss 1995). Coming up with a special project on your own can also improve your image within the organization. You will be viewed as someone with initiative, creativity, and drive—in other words, a grassroots leader. Be sure to check with your supervisor, though, before plunging into a project, and consider discussing it with your colleagues as well. See Chapter 3 on collaboration and working with colleagues for more on this topic. Projects that directly enhance the mission of your parent organization are most likely to be supported and provide the best opportunities for you to shine in the eyes of your administrators.

One more thing you can do to protect yourself is to develop a strong social support system. Research has indicated that people who have developed such systems are less negatively affected by stressful circumstances. Social support is beneficial to both physical and mental health and is related to lower levels of depression, anxiety, and other symptoms of psychological distress. Social support can bolster you during hard times by offering tangible assistance (actual resources such as money, information, or assistance on a project) or emotional support by reminding you that you have friends and family who love and respect you and who are confident that you can succeed in your endeavors whatever the obstacles (Hobfoll 2001).

Finally, people who stand the greatest chance of avoiding burnout are those who strike a healthy balance between work and the rest of their lives. Find something you love to do. Make a commitment to that interest and view it as equally important as your job (Cherniss 1995; Sapolsky 1998). In other words, get a life and make time to live that life. There may be periods when the stress of working becomes so overwhelming that you need to escape. Make sure you have created an escape route and use it. A temporary retreat to your non-job-related interests could refresh and rejuvenate you. Make time during your workday to get away. Do not eat lunch at your desk every day. If you must eat at your desk, take a short postmeal break to refresh yourself. Go for a walk. Read a book. Do something for a few minutes that takes you out of your work mind-set. You may even find that you return to work armed with a better, more productive attitude. In the end, time off from work may actually improve your work performance. It can enable you to view problems from a fresh, less stressed perspective and discover potential solutions that you had not been originally aware of.

Can we avoid stress on the job? We probably cannot. But we can take action to prevent that stress from turning into burnout and destroying our lives. Be aware of the symptoms. As soon as you begin to notice them, step back and do a self-analysis about the cause of your problems. Once you have identified the causes, examine your options. Then take some positive action to improve your situation. In other words, do not allow yourself to burn out. Fight back instead. Whether you choose to practice your organizational negotiating skills, reprioritize your job responsibilities, develop a special interest, or refocus your attention on off-the-job interests for a while, take some positive action. Remember that situations can change, and a seemingly insurmountable problem, even personnel problems, may become less of a barrier in the future as organizational priorities evolve in new directions or as people move to different positions and different environments. Watch for your chance to add your voice (and your projects) to whichever new initiative seems related to your personal and professional goals. And as an IL manager, keep your eyes on your colleagues and watch for symptoms in them as well. If you notice them, try to encourage your colleagues to do some self-reflection and to turn to the members of their social support system in an effort to reduce their own stress and vulnerability to burnout.

One of the primary rules for people involved in search and rescue is that you must take care of yourself first. You cannot help anyone else if you are hurt or incapacitated. You must keep this in mind when deciding how to deal with symptoms of burnout. Sometimes the only answer is simply to walk away. The burned-out individual must either leave his or her job or let go of whatever is impossible to accomplish under current circumstances or try to find nonconfrontational, less stressful ways to work with other employees or within the work environment as it is. Does that mean that burned-out people are less professional? It certainly does not. It means they are protecting the most valuable asset they have, their own personal well-being. The burned-out individual contributes little or nothing to the organization. Making an effort to avoid burnout allows you to maintain a high level of professionalism and productivity. In the end everyone profits—you, your organization, and most especially the people you have committed yourself to serve.

EXERCISES

*Mentoring*

Part A

1.  List the characteristics you would like to find in a mentor.
2.  Identify an area in which you would like to receive mentoring.

3. Locate someone who could serve as a mentor in that area and set up an appointment with that person to discuss your area of interest.
4. During that meeting explore the possibilities of forming a mentor/mentee relationship with that person.

PART B

1. See if your organization or professional association has developed formal mentoring programs and offer your services.
2. If no formal programs exist, identify an area in which you feel you have some personal expertise.
3. Locate newer professionals who may have less expertise or experience in this area.
4. Approach those newer professionals and offer your services as a mentor.
5. As time goes on, encourage both formal and informal mentees to complete the process by becoming a mentor to others.

*Teacher Appraisal Part A*

PART A

1. Think about the best teacher you ever had.
2. What were the characteristics that teacher exhibited that made him or her so effective?
3. Now design a classroom observation checklist that would help you identify those characteristics in someone whose teaching you are observing.

*Teacher Appraisal Part B*

1. Find an instructional Web site and/or an example of a print instructional support handout that you find particularly effective.
2. What are the characteristics or qualities that make this Web site or print handout effective?
3. Now develop a checklist that would help you evaluate another Web site or print instructional handout.

*Teacher Appraisal Part C*

1. Make a list of items you would include in your own teaching portfolio.

2. Compile the material.
3. Wait six months and review the material. What would you add or delete at this point?
4. Either alone or with a trusted colleague, identify areas that need improvement and develop a plan of action for the next year.
5. Review your portfolio and your plan of action at the end of that year. What growth and development can you identify?
6. Add or delete material and begin again from step 4.
7. Make this portfolio review a continuing part of your professional development plan.

*Stress, Burnout, and Renewal*

1. Imagine yourself in a stressful situation. What are you reactions to stress? Use this information to prepare your personal Stress and Burnout Alert chart.
2. Now examine the different aspects of your job. Which ones trigger your Stress and Burnout Alert symptoms?
3. Make a list of things you can realistically do to reduce the potential for burnout. Try applying one or more of these solutions to your situation. Do the potential burnout symptoms diminish in relation to these tasks? If not, look for additional solutions to the problem, including changing jobs or reprioritizing your responsibilities.

## READ MORE ABOUT IT

*Coaching and Mentoring*

Metz, Ruth E. 2001. *Coaching in the Library*. Chicago: American Library Association.
Wickman, Floyd, and Terri Sjodin. 1997. *Mentoring: The Most Obvious Yet Overlooked Key to Achieving More in Life Than You Dreamed Possible*. Chicago: Irwin Professional Publishing.

*Teacher Appraisal*

Bollington, Rob, David Hopkins, and Mel West. 1990. *An Introduction to Teacher Appraisal: A Professional Development Approach*. London: Cassell Educational.
Burman, Paul. 1993. "Fine-Tuning Classroom Techniques: A Peer Coaching Experience." *Research Strategies* 11(1): 42–46.
Chisom, Nancy Van Note, and Christine A. Stanley. 1999. *Peer Review of Teaching: A Sourcebook*. Bolton, MA: Anker Publishing Company.

Jarzabkowski, Paula, and Zelma Bone. 1998. "A 'How-To' Guide and Checklist for Peer Appraisal of Teaching." *Innocations in Education and Training International* 35(2): 177–182.
Levene, Lee-Allison, and Polly Frank. 1992/1993. "Peer Coaching: Professional Growth and Development for Instruction Librarians." *Reference Services Review* 20/21(2): 35–42.

## Stress and Burnout

Becker, Karen A. 1993. "The Characteristics of Bibliographic Instruction in Relation to the Causes of and Symptoms of Burnout. *RQ* 32(3): 346–357.
Caputo, Jannet S. 1991. *Stress and Burnout in Library Service.* Phoenix, AZ: Oryx Press.
Cherniss, Cary. 1995. *Beyond Burnout.* New York: Routledge.
Freudenbergen, Herbert J. 1980. *Burn-Out: The High Cost of High Achievement.* Garden City, NY: Anchor.
Kupersmith, John. 1998. "Technostress in the Bionic Library." In *Recreating the Academic Library: Breaking Virtual Ground,* edited by Cheryl LaGuardia. New York: Neal-Schuman Publishers.
Maslach, Christina. 1982. *Burnout: The Cost of Caring.* Englewood Cliffs, NJ: Prentice-Hall.

# 5

---

# Adding to the Knowledge Base through Research

*The more I learn, the more I realize I don't know.*

—Albert Einstein

## WHY DO RESEARCH?

How does a discipline move forward? As information literacy instruction specialists, how do we assess the success of our endeavors or explore new approaches that might increase our effectiveness? In other words, how do we take a step back from our day-to-day endeavors and explore the efficacy of what we do? Furthermore, how do we gather data that will support our efforts not only within our libraries but also as we market our services and ourselves to our community and institutional partners? The answer is through the research process.

Are there things about ILI that you wished you knew but are afraid to ask? Does the thought of conducting formal research send you running into the night screaming:

I do not have the time!
I do not have the money!
I do not know how to do research!

A little background reading, a lot of planning, and the right amount of collaboration with the appropriate people with the expertise you may lack will help you overcome these very legitimate fears. Many excellent books are available to assist you in gaining insight into the research process. Those in the social and behavioral sciences are particularly applicable to information science research. Pick out one or two that appeal to you. Make sure you find them readable and organized in a manner that matches the way you think and are suitable for your particular learning style. Do not waste your time on books that bore you or struggle with ones you do not understand. There are so many different research methods books available that you are sure to locate several that you will find engaging and interesting to read. For some suggestions see the Read More about It section at the end of this chapter. We hope that our book, especially this chapter, will also help you gain insight into this topic and encourage you to explore the research path.

Is the research path for you? How can you decide if you should add research to your already overcrowded schedule? With so much on your busy information literacy plate each day, the idea of taking the time to develop a research proposal, let alone carry out the project, may seem like an unrealistic, if not impossible, task. However, there are many worthwhile reasons to follow the research path. First you must ask yourself, Why does anyone do research? The obvious response is that people do it in order to answer questions. The researcher engages in an exploration, looking for new bits of knowledge. And he or she conducts this exploration in a rational, objective, and orderly manner, adhering to the mandates of the scientific method (Berger and Patchner 1988a).

A discipline stifles, atrophies, and may wither away if no one seeks new information to add to its knowledge base. Properly conducted research can contribute to the continued maturation of librarianship as a discipline and information literacy as an area of interest within that discipline (Heron and Schwartz 1995). One of the earmarks of a profession, after all, is having a growing body of theoretical knowledge (Berger and Patchner 1988a). So, well-designed and properly conducted research is essential to the continued growth and development of ILI as well as librarianship at large (Porter 1997). And in ILI there are still many, many unanswered questions about the efficacy of our IL programs and approaches that could inspire research topics. Here are some examples:

- Are particular types of instruction more effective than other types?
- Does effectiveness vary for different populations, in different environments, for different topics?
- Are we designing our Web-based tutorials in a useful and usable manner?
- Are students learning what we want them to learn?
- Are we teaching what they need to know?

In other words, ILI professionals who engage in research are generally looking for ways to improve what they do and how they do it.

Whether you are operating in an environment of fiscal bounty or budgetary constraints, you are accountable to your administration regarding the success and worthiness of your instructional efforts. ILI professionals need to engage in research in order to support their proposals for new ILI initiatives. More evidence needs to be amassed to show that ILI enhances the educational experience, improves productivity, and leads to a more self-reliant and knowledgeable population. ILI methodologies also need investigation. For example, how much real evidence is there that students do better in active learning environments? When looking for answers, do not forget to look beyond the field of librarianship. Researchers in education and psychology are exploring the same or similar questions. Look to the literature in those disciplines for possible answers to your questions or examples of research that can be applied or modified to information literacy instruction research.

Ask yourself, What data do I need to sell my ideas? Then look for that evidence. If evidence to support your contention exists, use it as ammunition when presenting your proposals to your administration. If there is little or no evidence in the literature, you may just have uncovered a potential area for research. Research findings can inform decision making and can result in better and more accountable services and programs.

This may all sound very reminiscent of the reasons for engaging in assessment. That is not surprising. Every time you assess the success of your instructional endeavors, even informally, you are actually doing a bit of research. All such undertakings, whether they are conducted to determine the success of an innovation or to help in making decisions about one instructional methodology over another, are looking for some kind of causal link between practice and outcomes and therefore qualify in some way as research (Porter 1997). Your assessment may be modest in scope and simple in design, but if the basic definition of research is to answer a question, then each and every assessment is really a miniresearch project. So you are probably more familiar with doing research, at least on some level, than you might think you are. However, although your day-to-day assessment projects could form the basis for a research project on a grander scale, they do not qualify as research unless they meet some basic criteria. Much of the research published on ILI tends toward the "How we did it good at our place" approach. Furthermore, much of the reported research is not always as methodologically sound as it might be (Powell 1997). There are much room for improvement and large areas of opportunity for any IL professional who wishes to move into the research arena.

What are the parameters that define research? First of all, researchers are skeptical. Researchers ask questions and may remain unconvinced about existing answers. They might formulate questions that have not as yet been explored or decide to investigate those that have incomplete or inconclusive answers. Researchers need proof or empirical evidence to support any statement. Some kind of data must be gathered and must be collected in particular ways that follow the accepted norms of scientific research (Del Balso and Lewis 1997).

Do not let the idea of scientific research frighten you. Although there are certain things that must be kept in mind in order for your project to qualify as research, there is a lot of room for variability based on discipline. Remember that research is done in all disciplines from the arts and humanities to the social and physical sciences. The objects of study and the methodologies vary widely. The humanist studies the products of human imagination, while the scientist studies events and behavior in the real world (Smalley and Pluto 1982). So, obviously the rules must be adjusted based upon the discipline in which the researcher is operating. Because ILI professionals are dealing with real people in real situations, our research seems most comparable to the type done in the social sciences. The rigor of laboratory research that is an earmark of the physical sciences is usually not required. For more information about how different disciplines are structured and the research process typically done in each see *Conceptual Frameworks for Bibliographic Education,* especially part 2, which discusses the social sciences; part 3, which deals with the humanities; and part 4, which addresses the sciences (Reichel and Ramey 1987).

What are the underlying rules and procedures that are common to research in all disciplines? All research (Berger and Patchner 1988a,b; Del Balso and Lewis 1997) must be:

1.  Objective: First and foremost is objectivity. The researcher is committed to using appropriate methods for data gathering and analysis and to presenting that data honestly and without bias. Researchers are systematic in the way in which they gather information. They try to understand the relationship between events and control for, or rule out, all other factors that could account for this relationship.

2.  Based on empirical facts: Second, the conclusions presented must be based on empirical verification. Conclusions must be connected to observations made—in other words, to the data that were collected. These ideas are not personal speculations. They have a basis in empirical fact.

3.  Cumulative: Third, research does not exist in a vacuum. It builds on already established work, and it lays the foundation for future endeavors. Researchers look for gaps in the knowledge base and formulate questions that will fill those gaps, or they attempt to replicate previous research that has inconclusive or contradictory results.

4.  Disseminated: Finally, research findings are shared. Researchers make a contribution only if their results are disseminated clearly, honestly, and in sufficient detail that other researchers can understand not only what was done but also how the data were interpreted. Anyone should be able to review the evidence presented and draw the same conclusions.

For some librarians, conducting research and publishing in peer-reviewed journals are required as part of their personnel review process. But even if this factor is not a consideration in your environment, engaging in research or at least becoming more knowledgeable about the process has other benefits as well. Understanding basic research methodologies makes you a better consumer of the research literature. It enables you to read with a more critical eye and gives you the ability to determine if the research methodology used is sound. Furthermore, as a knowledgeable research consumer who truly understands the process, you gain insight into the needs of all levels of researchers who utilize your library resources. Finally, the skills you acquire frequently improve your overall ability to think critically and analytically and may even enhance the way in which you, your library, and the profession at large are viewed in your community (Powell 1997).

## HOW DO YOU GET IDEAS?

Whether your job mandates that you must do research, or the desire to pursue a research path grows out of personal interest and curiosity, the first step is to decide what question you wish to answer. You may choose to focus your research on questions that concern you or your institution directly, or you may wish to concentrate on unanswered questions posed by previous research (Del Balso and Lewis 1997; Powell 1997). Ideas can come to you out of your daily interactions. You may be developing a new instructional program and wonder what instructional methods would be most appropriate for this type of situation. Or you become intrigued by a particular methodology and want to find out more about the effectiveness of that method in different settings. Other ideas grow out of your reading in the field. As you follow the literature, within and outside librarianship, particular notions or trends that you uncover may intrigue you. The results of some studies may point to other research possibilities or identify additional, as yet unanswered, questions.

Although it is wise to take a broad sweep in your current awareness reading, you cannot be expected to read everything there is in the field. Most people focus on particular aspects that are of special interest to them. Finding an intriguing idea that you think may lead to a researchable question requires reading the literature, attending conferences, and talking to colleagues with an open, curious mind. You do not have to look for a research topic actively. Wait for it, and it will come to you. What you want is a question or idea that intrigues you and that will hold your interest for the long haul (Del Balso and Lewis 1997; Gliner and Morgan 2000). Keep in mind that the research process can be a lengthy one, and you do not want to become bored with your question halfway through.

However, remember that you will be engaging in research not only to satisfy your own personal curiosity. You are hoping to find out something that will help to inform your colleagues and add to the knowledge base in the field. So you want to look for a question that is important to answer—one that can lead to practical applications and improvements and may have widespread appeal (Bordons and Abbott 1999; Gliner and Morgan 2000). In ILI research questions frequently focus on how to improve the instructional experience and develop more information-literate individuals.

Identifying your question is only the first step. Practical and feasible considerations must be taken into account. Foremost among these concerns is determining if your question can be answered through the research process. In other words, can your research idea be translated into a set of predictions about the relationship between variables, and are those relationships testable (Bordons and Abbott 1999)? Furthermore, you need to make sure that you have the resources (time, staff, funding, etc.) to carry out the task (Del Balso and Lewis 1997; Gliner and Morgan 2000; Powell 1997). Finally, your research design must adhere to accepted guidelines for the ethical conduct of research (Gliner and Morgan 2000).

## WHAT ARE THE STEPS IN THE PROCESS?

*Develop a Question*

Once you have identified your area of interest and have decided, at least on a general level, where you want your research to be focused, you must translate your ideas into a researchable question or group of questions upon which to concentrate. In order to do this, you must have a thorough knowledge of the field. You must be well read on the topic in question and be familiar with both known facts and accepted ideas. The more you know about the topic, the easier it will be for you to identify gaps in the field, studies that need to be replicated to verify questionable or contradictory results, and areas in which additional research is needed (Gliner and Morgan 2000; Powell 1997). There is no point in expending effort in reinventing the wheel. Obviously, to move from the general area of interest to the specific research process requires doing a well-designed and comprehensive literature review. Furthermore, it requires reading the research with a critical eye. Remember that skepticism is the cornerstone of science. Publication in a reputable referred journal does not always guarantee that the research was done properly. It is up to you, as the research consumer, to analyze the research report carefully. Pay special attention to the reasoning that went into the development of the research design, the adequacy of the methods used, and how well the data were analyzed and interpreted (Bordons and Abbott 1999; Fink 1998). The literature review enables you to examine the trends, fads, and theories represented by previous research. It helps to provide a framework for your study and provides background for your project (Berger and Patchner 1988; Bordons and Abbott 1999). In the early stages of your explorations, be sure to check out the *Reference Services Review* annual bibliography of ILI articles. The column can be a fast and easy way to get a snapshot of the areas that are currently of interest to ILI professionals. Another publication to review at this early exploration stage is *Research Agenda for Library and Instruction and Information Literacy*, developed by the ACRL Instruction Section's Research and Scholarship Committee (ALA. ACRL Libraries Instruction Section Research and Scholarship Committee 2004a).

Naturally, conducting a literature review is quite familiar to the information professional. When conducting a literature review for the express purpose of informing your research process, you are looking for several things. First and foremost, you want to determine that your question has not already been answered, thus negating the need for you to undertake the research. You are also trying to confirm that there are questions yet to be answered and that it appears that other people in the field would be interested in the discovery of those answers. You should also be on the outlook for techniques, methods, and instruments that have already been developed and successfully used that might be helpful to you as you conduct your own research. You can also use the literature review to identify colleagues who are working in the same area of interest and whom you may wish to contact for assistance (Bordons and Abbott 1999; Jaeger 1997; Westmeyer 1994).

The literature review is an iterative process. In general you will start off reading broadly in the field. You will then discover a subset of the literature that interests you, and you will begin to focus your literature review in this more narrow area. You will continue reviewing the literature until you are sure that your research area is worth pursuing and that it has not already been explored. Scanning the literature at a broad level is something information professionals do all the time in an attempt to stay current in the field and in the case of the IL professional, as a way to discover new and exciting ways to teach. As you scan, develop a research mind-set. Be on the lookout for researchable ideas. Keep that mind-set with you all the time, and your research topic will find you. It will be a question that you simply *have* to answer.

Be systematic and methodical as you review the literature. Make sure you keep good records of the material you read, including complete citations. Bibliographic management software can be helpful in keeping track of your readings and can be useful when you write your proposals or final research reports. However, manual methods work as well. Use whichever method you feel comfortable with that works for you. Inputting into the software or writing up those note cards may seem tedious and annoying to you, as you are excitedly reading on your topic. But force yourself to stop and do careful documentation as you go along. It will save you time, trouble, and heartache later when you need to locate specific citations for your reports, articles, or manuscripts.

A final word on literature reviews—frequently when a research question has multiple variables, the researcher discovers that there is nothing written on the topic. On the surface this seems like good news since no one has explored the question before. But keep in mind that your question must be relevant and of interest to others in the field. If no one has researched this question or anything related to it, it might be that the question is of minor importance. One way to make sure you find some context for your question is to explore the literature using a faceted approach.

Let us say you are interested in whether or not ILI utilizing active learning techniques leads to improved grades in middle school students. You cannot find anything on that particular combination of factors. So you look for any studies that show improvement in grades from any type of ILI at any educational level. You also look for studies that talk about the use of active learning techniques with middle school students. Finally, you try to find articles that talk about improved grades in middle school students, especially those that seem to be a result of anything resembling ILI principles. You can then take those findings and extrapolate from them to develop your specific, focused, research question. The result of these separate literature reviews should give you the background material you need to show why your research question is worth pursuing and may supply suggestions that will help you as you design your methodology for addressing that question.

*Make Predictions*

FORMULATE YOUR HYPOTHESIS

Once you have settled upon the question you wish to explore with your research, you need to translate it into testable terms. In other words, you must be able to describe the relationships you expect to uncover in

your research. You must clearly define the variables you will be study-
ing and indicate how those variables interact. The statement that links
your variables and describes this relationship is your hypothesis (Berger
and Patchner 1988; Bordons and Abbott 1999; Gliner and Morgan 2000).
The ultimate goal of your research will be to prove or disprove your hypothesis.

What constitutes a workable hypothesis? Here are some important
characteristics that you need to keep in mind (Berger and Patchner
1988; Bordons and Abbott 1999; Powell 1997; Westmeyer 1994):

1. Generalizability: The hypothesis should hold up in more than
   one situation.
2. Compatibility with existing knowledge: The hypothesis should
   be based on findings already cited in related literature. Even if
   your goal is to question previous findings, your research is still
   based on evidence that has already been accumulated in the
   field.
3. Testability: An experiment or situation can be devised that will
   test the truth or falseness of the hypothesis. In other words, the
   hypothesis will use variables that can be potentially measured.
4. Relational: The hypothesis describes a relationship between
   two or more variables.

An example of an ILI hypothesis would be as follows: Students who are
enrolled in an introductory biology course will locate more relevant articles on their research topics after completing an online IL tutorial than
students who are presented this material as part of their laboratory manuals. This hypothesis should be able to be generalized beyond the particular institution in which it is tested and might even be applicable beyond
the area of biology. Presumably, there is sufficient literature to support the
notion that the more active IL interventions represented by the tutorial
improve students' ability to locate relevant articles on their topic. Or the
researcher has identified the fact that more evidence is needed to support
this notion. The hypothesis is testable since some students can be selected
to participate in the online tutorial while other students are not given this
opportunity and must rely on the written material. The variables involved are the participation in the tutorial versus using the written material in their manuals and the number of relevant articles retrieved.

DEFINE YOUR VARIABLES

In order to write your hypothesis, you must first define the variables
under study. A variable is anything that can exist in one form or state at

one time and in another at a different time. In the case of people, it could also be considered a characteristic that is different in one person than it is in another (gender, age, school level, etc.) (Berger and Patchner 1988a,b; Westmeyer 1994).

Two types of variables are identified in traditional experimental research: the independent and the dependent variable. The independent variable is in some way under the control of the researcher. In other words, it is a variable that the researcher deliberately changes or manipulates from one setting to another. In the above example the independent variable is whether or not the student uses the online tutorial. A variable that changes as a result of this manipulation is the dependent variable. The dependent variable is what the subject of the experiment does. It represents the behavior exhibited as a result of the manipulation of the independent variable. This behavior or level of the dependent variable is what is being measured in the research. Again in our example the dependent variable would be the number of relevant articles located on a subject. Dependent variables can be scores from a test, survey, or questionnaire, readings from instruments (EKG, GSR, etc.), or measures of performance (Gliner and Morgan 2000; Westmeyer 1994).

A significant change in the dependent variable following manipulation of the independent variable may reasonably lead the researcher to infer a causal relationship between the two variables. In order for the researcher to be able to conclude that the change in the dependent variable was caused by the manipulation of the independent variable, changes in the independent variable must precede changes in the dependent variable. In addition, there can be no other plausible variables that could also explain the relationship between the two variables (Porter 1997). It is important for the researcher to account for these possible extraneous or confounding variables and to control for them as much as possible (Gliner and Morgan 2000). So if our research was designed properly and students who took the online tutorial found significantly more relevant articles than those who did not use the tutorial, we could extrapolate that using the online tutorial improved the students' abilities to locate relevant articles on their subject.

Here is another example of how this would look in ILI research. Let us say we are interested in seeing if a particular ILI in-person session improves students' understanding of how to select appropriate resources for a given topic. That is to say, one of the learning outcomes for the session would be that students could identify relevant resources for a given topic from a variety of resources available to them. Whether or not a student received the ILI would be the independent variable. Students who received the instruction would be considered the experimental group. Those who did not would be the control group. The dependent variable in this case would be the ability to correctly choose appropriate resources for a given topic. Some sort of postinstruction test or exercise would measure this behavior. The research hypothesis in this case would be that students who received instruction (the independent variable) would score significantly higher on the postinstruction test (dependent variable) than those who did not receive the instruction. Assigning students randomly to the experimental group (those who receive instruction) and the control group (those who do not) would help account for extraneous variables that could confound the results.

Another way to do this is to use the pre/posttest design and let students act as their own controls. In this case, the dependent variable would be differences in test scores between the pre- and postinstruction versions of the test. The hypothesis would be that students who participated in instruction (independent variable) would score significantly better on a posttest that measured their abilities to select appropriate resources than they did on the preinstruction version of the test. The difference in scores between the pretest and posttest is the dependent variable.

Variables must be defined in precise, measurable terms in order to meet the research criteria of objectivity and empirical verification. These operational definitions tell the researcher what activities or manipulations he or she needs to perform in order to measure the concept or variable. Good operational definitions are so clear that anyone following the same operational definition will measure the variable in the same exact way. Although precise operational definitions can somewhat restrict the ability to generalize the results, they are necessary if the researcher wishes to make meaningful predictions about the behavior under consideration (Berger and Patchner 1988a,b; Bordons and Abbott 1999). In the above example, the independent variable is defined as the presence or absence of a specific type of instruction. The dependent variable is defined as the difference in scores between the pre- and postinstruction tests.

## Determine Reliability and Validity

Another consideration when designing your research and defining your variables is determining the reliability and validity of your measurements. Reliability refers to repeatability. Can other researchers, using your operational definitions of variables and your means of measuring them, repeat the experiment and get the same results? Can you redo the experiment on multiple occasions and also get consistent results? If someone in another institution used the same pre- and post-test design to measure the effects of the same type of ILI in their institution, would they get the same results? If you replicated your study in your own institution but used students in history instead of students in English composition, would you get the same results? If the answer to these questions is yes, your experimental results are reliable.

Validity, on the other hand, refers to whether or not your research study is actually measuring what it is supposed to be measuring—that is, whether or not it is adequately testing your hypothesis. One way to improve validity is to design your research to control for the possibility that extraneous variables could account for your results. The sounder your research design, the more likely it will be that you have in fact adequately tested your hypothesis and that your results may have some practical application beyond the current research study (Bordons and Abbott 1999).

Another way to examine validity is to compare your measures against standards in the field. In the case of ILI it might be beneficial to look at ACRL's *Information Literacy Competency Standards for Higher Education* (ALA. ACRL Task Force on Information Literacy Standards 2004b) or those developed at your own institution to make sure you are selecting the appropriate dependent variables. This is yet another argument for the establishment of these types of standards and the importance of developing learning outcomes based on these standards at the outset of your instructional design process. In order to examine the success of your instruction, you need something to measure. These are your learning outcomes. Your learning outcomes inform and help you develop your hypothesis. If your hypothesis is that what you are doing improves IL, then you need standards as your starting point.

*Selecting Your Population*

Since ILI research is examining real people in the real world, the way in which subjects are selected for your study is crucial to the process. Types of research designs are discussed in a later section of this chapter. However, regardless of which research design you select, you must consider the methods you will be using to recruit subjects into your study. The first consideration is to develop your sampling frame. This is a list or description of the members of the population from which your sample will be drawn (Del Balso and Lewis 1997; Jaeger 1997; Rice and Ezzy 1999). Characteristics could include age, gender, educational level, prior IL experience, cultural or ethnic group, enrollment in a particular course, and so on. The most rigorous of research designs are dependent upon the use of random sampling. In this design there is an equal chance for any member of the target population to be selected for the study. This is to ensure that the subjects in the samples are representative of the population from which they are drawn (Berger and Patchner 1988a,b; Bordons and Abbott 1999).

Furthermore, selected subjects are randomly assigned to the different conditions of the independent variable involved in the study (Gliner and Morgan 2000). So for example, if you were interested in looking at the difference between collaborative, small group learning versus more traditional lecture-type classroom situations in a population of college freshman writing composition students, your population is made up of all students enrolled in writing composition classes. You would use some mechanism to randomly select your subjects from this population such as selecting every third name on the class rosters as your subjects or using random number tables to determine who will be chosen to participate. Once you have your group of subjects, you could randomly assign students either to the collaborative learning situation or the lecture-style situation. Obviously, there are all kinds of logistical and ethical issues involved in doing such a thing. The use of quasi-experimental designs discussed in a later section is a way in which researchers have tried to overcome these dilemmas. The important thing to remember is that poor sampling techniques may result in questionable research results that can diminish the validity and value of the study.

SAMPLING TECHNIQUES

There are many different types of sampling techniques available to the researcher. An excellent discussion of these various methodologies appears in *Qualitative Research Methods* by Pranee Liamputtong Rice and Douglas Ezzy (Rice and Ezzy 1999). Here are a few examples:

1. Homogeneous group sampling: Samples are selected to minimize variation and to maximize homogeneity in order to obtain in-depth descriptions of a situation, condition, or issue. Focus group participants are often selected this way.
2. Criterion sampling: Subjects are selected on the basis of a preset list of characteristics and/or criteria. Clearly, the criteria must be selected carefully in order to define subjects who can offer the most relevant and detailed data as possible. All students taking a particular course would fall into this category.
3. Snowball or chain: This technique is used as a subsequent stage of data collection. After the first set of subjects have been selected and participated in the research, they are asked to supply the names of others who they think would also be willing to participate. The characteristics of the original sample will

obviously shape the subsequent one. So snowball sampling often results in homogeneous groups. However, it is a good way to gather subjects from closed groups or networks. It is very useful for identifying subjects when you are not a member of a given group and have only limited access to it.

One final consideration is sample size. While it is difficult to make any definitive statement on the sample size needed in any given situation, the rule of thumb is to make sure the sample is large enough to be representative of the population yet not too large to be unwieldy. It should also offer the opportunity for collecting enough data to address the research question under examination (Bordons and Abbott 1999; Rice and Ezzy 1999). The actual size will vary depending upon the focus of the research. For example, usability research is predicated on the fact that only a few (three to five) subjects are necessary in each iteration of the process. Once the researcher begins to see a pattern in the responses, that is, a repeat in the type of responses being made, the usability researcher calls a halt to the research (Krug 2000; Nielsen 2000).

*Choose Your Research Design*

Once you have determined your research question, developed your hypothesis, operationally defined your variables, and described the population you wish to study, you must select a methodology for collecting the necessary data to prove or disprove your hypothesis. So the next step is to select your research design. Research designs are plans that specify how the independent variable will be manipulated and how potential changes in the dependent variable are measured. They also delineate ways in which possible plausible alternative hypotheses that might account for the results have been eliminated or controlled for. In other words, the research design includes a description of how extraneous factors or variables other than the independent variable or treatment have been reasonably ruled out as causing the observed changes in the dependent variable.

For example, if our hypothesis is that students who complete an intellectual property tutorial will be less likely to plagiarize on their papers, we must make sure that they have not had any other opportunities to learn the principles covered in the tutorial. One way to do that is to have each student complete a pretest on the subject to determine his or her level of knowledge prior to interacting with the tutorial. You would then have a baseline for each student. Any changes in the student's understanding of plagiarism and intellectual property issues could then be expected to be a result of completing the tutorial. Remember, the goal of the research design is to ensure that the manipulation of the independent variable is the only reasonable explanation for the resultant changes in the dependent variable. A further goal is that valid generalizations can be made from the study (Berger and Patchner 1988; Porter 1997; Powell 1997). If the tutorial under examination successfully decreases the incidence of plagiarism in your institution, would it also do so in other institutions?

The research design, therefore, gives a detailed description of how subjects will be recruited for the study, how they will be assigned to groups as appropriate, how the independent variable will be manipulated, and how the dependent variable will be measured. Researchers in ILI are frequently dealing with real people in real-life situations. This often limits how much control the researcher can ethically have over the manipulation of the independent variable. Furthermore, it may influence the type of data that can be realistically collected. The ILI researcher, like those in the social sciences, may have less control over the manipulation of variables than researchers in the physical sciences. Therefore, research in social science arenas is often referred to as quasi-experimental, observational, or naturalistic in approach. See below for details on these techniques.

Regardless of the type of the research design, data must be collected. There is a wide range of possibilities when determining how data will be collected. However, data collection can be described as falling into two major categories—quantitative and qualitative methods. Quantitative methods result in numbers. Qualitative methods are more descriptive in nature. Both can support hypothesis testing, and the selection of the type of data collection does not reflect upon the rigor of the study. The fundamental difference between quantitative and qualitative techniques is the format in which the data are collected (numbers or descriptions) (Grassian and Kaplowitz 2001).

Typical quantitative methods include multiple choice, fill-in or matching questions, questionnaires, surveys, and rating scales. Qualitative techniques include interviews, focus group research, observational techniques, and other forms of field-testing (Del Balso and Lewis 1997; Gliner and Morgan 2000; Grassian and Kaplowitz 2001; Porter 1997; Powell 1997; Rice and Ezzy 1999).

QUASI-EXPERIMENTAL

Regardless of the data collection technique utilized, you must assign subjects to different groups. In pure scientific research experiments, subjects are randomly assigned to either the experimental group (the one in which the independent variable will be manipulated) or the control group (the one in which the independent variable will not be manipulated). In terms of ILI research the experimental group would receive the instruction under examination, and the control group would not. However, when working with real people in the real world, this type of random assignment poses both logistical and ethical issues (Berger and Patchner 1988a,b; Powell 1997). The most difficult issue would be the ethics of denying instruction to a segment of the population, which, we hypothesize, will in some way benefit everyone.

One solution to this dilemma is to use naturally occurring groups in what is commonly called a quasi-experimental design. Typically, subjects in this type of design act as their own controls. One example of a quasi-experimental design is the pre- and posttest research strategy in which all subjects are tested prior to instruction (the control state) and again after instruction has been received (the experimental state). Since subjects serve as their own control, any differences between the pre- and the posttest scores are assumed to be a result of the instruction (Del Balso and Lewis 1997; Gliner and Morgan 2000; Powell 1997).

## NATURALISTIC APPROACHES

These approaches, which are often used in the social sciences, can be applied to ILI research and do not require manipulation of an independent variable. The goal of this type of research is to understand behavior rather than to predict it. Naturalistic approaches can include interviews, surveys or questionnaires, observations of real behavior, and document or product analysis (Bordons and Abbott 1999; Grassian and Kaplowitz 2001; Powell 1997; Westbrook 1997). Interviews, surveys, and questionnaires are used to find out what people think or feel about a situation. As a result the data collected from them are very subjective and personal. The data describe, frequently in the person's own words, how they would behave in a particular situation. As such, this type of data cannot always tell us what will really happen when the person is confronted with a real-world situation. Such first-person reports are also influenced by the fact that people know they are in a study. Subjects may try to provide answers they think the researcher wishes to hear or hide those they do not wish to disclose. Furthermore, they may make up responses if they do not know the answers to some of the questions (Gliner and Morgan 2000). However, interviews, surveys, and questionnaires can be used to gather information from a small, but representative, sample of a larger group, and the resultant data can be used to describe the characteristics of the larger population (Del Balso and Lewis 1997).

## QUESTIONNAIRES OR SURVEYS

Using these types of instruments requires very careful planning and design. If possible, the ILI researcher should enlist help from experts in fields such as education, management, political science, psychology, and sociology. Look for arenas in your environment where this type of data is collected—for marketing purposes, for demographics, for political analysis—and see if you can partner with these survey design experts.

When designing a survey or questionnaire, keep the following factors in mind. First, can you find an instrument that already exists that you can either use or adapt? If something already exists that has been tested for reliability and validity, you can save valuable development time. Your literature review should help identify potential instruments for your use. You might also wish to look at the Library Instruction Round Table's book on *Evaluating Library Instruction* (Shonrock 1996), which includes sample questions and surveys that may be adapted for ILI assessment and research primarily in the area of attitudes and perceptions. When looking for already developed instruments, keep in mind that many of them are copyrighted and that the use of these instruments may be restricted to those with certain credentials. These restrictions are partly to ensure the validity of the instruments. If instruments were freely available, some might review them in advance and prepare answers on their own or by consulting other resources. The instrument then would no longer test what it was designed to test. The bottom line is that although you might find an instrument that suits your needs, you may need to adapt it to fit your environment. And you must always confer with the copyright owner to get permission either to use or to modify the instrument.

Make sure that each item on the survey has a purpose and is clear and understandable to the respondent. Remember that even if an item is clear and understandable and has a purpose, it may not test for what a person knows or what he or she has learned. So testing the validity of each item against external standards is also crucial. (See section on validity for more on this topic.)

The shorter the survey, the more likely your respondents will complete it, so make each item count. Avoid ambiguities in your items. The best way to ensure your questions are clear is to pretest the instrument with people as similar to those you will be surveying as possible. Ask for feedback about any question that is unclear or difficult to follow. Also make sure you have not included any leading questions or questions that seem to indicate how the researcher would like to see them answered. Avoid double-barreled questions—those that ask more than one thing within a single question. These are difficult to respond to, especially if the person has a different answer to the various parts of the question. Be sure to include both positive and negative possible answers within your questions to avoid biasing respondents one way or the other. Instead of asking, "Would you use Expanded Academic ASAP to search for periodical articles?" ask, "Would you or would you not use Expanded Academic ASAP to search for periodical articles?"

Is the order of the questions appropriate? It is usually best to put sensitive questions at the end of the survey. Also it helps the respondent if questions are grouped by content so that the respondent does not have to switch from topic to topic. Whenever possible, all items using a particular format such as multiple-choice, fill-in, open-ended questions, and/or rating scales should also be kept together. This is less confusing to the respondent and also allows for more concise presentation of instructions for completion of each section of the survey. Appearance is important, too. So make sure that the survey is laid out in a pleasant and eye-appealing manner (Berger and Patchner 1988a,b; Del Balso and Lewis 1997; Gliner and Morgan 2000; Jaeger 1997).

Surveys can be administered via mail, e-mail, phone or in-person. Each method has its advantages and disadvantages. Mailing print surveys is probably the most cost-effective method but generally suffers from poor response rates. E-mail eliminates postal charges and offers the possibility of a quick response. However, there is that delete key. So again the response rate may be a bit low. Telephoning respondents tends to have a better response rate, if you actually reach the person. It appears to be harder to refuse to participate in a telephone survey than to either mail or e-mail. However, it may take several calls before you actually reach some persons. If they have caller ID, you may never reach them. Once you reach them, you will probably need to limit your phone call to just a few minutes, and you will need to reassure the person you are calling that you will not take up too much of his or her time. So although the response rate may be better with telephone surveys, they are more labor-intensive (Berger and Patchner 1988; Jaeger 1997).

Survey-type data can also be collected in person. One technique is to gather together a group of respondents in one place and ask them to fill out the survey all at the same time. While this is quite an efficient way to gather a lot of data in a short period of time, it is often difficult to get people together in this manner unless you are distributing a survey to a group that is already gathered together for some purpose, like a class. This is often why college students are the subjects of many experiments. However, using already established groups can diminish the possibility of obtaining a random sample as opposed to telephone, mail and e-mail approaches, which can offer more opportunities to randomize the people being surveyed. The in-person technique may rely on the willingness of people to participate and so may be biased by the fact that respondents are either self-selecting to participate (Berger and Patchner 1988) or are in an already established group.

Survey material can also be developed as a one-on-one interview. In this format, the respondent is asked questions by the interviewer, and the respondent answers verbally. Great care is needed not only in the formulating of the interview questions but also in the training of the interviewer. Interviewers must be skilled in eliciting the responses while remaining impartial and unbiased, so as to not influence the respondents (Del Balso and Lewis 1997).

Focus Groups

Focus groups are similar to both interviews and surveys. However, the questions are asked in a group setting. Typically, eight to ten people, who meet some sort of preset criteria for inclusion in the group, are brought together to participate in the research. There are several advantages to gathering data in this manner. First of all, you are collecting information from multiple people at the same time. You are ensuring that your questions will be answered since you are doing the surveying in person. The moderator or facilitator of the group can clarify any items that might be confusing to participants and can ask follow-up questions if participants' responses are unclear or incomplete. Furthermore, since the survey is done in a group setting, the participants themselves have a chance to hear each other's comments and discuss issues together. Focus group research also has a side benefit. It can serve as a marketing tool. The very act of inviting the library's constituents to discuss their opinions about the library, its resources and services, lets them know that their ideas are valued and will contribute to future decision making. If this decision making is, at least in part, based on the data gathered via focus group research, people in the community feel that their interests have been represented and considered. As a result, they are more likely to support whatever changes may be implemented (Gliner and Morgan 2000; Glitz 1998).

The following material on focus group research was drawn both from personal experience and from an excellent book on the subject called *Focus Groups for Libraries and Librarians* by Beryl Glitz (Glitz 1998). This book is invaluable to anyone who wishes to undertake this type of research as not only does it offer background information on the subject, but the author shows how this type of research can and has been applied in the library setting.

There are several considerations to keep in mind when designing a focus group research project. First, whom will you recruit as your participants? The answer to this question will rely in part on the type of information you are trying to gather and on whom will be affected by the decisions you are considering. Obviously, you want to gather participants who have some knowledge about the issues involved. In the case of libraries it might be interesting to gather data both from those who use the library and its services and from those who do not. So for ILI research your focus group participants might be those who have participated in instruction and those who have not.

Once you have selected the people you would like to include in your focus groups, you must decide on a mechanism for recruiting them. Personal contact either via telephone or e-mail seems to work well. However, keep in mind that people who agree to participate might not show up at the scheduled day and time. Offering incentives for participation can increase the odds of participants actually showing up for the focus group discussion. Food is always a draw. People may be more likely to appear if they know ahead of time that a meal or some kind of light refreshments will be offered. Thank-you gifts are also a nice touch. These can be small and might even be marketing items such as pens or notepads with the library's logo. You can also have one or two larger gifts that will be raffled off to all participants at the end of the research project.

Remember that people may have every intention of showing up for the group but may just forget the appointment. Scheduled follow-up calls or e-mails reminding the participants of their impending involvement are crucial. While the researcher should take care not to overwhelm or annoy the participants with frequent reminders, it is wise to plan for at least one follow-up call or e-mail a few days prior to the scheduled discussion as a courtesy and a reminder. Your participants can use this as an opportunity to confirm participation or to let you know that they are no longer able to attend. As a result, you will have a better idea about who is actually going to appear on the scheduled focus group day.

The second major consideration is the selection of a moderator or facilitator for the discussion. This person must be well trained in the process. She or he should be people-oriented, both a good communicator and a skilled interviewer, be interested in the topic, and be well organized. Furthermore, the moderator needs good short-term memory abilities as he or she must be able to process what is being said, ask for clarification as needed, refer back to previous responses as appropriate and keep the conversation on track (Glitz 1998).

The question of using an outside moderator who has no personal stake in the project, versus one who has in-depth knowledge and an understanding of the general environment has been a subject of much debate (Glitz 1998; Sevier 1989; Shoaf 2003). Although there are merits to both approaches, practical considerations may affect the decision. Professional moderators offer the advantage of being objective and experienced in this type of research. But a professional moderator can be costly, and the library may not have the budget to hire one. Using someone from within the library as the moderator is less expensive. Furthermore that person probably has in-depth knowledge about the issues at hand. However, this very knowledge can cause difficulties. It can be very hard for someone who is personally involved in the issues to remain as objective as necessary during the discussion. It is no fun to hear negative comments about your own library and its services. A further problem with using internal moderators is the possibility that your participants may not be as open and honest as they might with an outside facilitator since they do not wish to hurt the feelings of internal moderators.

A possible compromise is to use someone from within your parent organization who has some knowledge of the situation but who is not directly involved in the issues under discussion. Check with people who are involved in data gathering for your institution and see if they would be willing to help. In academic settings, education, management, political science, psychology, and sociology departments may be fruitful places to look for assistance. You may be able to find someone who would be willing to act as moderator for the good of the institution and may charge little or nothing in the way of a fee.

The nature of the questions being asked during the focus group discussion is, of course, a major consideration. The answers to these questions serve as your data. So care should be taken to make sure the questions are going to supply the data you need. Whether you use someone as your moderator who is personally involved, an outside professional, or someone from within your community but outside the library, you need to work with the moderator to make sure the questions are clear, are arranged in a logical order, and are relevant to your research needs. Experienced moderators can offer a great deal of assistance in the development of a logical flow to the questions and can help guide you in their development. Questions, for the most part, should be open-ended since prompting discussion is the goal of the project. It is also important to provide feedback to focus group participants who are interested in the cumulative results and to let them know what form the feedback will take, as well as when they can expect it. If you have taken the important step of applying for, and receiving, Internal Review Board approval for your project (see below), you will also be able to disseminate the results by preparing and submitting a manuscript describing both the process used and the results to an appropriate journal.

## OBSERVATIONS

Observing actual behavior offers the advantage of allowing the researcher to get firsthand insight into the way that people really behave. The researcher can see how people gather information, how they select the resources to use, how they develop their search strategies, how they evaluate both the resources and the products of their searches, and so on. However, the act of observation may influence the behavior. One cannot be absolutely sure that the person being observed is not performing for the benefit of the observer, exhibiting behavior that the observer is hoping to see. Would the person really behave in this fashion if he or she were not being watched? Of course, the researcher may choose to observe the behavior without the subject's being aware of the observation. This can be done in person or by means of computer logs and search records. Although observing someone without his or her knowledge may help resolve this issue, it opens up some ethical and privacy concerns. A further concern with observations is that they can be very time- and labor-intensive (Del Balso and Lewis 1997).

## PRODUCT ANALYSIS

This approach offers a way to see what people actually do with the information they gather. Although product analysis offers insight into how well the person accomplished a task, the researcher has no real way of knowing how the product was developed. In other words, the ILI researcher who does product analysis does not know if the student really applied IL strategies to gather the information for the product. A frequently used methodology, designed to assist with this concern, is to have students keep a research journal or diary in which they record the steps taken to research their papers. The resultant data give the researcher a more complete picture of the search behavior as they include both information about the process (the journal) and the final product (the research paper itself).

Obviously, great care needs to be taken in gathering data using observational methods and product analysis since these data can be highly subjective and dependent on the observer and/or the reviewer. Since the data consist of real behavior in the real world, they can be difficult to categorize. A great deal of preliminary work needs to be done in order to develop methods of coding the behavior being observed. Observers and coders also need training in the methodology to be sure not only that they each understand what is expected of them, but also that there is consistency among all who will be gathering the data (Del Balso and Lewis 1997; Westbrook 1997).

Clearly, each of these data-collecting methods has its particular values and concerns. Because none of them offer a perfect solution, many researchers choose to use a combination of techniques, both those that are experimental or quasi-experimental in nature and those that are more descriptive. A combination of techniques provides the researcher with a variety of data that, taken together, can give a clearer picture of the behavior being studied.

*Write Your Research Proposal*

After you have written your hypothesis, defined your variables, chosen your subjects, and selected your research design, you can move on to writing your research proposal and possibly requesting or applying for some kind of support to conduct the research. (See Chapter 6 for more on grant writing.) Even if you are not attempting to get funding or institutional support for your project, it is a good idea to take the time to write a formal proposal. It forces you to put your thoughts in order and to clearly outline what you plan to do. The proposal serves as a guideline for your work and represents the first stage in what should be the careful planning process that precedes a well-conceived research study. It can also be extremely useful when you are writing your final research report. In essence the proposal acts as an outline that you fill in with the actual data, results, and conclusions once the research is completed.

The proposal should include the details of the project and serves as a guide as you carry out your research. It encourages the researcher to clarify exactly what he or she plans to do and includes definitions of the variables to be studied, details regarding the conditions, settings, instruments, procedures, timing for collecting data about these variables, and how the data will be analyzed. The population that will be studied should be clearly identified and how that population will be recruited for the study should be described. Writing the research proposal can point out possible flaws in the research design and methods (Powell 1997; Westmeyer 1994). For example, how easy will it be for you to gain access to the population you wish to study?

Sometimes the question that you wish to answer is a fairly complex one. In that case, it can be useful to break the question into subsets or subproblems in order to design your research (Powell 1997). For example, let us say your hypothesis is that the frequency of library use by first-year college students is dependent upon whether or not they received course-integrated ILI. To help design the study, ask yourself, What do I need to know? In this case you need to determine three things—the frequency of use for students who received IL, the frequency of use for those who did not receive IL, and the difference in frequency of library use between the two groups. Breaking your research question down into its component parts can help you decide what data to collect and how you need to analyze them.

What are the parts of a proposal?

1. **Statement of the Problem:** The proposal starts with a statement of the problem, written clearly and in complete sentences. The problem statement should be straightforward, unambiguous, specific, and explicit. This is followed by a review of the literature focusing not only on what already is known on the topic but on how the gaps in the literature were identified and the ways in which those gaps led the researcher to the research question he or she is proposing to study.

2. **Research Design:** The next section should focus on the research design. This includes the goals and objectives of the study, the hypothesis being researched, definitions of the variables being studied, and the methodology being used to collect and analyze the data.

3. **Resources Available:** The following section describes institutional resources or other means of funding the research the researcher plans to call upon in the course of the research. Included in this portion of the proposal is information on personnel and budget.

4. **Anticipated Results:** Next comes a section on anticipated results followed by any possible limitations on the study. These limitations may be imposed by the methods being used, the setting, access to particular populations, ethical issues, and any other variables that might be outside the researcher's control.

5. **Supporting Documents (Optional):** Some proposals include support or back material such as documents from the parent institution that relate to the proposal and a list of suggested readings beyond the literature review. For example, if you are at an academic institution that has recently issued some sort of white paper on undergraduate students' lack of abilities to pursue scholarly research, this might be included to help bolster your idea of ILI research as a possible solution to this problem. Along the same line, you might also include additional readings such as ACRL's *Information Literacy Competency Standards for Higher Education* (ALA ACRL Task Force on Information Literacy Standards 2004). You might also include references to some of the documents highlighting the importance of information literacy published by accreditation agencies in higher education such as the Middle States Commission on Higher

Education (MSCHE) and the Western Association of Schools and Colleges. Furthermore, references to documents describing ILI efforts at other comparable institutions might also add credibility to your proposal.

6. **Timeline:** Finally, a timeline can be extremely helpful to include in your proposal—both to your reader and as a guide for helping the researcher stay on track. It should include benchmarks that indicate how much and what progress should be expected at particular points along the way.

Note that grant proposals follow a very similar process. See Chapter 6 on grants and grant writing for more details on writing proposals for funding.

*Collect and Analyze Your Data*

Once you have completed your proposal, it is time to test your hypothesis by conducting your research and collecting the resulting data. The type of data that you collect will be determined in part by the questions that your research is trying to answer and the research methodology you have decided upon. This is also true for the ways in which you decide to analyze your data. Statistical analysis is a complex and complicated procedure, and it is wise to seek assistance from experts in the field. However, remember that just because your data can be analyzed in a number of ways does not mean that you need to utilize all those different analyses. The statistical methodology selected and the means of presentation (tables, graphs, figures) should improve the assessment of the results and make it easier for the reader to understand your findings (Wilkinson and Inference 1999).

Computer programs have made it easier to manipulate and massage your data quickly and in a number of different ways. Always keep your research questions or hypotheses in mind when deciding upon how you will be analyzing your data. Do you need that statistic to address the research question? If not, why provide it? Try to avoid statistical overkill. Do not analyze the data to death just because you can easily do so. You do not want the number and variety of the statistical analysis provided to overwhelm your findings and make it difficult for your readers to focus on what is important. Choose statistical methodologies that relate to your original hypotheses and can prove or disprove them. All other statistics are irrelevant. Although they might be somewhat interesting, especially in the case of unanticipated results, you do not want these serendipitous findings to overwhelm your reason for doing the research in the first place.

*Publish Your Paper*

Once you have completed your research, collected and analyzed your data, and interpreted the results, you should communicate your findings to your colleagues. Remember that the fourth principle of scientific research is disseminating your results. If you have received grant funding in support of your research, you may very well be required to disseminate your results in some way. Here is where preparing a thorough research proposal comes in handy. Your research proposal should provide the foundation for your research paper. It should contain background information and a literature review supporting the necessity of your research. The proposal should also have a complete description of your research methodology, including definitions of your independent and dependent variables, how you selected your subjects, how the independent variable varied among groups, how you measured changes in the dependent variable, and so on. (See Chapter 6 for details on the parts of a grant proposal.)

The bulk of the new material for your paper, of course, will be a description of the findings and the discussion of these findings. Ultimately, you will have to indicate whether you feel your findings support your original hypotheses. Although it might be difficult for the researcher to publish findings that disprove his or her original ideas, keep in mind that one of the goals of research is to be cumulative and to contribute to a growing knowledge base in the field. So it is as important to report negative findings as it is to report positive ones (Berger and Patchner 1988a,b).

Research papers often end with a "Where do we go from here?" segment. Research is really an iterative process and each study can be both the end of one research trail and the beginning of a new one. Your results may include some unexpected findings that could suggest further arenas for research. You may have answered some questions and uncovered new ones that still need to be answered. There is always more to know. So as one project ends, another can begin (Del Balso and Lewis 1997).

Selecting an appropriate journal in which to publish your results or a professional conference at which to present them can be somewhat tricky. Your literature review should give you a good idea of which journals and what organizations might be interested in the topic you researched. Keep in mind that the criteria for accepting a paper for presentation or publication can be somewhat subjective. The peer review process, which is intended to ensure the quality of the material being published, can also be affected by personal bias. For example, reviewers who do not agree with your results may be more critical than those who find your results acceptable (Bordons and Abbott 1999).

Kenneth Bordons and Bruce Abbott offer the following advice for increasing the odds of getting your paper published (Bordons and Abbott 1999):

1. Make sure your methodology is sound. Most papers are rejected on the basis of design flaws.
2. Tackle important questions. Make sure the research you undertake will lead to information that people will care about. If your research is too esoteric, no one will care about your findings.
3. Write clearly, logically, concisely, and to the point. Reviewers who find it difficult to understand your points or are confused by what you are trying to say may react unfavorably to the paper.
4. Do not attack other researchers. If your findings disagree with previous findings, concentrate on the differences in the data. Do not cast blame on the integrity or ability of the previous researchers.
5. Appearances matter. Submit a neat, clean manuscript that exactly follows whatever directions to authors that the publication or conference provides. A sloppy manuscript reflects poorly not only on the writer but on the information being presented in it.
6. If you feel you were reviewed unfairly, write to the editor for reconsideration.
7. Do not be discouraged if in the end your paper is rejected. Remember that some critiques may be valid. Use the reviewers' comments to improve your study. You may have to do some rewriting to make your points clearer, or you may even have to do some additional research before resubmitting your material either to the same journal or to a different one. The net result may be an even better research study than the one you began with.

The **Read More about It** section at the end of this chapter contains several references to material offering excellent advice and checklists on how to prepare the research paper. Chapter 6 offers similar advice related to funding proposals to granting agencies.

ETHICAL CONSIDERATIONS AND OTHER
POTENTIAL PITFALLS

As mentioned in the previous section, it is as important to report negative findings as it is to report positive ones. In a sense, the suppression of findings that are surprising to the researcher or actually counter his or her hypotheses is an unethical or fraudulent act. It hinders the accumulation of knowledge.

Obviously, deliberately altering the results of an experiment in order to make the data support the researcher's ideas is also a fraudulent act and damages the essence of the scientific process (Woodward and Goodstein 1996). However, the researcher who allows cultural or personal values to influence his or her research is also undermining the validity of the research being reported (Bordons and Abbott 1999). One of the four principles of research is objectivity. The researcher who allows personal beliefs to affect the selection of subjects for the research, the way in which questions are asked or variables are manipulated, and the interpretation of the results is doing a disservice to the discipline he or she is trying to advance (Bordons and Abbott 1999).

While fraud, either inadvertent or purposeful, is clearly a concern, the ethical use of human subjects is an even larger issue to the ILI researcher. It is important to find out if your institution has procedures in place relating to the use of human subjects. Many organizations have Internal Review Boards that must pass on research designs before they can be implemented. For example, UCLA's Office for the Protection of Research Subjects offers an online training program for researchers (UCLA Office of Human Subject Protection 2004). Certificates of completion for this program are required of all Primary Investigators (PI) who are applying for IRB approval.

The ethical treatment of human subjects revolves around the principle of "do no harm." Being a part of the research should in no way jeopardize subjects (Berger and Patchner 1988a; National Commission for the Protection of Human Subjects of Biomedical and Behavioral Research 1978; Sieber 1992). Confidentiality of the data should be maintained at all times. Anonymity is also required. Research participants should receive a guarantee that there is no way for their names to be associated with any particular piece of data.

A major component of the ethical use of human subjects is that participation in research should be voluntary. In order to comply with this requirement, individuals must be given an explicit choice about whether or not they want to be involved in the research (Berger and Patchner 1988a). Therefore, participants should be given as much information as possible about what will be going on during the research and should be given a consent form to sign. In the case where disclosing certain aspects of the design in advance of the research could compromise the results, debriefing of participants after the research is completed becomes extremely important. If participants seem distressed by having been in the study, postresearch counseling should be provided (Bordons and Abbott 1999; Del Balso and Lewis 1997; Powell 1997;

Gliner and Morgan 2000; Rice and Ezzy 1999). In the case of ILI, if participants were in a group that did not receive instruction, this might be the point at which you could offer the instruction to those who feel they might profit by it.

Although the necessity to protect human subjects seems more clear-cut in medical and psychological studies, we must remember that harm can take the place of emotional or mental stress or financial hardships. Students and employees are on the list of protected subjects for very good reasons. Students might feel that participating in a study will affect their grades. Employees may feel their participation will reflect on their work status. UCLA's certification program, mentioned above, has separate sections for those engaging in medical research and those involved in social science research to help identify the issues that are associated with each type of research. Working with the IRB on your campus will ensure not only that your study is ethically designed and your subjects are protected but that your results can safely and legally be disseminated to your colleagues, who can benefit by the work you have accomplished.

## FINAL REMARKS

Research is hard, but it is also exciting. There is no question that it takes time, energy, and frequently money. But the benefits to both the profession and the individual are enormous. If you decide that the research path is for you, remember that you are not alone. Your literature review should point you to people with whom you can confer when the research road gets rocky. Look both inside librarianship and outside the field for assistance. Seek help from people within your own organization who have expertise in the various aspects of the research process. Consult with your institution's Internal Review Board to find out what you need to do in terms of using human subjects in your research. Although your research study may at times seem to be consuming your life, you will find the adventure well worth the effort. There is no bigger thrill than discovering something new, uncovering some bit of information that has previously gone unnoticed, or adding empirical support to show that some of our ideas or practices really work. And then, of course, there is the equally important discovery that other ideas or practices may not work as well as we had thought and need to be modified or discarded. Research in ILI can make a difference in how we understand the world around us and how we apply that new understanding to enhance learning as well as our interactions with our learners. The more we know about how ILI works, the better we can help people become more proficient information seekers, users, and evaluators.

## EXERCISES

1. Locate the Internal Review Board or Office for the Protection of Human Subjects at your institution. Review the mechanisms needed to obtain IRB approval for your research. If appropriate, take any training offered and/or required that would allow you to become certified at your institution as a researcher who is authorized to submit proposals for research using human subjects.

2. Obtain the most recent annual bibliography of ILI articles from *Reference Services Review* journal. Identify two or three research areas that interest you. Do a preliminary literature review on these areas and identify areas that might benefit from further research. Draft a possible hypothesis that addresses your research question.

3. Explore the research literature in education and psychology. Pay special attention to instructional techniques that explore improving learning outcomes. Can you adapt any of this research to the field of Information Literacy Instruction?

## READ MORE ABOUT IT

ALA. ACRL—Instruction Section—Research and Scholarship Committee. 2000–2002. *Research Agenda for Library Instruction and Information Literacy.* ALA 2002 [cited September 11, 2004]. www.ala.org/ala/acrlbucket/is/iscommittees/webpages/research/researchagendalibrary.htm.

Del Balso, Michael, and Alan D. Lewis. 1997. *First Steps: A Guide to Social Research.* Scarborough, Canada: Nelson.

Gliner, Jeffrey A., and George A. Morgan. 2000. *Research Methods in Applied Settings: An Integrated Approach to Design and Analysis.* Mahwah, NJ: Lawrence Erlbaum.

Glitz, Beryl. 1998. *Focus Groups for Libraries and Librarians.* New York: Forbes.

Librarians Association of the University of California. 2004. *Research Page.* University of California Office of the President (UCOP) 2003 [cited 5 July 2004]. www.ucop.edu/lauc/research.html.

Powell, Ronald R. 1997. *Basic Research Methods for Librarians.* 3rd ed. Greenwich, CT: Ablex Publishing Corporation.

Wilkinson, Leland, and Task Force on Statistical Inference. 1999. *Statistical Methods in Psychology Journals. American Psychologist*: 594–604.

# 6

## Grant Writing and Grants

*Money is better than poverty, if only for financial reasons.*

—Woody Allen

## WHAT ARE GRANTS?

Diversity grants, research grants, leadership grants, instructional improvement grants, professional development grants, grants for nonprofits, federal grants, innovation grants—are you dizzy thinking about all of the possibilities or just overwhelmed by the complexity and size of grant proposal requirements? You may be tempted to go for a grant if you have just gotten a new job, or if your responsibilities have changed recently and now include IL-related projects or research. Or you may have gotten some new and exciting ideas at a conference or by reading an article, a Web page, or a book. Giant books like the *Annual Register of Grant Support* and the *Foundation Directory* come out every year. Many granting agencies and groups offer tempting Web sites devoted to grants and grant proposal writing. So it is easy to think that you are missing out on lots of free money and the prestige you may earn by getting a grant. Are you? Maybe and maybe not.

What are grants, anyhow? An honor or a costly burden? Free money or more trouble than they're worth? Headaches, budgeting nightmares, wasted time and effort, or a way to test out a theory, create a product, get time off to write a book? Only for charitable groups, schools, teaching faculty, and scientists, or also for individuals, groups, organizations, and institutions?

Grants have grown enormously in number, size, and diversity over the past century (Kaplan et al. 1996; Print and Hattie 1997; Wilson 2003). They can be especially significant in enabling experimentation and change, even during negative budgetary times, and they can be very tempting, both for the money and for the prestige.

In this chapter we delve into competitive grants and grant writing for the purpose of research and other projects related to ILI. We do not cover grants for pure scientific research, although some of the topics covered can be applied to the pure sciences. Nor do we cover fundraising to support institutions or organizations, also known as "development." Our goal here is to demystify the grant process and provide tips and techniques to help IL librarians succeed in identifying feasible and useful projects, selecting appropriate grants, writing proposals, and following up on their own or in partnership with others. As you read this chapter, keep in mind that grant writing is a learning process. Each small success will help you feel more confident and can lead to further success, though you will need to get over that first hump, writing your first funded proposal. If you start with a small project and an internal funding source and show that you can fulfill the aims of the proposal, you will be well on your way to being an increasingly successful grant writer.

## WHAT IS THE HISTORY OF GRANT SUPPORT?

Grants have a long history. The first printed use of the word "grant" as a gift given by someone in charge of a fund appeared in 1380 (*Oxford English Dictionary* 2004). Formal, charitable giving dates back to Roman times, though private foundations developed much later (Kalas 1987).

> The concept of a private foundation, as it exists today, can be traced to the English Statute of Charitable Uses of 1601, which extended tax privileges to individuals or to groups providing financial support for service activities. . . . In essence, all organizations that form the basis for what is now known as the grant system can trace their roots to this statute. (Kalas 1987, p. 18)

The Lewis and Clark expedition received the very first U.S. federal funding in 1803, though the first official federal grant was awarded to Samuel Morse in 1842, "to field test the electromagnetic telegraph system and explore the feasibility of the system for public use" (Brewer, Achilles, and Fuhriman 1998, p. 1). It was after World War II, though, that large-scale U.S. federal support for individual and group research really took off, with the passage of legislation such as the National Defense Education Act (1958), the Civil Rights Acts (1957, 1960) and the Elementary and Secondary Education Act (1965) (Brewer, Achilles, and Fuhriman 1998). Many federal acts since then have provided support for various kinds of research and other activities, though there are many types of funding agencies besides the U.S. government.

## WHAT IS THE PURPOSE OF GRANTS?

Grant purposes vary widely. Some support training, while others support research or product development or a wide range of projects. Any librarian, with or without faculty status, can apply for grants. If you have faculty status, you are expected to conduct research, just as teaching faculty do. In fact, those who teach at all types of institutions, K–12 and up, often apply for grants to support research and teaching as a matter of course. Librarians in public libraries also apply for grants to support their work.

When you write a grant proposal, you are doing just that—putting forth your ideas and proposing support for them. You are trying to convince the reader that your ideas are important and useful. Most of all, you want a grantor to give you money to support your ideas (Kalas 1987). Grantors generally view grant making as a public good, and proposal developers, too, may see themselves as agents of social change (Kendrick 2001). Of course, views of what is actually beneficial or a public good can certainly vary from one individual or organization to another, and you may want to be careful about the purposes for which you will and will not seek funding (Becker 2003).

For ILI, the most important forms of grant funding are "seed" funding to start or pilot a project or product, full project/product support, and research (problem-based and theory-based) support. However, there are many important differences between project proposals and research proposals (both theory- and problem-based).

## HOW DO YOU COMPARE THEORY-BASED RESEARCH, PROBLEM-BASED RESEARCH, AND PROJECT PROPOSALS?

What is the difference between theory- and problem-based research? Theoretical research may deal with challenging or elaborating upon an idea or a widely held belief, while problem-based (or problem-solving) research is based upon real-world observation (Caplovitz 1983). New technology like Personal Digital Assistants (PDAs) offer many opportunities for problem-based ILI research funded by grants. Stephenson and Bartel are investigating the use of PDAs among medical and health researchers, in order to "understand how to accommodate the information needs of health scholars, and to work with these scholars to develop useful statistical health research materials for use in a PDA environment" (Stephenson and Bartel 2004). One type of research like this may lead to, or even derive from, the other. For instance, your study of real-world observations of how people use online IL tutorials may lead you to reexamine some long-held educational theories.

You may be able to get some internal funding for problem-based research, as long as the funder sees potential for direct benefits. If not, and if the effort is worthwhile, you may need to take the external funding route. If you decide to apply for external funding, be aware of the fact that there may be restrictions on who can apply for a research grant as the primary applicant or "Principal Investigator" (PI). Some institutions permit only faculty to apply for grants as PIs. If you are in an academic library and you do not have faculty status, you may not be permitted to serve as a PI on an external grant unless you can get special permission to do so. However, these restrictions may not apply to a project proposal, particularly one submitted to an internal funding source.

## WHAT DISTINGUISHES INDIVIDUAL FROM TEAM PROPOSALS?

Project proposals may be shorter than other kinds of research proposals (theory-based or problem-based) and generally require less effort to put together, as they may not require a research hypothesis, a literature review, and other paperwork, such as Internal Review Board (IRB)/Human Subjects Protection forms. You may be able to get internal funding from your own library or institution for a project. Writing these less complex and detailed proposals offers an excellent opportunity both to practice your grant-writing skills and to demonstrate that you can get funding and can complete a project as promised.

Generally, ILI librarians tend to focus on projects or on problem-based research and then use their research results to extrapolate, verify, or dispute educational theories, particularly those related to libraries, information research, and information resources. For example, as an individual ILI librarian, you may want to request support for a study to assess the effectiveness of your instructional materials or to develop a model ILI program or for a statistician to help you design and then analyze data on assessment of learning outcomes for an existing program. You may want to request release time to pay for a reference desk substitute so that you can spend more time on a special project, like developing an IL credit course. Or you may want to hire consultants to provide specialized training in game-based learning and Web site design. You could request help for your colleagues to learn and try out new instructional approaches, like using online chat and discussion boards in place of some in-person group instruction. Or you may want to hire an expert to help you design assessment instruments to measure the effectiveness of new instructional approaches. You could also request funding for a programmer to work on the technical aspects of an interactive tutorial, or a Web designer to improve the readability and usability of your ILI tutorial.

Teams of ILI librarians or entire libraries, institutions, and organizations may also want to apply for larger grants for IL purposes. For instance, the UC Berkeley Library, in collaboration with other campus groups, including the Office of Undergraduate Research, received a Mellon grant to fund a Faculty Institute on Undergraduate Research. Faculty participating in this institute receive $5,000 each and make four commitments, including one to "[d]evelop or revise a syllabus that incorporates a research project requiring the use of library resources," with the aim of integrating information literacy into their curricula (University of California, Berkeley 2004). Some libraries, such as the California State University Library, offer grants of their own for teaching faculty to work with librarians on this same sort of effort (California State University 2004).

## WHAT ARE THE BENEFITS OF GRANTS?

Tempting and exciting, grants offer many personal and institutional benefits, as well as fresh means of experimenting with, and achieving, IL goals. Any sort of grant funding offers a way to test out a new idea and even experiment with applying technology to solve a lingering problem. For instance, you might want to create a series of Web tutorials to help high school students and transfer students learn some information research basics before they come to a college or university campus library. Grant funding could help you begin by supporting creation of one or two tutorials to use as models for the remainder of the series. You may want to build in some assessment, as well. Once you have completed a grant-funded activity or project, you may also be able to present your work (successful or not) at conferences and publish articles, essays, or even a book about it. (See Gitlin and Lyons 1996, p. xiii, and Brewer, Achilles, and Fuhriman 1998, p. 5, for generic benefits of grants.)

Can you get grant funding for research or for a project? Yes! Should you do it? Maybe, if there is a real and pressing ILI problem and a need for special internal or external funding to address it. How do you find out about needs? Conduct a grants needs assessment and ask some hard questions before you plunge in.

CONSIDER THE POLITICS OF GRANTS

Why should you conduct a needs assessment before applying for a grant? Though there are many positive aspects to obtaining grants, think carefully! Before you jump on the grants "bullet train," consider the many steps involved just in preparing for, and writing, a grant proposal. First, you will need to identify and describe the important problem or issue you want to address. Then you will need to investigate and document any prior efforts to address this problem. Once you have laid this groundwork, you will need to come up with some new approaches. The next step is to consider whether you actually need a grant in order to try out one or more new approaches. As you think about applying for an internal or external grant, consider your capabilities, your available time and resources, and the kind of support you can expect of your group or institution. Once you have gathered all of this information, you will need to weigh it against the many drawbacks of grants.

*Needs Assessment Specifics*

A grants needs assessment is similar to general ILI needs assessments (see Grassian and Kaplowitz 2001), with additional focus on costs, time needed for all aspects of addressing the problem, potential partnerships, approvals, and so on. The following nine questions may help guide you in this process.

1. **Is there a problem, and if so, what is it?** Grantors reject about 44 percent of grant proposals because they are not convinced that the

---

**Figure 6–1**
**Grants Needs Assessment Questions**

---

1. Is there a problem, and if so, what is it?
2. What are the existing remedies for the problem?
3. Are the existing remedies working or not? If not, why not?
4. What ideas do you have for new or different remedies for this problem?
5. Would an infusion of funds help you implement these remedies?
6. How much time do you have to spend on writing and implementing a proposal to address this problem and then evaluating and disseminating the results?
7. What are your qualifications for addressing this problem, and should you do it on your own, or in consultation, cooperation, or collaboration with others? (Gitlin and Lyons 1996, p.136)
8. Will your administration support your grant application efforts to address this problem?
9. If your administration approves this effort, how can you find a good fit between your project or research and a granting agency and grant?

---

proposal addresses a significant problem (Coley and Scheinberg 1990). So, any discussion of the grant process must begin with why you would want to undertake a particular project. See Chapter 5 for ways to come up with ideas for grant-funded projects. Or consider brainstorming about IL services, issues, and problems you would like to solve or investigate. Consider selecting a new problem, one that has not been addressed before or has received little attention. This approach may get the attention of the granting agency and will make it a lot easier to supply supporting documentation regarding this gap, in a literature review (Caplovitz 1983, p. 10). Make sure it is a real and serious problem, which would benefit from some concentrated attention on a possible solution. Once you have selected a problem, describe it in detail, in writing, including any recent or cumulative changes that make it an acute problem now.

2. **What are the existing remedies for the problem?** Do an environmental scan and list the various approaches currently used to address this problem. For instance, what happens when dozens of students in research methods courses come to the reference desk one by one needing ILI? The IL coordinator contacts the instructor, discusses the problem,

and offers "one-shot" course-integrated group sessions, a Web page for the course, and a tailored exercise.

3. **Are the existing remedies working or not?** If not, why not? Classroom assessment techniques may reveal the effectiveness of one-shot group instruction sessions. When exercises are corrected, or if you give a pre- and posttest, you will get a good picture of performance and can hone in on common errors or common areas of misunderstanding. Analysis of these types of assessments will give you and grantors solid evidence as to whether or not existing remedies really are working and what areas need to be beefed up. Your creative ideas for fixing these specific problem areas can form the basis for your grant proposal.

4. **What ideas do you have for new or different remedies for this problem?** Do you want to do research or get support for a project or product? Think about what may be so special about your project or research. Do you want to try doing remote instruction for PDAs? Do you want to team up with a computer trainer to develop ILI for staff at your institution, organization, or corporation? What about partnering with librarians in other types of libraries to offer sequential ILI for your various populations? How would these groups benefit from these efforts? What is new and different about them, and what will happen if you do not get funded? For more ideas, see Chapter 5 in this book.

5. **Would an infusion of funds help you implement these remedies, and if so, approximately how much money will you need?** Grant proposals are rarely fully funded, so you need to show what can and cannot be accomplished with various amounts of funding. Break your project down into as many small functional parts as possible. Create an outline with a few words of description and justification for each segment or a label—essential, important, or nice-to-have. Then, try to provide an estimate for each segment so that even if you get just partial funding, you will be able to proceed.

6. **How much time do you have to spend?** This is a given: You will need to invest *a lot* of time and effort just to prepare an effective grant proposal and even more time to implement it, evaluate it, and report on, and disseminate, the results. After you have identified an important issue or problem, you must document the need to address it, come up with some alternative means of tackling the problem, including cost estimates, and then identify potential grantors and specific grants.

Now what? Next, you will need to decide who will actually write the proposal—one person or a group—and who will answer the grantors' questions, if need be, as they review your proposal. Someone will have to request official approval to apply for a grant, prepare required and optional supporting documents, get any necessary signatures, make copies of all documents for all partners (as well as for the granting agency), assemble documents in packets, and mail packets prior to the deadline.

Then, if you get a grant, as the principal investigator (PI) or Co-PI, you will probably have to do a lot of the work you described in your grant proposal. You may have to allot time for additional work, as well, including interviewing, hiring, training, supervising, and handling all administrative paperwork for others who may also contribute to the effort.

Are you finished? Not quite. After you have completed the grant-funded work, you will have to document what you actually did with the funds, and you will need to evaluate the effectiveness of your project or research study. You will then have an opportunity or, perhaps, an obligation to disseminate the results by preparing and delivering poster sessions or papers at conferences or by writing journal articles.

Each and every part of this process can take a lot of time, before and after you get any funding—if your proposal is approved, that is.

7. **What are your qualifications for addressing this problem, and should you do it on your own or in consultation, cooperation, or collaboration with others?** (Gitlin and Lyons 1996, p. 136). Because the entire grant process can be so time-consuming from beginning to end, you may want to consider working with others to research, write, implement, evaluate, and disseminate the results. Partnering with others, like businesses interested in improving the information literacy skills of their employees, may strengthen your grant proposal with faculty or with community organizations (Locke, Spirduso, and Silverman 1993, p. 159; Ruskin and Achilles 1995, pp. 35, 43). You can do an advanced search of Guidestar, a free national database of nonprofits, to identify organizations in your city or state that might be interested in partnering with you (2005). You may also want to join with those in other types of libraries to develop sequenced ILI grant projects and proposals. Broad community support can be very impressive to grant makers. If you decide to work with partners, though, be sure to work out in advance precisely how the partnership will operate. Clearly identify each partner's role. Will each partner bear an equal share of the work, any additional expenses, and responsibility for personnel? How will you work out problems if administrators and priorities change? What will happen if one of your partners does not contribute fully or in a timely fashion?

8. **Will your administration support your grant application efforts to address this problem?** Make sure that you have gotten administrative approval to proceed with the sometimes onerous and time-consuming task of preparing and then implementing a detailed proposal. Some administrators are very much in favor of grants, but if your proposal is not fully funded, they may not be willing to provide you with sufficient release time to complete the project. Most administrators will also want you to be particularly wary of making permanent or long-term commitments in grant proposals for limited-term grants, as your institution might have to absorb additional unexpected financial commitments, such as serial subscriptions and maintenance of Web sites. You will need to get a firm commitment in writing regarding administrative support and include it in your grant proposal as evidence of supplementary support, particularly if your administrators are pressuring you to apply for grants. Why would administrators do this? Some may view winning grants (or even applying for grants) as evidence of the fact that their library is forward-looking, that their librarians are risk-takers, experimenters, and on the cutting edge. These are good arguments for increased funding and support from their own higher-up administrators. However, if their staff is stretched too thin by too many poorly thought-out or poorly designed, and ill-supported projects and grants, there is great danger of decreasing morale, increased stress, and burnout among all staff in the library and one failed grant proposal/experiment after another. Wise and responsible administrators must pick and choose, asking hard questions about proposed grant-supported projects. They must strike a delicate balance between risk-taking and innovation through the use of grants, and support both for staff wanting to take the grants route and for the others who may need to take up the slack of day-to-day activities. This, in itself, offers an opportunity, if not a necessity, to review those day-to-day activities and priorities to see what can be done better and faster and with less staff and what can be done away with entirely. Again, an examination of this sort should be done in a participatory, democratic way, utilizing appropriate CPS techniques, if staff are to buy in and support changes.

9. **If your administration approves this effort, how can you find a good fit between your project or research and a granting agency and grant?** Check to see who is supporting published research and conference papers in your area of interest (Locke, Spirduso, and Silverman 1993). Most importantly, ask yourself whether or not your proposal fits in with the library's and institution's goals and, in turn, if they all fit the goals of the granting agency and that grant. How can you find out? Talk to whoever you can at the granting agency about previous grants

funded by this agency and study them. What made those grants successful? If this group funds research grants, find out how they define "research." (See Chapter 5.)

*Drawbacks of Grants*

Once you have answered all of these questions, you will have much of a grant proposal already outlined, if not fully written. (See sample proposals on the CD that accompanies this book.) However, if you have gotten this far, and you are still considering applying for a grant, consider further the many potential burdens and problems related to grants. The following eight caveats are drawn in part from a number of publications (Ruskin and Achilles 1995; Brewer, Achilles, and Fuhriman 1998; Sladek and Stein 1981; Gitlin and Lyons 1996).

1. **You will need to be very familiar with the grant requirements, as you may need to administer the grant yourself.** Check to see if your library and your institution or organization has a research office or grant administration office. If so, are there specific policies and procedures you need to follow in order to apply for a grant? Some institutions tack on a fixed percentage of the total grant to pay for services rendered by their grant administration office. If you must administer the grant yourself, this may include handling a large amount of paperwork, as well as payroll, bill paying, and keeping financial records. A grants office does cost, in terms of overhead, but often it earns its pay when it comes to external grants.

Research grants that involve testing or querying people may require Internal Review Board (IRB)/Human Subjects Protection (HSP) approval prior to submission, particularly if the investigators want to determine and disseminate generalizable results. IRB/HSP Committees will want to know details of recruitment, activities, risks (including psychological—e.g., anxiety), plans for ensuring informed consent, and so on. (Gitlin and Lyons 1996). They may need to review and approve any survey or assessment instruments you design, and they may require you to devise and provide an informed consent form to each person you ask to complete a survey or questionnaire. One of your administrative duties in relation to the grant may be to ensure that you are aware of, and are complying with, these requirements.

2. **You may need to conduct some sort of marketing or public relations effort both within and outside your own department.** You may need to help your colleagues and supervisors understand the benefits of having funding to pursue this particular project or research. In fact,

you should not embark on a grant proposal until you have a good idea of how your colleagues and administrators will view this activity, as it will take you away from some of your other duties, possibly burdening other staff. If your supervisor/administrator pressures you to apply for a grant to solve an instructional problem or to impress her or his supervisors, you should consider carefully how you can protect yourself from overwork and unrealistic expectations. Grants bring in funding, but they also require lots of extra work and may drain staff time and other resources unexpectedly. This can result in resentment and professional jealousy among colleagues, support staff, and even administrators (Kalas 1987). So, remember to do your political homework before seeking grant funding for any purpose. If you do not, you risk disapproval and rejection by your administration and/or your colleagues at work, not to mention a lot of wasted time and effort. See Chapter 3 for ideas on working with your colleagues.

During and after the grant period, you may have to market the completed product or problem solution. If you and your partners have created a new ILI tutorial, for instance, you will all have to work hard to inform your users of its benefits and make it stand out so people will make use of it.

3. **You will actually have to conduct the research or other work, and you would be well advised to keep track of your milestones and the time you are investing.** Even the smallest accomplishments can add up and make the entire project seem less overwhelming. Your supervisors may be particularly wary of the time investment needed for technology-related projects. It may help to track your time investment in small aspects of the project, as you will be able to show how you are building your skills and taking less time with each iteration or aspect of your project. It will certainly take time to keep track of accomplishments, though, and to report progress to administrators and colleagues alike.

4. **You may have to negotiate in a variety of areas, for supplementary funding, release time, and from colleagues, use of equipment, software and supplies, and space to store materials and records.** You may end up spending much of your own personal time on it if you do not receive any or enough release time to work on the project. This can cause stress and build resentment toward administrators, particularly if they have pressured you to apply for grants in the first place, as mentioned earlier. You will also have to keep track of expenditures and do your best to keep costs down and within the grant budget. Remember, if you are able to use equipment at work, that, too, is an in-kind contribution to the grant effort and should be listed as such in the proposal.

5. **You may need to persuade someone or some group to help you in one way or another.** Often, projects do not progress quite as expected, or partners may not be as devoted to the project as you are. If you reach this point, you will need to strategize about whom to ask for help, when, and how much. You may want to consider when would be the most politic time to ask for advice and to let your colleagues know about the significance of your project or research. The more you keep your colleagues informed and involve them in the process, the more support you are likely to receive and the more valuable feedback you are likely to get as well.

6. **You will need to evaluate progress, based on the timeline in your proposal.** You will need to decide if you and any other grant project staff are moving along at an appropriate speed, accomplishing all you have set out to, within the time frame you set in your proposal. If not, you may need to reassign work or take on additional work yourself that you may not have planned to do at first. What about working on grant projects on your time? You will very likely be putting in some or much of your own time on grant projects. This is a given and becomes more certain only if the project ends up ballooning in ways you did not predict or if you are unable to obtain sufficient release time to work on it. Keep a record of how much of your own time you are spending on a grant-funded project. Why? If you are successful, administrators may want you or other staff to pursue other grants to support projects or research, and they need to know the real cost in time to develop an interactive IL tutorial, for instance. Without this sort of information, they may have quite unreasonable expectations about what can be done in the future. So, be careful about what you wish for, as the "glow" of receiving a grant can fade quickly as your work and even personal time get eaten up to meet deadlines and show progress.

7. **You will need to evaluate the quality of your efforts and those of anyone working with you on the project and act as a personnel manager as well.** In addition to writing job descriptions, interviewing, and hiring grant-supported personnel (students or staff), you will need to train, supervise, and evaluate them. In essence, you will need to be a people manager as well as a project manager. You may need to set aside some time to work more closely with one or two people individually, to encourage them and help them with problem areas. From the very beginning, it is important to ensure that all participants in the project understand that it is a team effort and that the project will need to coalesce into a unified whole at some point, even if each person is working independently on a portion of it. This is delicate and tricky, as, above all, you need to maintain a team spirit and make sure that each member of the team knows that her or his contributions are much appreciated. You

may need to provide this reassurance throughout the project, as it is easy to lose track of the overall goal as you get caught up in the many small details of each aspect of a project.

8. **You may encounter unrealistic expectations from administrators.** Those unfamiliar with implementation details may assume that projects such as interactive IL Web tutorials are quick and easy to create. Quality products take time, so be sure you take the time to keep administrators informed of details and progress in meeting goals. Keep track of all time spent on each aspect of a project and prepare yourself, the project staff, and administrators for the possibility of unforeseen delays.

After reading all of this, with your eyes wide open, and with administrative approval, you have decided to apply for a grant—what next? Now you must spend some time researching granting agencies and specific grants.

## DISTINGUISH AMONG TYPES OF GRANTING AGENCIES

Find the right fit! Funding sources differ greatly in purpose, operation, and size, as well as number and dollar amount of grant projects funded. Some fund institutions, organizations, or groups only, while others fund individuals.

Many funding agencies offer more than one type of grant, and specific grants can vary greatly in size, scope, and format. Funding agencies often receive many more requests for funding than they can support, even if they wanted to fund every one of them. So, you may need to cobble together partial funding from a number of different sources, request funding for part of a project at a time, or be prepared to do a small pilot project first. Many grant agencies ask that you list all support already promised or formally committed for a particular project or study and may even give preference to those that have additional support committed (in writing) from one or more other sources. Grantors particularly like to see that the applicant has received prior grants and has successfully completed proposed projects or studies.

*Internal and External Grantors*

Most grant-funding sources fall into one of the following categories (*Annual Register of Grant Support* 2004; *Bread Game* 1973; Gitlin and Lyons 1996; Lauffer 1984; Peterson 2001). (See also *The Foundation Directory* 2005; Kiritz and Mundel 2002; and Peterson 2001 for detailed information on many different types of funding sources.)

| Internal Funding Sources | External Funding Sources |
|---|---|
| Corporate/Institutional (including departments on the local level) | Corporate/Institutional |
| Individual Endowments | Individual Endowments |
| | Professional Organizations (national, state, regional, and local) |
| | Private Foundations |
| | Community Foundations |
| | Family Foundations |
| | Government (all levels) |

*Corporate/Institutional*

Are you a first-time grant applicant? You may want to gain valuable grant-writing experience by beginning with internal grants offered by local grant sources. Various departments or units within your own library, organization, or institution (internal grants) may offer minigrants. Small pilot studies are ideal for this sort of grant. At UCLA, the Office of Instructional Development offers internal undergraduate instructional improvement grants available to librarians and faculty at all levels. One of the authors of this book and a UCLA Applied Linguistics/TESL lecturer together received a grant for $7,500 to develop an interactive information literacy tutorial originally intended for ESL students as a test population but now broadened to serve all UCLA undergraduates, though the full grant request was for $29,560 (Grassian 2004b).

*Professional Organizations*

If you get a minigrant of some kind and complete your project successfully, go up a step. Apply for a grant offered by a local or regional professional organization. The Librarians Association of the University of California (LAUC) offers research grants to UC librarians on a competitive basis, and the LAUC Web site provides a list of all LAUC grant proposals as well as copies of some proposals. (LAUC 2004a; ALA. ACRL. CARL n.d.). The California ACRL Chapter (CARL) also offers an annual grant for "research" (ALA. ACRL. CARL n.d.). See the CD that accompanies this book for the LAUC grant proposal that supported the authors' previous book, *Information Literacy Instruction: Theory and*

*Practice.* LAUC has also mounted a useful list of alternative research grant-funding agencies for librarians, called "Research Resources for Librarians" (LAUC 2004b).

On a larger scale, the American Library Association (ALA) also offers a number of different types of grants, including Diversity Research Grants, a program that began in 2002. The 2003 research topics included "Coalition Building across Affinity Groups" and "Cultural Biases in the Organization of Information." Though the research topics change from year to year, you may be able to develop an ILI proposal that would fit under either of these two topics (Davis 2003). The 2004 Grolier National Library Week Grant, sponsored by Scholastic Library Publishing and administered by ALA's Public Awareness Committee, provides $5,000 "for the best public awareness campaign during National Library Week . . . that promotes Equity of Access" (ALA 2003b).

## Foundations

Those who have already been awarded one or more grants may want to expand their funding horizons by investigating foundation grants or U.S. government grants. Just keep in mind that paperwork and other requirements generally increase dramatically with the size of the funding source, and each funding source may have a large variety of grant opportunities.

Foundations may be general-purpose or special-purpose. General-purpose foundations award grants in many different areas, in contrast to special-purpose foundations. Private foundations also offer grant opportunities for ILI. Often, they start as "individual endowments," like the Tocker Foundation, established in 1964 by Philip Tocker and his wife, Olive. Since 1992, this foundation has focused on accessibility issues for small rural libraries in Texas with populations of 12,000 or less (Tocker Foundation n.d.). You can search through the Foundation Center's Web site alphabetically or by topic, for annotated descriptions and links to private foundation Web sites (Foundation Center 2004b).

## Individual Endowments

These are grants that consist of the interest generated from a sum set aside or willed by individuals, usually for specific purposes or specific types of individuals or groups. For instance, the Carol McMurry Library Endowment funds Library Leadership Institutes in Wyoming (Wyoming Community Foundation, Carol McMurry Library Endowment n.d.). The

Bill and Melinda Gates Foundation has funded a number of library grants for Internet access. In June 2003, Libraries for the Future was awarded a three-year $1.05 million Gates Foundation challenge grant to go beyond providing access by developing a ten-state network. The network, *EqualAccess Libraries*, is "a new initiative designed to transform libraries into information and education centers, based on the needs of their communities" (Bill and Melinda Gates Foundation 2003). However, there may be many subdivisions under each type of granting agency, as well. For instance, the Mellon Foundation offers numerous grants in the areas of higher education, museums, public affairs, and so on (the Andrew W. Mellon Foundation n.d.). In the higher education arena, there are eight different Mellon Foundation grant subcategories, including "Teaching and Technology," which "supports promising research on university level online learning and distance education" (the Andrew W. Mellon Foundation 2003).

### Government Grants

The U.S. federal government supports a vast array of contract and grant funding for businesses, for institutions, for organizations and groups, and for individuals. When it comes to the U.S. federal government, the "superbeast" funding agency (*Bread Game* 1973), we must first distinguish between contracts and grants, as the rules and regulations for each differ. Contracts are for the purpose of procurement, while grants provide assistance (Kalas 1987). What does this mean?

#### PROCUREMENT

Federal agencies may want to acquire a product or learn something. When they do, they describe the details of what they want in the form of a Request for Proposals or RFP for a contract. Firms or individuals then submit proposals to meet the RFP. The agency reviews the proposals and contracts with the winner to provide a product or service that will meet the details of the RFP. Many rules and requirements must be met for contracts. Those who do not meet the contract requirements, including completion date, can be sued. The same is not true for grant recipients, as they may never complete their projects or studies and cannot be sued (Caplovitz 1983).

#### ASSISTANCE

The U.S. federal government offers grants to assist individuals, institutions, organizations, and groups in almost every area of enterprise and research. In fact, you may be quite surprised to discover the extent of this funding and how many programs, institutions, and individuals the federal government supports. For instance, the U.S. Institute of Museum and Library Services (IMLS) and the U.S. National Endowment for the Humanities (NEH) offer a number of grants for individuals and institutions, including some highly promising for ILI. The document "Keeping Librarians on Top of Their Game: Federal Grants for Continuing Education and Training of Library Staff" states that IMLS has provided $18 million in matching grant funding for four types of National Leadership Grants to libraries and museums:

1. Continuing Education, Curriculum Development and Training
2. Preservation or Digitization
3. Research and Demonstration
4. Library–Museum Collaborations (U.S. IMLS 2003)

In federal grant lingo, a "demonstration" is like a pilot project, in which a grantee hopes to demonstrate how something would work on a smaller scale and then project or propose its extension on a larger scale. So all of these types of grants offer great opportunities for ILI, with the exception of #2, preservation or digitization. Though #4 is the only type of grant that specifically mentions collaboration, you may want to consider a collaborative grant for #1 and #3 as well. In 2000 Durrance and Fisher-Pettigrew received an IMLS National Leadership Grant to develop means for librarians to evaluate their community outreach efforts. They developed a Web site called "How Libraries and Librarians Help," which includes "Putting Outcome Evaluation in Context: A Toolkit," as well as best practices and more (2000). You can find a monthly list of highlighted IMLS grant-funded projects on their Web site (U.S. IMLS 2004).

The U.S. National Endowment for the Humanities (NEH) offers many different grant opportunities for study, research, planning and implementation. Of particular interest for ILI are the "Implementation Grants for Humanities Projects in Libraries and Archives." All application materials are online, including criteria for awards and an online application form. NEH estimates that it will take you about two hours to complete an online cover sheet, and you can even "test-drive" the online application forms. The FAQ (list of Frequently Asked Questions) provides much useful information, including how much time it will take before you find out whether or not your grant has been funded—four to five months for consultation grant applications, and six to seven months for planning and implementation applications (U.S. NEH n.d.).

U.S. Department of Education grant opportunities may be of interest regarding IL, especially as part of overall outreach efforts for sequential IL programs, for instance: "21st Century Community Learning Centers" was appropriated close to $1 billion for 2004. "The focus of this program, re-authorized under Title IV, Part B, of the No Child Left Behind Act, is to provide expanded academic enrichment opportunities for children attending low performing schools" (U.S. Department of Education n.d.).

---

**Figure 6–2**
**Where Can You Find Lists of U.S. Federal Grants?**

---

1. Federal Grant Opportunities (FedGrant) (U.S. 2004a). Provides electronic forms for many grantors, as well as applicants, a means of searching for grants by keyword, and a grant applicant notification form.
   Example of grant listing:

   > Fund number : NEH-GRANTS-020204-005
   > Title : "Summer Stipends" (U.S., NEH 2004)
   > Brief Description: $5,000 grants to individuals for two-month full-time work research and writing related to the humanities, including curriculum development, studies of teaching methods, writing textbooks, and more.

2. Federal Register. "official daily publication for rules, proposed rules, and notices of Federal agencies and organizations, as well as executive orders and other presidential documents" (U.S. GPO 2004).
3. U.S. Department of Education—Grants and Contracts (U.S. Department of Education 2004a). Examples of grants for individuals include those for "Education Research," for those who "have the ability and capacity to conduct scientifically valid research" in such areas as education innovation reform (U.S. Department of Education 2004b).
4. Catalog of Federal Domestic Assistance (CFDA). Provides a database of funding programs available to state and local entities, along with guidance on proposal-writing (U.S. 2004b).

## HOW DO YOU FIND SPECIFIC GRANTS?

Once you have decided on the type of funding agency to investigate, the next step is to find specific grants that would be suitable. Worksheets and online tools can help!

Worksheets can be very handy when researching grants, to help you compare and keep track of grant requirements, especially deadlines. In fact, check the deadline first for each grant, as you find some that match your interest area. Then, be sure to allow plenty of advance time for planning. Write or type the deadline dates for particular grants in large block numbers and paste them up everywhere. A grant submitted after the deadline is usually rejected without a second glance, so you may want to create and maintain your own database or table or use print worksheets like Bauer's "Foundation Research Worksheet" (2000, p. 123) and "Corporate Research Worksheet" (2000, p. 128) to help you select appropriate grants with deadlines you will be able to meet. You may also be able to use some searchable grant databases to identify funding agencies and opportunities, though some, like SPIN, IRIS and COS are available only through institutional subscription (SPIN, n.d., IRIS 2005, COS 2005).

Make note of the funding range for each grant. Granting agencies that fund $100,000 to $1+ million grants are not likely to consider your proposal for an $8,000 grant, no matter how good it may be. So be sure to match your grant proposal to an agency with the appropriately sized resources and sizes of grants, as well as types of grants.

Pay attention to the date that funding begins. You may have to apply six months to a year in advance. A lot can change in a year, including estimated costs, not to mention new technology. At some point, though, you will need to estimate how much money you will actually need for your proposal. Fluctuating costs and unpredictable technology make it important, if not essential, to be prepared to scale back to just a portion of your original proposal, based on how much funding you receive in the end.

*Personal Contact Can Make a Difference*

Once you have a list of possible grants that fit your interest area and an estimated budget, you will certainly have questions. Some grants are designed with very specific projects or activities in mind, while others are more open-ended. Sometimes it is hard to tell exactly what the grantor wants. Grant guidelines may seem unclear or they may be vague or laden with jargon. If a granting agency funds "research," how do they define that term—pure research, applied research, research to prepare for, and write, a publication, or? (See Chapter 5.)

**Figure 6–3**
**FOUNDATION RESEARCH WORKSHEET**

**Foundation:** _____ **Deadline Date(s):** _____

Create a file for each foundation you are researching and place all the information you gather on this foundation in the file. Use the Foundation Research Worksheet to do the following:

• Keep a record of the information you have gathered
• Maintain a log of all telephone and face-to-face contact with the foundation
• Log all correspondence sent to and received from the foundation

Foundation address: _____    Name of contact person: _____
Telephone number: _____    Title of contact person: _____
Fax number: _____

Place a check mark (√) next to the information you have gathered and put in the file for the foundation.

___Foundation description from *Foundation Directory* or other source such as DIALOG, SPIN, etc.
   Note source: _____
___List of grants from IRS Form 990 or *Foundation Grants Index*
   Note source: _____
___Application information/guidelines
   ___sent for ___received
___Foundation's annual report
   ___sent for ___received
___Foundation's newsletter/other reports
   ___sent for ___received
___Foundation funding staff history
___Written summary of each contact made
___Grantor Strategy Worksheet

**Record of Face-to-Face and Telephone Contact:**

| Date Contacted | Contacted by | Foundation Contact | Results | Action |
|---|---|---|---|---|
|  |  |  |  |  |

**Record of All Correspondence Sent and Received:**

| Date of Correspondence | Purpose of Correspondence | Results/Action |
|---|---|---|
|  |  |  |

Reprinted with permission of John Wiley and Sons, Inc., from *Successful Grants Program Management*, by David G. Bauer, p.123. © 2000.

**Figure 6–4**
**CORPORATE RESEARCH WORKSHEET**

**Corporation:**_____ **Deadline Date(s):** _____

Create a file for each corporation you are researching and place all the information you gather on this corporation in the file. Use the Corporation Research Worksheet to do the following:

• Keep a record of the information you have gathered
• Maintain a log of all telephone and face-to-face contact with the corporation
• Log all correspondence sent to and received from the corporation

Corporation address: _____    Name of contact person: _____
Telephone number: _____    Title of contact person: _____
Fax number: _____

Place a check mark (√) next to the information you have gathered and put in the file for the corporation.

____Description of corporate giving program from *National Directory of Corporate Giving, Corporate Foundation Profiles,* or other source.
    Note source: _____
____Required proposal format, grant application/guidelines
____Corporate foundation's 990 IRS tax return
____List of corporate officers, sales representatives
    Note source: _____
____Corporate product information (the Standard Industrial Classification Code)
____Profits/dividends information–financial status of corporation from Dun and Bradstreet's *Million Dollar Directory,* credit rating service, or other source.
    Note source: _____
____Corporate funding staff history
____Information obtained from Chamber of Commerce (number of employees, payroll, etc.)
____Written summary of each contact made
____Grantor Strategy Worksheet

**Record of Face-to-Face and Telephone Contact:**

| Date Contacted | Contacted by | Foundation Contact | Results | Action |
|----------------|--------------|--------------------|---------|--------|
|                |              |                    |         |        |
|                |              |                    |         |        |

**Record of All Correspondence Sent and Received:**

| Date of Correspondence | Purpose of Correspondence | Results/Action |
|------------------------|---------------------------|----------------|
|                        |                           |                |
|                        |                           |                |

Reprinted with permission of John Wiley and Sons, Inc., from *Successful Grants Program Management,* by David G. Bauer, p.128. © 2000.

So, save yourself a lot of time, trouble, and embarrassment. Before you settle on which grants to pursue, ask questions. Talk in person or by phone to someone of authority within the granting agency. When you do, ask questions about previously funded grants, their purpose, the timeline, and the amount of funding. Ask to see some proposals that have been funded by that agency in the past. This step can save you a lot of time and trouble, as you will learn what sorts of proposals have been funded and what the granting agency wants to see in a proposal. Of course, when inquiring about grants and requirements, remember to be courteous, even if you have to go through many-branched voice mail systems, many people, and many steps to get to someone who can answer your questions.

Talking to grant representatives in advance is not cheating. It is just doing your homework (Kreeger 2000). In fact, grant administrators really appreciate it when you check with them in advance on what their agency wants to see in a grant and what it does not want to see, as reviewers would much rather spend time reviewing strong applications than those that are ill-prepared, incomplete, or poor fits with the goals of the grant and the granting agency.

## WHAT DO REVIEWERS LOOK FOR?

Reviewers want proposals that match the grantors' goals (McGowan 2003). They want succinct proposals that grab you, that are written in clear and simple language, with realistic budgets and timetables. You must assume, though, that anyone reading your proposal has little or no knowledge of its subject matter and the need for your project. Make your proposal look clean and attractive. It should be double-spaced, with no typos, and with plenty of white space. Because individuals reviewing a proposal may come with differing areas of expertise and backgrounds, it is important to cover both the qualitative and quantitative aspects of your project in your proposal (Caplovitz 1983).

Reviewers will look for many of the following features, drawn in part from a number of publications (Bauer 1998; Brewer, Achilles, and Fuhriman 1998; Coley and Scheinberg 1990; Lauffer 1984; Molfese, Karp, and Siegel 2002; Ruskin and Achilles 1995). Note that there are many parallels here to research proposals and that research proposals are often supported by grant funds. (See Chapter 5 for details.) If you are applying for a grant in support of research, you may certainly want to repurpose or adapt your research proposal as necessary, to suit the differing requirements or focuses of particular grants. However, grants may also be for projects, as well as for problem-based or theory-based research, as mentioned earlier in this chapter.

• **Immediate indication of the significance, urgency, and severity of the problem and the impact of the solution.** Does the project have merit, and is it needed? Is it imaginative, innovative and important? Speak positively, but remember to provide supporting evidence. Conduct a survey and use the results—nothing speaks louder to some funders than quantitative results that clearly indicate a need or a gap. Indicate the project's potential as a model or as a pilot study, which may be extended, expanded, and applied in other circumstances or populations to good effect. How will the project increase the knowledge base in a particular field? Have you provided sufficient justification for it?

• **Quality of planned program or project (design) and quality of management plan.** Does it seem likely that you will be able to accomplish the goals of your proposal? Write a simple, clear description of the program and methodology. Show that you propose to use a variety of approaches and that you have investigated and will make good use of any available community resources. ("Community" may be taken broadly or narrowly here.) Indicate how you will evaluate the quality of project contributions on an ongoing basis and monitor progress on the funded proposal. Indicate the benefits but also the drawbacks of your proposal—its feasibility and risk factors. Ask the reviewers to consider what will happen if your proposal is not funded.

Consider offering an alternative plan (Molfese, Karp, and Siegel 2002) or a staged plan with separate descriptions, plans, and budgets for each stage (Caplovitz 1983). Some applicants may be afraid to do this, thinking that it is an invitation for incomplete funding. Most grant proposals are not fully funded anyhow, so you will probably need to figure out in advance what you will do with partial funding. By proposing a multipart project, you will not be left in an all-or-nothing, take-it-or-leave-it position if you do not get full funding. In addition, you will not be committing yourself to a large project that receives only partial funding. In any case, do not promise more than you can realistically achieve with the kind of funding you get. Partial funding can be much better than no funding, or much worse, depending on how realistic you are with the funders, with administrators, with colleagues, and with other project staff.

• **Project Personnel, preferably those with a proven track record.** Are you and the other project staff qualified to do the work? Indicate why you are the best person to undertake this project (Gitlin and Lyons 1996). In addition, remember to include two- to three-page résumés for each of the project staff, including yourself, with narrative summaries or biographical sketches at the beginning of each résumé, tailored to the needs of the proposal and positions each project staff member will hold (Kendrick 1997). Or write a brief one-paragraph description of each person's educational qualifications, including degrees, instruction experience, major publications, and any other related research efforts undertaken. Remember, grantors like to see that you have received other grants and support from others, so provide information on each person who will be involved in the project, particularly evidence of her or his expertise and ability to manage and bring other projects to fruition/completion.

• **Attention to cultural diversity/sensitivity issues.** Though it may not be a stated requirement for all grants, it is important to consider these issues in relation both to the problem and to your proposed solution. Will your ILI project address deep-seated needs of underserved minority groups or individuals? Have you accounted for cultural differences in your project design and language? If there is a sizable Spanish-speaking community in your area, for instance, have you included a funding request for Spanish-language translation of your ILI materials and testing among Spanish-speaking community members?

• **Facilities and equipment.** Indicate what you will be permitted to use in-house without charge, including your desktop computer, a photocopier, a scanner, a fax machine, your desk telephone, meeting space, work space, and supplies. These resources actually count as donations toward the project and may make any requests for additional equipment seem more reasonable. Documenting them will also make your proposal stronger, because you can list your institution, organization, or corporation as a grant proposal partner.

• **Adequacy of support.** Remember, your own time is not free. If you get time off (release time) from your employer, the sponsoring organization or institution to work on this project, include the dollar equivalent of your salary and benefits as "in-kind" support from your institution. The same is true for other project staff.

It can only help to have strong commitments from other institutions, groups, or individuals as well. Partnerships offer an excellent opportunity to demonstrate support from other groups or institutions that serve the same population. Interested groups or institutions can be full partners by providing staff time, money, equipment, space or other types of support. Or they may provide letters of support that indicate the need for the project and how it will benefit them and their constituents.

If approved by library administration, grant application partners like computer center staff, faculty, or schools can support mutually beneficial endeavors. Multnomah County Library in Portland, Oregon, developed a close relationship with 250 K–12 schools in the county in support of library media specialists (Minkel 1999). This is a good example of local collaboration, but you can also collaborate more broadly. For example, Bransford, Brophy, and Williams suggest looking into organizations like the Center for Innovative Learning Technologies, whose goal is to increase collaboration on issues related to technology and learning and who provide seed grants for this purpose (2000). In addition, every U.S. state has Federal LSCA (Library Services and Construction Act) funds which "provide formula grants to the States to assist public libraries in establishing, expanding and improving library services" (U.S. n.d.), and LSTA (Library Services and Technology Act) grant funds focused on information access and empowerment through technology. LSTA funds are now administered through the Institute of Museum and Library Services (U.S. IMLS n.d.). Those who control any of these funds may be amenable to multitype library grant requests, such as school and public library collaborations. The U.S. Institute of Museum and Library Services is another avenue for grants for libraries and also encourages library/museum collaboration proposals (n.d.). The U.S. Department of Education offers technology innovation challenge grants (2000). For large projects consider applying for other types of federal or nonprofit corporation grants (Kight and Perry 1999). For small projects, consider establishing ties with local businesses or academic departments at a college or university in the area. Finally, watch for staff changes in all of these situations, as there may be new opportunities for partnership, collaboration, and grantsmanship.

• **Cost-effectiveness.** Construct a reasonable, detailed timeline and indicate how you will keep track of your progress (milestones). If it succeeds, can your project serve as a model for others? (Foundation Center 2004a) If you can convince reviewers that it can, you will have a good cost-effective argument for funding your proposal. This is very tempting, but it could backfire. The "model" argument is fairly common, and researchers in various disciplines propose models of various types, but how many models are actually adopted and used widely? Avoid stating that your project will be a model for all other projects or programs like it, unless you really think it will be so new and different, with such common applicability and adaptable design, that many will want to emulate it. Instead, suggest that your project can be a pilot, and if it is successful, it or some of its features could serve as a model for others. Be specific about which others and how and provide some evidence that this is a distinct possibility.

Hurry up and wait. Even if you take all of this into account, deadlines may still trip you up, as "There is no such thing as a late proposal" (Brewer, Achilles, and Fuhriman 1998, p. 17). If you submit a proposal after the deadline, the grantor will toss it or return it to you, unopened. So, be sure to follow mailing instructions and meet those deadlines! Of course, some grants are available year after year and often maintain the same deadline each year. So if you miss a deadline one year, you could apply for the same grant the following year.

After you have submitted a grant, you will probably have to wait a number of months or even a year before you find out if your grant has been funded, even when you submit your application on time. During this time the granting agency may send you some questions or some requests to make alterations and resubmit your proposal. Then, even if your grant is funded, it may be a number of months before you will have access to the funds. So, you need to plan way ahead for grant funding, often a year or more in advance of the start of a project, especially for onetime grants that are not available at repeated intervals.

WHAT STRATEGIES HELP IN WRITING THE PROPOSAL?

Granting agencies generally look first at the proposal topic, then at the amount of money requested, and then at the qualifications of those requesting funding.

So, market your ideas! Almost anyone can prepare a proposal that meets all the requirements of a particular grant and that has all the required pieces. However, if you want to get funded, you will need to stand out from the rest of the applicants who have also submitted all of the required pieces. Your job is to grab their attention. Let the granting agency know how this project differs from any similar projects, why it is needed, what success will mean, and why your proposal is a valuable, cost-effective contribution.

It might help to think of your grant proposal as a kind of short story, where the first few lines need to suck the reader in so she or he feels compelled to read to the end and to fund your project (Caplovitz 1983). Cut out needless words and overblown language and make your proposal as succinct and crystal clear as possible. If you are unsure of something, do not put it in your proposal, unless it is a research question you are investigating. Be specific. If your proposal is vague, the granting agency will wonder what it is being asked to fund and why and will set your proposal aside in favor of the competition.

In other words, let your enthusiasm for the project shine through but back it up with documentation about need and significance and focus on the positive. "Try to elicit admiration, not pity" (Solomon 2001, p. 45). You may have tried very hard to solve the problem of hundreds of unprepared high school students asking for very basic help at the reference desk one by one each Saturday. What have you tried so far, what has succeeded, and how is this proposed solution different? What makes this a cost-effective solution? If your project succeeds on a pilot basis, how could it be extended in a cost-effective manner? Why are you and the project team qualified to address this problem, and what is your project completion track record? Remember that individuals reviewing a proposal may come with differing expertise and background, so it is important to cover both the qualitative and quantitative aspects of your project in your proposal (Caplovitz 1983).

Bear this in mind, though: Grantors are rather skeptical of grant proposals, probably because of the large numbers of proposals they receive. They are keenly attuned to weak arguments, lack of substantiating data, overblown claims and inflated budgets relative to the work proposed. So, be sure of what you say, provide data to back it up, and avoid making grandiose promises. As noted above, a better approach would be to start small and focus on your proposal as a pilot project that, if successful, could be extended in scope or scaled up to meet larger needs and a larger population.

Beware of jargon and do not make assumptions. Be aware of the review process for grants. Generally, grants are reviewed by a group of people within the granting agency or by an external panel of reviewers recruited for this purpose. Grant reviewers will need to understand every word of your proposal and grasp its significance. You should assume that they know little or nothing about your field. Be wary of jargon and be sure to describe issues, themes, and previous or related projects in clear and simple terms. Remember to spell out acronyms the first time you use them and provide a glossary of terms that may be new to the reviewers.

All of these points should be useful to you as you prepare multipart grant proposals.

## WHAT ARE THE PARTS OF THE TYPICAL GRANT APPLICATION?

It is easy to feel overwhelmed by the many required pieces of most grant proposals. Though you will need to work hard on each part, effective proposals can be short. For instance, Caplovitz offers a powerful two-page sample proposal, "Ecological Bases of Racial Experiences and Attitudes," along with a brief analysis (1983, pp. 20, 22). He also offers a rare look at one of his own losing proposals, "The Causes and Consequence of Divorce," submitted twice and turned down both times. The reviewers' "pink sheets" (rejection comments) and his own responses to them offer quite valuable insights into the process. He concludes that one must be attuned to the sophistication and interests of the reviewers, especially when it comes to descriptions of methodologies (including forms of statistical analysis). He also admits that in the end, even if one covers all points completely, there is still a good possibility that almost any given proposal will not be funded (Caplovitz 1983). Locke, Spirduso, and Silverman provide sample nonlibrary-related proposals annotated with helpful comments (1998, pp. 185–296); see especially Proposal 3: "Quasi-Experimental Design: Teaching Children to Question What They Read: An Attempt to Improve Reading Comprehension through Training in a Cognitive Learning Strategy" (1998, pp. 249–270). As you read this lengthy proposal, you may ask yourself over and over, "What is the technique the author proposes to test?" The answer does not appear until page 256, far into the proposal. Coley and Scheinberg provide separate portions of a sample proposal, with detailed critiques following each one, including "Agency Capability," "Needs/Problem Statement," "Goals and Objectives," "Project Activities," "Evaluation," and "Timeline" (pp. 112–124). They contend that omitting relevant information is the biggest problem in proposal writing, another excellent reason to ask someone with no prior knowledge of the topic to read your proposal. It does help to pay careful attention to the multitude of details, large and small, that constitute the typical grant proposal.

How should you structure your proposal application? Grant proposals do not follow a single format but usually include vital components that summarize, provide detailed explanations and justification, list project staff, and a detailed budget.

---

## READ THE GRANT GUIDELINES CAREFULLY AND THOROUGHLY.

---

These words are in caps, underlined, and in a box for a reason. It is easy to make assumptions based on grant titles, granting agencies' reputations, and grantors' potential interest in the promise of your grant proposal. Do not make assumptions about any part of a grant proposal. The parts required and the order in which they need to appear may vary widely from one grant to another. When you read the grant guidelines, you will find out which types of documents are required for a particular grant, which forms must be filled out and signed by appropriate individuals, the order in which these documents must appear in the proposal packet, their titles, their length, what must be included and what is optional, and the deadline for submission. If you need to get signatures, allow time for lobbying for support, for preparing the documents for signature, for submitting the documents to be signed, for following up to make sure they are signed, and for making the required number of copies, including one for yourself.

Grant proposals fail for many different reasons, often for more than one reason. So, the message here is read, read, read, and carefully study the grant requirements, word for word, before, during, and after you have prepared your grant proposal and before submitting it.

It helps to use the same language the granting agency uses in its call for proposals. As mentioned earlier in this chapter, you may want to create or adapt a checklist of required items for each grant, modeled on such worksheets as Bauer's worksheets (2000, pp. 123, 128). If you do this, leave a column at the left where you can check off each item as you complete it. Remember to tailor each application to the funding agency to which you are applying, break your proposal into manageable, separately fundable parts, and include a backup plan of what you would do if you only get partial funding, or if the work does not pan out as expected (Kreeger 2000).

Many how-to publications regarding grant writing list the common elements of a grant proposal (*The Bread Game* 1973; Brewer, Achilles, and Fuhriman 1998; Caplovitz 1983; Coley and Scheinberg 1990; the Foundation Center 2004a; *A Guide to Research . . .* 1983; Lauffer 1984; Locke, Spirduso, and Silverman 1993). Following is a list of the six most common proposal components. Again, this list parallels but is not necessarily identical to the list of research proposal components. If you have already written a research proposal, or even an internal project proposal, match up its sections to the components below, check the interest areas for each grant for which you are applying, and tweak those sections accordingly. This is actually an important and useful exercise, as it allows you to see rather quickly whether or not you have a good grant proposal fit for your research or project interests.

**1. Cover sheet or cover letter:** Many granting agencies require grant applicants to fill out a cover sheet form which has many different sections.

---

**Figure 6–5**
**Parts of the Proposal**

1. Cover sheet or cover letter
2. Executive Summary
3. Project Narrative or Research Plan
4. Budget summary and detailed budget with rationale
5. Project staff
6. Appendixes

You must be sure to fill out each and every section in the form, as required, or your proposal will not even make the first cut. Some grantors simply list the information they require and ask for a cover sheet but do not provide a form. Some request an Executive Summary.

**2. Executive Summary:** Begin with a short, descriptive title. Then provide a clearly written, attention-getting abstract or summary of your proposal, composed of about 60 percent facts and 40 percent "spin" designed to engage the reader (Kendrick 1997). Include the following:

- a brief description of the problem
- the significance of the problem and who is affected by it
- a brief history of other attempts to address the problem (if any)
- why those attempts may have failed partially or wholly
- a succinct description of the solution you propose, with a brief timeline
- why and how it will alleviate the problem, that is, your goals and objectives
- if and how the results may be generalizable (applicable to a larger population)
- how much it will cost (total amount requested)

Following the abstract, list the names, addresses, and signatures of requestors or principal investigator (PI) and co-PI, if any. Then list the name(s) and address(es) of the sponsoring institution(s), if any. Finally, provide a brief list of personnel (staffing needed) along with their qualifications including the PI and co-PI, if any.

**3. Project narrative or research plan:** Describe your project or research in detail in this section but make it interesting, even gripping, or you will lose the grant reader's attention. Depending on the grant, this section could be fifteen to forty pages long (Caplovitz 1983) and, if for research, could be an adapted version of your research proposal.

Begin with a brief introduction and overview listing your specific aims. Then state the need or problem and the significance of your proposal or project in more detail than you did in the abstract. Consider including detailed demographic information regarding those most affected by the problem, such as ethnicity, language, and income (Coley and Scheinberg 1990). Be clear about the nature of the problem, or you may end up among the 33 percent of proposals rejected for lack of clarity about the problem (Coley and Scheinberg 1990).

Continue by providing historical rationale. Explain why and for how long the problem has existed. Identify approaches and solutions to date, as well as limitations. Include a literature review of the most significant materials, including both recent and older items that help illustrate the need and/or gap you intend to fill. Insufficient documentation of the problem accounts for over one-quarter of proposal rejections (Coley and Scheinberg 1990; Gitlin and Lyons 1996).

Next, list your detailed goals and objectives, followed by a detailed description of the methodology you intend to use and why it is appropriate. Include procedures, implementation plan, control and decision-making process, and a timeline. About one-third of proposals are rejected because the methods are unclear or do not convince reviewers that the proposed method is appropriate or fits the scope of the problem (Coley and Scheinberg 1990; Gitlin and Lyons 1996).

Now, detail your project evaluation plans. About one-quarter of proposals are rejected because they do not include clear program evaluation plans (Coley and Scheinberg 1990) or because their objectives are unclear or do not seem to be measurable (Gitlin and Lyons 1996). Describe how you will determine whether the grant goals and objectives have been met and whether or not the work was completed as expected, within the proposed timeline. About 20 percent of proposals are rejected because the timeline seems unreasonable (Coley and Scheinberg 1990). It would be helpful to the reviewers (and later to you) to list benchmarks or indicators that will tell you what you have achieved along the way (Solomon 2001). You may even want to go much further and provide the kind of information Coley and Scheinberg include in their ten-part "Outline for an Evaluation Plan," including a description of the evaluation design, a sampling plan, data analysis techniques, and reporting procedures (1990, p. 77).

Then, state how you plan to disseminate the results of your project. Will you write an article and submit it to a journal or magazine? Will you write a procedures manual or training manual for others who may carry on your work or extend it? Will your project result in other "deliverables," such as interactive Web pages, pathfinders, tutorials, or point-of-use guides? Will you write a report to the grantor? Frequently, this is a requirement of the grant.

Finally, indicate what will happen to your project when the grant funds run out. About half of all proposals are rejected because they lack a "plan for self-sufficiency" (Gitlin and Lyons 1996). How will it be maintained? Will someone need to do more research? Most journal articles reporting on the results of research studies identify related areas or questions needing further study. If more funding will be needed to maintain and continue the project (beyond the scope of this grant), describe any plans you may have to gain further support.

**4. Budget summary and detailed budget with rationale:** Have you grabbed reviewers' attention with an urgent IL need? This is good, but it is not enough. Now you must tell them how much it will cost to meet that need and why it is reasonable, as 43 percent of grant proposals are rejected because applicants have been unclear about how the money will be used (Coley and Scheinberg 1990). So, spend some time working on the budget estimate. Make it easy to read and easy to follow (Solomon 2001). Grantors read the budget summary and narrative carefully to see what can be cut without destroying the entire project. They will be looking for flexibility, meaningful justification, sufficient details, a project that is reasonable, not too ambitious, and cost-effective (Sladek and Stein 1981).

Four funding categories usually appear in grant budget requests: direct costs (including salaries, benefits, equipment, and supplies), indirect costs (including utilities, maintenance, and janitorial services), cost sharing (matching funds), and program income (if any) (Sladek and Stein 1981). Your institution may have a set percentage for some of these categories, but the grant guidelines should tell you what kinds of expenses you may or may not include in your proposal.

Some expenditures may be unallowable under the conditions of a particular grant or a particular granting agency. For example, the U.S.

---

**Figure 6–6**
**Common Grant Proposal Budget Items**

Following is a list of possible budget items drawn in part from several different sources (Brewer, Achilles, and Fuhriman 1998; Lauffer 1984).

- Personnel, including salaries and percent of full-time equivalent (FTE)
- Benefits
- Consultants and honoraria
- Operating expenses
- Facilities
- Equipment
- Supplies
- Travel and per diem
- Services
- Postage
- Telephone
- Stipends

government has four "allowability" tests: "the cost must: (1) be reasonable; (2) be allocable; (3) be consistently treated; (4) conform to any limitations or exclusions in the sponsored agreement" (Sladek and Stein 1981, p. 182). Document all expenditures and show how the money was used, in any case, or you may not be reimbursed during or following the funding period.

To reiterate, read the grant guidelines. Then make a list of the types of budget items you need to include. Think about what you need to get the job done, why you need funding at all and at what level, and the range of funding provided in the past for this particular type of grant. Include a budget narrative that describes and explains briefly the significance of each proposed expenditure, as well as other options you may have already explored. Describe the most important pros and cons of these alternatives and why you settled on the items you are proposing (Sladek and Stein 1981). If you ask for release time for yourself, request funding for a replacement at a lower level than your own salary. For instance, you might ask for ten hours of release time a week for a six-month period, and request ten hours a week for a lower-paid library school student to replace you at the reference desk for those six months.

Again, if you are given release time (leave with pay) to work on this project, your salary and benefits count as support and should be calculated and included in your proposal. You may also want to discuss other budget items as well, including institutional support, direct, indirect, or overhead costs (including facilities, equipment, and other support), in-kind (noncash) contributions and costs, and any out-of-pocket expenses you anticipate (Sladek and Stein 1981). Over 40 percent of grant proposals are rejected because they do not identify commitment and support to be provided by others (Gitlin and Lyons 1996).

**5. Project staff:** As we mentioned earlier, you will need to provide a complete list of project staff along with their qualifications to do the work proposed. In addition, indicate who will handle the grant funds and their qualifications for doing so. Remember to consider budgeting for consultants for various aspects of the project. Skilled consultants can be highly useful in designing valid questionnaires, for example, or in doing statistical analyses of survey results. If you do include one or more consultants, provide full information about the individuals you would hire, including their names, their expertise, their institutional or organizational affiliations (if any), and an estimate of their fees.

**6. Appendixes:** Consider adding documentation to illustrate the unusual nature of your proposal, such as additional statistics and interviews of potential individual grant recipients, and letters of support (with contact information) from groups that would benefit as a result of the grant project (Ruskin and Achilles 1995). Also, be sure to include here any necessary approval signatures, including internal administrative approval and any required Internal Review Board/Human Subjects Protection approvals. Remember, it takes time to get approvals, and they always need to be in writing, so plan ahead, and keep in mind that IRB/Human Subjects Protection procedures and regulations may vary somewhat from one institution or organization to another. For example, in addition to review of full research studies, some institutions require IRB/Human Subjects Protection review for each and every survey or questionnaire distributed to anyone, internally or externally.

## WHAT DO YOU DO BEFORE SUBMITTING THE FINAL PROPOSAL?

Should you prepare these documents in the order listed above? The answer? READ THE GRANT GUIDELINES.

You have all of the pieces of your grant proposal, in the required order. Are you finished now? Not yet. Get one or two colleagues to read your proposal for typographical, grammatical, procedural, content, or other errors. Ask them to play the role of reviewers and give you feedback on each of the items reviewers generally look for listed above.

## WHAT IF THE GRANTORS ASK QUESTIONS ABOUT YOUR PROPOSAL?

This is a good sign! It means that you have passed the first review and that the reviewers are considering recommending some funding, that is, if you answer their questions satisfactorily. It does not help to get angry with reviewers for asking you questions about your proposal. We are all so familiar with our own areas that it is easy to use jargon unintentionally and to make assumptions about various aspects of our projects. If you truly want to be funded, you must be prepared to compromise by limiting the scope of your proposal (Sladek and Stein 1981; Stewart and Stewart 1984). So, prepare for questions and negotiation, rather than just "winging it." Know all of the details of your proposal and be prepared to justify each or to compromise, diplomatically and rationally.

Remember, any changes you agree to as a result of a compromise or negotiation with the grantor will directly affect what you can expect to accomplish. Also, this clarification and negotiation process may even continue through the final steps of the process. It can be quite delicate, as you must balance what you truly need in order to accomplish the task at hand with the available resources. If you do not have sufficient resources, you should cut back on your plan, slice it into pieces, or even turn down the grant on the basis of insufficient funding to carry out the plan.

## BESIDES CELEBRATING, WHAT DO YOU DO IF YOU ARE FUNDED?

*But What if You Get Only Partial Funding?*

More often than not, grants receive only partial funding. Why does this happen? There may be a lot of competition for a particular grant during a given year, and unfortunately, there is no way to predict this. Your budget may seem padded and not well justified. You may have made some mathematical errors in calculating your budget. Or, it may just be the "Grantor's desire to demonstrate power" (Sladek and Stein 1981, p. 80).

In some cases you may be able to negotiate for additional funding right away. Prior to the widespread use of e-mail and fax, three-quarters of all grant negotiations were conducted by telephone. Today, e-mail and fax are much more efficient and cost-effective means of negotiating. Sometimes the grantor will ask the applicant to submit a revised proposal that will cost less and perhaps be smaller in scope. In other cases, the granting agency may specify which portions of a grant they will not be able to fund. You may then choose to negotiate in a variety of ways, including substituting one chunk of your project for another, renting as opposed to buying equipment, purchasing used, rather than new equipment, or getting donations (Sladek and Stein 1981).

It is possible that you may be awarded partial funding with no possibility of negotiation. You then face a difficult decision. Do you want to accept the funding granted and work on the project anyway or reapply at a later time? Or should you turn it down and hope for a more favorable response from a different granting agency? These are the kinds of decisions best made in concert with your supervisor and other administrators. You may be able to negotiate with your administrators for some supplementary funds and some release time to allow you to work on this project, even without full funding. You may also be able to apply for other grants, using this partial funding as evidence of matching support.

If you submitted your proposal as a staged project with plans and budgets for each stage, it will be much easier for you to decide which portions of your proposal you will be able to complete with the funding you have received. If not, create your own separate plan B! Break your proposal down into ordered steps. Consider which steps you could accomplish as a chunk, given partial funding, and draw up a timetable. If you take this approach, you will need to indicate what is absolutely essential in order to do any of it. Try to maintain a balance among the factors of performance, cost and time (Brewer, Achilles, and Fuhriman 1998). Be diplomatic and positive but make clear to the granting agency that you will be able to accomplish only part of your original proposal if you do not get full funding, and you may not be able to complete the entire project during the time period described. However, if you can complete the first chunk well with the funding you get, on time and within budget, you can use that as strong evidence to request additional funding for the remainder of the project or for the next chunk.

The key factor is whether or not you will be able to accomplish what you agree to, given the funding and support you get. If not, then you should consider turning down an underfunded grant.

### What if You Get Funded for More Than You Requested?

This happens on rare occasions, usually because the scope of the work proposed has expanded unexpectedly or because of budget errors, increased costs, or changes in regulations (Sladek and Stein 1981). The same caveat applies for extra funding as for partial funding. Do not take a bigger bite than you can chew and swallow. Make sure that you check with your administrators and colleagues and agree to accomplish only what you can handle.

### What Happens After You Are Funded?

First, celebrate! Then face facts. After you receive grant funding, you will need to begin implementing your proposal, so have your plans all set up and ready to go in advance. What can you actually start doing as soon as you find out you have been funded? If you have planned ahead, you should be prepared to hire part- or full-time staff or students to work on your grant project. Before you have the funds in hand, you can prepare job postings (you may have to make some adjustments if you get only partial funding), interview questions, a way to keep track of transactions and balances, a list of implementation procedures, a list of documents that need to be retained, and an outline of items to be covered in a final report to the granting agency (Brewer, Achilles, and Fuhriman 1998).

*Can You Change the Terms of the Grant during the Funding Period?*

Beware—this could be a problem. Some granting agencies are sticklers about the terms under which a grant is approved and will not permit any changes, while others allow more leeway. Once you have received a grant, though, you may be able to influence the grant maker's thinking, focus, process, and documentation. You may need to interact with the grantor, if you find out that reality is quite different from what you anticipated in your grant proposal. At that point during the grant period, you may want to lobby the grantor to make changes in the granting process or documentation, to reflect this "new" reality. The grant process, though often encased in very specific rules, can be a living entity, subject to the direct influence of grantees. This influence, in turn, may result in changes in the social direction of the grant or grantors, as well (Kalas 1987).

*How Do You Report Results or Lack of Them?*

Many granting agencies require a final report at the end of the funding period. In this report you will need to describe your accomplishments and explain why some portions of your project may not have turned out the way you expected or were not completed on time. You may also have to provide interim reports for multiyear projects in which you can show reasonable progress toward the ultimate goal. Keep in mind that the PI will be held accountable for funding expenditures, for progress toward the goal outlined in the proposal, for expenditures to support the project, and for the final outcome. It will be much easier to write your report if you keep a notebook or file handy with the original proposal and all appendixes, your award letter with the approved budget, and a list of items purchased with grant funds, along with receipts (Brewer, Achilles, and Fuhriman 1998).

WHAT HAPPENS IF YOU ARE TURNED DOWN?

After all of your hard work, your grant has a very good chance of *not* being funded. Cheer up—you are not alone! Seventy percent of first-time applicants for U.S. National Institutes of Health (NIH) grants are rejected (Locke, Spirduso, and Silverman 1993, p. 147), and "[t]he overall

[NIH grant] success rate in 2000 was 31 percent, up just 3 percent from what it was in 1996, and more or less where it has been for 10 years" (Hollon 2001). Those in the social sciences fare no better, with a 30 percent success rate for National Science Foundation grants for law and the social sciences (Hosch and Oliveri 1998, p. 517). Does this mean you should give up? No. Do not be discouraged. Some claim that half of all funded proposals are resubmissions (Coley and Scheinberg 1990), so you may still have a good chance of getting funded.

Why are there so many outright rejections? There may be many reasons for rejection in addition to unpredictable strong competition and limited grant funds, including missed deadlines and not following the grant guidelines, among others. These may seem minor, but any one can destroy your chance for approval.

---

### Figure 6–7
### Common Reasons for Grant Rejection
Following is a list drawn in part from several different sources (Gitlin and Lyons 1996; Kreeger 2000; Locke, Spirduso, and Silverman 1993).

1. Deadline missed
2. Guidelines not followed
   - too many pages
   - wrong size font
   - wrong forms
   - incomplete forms
   - missing forms
   - missing approvals
   - not enough copies
   - misspelled text
3. Proposal unclear
4. Proposal incomplete
5. Proposal writer took position with which reviewers disagreed
6. Poor writing quality—incomprehensible text
7. Typographical and grammatical errors
8. Nothing out of the ordinary
9. Methodology flawed or inappropriate for the study
10. Literature review incomplete—missing important citations
11. Applicants do not seem qualified to carry out the project
12. Proposal not a priority for the granting agency this year
13. Budget unrealistic
14. Cost ineffective

What to do? Ask program officers to help you write your grant proposal to begin with, by asking them to react to your ideas, to review your drafts, and to provide examples of proposals they have funded in the past (Sladek and Stein 1981). Be sure you do not overburden them, though, as many grant seekers will be eager to get their help. So, contact them very early in the process and only later if you truly need their help with the specifics. In any case, learn from your mistakes or the apparent poor fit with that granting agency, and try, try again with that agency or with one that is a better fit (Stewart and Stewart 1984).

If you do contact program staff at a granting agency, remember to send a thank-you letter telling them that you appreciate their time and effort in reviewing your proposal, whether or not they approve all or part of it. If your grant is rejected, ask for details about why it was rejected, including reviewer comments or suggestions for improving it for the future, as well as copies of top-ranked proposals (Brewer, Achilles, and Fuhriman 1998). Keep in mind, too, that reviewers for a particular grant may change from year to year, so it is certainly possible to resubmit and get an entirely different response, though you should consider making some changes based on reviewer comments.

Whether or not your grant is reduced, increased, or funded at the level requested, you may find that at the end of the grant term, you have not expended all of your grant funds. In many cases, if you have good reasons for not using all of the funds, you may be able to carry them over to the next grant period. It never hurts to ask about carrying forward unexpended funds. Just be sure you ask the person who can approve or deny your request with appropriate authority, or you may see badly needed grant funds disappear unnecessarily.

ENDGAME

Just remember, no matter the size, each successful grant, "underpromised" and delivered on time, or "over-delivered," contributes to your credibility, your reliability as someone who can and does get the job done. So, be conservative when estimating how much you will be able to accomplish and by when, given specific funding, and then work hard to reach your goals early and more fully than expressed in your written proposal. This strategy will certainly improve your chances with other grants and offers many opportunities for personal and professional achievements and satisfaction. So, think about it, investigate, and consider possible problems carefully. Get administrative approval, start small, and go for it!

EXERCISES

1.  Identify three different granting agencies that might fund a grant to an individual librarian to address "information illiteracy" among Web-savvy high school students and college freshmen.
2.  Find one federal grant, one foundation grant, and one private endowment grant that would accept an IL-related proposal. Draw up a table listing the most important factors to keep in mind regarding each grant.
3.  Write the first paragraph of a cover letter for a grant proposal to develop an interactive IL tutorial for elementary schools, another for high schools, and a third for college undergraduates.
4.  Make a list of five potential grant partners in your community, for instance, local governmental offices, schools, organizations, businesses, colleges and universities. Indicate what strengths each potential partner would bring to a grant.
5.  Come up with a list of items to include in a budget for a partnership between a school library, a public library, and an academic library, to develop a sequential IL program for college-bound high school students.
6.  Write a two-page memo to an administrator, requesting internal funding from your institution to develop a basic IL tutorial. Include an estimated breakdown of all direct costs and any indirect costs you can identify.

READ MORE ABOUT IT

*Annual Register of Grant Support: A Directory of Funding Sources.* 2004. Medford, NJ: Information Today.

Brewer, Ernest W., Charles M. Achilles, and Jay R. Fuhriman. 1998. *Finding Funding: Grantwriting from Start to Finish, Including Project Management and Internet Use.* 3rd ed. Thousand Oaks, CA: Corwin Press.

Coley, Soraya M., and Cynthia A. Scheinberg. 1990. *Proposal Writing.* Newbury Park, CA: Sage.

The Foundation Center. 2005. Proposal Writing Short Course. http://fdncenter.org/learn/shortcourse/prop1.html [5 June 2004].

*The Foundation Directory.* 2004. New York: Foundation Center.

*The Foundation Directory Part 2.* 2004. New York: Foundation Center.

Gitlin, Laura N., and Kevin J. Lyons. 1996. *Successful Grant Writing: Strategies for Health and Human Service Professionals.* New York: Springer Publishing Co.

Kendrick, Jim. 2004. Newsletters. P2C2 Group. http://www.p2c2group.com/s-news.html [14 June 2004].

Kight, Dawn Ventress, and Emma Bradford Perry. 1999. "Grant Resources on the Web: Where to Look When You Need Funding." *College & Research Libraries News* 60(7): 543–545.

LAUC. 2002b. *Research Resources for Librarians.* www.ucop.edu/lauc/research/resources.doc [9 September 2004].

Molfese, Victoria J., Karen S. Karp, and Linda A. Siegel. 2002. "Recommendations for Writing Successful Proposals from the Reviewer's Perspective (Shop Talk)." *Journal of Research Administration* 33(3): 21–25.

Ruskin, Karen B., and Charles M. Achilles. 1995. *Grantwriting, Fundraising and Partnerships: Strategies That Work!* Thousand Oaks, CA: Corwin Press.

Solomon, Gwen. 2001. "Deconstructing a Grant." *Technology & Learning* 21 (11): 44–46.

U.S. 2004b. *FedGrants.* www.fedgrants.gov/ [4 September 2004].

# 7

## Marketing, Publicity, and Promotion

*Doing business without advertising is like winking at a girl in the dark. You know what you are doing but nobody else does.*
—Edgar Watson Howe (1894–1956), U.S. comedian, vaudeville juggler

Does anyone visit your ILI Web pages? Do they complete your ILI Web tutorials? Have you offered an ILI session where no one showed up? Is there little demand for course-related or course-integrated ILI in your institution or organization?

Why does this happen? In some cases, it may be that we have decided on our own what is best for our user population, rather than developing and offering what our potential audience wants to learn and in the ways they want to learn. But how many of our users even know what we mean by "information literacy," much less what we are trying to accomplish with ILI? How many understand that links labeled "instruction" or "tutorial" will help them learn how to find useful books and articles, evaluate the tools they use and the items they retrieve? Will they know that taking an IL class, completing an IL tutorial, or exercise will save them time and help them end up with better papers and conduct more thorough research (i.e., better grades) or help them learn how to learn for future information needs? If your answer to any of these questions is no, your program participation may very well increase if you market, publicize, and promote it widely. Marketing allows us to find out and respond to what our users want to know. Publicity and promotion can help raise their awareness of what we have to offer.

WHAT IS MARKETING?

According to Nims and Weiss, "marketing" is a planned analytical process that includes market research, analysis of the competition as well as your own organization or company, product and service development, program evaluation, and program revision, and is user- or customer-driven (Nims 1999; Weiss 2000). The *Oxford English Dictionary* defines "marketing" as "the action, business, or process of promoting and selling a product, etc., including market research, advertising, and distribution" (*Oxford English Dictionary* 2004). Clemente says it is an active promotional effort to communicate information about a product or service (1992). Taken together, this is very similar to the initiation and program planning process for ILI described in Chapter 6 of *Information*

*Literacy Instruction: Theory and Practice* (Grassian and Kaplowitz 2001), though it needs to go beyond potential customers and reach decision-makers as well. You need to "recruit" interest in your quality services and products so you stand out from the ever-increasing crowd of commercial, personal, and other sites designed by those without ILI training or qualifications.

WHAT ARE PUBLICITY AND PROMOTION?

In contrast to marketing, the main function of publicity is to create "a positive image about a company, its products, services, or people via the use of *nonpaid* forms of communication" (Clemente 1992, p. 284) *or* through paid advertising. News stories about your library's new IL program would be free publicity, while an advertisement about it in a local newspaper would be paid publicity.

Terms like *publicity* and *promotion* can get a bit fuzzy. Some would consider paid advertisements, such as newspaper, magazine and Web page banner ads to be a form of promotion, though paid ads are usually shorter than public relations information, primarily because advertising costs money. The advantage of a paid advertisement is that the content and design of the ad itself are under the control of the person or group paying for it. In contrast, you have to release control when it comes to free publicity (also called public relations).

*Free Publicity (Public Relations)*

Often a publicist sends out or distributes information about a product or service and hopes that news organizations and others will include it in announcements, articles, and broadcasts. The person distributing this public relations information usually has no control over whether a person or group will actually use the information, how much of it they will use, and how they will use it. This can be difficult to accept and sometimes can take you in unexpected directions. Heinz's experience with green ketchup offers a good example.

In 2000, the H. J. Heinz Co. got $10 million worth of free publicity for its launch of Heinz EZ Squirt ketchup because of the novelty of green ketchup. This free publicity amounted to more than three times what Heinz spent on media advertising for EZ Squirt. But it was not quite the same as paid advertising, as the green-ketchup story leaked two months before Heinz was ready. This meant that stores did not have enough of the product to meet demand, and all the media attention focused on the fact that it was green, rather than on the kid-friendly bottle, Heinz' original marketing goal (Neff 2002). So, timing is important, whether you use paid advertising or get free publicity.

*Promotion*

Promotion is different from free publicity (public relations). Promotion is "simply employing creative ways to make library products and services visible to users" (Nims 1999, p. 251), like giving away pencils that have your library's ILI url on them, along with a catchy phrase, or developing brochures, flyers, and posters advertising your library's ILI products or services. ALA's "@your library" campaign toolkit, "PR Tools and Resources," offers some good examples of promotional approaches and eye-catching wording, like "Research made easy @your library." They also include other useful links, like "Creating Your Own [Marketing] Campaign/View Webcast," developed in conjunction with 3M Corporation (3M 1995–2003). In addition, ALA's AASL has published a handy *Toolkit for School Library Media Programs* with many promotional examples and ideas for working with various groups (ALA. AASL 2003). Libraries may also add descriptions of their own "@your library" activities to a searchable database under "Participating Libraries" on the "@your library" Web site. Although "information literacy" is not a searchable "story type," a search under "Web site" retrieved a number of results, including the Colorado State Library in Denver, which "named its information literacy and program standards for school libraries 'Colorado Students Achieve Power @ your library'" (ALA 2003c). ALA even offers a "READ" CD that allows libraries to create customized READ posters, where you can insert pictures of influential local personages, like the owner of a supportive local business, the city mayor, or the president of your college or university.

Keep in mind, though, that promotion and traditional paid advertising often do not persuade people about products but rather serve as reminders of brands already developed, primarily through repetition (Ehrenberg et al. 2002, p. 7; Ries and Ries 2002). Libraries may just need to remind people of their reputation for quality, their trustworthiness in relation to other, newer competitors. Yet, new marketing, publicity, and promotion books and other resources for libraries appear almost daily. Why?

WHY MARKET?

Why do we need to market? The user, customer, or client lies at the heart of the answer. As Siess puts it, "The customer has the ultimate power—to ignore us completely" (2003, p. 4). Why do they ignore us?

Let's face it—like it or not, we are in direct competition with both free and fee enterprises like "about.com" ("What you need to know about" 2003), AskJeeves (2003), Google Answers (2003), and e-training/e-learning sites like Barnes & Noble University (2004) and MIT (2003). In our Web-centered world, the competition for "eyeballs" is very intense. So, our goal must be to help people learn to question our competition. How reliable is it? How does it work? Are you paying for something you can get for free? What is the scope of these services? Who is actually trying to answer your users' questions? Do they just try to provide answers, or do they aim to help people learn how to learn?

MIT gives its courses away for free on its Web site. There you can find their "Survival Skills for Researchers" course, with a slide show giving a fairly good overview of a literature review and how and why to conduct one (2003). Does their course help students learn how to select a database appropriate to their needs? Do they help students learn criteria for evaluating research tools? Do they discuss the visible versus invisible Web? Do they help students learn the differences between scholarly and popular materials? In short, no. They do realize the value of personal interaction with instructors, however, who can respond to questions like these, so that is what they restrict, rather than the course content. In fact, over and over, marketing experts emphasize the personal touch, the need for intermediaries, those who can figure out what you want and need and then help you find it or, in the case of ILI, learn it. As Siess puts it, "Satisfying your customers is simple. Exceed their expectations" (2003, p. 9). We need to "recruit" interest in our quality services and products so that we stand out from the ever-increasing crowd of commercial, personal, and other sites designed by those without IL training or qualifications.

Make your ILI services essential and irresistible. When you market, emphasize relevance by providing brief definitions of IL and focus on how librarians can help people learn critical-thinking skills that will be useful right now and for a lifetime. This can be particularly effective when there are new educational endeavors, such as learning communities (Nahl 1999), newly revised General Education (GE) courses, or First Year Experience (FYE) undergraduate courses. The University of South Florida offers a useful definition of a learning community and points out that within a learning community, both faculty and students participate in the learning process:

> The Learning Community is an innovative, interdisciplinary . . . program. . . . It is an academic and social community that employs a unifying theme and active learning to develop higher order thinking skills and collaborative inquiry. The Learning Community

is a supportive environment that fosters a respect for multiple perspectives and personal and community responsibility. Faculty and
students continuously and self-reflectively work to build and improve upon the unique environment of their Learning Community.
(University of South Florida 1998)

Proactive efforts to integrate IL into Learning Communities may be
most effective when the librarian joins the Learning Community team.
This may mean more than just the occasional visit to an instructor's office to talk about IL needs and the benefits of ILI. At UCLA, attending
all lectures of a freshman three-quarter-long GE Cluster course, Frontiers in Human Aging, offered one of the authors of this book many opportunities to provide IL help to faculty as well as students, on the spot,
as well as on the class discussion board. It lead to several brief ten- to
fifteen minute interactive presentations to the entire class of 120 students, as well as one-and-a-half-hour one-shot sessions to seminars of
20 students each, and the introduction of a one-unit adjunct IL course
designed to support the curricula of all six Cluster seminars.

This is very high touch, as it requires a librarian to devote much in-
dividualized time and energy to a single course, with a relatively small
number of students, within the context of a large research university
with limited librarian staff. What would happen if faculty teaching
other GE Clusters or faculty in other departments wanted the same
kind of in-depth attention? How could we handle it with a limited
staff? These questions often lead one to wonder whether and how much
to market IL.

In order to do this sort of marketing at the most opportune moment, though, librarians need to be in on curriculum proposals and
planning from the ground up. It is important to maintain a continuous
environmental scan for new trends, new curriculum interests and developments, and new staff at various levels. In higher education it may
be easier to do this if you have faculty status and can serve on curriculum committees. If you are not at the same official level as faculty, you
will need to work harder and be more proactive in getting involved in,
or starting up, new projects or efforts. If you sit back and wait, chances
are that you and the library will be forgotten and left by the wayside.

Ask if you can be appointed to the training and development
group, the instructional technology group, or the campus curriculum
committee. Stay on top of new courses and initiatives and raise consciousness about the benefits and potential for ILI in all new endeavors.
Is the campus revising General Education requirements? Is there a new
push to focus on undergraduate research? Is the Political Science Department proposing a new minor in complex human systems? Is the

Sociology Department reexamining and altering its course sequence, structure, and curricula? How can IL fit in?

If you are not able to get on these committees yourself, ask your administrators if they can serve as ex-officio members, or if they can get meeting minutes or, at least, agendas. Is this enough? No. You need to be even more proactive, in friendly, diplomatic ways. Develop a marketing survey for faculty, for instance, and make it interesting and worth their while (Barker, Nancarrow, and Spackman 2001). Ask them what research materials they pay for and how they identify them. Respond to each with ways to get to some of these materials more quickly and for free. Offer to go to their offices and help them learn how on their own computers. Ask them how much time they are spending one-on-one with students, teaching them how to conduct information research, teaching them the differences between popular and scholarly materials, what the peer review process is and its significance. Ask if they know that the library can help save them time by addressing this problem in many ways. Provide a menu of various kinds of ILI help (see the example on the CD, "Use Teaching Fellows ILI Help as Example"). Talk about the need to come up with expected learning outcomes together and to provide enough advance notice and feedback so that those outcomes can be achieved.

IL librarians frequently wonder how much advance notice they should require in order to plan and develop instruction. On the ILI listserv, librarians have debated whether or not to require or request a minimum of two weeks' advance notice for course-integrated synchronous group instruction. Some librarians feel very strongly that two weeks' advance notice is vital for all instruction; any less, they believe, shows a lack of respect for the librarian's need to prepare quality instruction and for the fact that they have many other responsibilities (Presti 2000; Ream 2000). Others require one week's notice or try to be more flexible (Holmes 2000; Pusey 2000).

Do you need advance notice, and if so, how much? It depends on a lot of factors. If you are invited to come to the regular classroom, you will not need to worry about finding a place to teach an in-person session. If not, you will need to arrange for a room with sufficient space and equipment and possibly for someone to teach the class whenever it is scheduled. Whoever teaches it will need to develop goals and objectives, design an outline, research relevant examples, prepare handouts or Web pages, and, possibly, a slide show using presentation software. What if you have taught the same sort of synchronous session before, on the same topic, though? Would you need a lot of preparation time and two weeks' advance notice for a one- to two-hour instruction session? Some even claim that overpreparing can reduce the effectiveness of your instruction (Wankat and Oreovicz 2000). But what if your administration caters to teaching faculty and wants you to teach as much as possible, no matter when they ask you to teach or what they want you to teach?

There may be occasions when you will need to do some ILI on the spot, with little or no advance notice. It may help to remember this: Even if you are brand-new to ILI or just out of library school, you still have a lot to offer. You may not even be aware of how much you know about information tools and materials until you try to help others learn about them and about IL strategies. We need to sell ourselves and our expertise as much, if not more, than we sell the content of what we can do to help people become information-literate. This is particularly true for those who do not make much use of ILI options. If you find yourself in this situation, try "cross-selling" (Siess 2003). When providing a service in one area, like reserves or the reference desk, mention ILI, and demo or provide other materials or resources that might be of interest. Jump on any opportunity, large or small, to raise consciousness about information illiteracy and the need for ILI, and you may be surprised at how your tiny successes can build and lead to major ones.

You can also create opportunities for consciousness-raising, rather than just waiting for them to drop into your lap. Write news releases and public service announcements (PSAs) about the benefits of ILI, put an exhibit together, hold a special event related to ILI, or create some supplementary ILI material to accompany special events.

Exhibits can be challenging to develop and mount attractively. Their visual impact can grab attention quite effectively, as can special events on topics of interest to your users. Once you have someone's attention, direct it to the benefits of ILI. Create some informational crossword puzzles using puzzlemaker.com (2003). Hold a contest by asking intriguing historical or biographical questions related to the topic of the exhibit. If your exhibit consists of drawings or paintings by homeless people, or if your special event will teach people how to do ballroom dancing, provide a list of reference books and Web sites related to these topics. In 1990, for example, the North Haven Memorial Library in North Haven, Connecticut, offered a public awareness fair during National Library Week. At each of a variety of booths, users learned first-hand about book topics, including Chinese handwriting and weaving demos (*Great Library Promotion Ideas VI* 1991). These supplementary materials could be mounted on a Web site or made available as paper handouts. They are important because they represent another way that librarians can add value to a service, beyond what a clerk or library assistant or a museum staff member can do. The idea is to use every opportunity you can to illustrate the value and benefits of knowing how to learn about a topic, in practical terms and in ways that will appeal to your audience. Of course, you should evaluate the effectiveness of these PR efforts (*Part-Time Public Relations with Full-Time Results* 1995) and do some market research to make sure you are addressing the needs and interests of your potential audiences.

WHAT IS MARKET RESEARCH?

Ongoing marketing research/needs assessment can serve as an excellent public relations tool in itself, as simply posing questions can help raise consciousness about the need for ILI and ILI offerings. Be careful about question design, though, as your goal is to improve or build trust in your organization and your products. ARL's LibQual survey instrument attempts to measure user satisfaction with library services, particularly, trust in libraries—do users get the kinds of services they expect, based on their perceptions of promised service? (ARL 2003; Papadopoulou et al. 2001). Are there poorly designed questions with inadequate alternative responses in this well-known survey? Though well-intentioned, surveys that include poor questions can produce added frustration, thus decreasing user satisfaction and conveying a negative image of the library.

Experts in questionnaire and question design recommend starting by figuring out why you want to do a survey in the first place and what you want to find out (Leung 2001; O'Rourke and O'Rourke 2001). Good survey designers have a reason for asking each and every question and also have a plan for analyzing the results before collecting the data (O'Rourke and O'Rourke 2001). Try to get funding for a professional to review your survey and your questions to make sure they are "relevant, appropriate, intelligible, precise and unbiased" (Leung 2001, available online). If you want to prepare your own survey and questions, experts offer many useful question and survey design tips. Some may seem obvious on the surface, like asking for just one piece of information in each question (Leung 2001), using mutually exclusive categories (O'Rourke and O'Rourke 2001), and showing sensitivity to the fact that most people will want to answer "no" to questions about socially undesirable behavior, like plagiarism (O'Rourke and O'Rourke 2002). It is also easy to make mistakes in question design because those who are very knowledgeable about a topic often use jargon familiar to them and make assumptions about what novices know. (See Figure 7-1 for examples of poorly written and better questions. Read carefully, as there are small, but important, differences between some of the poor questions and their better equivalents.)

## Figure 7–1
## Tips for Improving Survey Questions

| Poorly written questions | Better questions |
|---|---|
| 1. When doing research for a paper, how often do you use general search tools like Google and licensed databases, like PsycInfo? | 1a. When doing research for a paper, how often do you use general search tools like Google?<br><br>1b. When doing research for a paper, how often do you use licensed databases, like PsycInfo? |
| 2. At what point in the quarter do you usually begin doing research for a 12–15 page paper, if you need to have at least 10 references?<br>　a. Week 1<br>　b. Weeks 2–3<br>　c. Weeks 3–5<br>　d. Weeks 5–6<br>　e. Weeks 6–8 | 2. At what point in the quarter do you usually begin doing research for a 12–15 page paper, if you need to have at least 10 references?<br>　a. Week 1<br>　b. Weeks 2–3<br>　c. Weeks 4–5<br>　d. Weeks 6–7<br>　e. Weeks 8–9 |
| 3. How often would you say you have used plagiarized material (other people's ideas or words) in a research paper without citing them?<br>　a. Once<br>　b. Twice<br>　c. Three to five times<br>　d. More than five times<br>　e. Never | 3. Occasionally, students forget to cite when they use other people's ideas or words in their research papers. How often would you say you may have done this?<br>　a. Once<br>　b. Twice<br>　c. Three to five times<br>　d. More than five times<br>　e. Never |
| 4. Where can you find a list of all the books your library owns about earthquakes?<br>　a. Amazon.com<br>　b. The OPAC<br>　c. Google<br>　d. Science Citation Index | 4. Where can you find a list of all the books your library owns about earthquakes?<br>　a. Amazon.com<br>　b. The library catalog<br>　c. Google<br>　d. Science Citation Index |

You may wonder why you would ask content questions like those above when doing market research. The market for ILI consists of learners, teachers, administrators, and other potential supporters (e.g., those who want to hire information-literate individuals). This means that the more information you have about how, when, and why people use information resources, the better you will be able to plan to fill learning gaps. We are so inundated these days by poorly written questionnaires, pitches for donations with surveys as come-ons, and e-mail spam, that many people are suspicious and reluctant to respond to any survey ("We Value Your Feedback . . ." 2003). So, be sure to test your survey questions on people from your potential audience, as well as colleagues, clearly state why you are conducting a survey, and work with professional survey designers to validate the questions before finalizing them.

How can technology help? Needs assessments for ILI can be conducted electronically on a Web site with a simple form or by using survey software like Web Surveyor (2003) or survey sites like Zoomerang (2004). You can also conduct live chat or in-person focus groups or distribute paper surveys. Some even suggest using avatars (virtual images or characters that represent real people) and natural language in virtual landscapes, to imitate human interaction with customer service or specific business agents in a mall or business. This is like having very knowledgeable salespeople who can also help with the ordering process (Papadopolou et al. 2001, p. 329).

If we take a strictly user-centered approach, marketing research would come first at regular intervals, followed by product and service development, then publicity and promotion about our products and services. Evaluation and revision of our programs and materials would take place regularly and would be dictated by what users want to know. As Nims (1999) points out quite rightly, however, some question whether users really know what they need to know or what they can learn from IL librarians. This is a legitimate concern, so why not respond to it by offering IL instruction you and your colleagues believe is important and at the same time develop a marketing plan that would provide a more learner-centered approach and that would evaluate learning outcomes for all of your instructional programs and materials.

Regardless of the method and format you use, you should conduct some kind of assessment regularly, take the results seriously, and use them to realign your program goals and objectives. Needs assessment by itself, though, will not necessarily make for an effective program or product with high impact unless users know it exists and grasp its value.

## MARKET LIBRARIES OR MARKET LIBRARIANS?

Some claim that ALA's marketing efforts are passive, in that they focus on the library rather than the librarian, with the "@your library" campaign at the center (Sass 2002; Shamel 2002). SLA, in contrast, focuses much more on marketing librarians and improving their image, because librarians working for businesses need to work hard to justify their value, their contribution to the bottom line, as employees can find lots of information on their own these days, especially through the Web (Shamel 2002). SLA has even developed a list of core competencies for special librarians, in support of the librarian as an individual professional (Shamel 2002; Special Libraries Association 2003). ACRL, on the other hand, has focused on the learner by establishing core competencies for students in higher education. What is missing is a list of core competencies for all librarians, with special competencies to follow for librarians in various subfields, though Shonrock and Mulder did address this for academic instruction librarians in a 1988 survey (Shonrock and Mulder 1993).

One can guess why this gap exists, though. ALA supports all kinds of libraries and librarians, and public libraries play a big role in the association. For public libraries, the institution of the library is of major importance, including the building, the services, the staff, and the communities they serve. Special libraries tend to focus more on personalized service and are more dependent on personal efforts by individuals to demonstrate their worth. Generally, they appeal to a smaller cross-section of the population within their own spheres and often have an entrepreneurial orientation geared to showing how they contribute to the bottom line and how they are at the forefront, continually promoting the next new thing. This "next new thing" approach is more important in the special library world, where user population turnover may not be as rapid as in other environments. A constant flow of new users in academic and public libraries goes far to ensure that librarians are needed on an ongoing basis. In special libraries, where the user base remains constant for longer periods, librarians need to prove their continued worth to those who may have learned to find useful information on their own. The fear may be that once they have "sucked the librarian dry" of information-seeking and evaluation skills, they can throw her or him away, save money, and do the same on their own.

There are certainly lessons for all librarians and libraries to learn from both of these approaches, as a blended approach that supports and enhances the images of libraries (physical and virtual), as well as librarians, may be best, especially for ILI.

This discussion of the librarian's image brings us back to the issue of publicity and promotion for ILI, as image is an integral part of this entire endeavor. It is certainly easier and more comfortable for us to gear our efforts toward publicity and promotion, rather than the full marketing process. After all, it allows us to keep control of our products by focusing our attention on where, when, and how we can tell people about them. If we can open ourselves to a more learner-centered approach, though, as Nims (1999) suggests, we can precede both free (public relations) and paid publicity and promotion with a marketing plan that begins with user-driven market research. Then we can develop materials and programs that our users want and need, *followed* by public relations, then paid publicity and promotion, and finally, evaluation and revision.

## WHAT STRATEGIES AND TECHNIQUES MAKE FOR SUCCESSFUL MARKETING PLANS?

If you need to publicize or promote your IL expertise and your wares, whom should you target, where should you start, what approaches should you use, and when should you stop?

You need a marketing plan to put all of this together. Marketing plans generally aim to sell a product, increase use of a product, or raise consciousness about the value of a product or a "producer" through assertive techniques. A marketing plan combined with creative-thinking techniques can help you develop, organize, and mount more effective advertising of programs and services that users want and need. But start with your users first, rather than just publicizing a product or service you yourself have picked out or offer. Ask them what they want and need and listen to their answers. Then, focus on the benefits, what your users would get out of using them (Wagner 2003).

For ILI, this means doing needs assessments that ask users what they want to learn about or learn to do, what kinds of help they need and want. Examples of ILI benefits include saving lots of time, getting good grades on research papers, eliminating or decreasing frustration, and becoming a powerful information researcher by learning how to learn about information resources in any format.

Some marketing experts even recommend keeping a "file of customer likes, interests, and personal information" to help you lend a personal touch and counteract the impersonality of the Internet (Siess 2003, p. 5). In any case, once you know what your users want, and you are ready for change, you can develop a marketing plan, with the agreement of your administration and colleagues. The plan should include how you will address your user groups' ILI needs and wants in light of the competition, what kind of image you want to project, how you will name and brand your products and services, and how you will publicize and promote the results, using the various tools mentioned above. A word of caution here, though—it is much better to offer just a few products than to offer something you cannot deliver. When you do offer products, make sure that anyone can tell whose products they are.

*Brands and Branding*

What is a "brand"? A brand used to be a mark that meant, quite simply, "This is mine." Brands go back at least to Greek and Roman times, possibly even before there were written languages (Drawbaugh 2001). Cattle (and even slaves) were branded to indicate ownership. Over time, brands became associated with particular products, people, or groups, which conjured up images, both positive and negative. They became symbols, sometimes quite powerful. Many publications on branding often cite Coke as an example of an extremely powerful brand, recognizable worldwide as a positive product to some and as an extremely negative

---

**Figure 7–2**
**Planning for Marketing**

1. Do you know what your potential audience wants to learn?
2. Have all key people been consulted before you begin to market your products(s), including colleagues who may be affected by successes?
3. What are you planning to market?
4. To whom?
5. To what end?
6. How will you market?
7. How will you know you have reached your goal (expected learning outcomes)?
8. When and how will you know you have done enough marketing for the year?
9. What else do you need to take into account in planning a marketing or publicity campaign?
10. How will you judge success and make any necessary revisions to the plan?

representation of Western civilization to others (Mosbacher 2002; Ries and Trout 1989).

Most would agree that in today's world, "branding" usually refers to the following definition: "To set a mental mark of ownership upon" (*Oxford English Dictionary* 2004). Those who create brands, especially for the Internet, would be very happy if their brands also fulfilled another OED definition: "to impress (a fact, an event) indelibly on one's memory."

"[A] brand is a concept in the mind of the customer" (Rowley 1997, p. 246). Brands are images—corporate, product, or service—sometimes powerful enough to develop a cult following, which can even result in rather outrageous events, like a mass "wedding" of 250 people and their Mazda Miatas (Wells 2001). Unfortunately, though, many new brands fail. Why? "Most commonly . . . the reason for failure is simply that the new brands do not offer the consumer anything of interest that he does not have already—they are not differentiated meaningfully from existing products" (Murphy 1987, p. 10).

How do you create a successful brand? What would make people turn to your ILI programs and materials for help? This is where market research comes in. After you have identified the competition, focus on your potential customers. Examine the kind of advertising your competitors do and then survey people to "find out how they think about your kind of product, what language they use when they discuss the subject, what attributes are important to them, and what promise would be most likely to make them buy your brand" (Ogilvy 1983, pp. 11–12).

Check with the people you want to attract. Find out who your competitors are and where they are weakest. Start by asking yourself what words you would use to describe your IL programs and materials. Then ask your users where they turn for information research help and what they call this help. You can do this by conducting brief one-on-one interviews, through focus groups, or through paper or online surveys. Compare survey results with areas of weakness in the competition. With the results in hand, try matching your users' language with the various benefits of IL. Do they talk about being able to find factual information they can count on? Tell them they will know where to get reliable factual information. What about going to one place to find answers to reference questions? Tell them that information is power and that they will know where and how to find answers to almost any question. How about finding reliable, high-quality Web sites? Promise they will become discriminating Web searchers and be sure that what you offer is quite distinct from the competition. Most importantly, in order to attract people, offer "A significant point of difference [which] must be

recognisable by consumers;
desirable;
based on an 'element of familiarity';
credible on delivery;
communicated in all aspects of presentation."
     (Blackett and Denton 1987, p. 78)

Take advantage of nostalgia for libraries. Remind people of the quality service and products they have found in libraries. Tell them that as library and ILI users, they belong to a special group or "club" of those who are knowledgeable, up to date, and information-wise (Langer 1997). Just remember that people want value for their investment in time or money and will hold you to your promises. If you promise something and then do not deliver it, your user base will desert you for the competition.

*Image*

What sort of image should you project? There is no end of advice on this topic. Consider the Jungian approach in which organizations and products all have qualities in and of themselves and project one of twelve archetypes, including "Caregiver," "Regular Guy/Gal," "Lover," and "Sage" (Mark and Pearson 2001). If you can identify your organization's and products' archetypes, you can then gear mottoes and marketing strategies to each. For instance, if your organization is the "Sage" type, your motto may be "The truth will set you free" (Mark and Pearson 2001, p. 88). The organizational characteristics of this archetype could then include "help the customer make smarter decisions" (Mark and Pearson 2001, p. 90), and marketing strategies would include ads with something missing, to get attention and to "make the customer feel smart for knowing [the answer]" (Mark and Pearson 2001, p. 97), as well as ads in which experts recommend something. The Center for Applications of Psychological Types offers validated instruments (for a fee) to help you figure out what is your own or your organization's archetype (2003).
     Whether or not you use a Jungian approach to analyzing your organization's current image, ask yourself if you are projecting an image of quality. As you work toward revising perceptions of the organizational image, focus on what is good about your product or service, rather than what is bad about the competition (Ogilvy 1983). This approach fits in very well with ILI, as quality is what we have to offer and what the competition lacks. Librarians know what to look for, how to judge the authority, reliability, accuracy, and recency of information of all kinds, in all formats. We know there is always a point of view, and

we know where and how to uncover it. We may not know and remember every fact or bit of information there is, but we know where to look for it, how to identify, locate, and pull together diverse relevant data, and how to evaluate it, at least generically. This is what we can promise our learners—the chance to learn how to learn, to approach all sorts of information and information tools with a questioning attitude and with solid evaluative criteria. Again, and this bears repeating, promise only what you can deliver, or you will lose the trust and confidence of your "customers," and it is much more difficult to get new customers than to keep satisfying your current customers.

*Categories and Names*

How do you actually go about doing all of this? You could come up with a new category and a new name for your product or service (Ries and Ries 2002). Be careful about the name you use, though, especially if you have learners from different cultures, or if you want to publicize your ILI offerings via your Web site. Interesting and attractive-sounding names in one language or culture can be meaningless at best or negative and insulting at worst, in another language or culture. For instance, note the failure of Pepsi's advertising slogan in Taiwan, where "Come alive with the Pepsi generation" was translated as "Pepsi will bring your ancestors back from the dead" (Haig 2003, p. 163). So, just as you would test your instructional materials and Web site for clarity, ease of use, and other usability features, you must vet your name and slogan with various user groups for what may be negative cultural or linguistic nuances that you do not intend.

HOW DO YOU PROMOTE ILI?

Once you come up with an acceptable name and slogan (if you decide to use one), some influential experts suggest that you use public relations (particularly via news media) as your first approach. Paid advertising, they suggest, works best as reinforcement for what public relations has already placed in the prospect's mind. In fact, according to Ries and Ries, no one trusts advertising anyway, so why would we expect it to be effective as a first stop for marketing anything? (Ries and Ries 2002, p. 95). Of course, these days, many do not trust the news media either, but it certainly does make sense to try free means of publicizing ILI programs and materials before spending money on advertising and promotional gimmicks. Have you established a new IL course within an academic department? You will have to let go of the content, though, as journalists will pick and choose which parts of the story to tell and may not get it all right. Still, they will be telling at least part of the story, and this is bound to get you some attention. So, start by telling the student newspaper about your new (or newly named) ILI product or service. Interest them in writing a story about its benefits. Get a local newspaper to write up the new IL initiative you have started at a public library. Remember, too, to use your Web site for marketing, as "The website, when the purpose is promotion, becomes a shop window" (de Saez 2002, p. 154). What will you put in your shop window? A cluttered window attracts little attention. Make your shop window speak clearly and distinctly, by focusing on your major products or services. Turn it into a "motivational web site" that engages learners (Weaver 2001). Remember—"Cost to the user includes time spent at the site" (de Saez 2002, p. 155).

How do you get news coverage? Call or e-mail journalists with a hook of some kind. Anniversaries of all kinds often get news coverage as they cause us to reflect on what happened at the time and what has happened since then. Has your IL initiative been in place for two years? What was it like beforehand, and what progress have you made? Have administrators changed? A one-year anniversary is a good time to point out milestones, accomplishments of the previous year, and goals for the future. Is it time for an accreditation review? Are there IL standards against which your institution or organization will be evaluated? What changes in ILI have taken place since the last review or evaluation?

Be patient as you undertake this effort. It takes time to build a reputation, to get the word out about IL and the benefits of ILI. Some advertising experts cite a McGraw-Hill ad as "one of the best print ads to ever summarize awareness from a customer's . . . point of view":

> I don't know who you are.
> I don't know your company.
> I don't know your company's product.
> I don't know what your company stands for.
> I don't know your company's customers.
> I don't know your company's record.
> I don't know your company's reputation.
> Now—what was it you wanted to sell me? (Dowling 2001, p. 137)

*Define Your Audience*

IL librarians need to promote their products and services just as businesses do, to the extent the budget will allow. You will need to promote your wares and expertise directly and indirectly to potential "customers."

Who are your customers? This can be a difficult question to answer now that the Web has turned our world into a global village. We may need to "sell" to many different levels and types of customers, including administrators within and outside the library, instructors, students, community leaders, businesspeople, and the general public. Discuss this with administrators and other stakeholders in your institution or organization to help to determine who are your primary, secondary, and other user groups. It may be useful to segment your potential customers into logical groups (Dowling 2001). This may seem easy for some libraries, where "natural" groupings include undergraduates, graduate students, faculty, and staff (academic libraries), and children, young adults, adults, senior citizens, and staff (public libraries). It may take more analysis and thought to pull out other market segments, like transfer students, non- or limited-English speakers, distance learners, hesitant technology adopters, and so on and then identify the competition for each group of these "eyeballs." Once you know who your customers are, you will need to come up with different pitches for different audiences and a variety of approaches, both direct and indirect.

Direct marketing of noncredit ILI to learners can be expensive and not very successful. A common approach, instead, is to offer your services and hope for collaboration. Most often, ILI librarians reach out to IL funders or program decision makers and to course developers, the instructors. However, tiptoeing around diplomatically, trying to help instructors see the light and require IL or incorporate it fully into *their* curriculum can be extremely frustrating and ineffective. This is partly because until recently they often saw it as an overlay on their curriculum and did not want to give up what they saw as precious in-person class time. IL librarians, too, may forget to offer a full IL menu of options, rather than focusing on a particular comfortable or familiar approach, especially, getting time during a regular class session.

Word of mouth can be very important here, and you can help it along by leveraging even your smallest successes. Were you able to work with high school and community college librarians to introduce them to your free OPAC and some of your licensed databases? Encourage them to go back to their schools and pass this information along to the students, staff, and teachers. Then contact other high school and community college librarians and teachers. Tell them about their colleagues' new skills and knowledge and offer to work with them as well. Maximize all of this by talking with your administrators and the local news media about connecting different educational levels and sequencing ILI. Put news items about your efforts on your institution's Web site and include summaries or checklists of what you covered in synchronous group sessions. "Make your brand a source of information that prospects cannot find elsewhere" (Ries and Ries 2000, p. 95). This kind of outreach, these small successes, build on one another to create a climate of IL appreciation, expectations, and demand for your help and that of your colleagues.

*Deal with the Competition*

You can turn problems into solutions, however. If peers and experts are your competition, develop a database of peers and experts to help people get to them (Siess 2003). You may or may not agree with the following approach, but at least one person claims we should capitalize on the stereotype of the librarian with bun and glasses by using that image in a promotional ad:

> Imagine this: The business manager is lost in a sea of papers calling for answers. Enter, the librarian with the hair and the glasses to save the day. At least the viewer will understand who the hero is. (Shamel 2002, p. 70)

The opposite approach would be to use Rachel Weisz's character in *The Mummy*, who boldly says, "I . . . am a librarian" (1999), or Parker Posey's librarian-wannabe character in *Party Girl* (1995), or *The Lipstick Librarian*'s approach, whose motto is: "She's bold!! She's sassy!! She's helpful!!" (Absher 2004).

You can also promote your ILI program assertively by going outside the usual sphere of the physical library or even the library's Web site, mounting ads on nonlibrary Web sites, offering help to businesses, to schools and community organizations (including campus organizations and groups), to legislators, and to others, in settings outside the traditional library.

Wells Fargo Bank was the first bank to offer its services in grocery stores. Some stores like Wal-Mart have essentially become "portals" for one-stop shopping, selling groceries as well as clothes and other items sold in department stores. Why not bring our services to the people electronically or otherwise, instead of expecting them to come to us?

Coffee can be a big draw. Librarians at Hewlett-Packard have a "Coffee Schmooze" the first Monday of each month. They bring in a gourmet coffee cart, rearrange some library materials to look like a bookstore, and invite staff to get a free cup of coffee and ask questions about their research projects and library resources (Dworkin 2001, p. 52). ALA's Campaign for America's Libraries, while disparaged by some as too focused on libraries, as we have mentioned, has inspired many to take marketing, publicity, and promotion more seriously. In early 2003, academic librarians established an ALA listserv "AcademicPR." Coffee shops and food/drink policies in academic libraries constituted a major thread on this list in 2003 (Goodson 2003).

Germain offers ninety-nine interesting public relations ideas for getting users' attention, for example, sponsoring an alternative rock/poetry festival, setting up a booth at campus job fairs, and creating a library newsletter (2000). These ideas are aimed primarily at academic libraries, but many of them could be adapted for use in a variety of environments. Some libraries have taken novel approaches to promotion. The Loveland Public Library in Colorado, for example, put notices about its new Technology Center and its training facility in city utility bills and received tremendous response (Carpenter 1998).

Each year ALA presents the John Cotton Dana Library Public Relations Awards to libraries with outstanding programs in library public relations. In 2004, for instance, the Dr. Martin Luther King Jr. Library (San Jose, California) won an award "for a building dedication campaign, highlighting a groundbreaking partnership between the San Jose State University and the city's public library" (H. W. Wilson 2004). At ALA annual conferences, the Library Administration and Management Association's (LAMA) Public Relations and Marketing Section offers a "Swap & Shop Best of Show Award" for all kinds of public relations materials, like newsletters, educational materials regarding diversity, bibliographies, orientation materials, and more (ALA. LAMA. PRMS n.d.). You might want to look at the programs and materials that win these awards each year and consider how you could adapt some of their ideas to an ILI promotional effort, particularly during National Library Week, or whenever there is a major change in your library's offerings, like a new OPAC.

As you consider these and other creative promotional ideas, the following questions may guide you in developing an organized and more effective promotion campaign.

*Answer the Questions*

**1. What are you planning to promote?** It is important to discuss with administrators exactly what you will be trying to "sell," what sort of staff time will be necessary, and how much it will cost before you begin. Are you hoping to establish a brand-new IL program? Would a pilot project do for starters? What sort of staff time and budget can be devoted to this effort? Have you identified grant funds for which you might apply to fund a pilot project? You will have a much greater chance of success if you build a strong foundation of administrative support from the beginning.

**2. To whom and to what end?** Make lists of places to publicize or promote the existence of your instructional products and services and plan to take a personal, proactive approach. Call, meet with, make presentations to, e-mail, or write letters to administrators, teachers or faculty, community leaders, businesspeople, legislators, and other decision-makers. If you are planning to promote stand-alone library-initiated sessions and materials, individual users may be the most important target. For course-integrated or course-related IL, teachers or faculty may be the best target. However, if you really want to become a change agent and impact an entire institution or set of institutions, you will need to aim higher—at principals, deans, vice-chancellors, nongovernmental groups, clubs and organizations, legislative bodies at all levels, or accrediting agencies.

In the academic environment, accrediting agencies wield significant power and influence over entire institutions in a region. Lobbying these agencies and publicizing the significance of IL standards may result in adoption of IL accreditation standards or their incorporation into existing standards. This top-down approach could result in long-term change as IL becomes integrated into the basic curriculum from K–12 through college and university education. This, in turn, could have a strong positive impact in the public library environment, where parent groups, citizens' groups, and businesses may begin to see the value of information literacy competency.

Whatever the environment, a crucial question remains: Have you geared the tone and style of the publicity to the target audience(s)?

**3. How will you promote IL instructional products and services?** Have you identified the highest-impact forms and avenues for your audience(s), as well as secondary approaches? Do you know their costs and deadlines, contact persons, and limitations on length of publicity, if any? Which of these forms would be best for onetime instruction as opposed to an ongoing, large-scale program: paper flyers, posters, announcements on a variety of Web sites and listservs, brochures, handouts, newspaper ads, radio ads, billboards, or press releases?

**4. What will you include?** Do you have all the facts correct? Have you included all of the essential information, including a catchy title or hook, brief description of offerings, times, dates, places, contact person(s), e-mail address, phone number, fax number, mailing address, urls for Web pages, registration information, and deadlines? Have all groups and individuals involved in the program and sessions or in developing materials had a chance to review the publicity?

**5. When and how will you know you have done enough marketing**

**for the current goal?** Some fear that if we market our wares too well, we will end up with more business than we can handle well. It is difficult to know how much marketing may be enough or too much. One way to gauge interest is to test out a program, new or revised, with a pilot project and plan to scale up to a larger program if the pilot is successful. If you define your goals and capabilities carefully before beginning the marketing process, you should have a much better idea of when and how to stop or alter marketing to meet the current goal.

Brainstorming, focus groups, and other creative-thinking techniques can also help you determine your group's or institution's answers to these questions. (See Chapter 3 for more on creative-problem solving techniques.) These answers may very well change over time, even for the same institution or group, as technology evolves and as other circumstances change, such as the size of the user population and the extent of distance learning efforts.

Creative-problem solving techniques are useful in determining other important marketing factors as well. "Branding" through the use of logos that are more natural than representational (abstract) (Henderson and Cote 1998), headers, or other distinctive features like size and color of paper, templates, or use of particular fonts or clipart, for example, can help learners identify items developed and offered by a specific producer—your library (Hart 1999). ALA even offers a page where you can download the "@your library" logo for free in various languages (ALA 2003a). You can also ask user focus groups to come up with meaningful "power words" to use in marketing campaigns to that user group (Hart 1999). Once you have drafted your marketing materials, ask a naive user to take a "15-second test" to see if the main point gets across (Hart 1999, p. 41). Then continue to check on the effectiveness of

---

**Figure 7–3**
**Marketing Tips for a Shoestring Budget**

---

1. Involve others in ideas for marketing your program
2. Personal contact sometimes works best—attend faculty and Friends of the Library meetings
3. Try to identify pro-library faculty, community members, and business people, and try out your new program on them
4. Word of mouth may be the only marketing you need
5. Other ideas include flyers in mailboxes, ads in the institution's newsletter or the local newspaper, or self-test questionnaires or surveys.

your marketing plan and materials and be prepared to revise them often if necessary.

The "Tuna Story" is a famous case in point regarding "outside-the-dotted-lines" marketing strategy. As the story goes, Ben Sonnenberg, a public relations pioneer, morphed a perceived disadvantage into an advantage by changing the public's perception of what constitutes high-quality canned tuna. When most canned tuna on the market was pink, one company was having a hard time selling canned white tuna. Ben's solution was a new slogan: "Guaranteed not to turn pink in the can!" (Culligan and Greene 1982).

In ILI, when users are no longer attracted to classes labeled "How to Use the Web," when they use the Web first in searching for information of any kind, and when they do not distinguish between Web sites and licensed databases accessed via the Web, it may be time to try offering instruction on using the Web for research through the Web itself. A number of libraries are now developing or offering Web-based tutorials, some at a simple level and others quite sophisticated, to meet this need. Some libraries are offering "library fairs" in place of typical fall orientations or tours, where different segments of the library offer games and activities that teach students about those areas (Riley 2003). How successful are they? It is difficult to tell, but at least they are trying something new with good IL instructional intentions in mind, and they deserve credit and attention for doing so. In fact, many forms of instruction can be offered through the Web, including workbooks, exercises, PowerPoint presentations, and copies of paper point-of-use guides, and new forms are developing all the time, such as instant messaging, chat, and discussion boards.

*Anticipate Success*

All of this, of course, is very positive and upbeat—promote, promote, promote. What happens if we drum up too much business, though, or worse yet, if the budget is cut after we drum up lots of business? We must prioritize in advance of budget cuts, and we must publicize our worth. Too much ILI business sounds scary and overwhelming. Contingency plans could include the following. It may help to remember that there are only so many hours in a day and only so much one person can do. If there is too much for you to handle on your own, you do have options. First, your colleagues at the same institution may be able to help out. Second, you can use the demand to request more support. Third, you can ration your services on a first-come/first-served basis. Finally, you can make good use of this interest to spread the word about the significance of your ILI services. To do this, you will need to publicize your ILI worth.

You will need to come out from behind your OPAC, your Web sites, your reference encounters, and your classrooms and help your clientele understand the intrinsic value of your time and services, as well as their extrinsic value—what they cost. How do you do this?

**1. Value your own time and effort.** Let people know what it takes to put together a high-quality ILI group session, in terms of preparation time, intellectual effort, teaching time, and follow-up with evaluation and revision. Insist on sufficient advance notice. If you do not get sufficient advance notice for a customized session, let people know that you will be using a generic outline and examples and why.

**2. Include ballpark estimates of the cost of research resources and the cost (in terms of time and effort) of preparing usage guides for these resources.** For some time vendors have provided inadequate online help to accompany expensive licensed research resources. We can work with vendors to provide more useful help, but if we do so, we should get a discount on our licenses and/or bill the vendors for our efforts. If vendors are not amenable to this arrangement, we should at least let our clientele know the cost in time and effort for us to do the vendors' work for them. We should also let our users know what will be delayed or dropped in order for us to do this work. It does not come for free. There is always a cost.

**3. Be inviting, but be careful to promise only what you can deliver.** Know your limitations and those of your colleagues—resources, people, and space. Do not make promises that other people must keep without your checking with them first. If you plunge ahead recklessly, you risk losing instructor and administrator trust and colleague support. The most popular restaurants insist on a month's advance reservation at a minimum, and some will take reservations beginning only a month to the day before you want to go. This in itself increases the demand and the mystique. So, be sure to let everyone know how much demand there is for your services and the need for advance reservations. In other words, you need to plan in advance so you can handle the business you get, by thinking long-term, by learning to say no when necessary, and by setting guidelines and limitations.

**4. Help your clientele learn to focus on expected learning outcomes, rather than tools.** This can be their first and most immediate lesson. Ask faculty, teachers, and users themselves what they hope to get out of your ILI programs, sessions, and materials. Help them identify their own ILI needs by providing examples of outcomes. Then share your intellectual IL planning process as you work backwards from the outcomes to determine which tools and methodologies will help learners achieve those outcomes most effectively.

In a sense, all of this is part of an essential, coordinated, overall marketing plan. Many libraries are developing and using marketing plans, as they awake to the fact that easy access to information via tools like Google has eroded the concept of libraries and their resources as the place to go for information, physically or virtually. Even academic libraries are getting into the marketing business, as evidenced by the great interest in the ACRL listserv ACADEMICPR, mentioned previously. There, a number of academic libraries have posted copies of their marketing plans, eagerly snatched up by those who have just begun thinking about developing one. Examples include Scott Community College (Bettendorf, Iowa), the University of Nevada, Las Vegas, University of Florida, and County College of Morris (Randolph, New Jersey). IFLA, the international library association, even established an annual IFLA 3M International Marketing Award with three objectives:

- Reward the best library marketing project worldwide each year
- Encourage marketing in libraries
- Give libraries the opportunity to share marketing experiences (IFLA 3M International Marketing Award 2004)

The Houston Public Library won the first award in 2002 for "The Powercard Challenge," with the Calgary Public Library in Calgary, Alberta (Canada) in second place for "Rediscover Your Calgary Public Library," and the Queens Borough Public Library (New York) in third place for "The Opening and Promotion of the Flushing Library," as reported in the July 2002 newsletter of the IFLA Section on Management and Marketing (IFLA 3M International Marketing Award 2004).

GO FOR IT!

There are many options for instructional modes and many different parameters to consider. Which ILI forms you choose in the end may come down to the current administrative culture, the risk-taking climate in your environment, and your ability to engage both your administrators and your colleagues in dialogue and experimentation. Openness to change, flexibility, and a spirit of objective scientific inquiry into effectiveness within a given environment, for a given audience, and under given circumstances, are essential. Just keep in mind that the best ILI may be a waste of time and effort if people do not use it because they do not know about it and its benefits. Effective marketing, publicity, and promotion may be the key to at least a fair trial of your instructional program.

EXERCISES

1. Your library is about to make a drastic change to its IL program. Instead of doing one-hour standard introductions to the online catalog and licensed online periodical indexes, where students are inundated with numerous facts and mechanics, the library would like to offer voluntary sessions using a blend of concepts and mechanics and focused on the concept of the *Visible* vs. *Invisible Web*. Come up with five different ways to market this program and a list of criteria for determining its effectiveness. Be creative! Be wild!

2. The *Web of Science (WOS)* has just been made available to the public through your institution's Web site. *WOS* consists of three parts—*Arts & Humanities Citation Index, Science Citation Index*, and *Social Science Citation Index*—and goes back to 1975. Your user population can do a general search for an author or topic or a cited reference search. PsycInfo, a database of psychology research materials, including journal articles and book chapters, has been available through your Web site for several years. Many users outside the field of psychology use PsycInfo fruitfully. Design a piece of publicity (text and/or artwork) that will draw your clientele's attention to the advantages of using both of these databases over general Web search tools like *Google, Yahoo!* and *a9* (Amazon.com, 2004).

3. What is the "right image" for ILI librarians and an ILI program? Write a publicity piece (ad) for an ILI program. Then write a short plan (three paragraphs) describing how you would market this program.

4. If you had to pick three items to highlight in your ILI Web site "shop window," what would they be? How would you word and position them? What kinds of graphics would you use? How would you grab attention, yet avoid crude or overly flashy gimmicks?

READ MORE ABOUT IT

Germain, C. A. February 2000. "99 Ways to Get Those Feet in the Door." *College and Research Libraries News* 61(2): 93–96.

Haig, Matt. 2003. *Brand Failures: The Truth about the 100 Biggest Branding Mistakes of all Time.* London, UK; Sterling, VA: Kogan Page.

Mark, Margaret, and Carol S. Pearson. 2001. *The Hero and the Outlaw: Building Extraordinary Brands through the Power of Archetypes.* New York: McGraw-Hill.

Murphy, John M. 1987. "What Is Branding?" In *Branding: A Key Marketing Tool*, edited by John M. Murphy, pp. 1–12. New York: McGraw-Hill.

Ogilvy, David. 1983. *Ogilvy on Advertising*. New York: Vintage Books.

Orava, Hilkka. September 1997. Marketing Is an Attitude of Mind. In *Adapting Marketing to Libraries in a Changing and World-Wide Environment*, pp. 84–89. Papers presented at the 63rd IFLA conference, Copenhagen.

Ries, Al, and Laura Ries. 2002. *The Fall of Advertising and the Rise of PR*. New York: Harper-Collins.

Ries, Al, and Jack Trout. 1993. *The 22 Immutable Laws of Marketing: Violate Them at Your Own Risk!* New York: HarperCollins.

Shamel, Cynthia L. July/August 2002. "Building a Brand: Got Librarian?" *Searcher*, 60–71.

Siess, Judith A. 2003. *The Visible Librarian: Asserting Your Value with Marketing and Advocacy*. Chicago: American Library Association.

*8*

---

# Learning to Manage Technology

*Any sufficiently advanced technology is indistinguishable from magic.*
—Clarke's Third Law. Arthur C. Clarke. *Profiles of the Future*, p. 36

## MAGIC IS IN THE EYE OF THE BEHOLDER

In advanced technological societies like the United States, many of us take our technological tools for granted, particularly our computers. Yet, the personal "microcomputer" was an astonishing innovation, and so was its proliferation in the late 1970s and early 1980s. Suddenly there were personal computers (PCs), which could be placed on desktops, rather than a machine taking up an entire room. With some training for PCs (or very little training for Macintoshes), nontechnical people could learn to use them, at least for basic word processing. Since then, shrinking computer chips with greatly expanded capacity, ever-faster machines, and increasingly complex software have mesmerized and energized us.

Now there is a workstation on almost every employee's desk, lap, wrist, pocket, and soon, cell phone. We teach in electronic classrooms and remotely, and technology-based IL materials and instruction pour forth, as IL librarians design interactive IL Web tutorials and exercises, online courses, pathfinders, and other instructional materials. (See Grassian and Kaplowitz 2001, Chapter 9, for examples.) Since computers first appeared in libraries, though, someone has had to plan for, manage, train, and provide technical support for hardware, software, networks, proxy servers, and more. In other words, a lot of work goes on behind the scenes to set up and maintain the technological stage and create the technological magic we now take for granted. ILI librarians often find themselves immersed in various aspects of technology management and support, including designing, using, and providing support for electronic classrooms and distance learning, figuring out how to keep up with technology and how to train and support other library staff, lobbying for improved products, establishing and maintaining instructional technology partnerships, and even managing technostress and technoaddiction problems in themselves and other library staff. How do they manage to do all of this and, in many cases, also fulfill other responsibilities?

## WHAT IS LINE TECHNOLOGY MANAGEMENT?

Some libraries are closely linked to their own or their institution's computer center, which provides technical support. In others, technology management may be assigned to, or default to, one or more librarians with some technical expertise, while still others may hire librarians specifically for their technical expertise. Some very large institutions have layered levels of technical support, where one or more people in a department are responsible for basic technology-related problems and call in the "big guns" only when major problems arise or for equipment replacement, network upgrading, or other issues. In past years the librarian-technology manager may have simply been the library staff member who was most interested in computers. These days, the more tech-savvy staff may or may not be librarians, though most would agree that, in general, the level of technical expertise among librarians continues to grow as electronic resources proliferate. This chapter provides help for the librarian with average technology skills who wants to learn how to be a technology manager for IL. The chapter also addresses topics of interest to the highly skilled techie librarian who needs to learn about managing technology, specifically for ILI purposes.

*Responsibilities*

Technology management responsibilities for IL can vary greatly from one library to another, ranging from minimal hardware and software support to networking responsibility and database licensing, to Web page content development and complete interactive Web site design, development, implementation, and maintenance. Some IL technology managers may have to juggle even broader responsibilities, such as maintenance of wireless networks and instruction in e-mail systems (Pfohl and Hayes 2001), while others may also be "instruction managers," in charge of overall ILI within their library or institution, organization, or corporation (Woodard and Hinchliffe 2002). The technology manager may also need to make decisions (or at least provide advice) on issues of access, including filtering, marketing and publicity, technical support staffing (student or other), and electronic classroom issues. All of these duties need to be placed in the context of advancing the institution's and the library's IL mission and goals, as well. At the very least, these tasks require excellent communication skills and the ability to collaborate with others fruitfully.

Many IL librarians have stepped forward enthusiastically and embraced these new responsibilities, and, better yet, they have taken the time to share their knowledge and skills with those who are new or struggling. Billie Peterson, for example, writes an excellent column on technology for each issue of *LIRT News*, answering technology-related questions clearly, simply, and thoroughly (ALA. LIRT, 2004). Roy Tennant, a librarian at the University of California, Berkeley, has shared his knowledge in highly useful articles like "Web Sites by Design: How to Avoid a Pile of Pages" (1997). This particular article, though dated now, is worth noting, as it was published in *Syllabus Magazine*, whose broad subscriber base is certainly not limited to librarians.

Yet even with the most minimal Web site or other technology-related responsibilities, IL technology managers tend to morph, almost unnoticeably, into technology gatekeepers for the rest of the staff and for administrators, as well as for learners. They may maintain and upgrade equipment and software for an entire library or just for an electronic classroom. They may also write budget proposals for equipment and software as well as for additional staff and for support and training. They filter and forward information about new technology (hardware and software) and usage tips, develop instructional technology partnerships, train other staff, and even provide aid to "technostressed" or "technoaddicted" staff and users. They face frequent interruptions and intense time pressures to install, troubleshoot, repair and otherwise maintain equipment, and train others. All of this demands a high tolerance for frustration and the patience of an "Uber-Job." For long-range planning, the IL technology manager must also have some knowledge of the latest developments in, and capabilities and costs of, various types of computer hardware and software, as well as other sorts of equipment like videocassette recorders (VCRs), LCD panels, data projectors, scanners, DVD players and PDAs.

All of these pressures and time-critical responsibilities make technostress and burnout a very real danger for IL technology managers (Kupersmith 1998). This is especially true when the IL technology manager also has other responsibilities, like reference service and ILI. If you are in this position, you may want to take a few proactive steps to help and protect yourself.

First, as Stover recommends, set some reasonably flexible boundaries (1999). If you do not have an office with a door you can close, make a sign that says DO NOT DISTURB BETWEEN____&____(EXCEPT IN CASE OF EMERGENCY) and put it up near your desk for two-hour intervals several times a week but keep shifting the intervals around. Or buy a standing folding screen, put it up behind you, and put the sign on the screen. Look for other technology managers, within and outside the library, to chat, vent, learn about new technologies, and share problems and ideas. Or set up a listserv to do this electronically. This sort of support group can also lead to joint instructional endeavors or joint proposals to develop programs or materials that utilize technology in innovative ways. In 2003, for instance, the UCLA Office of Instructional Development put out a call for ideas for "blended instruction" for high enrollment courses to help meet pedagogical goals. ("Blended instruction" refers to teaching courses utilizing various forms of technology, in place of some in-person meetings.) If you have some technology background, you can write proposals like this yourself, using language familiar to those reviewing the proposals. Or better yet, you could write a joint proposal with a technical support staff member who is not a library employee and/or with a faculty member.

In order to do this work well, you will need to keep up with technological advances, but how? Try to attend conferences and workshops or get training in new technologies and new approaches to managing technology. Read Billie Peterson's highly informative "Tech Talk" column, recommended above, in each issue of *LIRT News* (for instance, "Open URLs" 2004). Attend LITA's "Top Technology Trends" program at each American Library Association conference or read reports on this outstanding program on the LITA Web site (ALA. LITA 2004). Keep your eyes and ears open for new technological products and new directions in instructional technology. When you learn about new technologies, discuss what you learn with your colleagues, demo it, and try to apply useful techniques. Look into new uses for the technology already available to you or propose upgrading or adding new technologies as appropriate. Do you need to do it all yourself? No! Try to get some help. Propose hiring a student assistant part-time to help out with technology-related problems. Most high school and college students are quite computer-literate, and many may be interested in a technology-related job in order to get résumé-level experience, and at a lower cost for your institution or organization than a professional. Other library staff may also be interested in working with technology-related issues and problems on a part-time basis as well.

If you try to do it all on your own, beware! You could burn out quickly, become irritable, and snap the 10th, 20th, or 100th time someone wants you to install a new printer driver, help him or her ftp a file, set his or her browser preferences, and so on. As Kupersmith points out, the IL technology manager serves as an example to the rest of the staff. Her or his attitude toward technology and change is catching and can help reduce stress among the rest of the staff (Kupersmith 1998). So, keep your cool by maintaining a balance between protecting yourself and helping other staff learn how to help themselves, so they call on you primarily for major problems or questions.

*Budget Issues*

"How much is it going to cost?" is often the first question administrators ask regarding technology. In 2001, Hinchliffe estimated a cost of $50,000 to $100,000 to establish a new electronic classroom, plus additional costs for major remodeling or equipment purchases (2001, p. 99). She estimated "$4000 annually for parts, supplies and staffing for a 'plug and show' [demo-only] classroom, and $19,000 annually for a computer classroom" (2001, p. 117). Equipment costs have declined since 2001 and continue to do so, but someone needs to select from the many technology choices for development and for instruction, even for institutions or organizations that utilize a single platform (PC, Mac, or Unix):

- lease or buy?
- proprietary brand or clone?
- laptop or desktop?
- local printers or networked printer?

In 1996, Tim Berners-Lee, the inventor of the Web, said that a "web year" was about three months (Whatis.com 2002). It is certainly not getting any longer. What implications does this have for equipment purchase or leasing? The three-year equipment lease or purchase rotation common in some libraries may explain why library machines are often outdated and slow.

The IL technology manager must address cost-related issues fairly frequently. She or he must have the ability to identify critical pieces of information, focus on key issues, discuss criteria for usage, purchase, rental, or lease of equipment and software, and make recommendations, including a proposed budget. All of this decision making should be based on staff needs, desires and comfort levels. Can several staff members share a networked printer, or does each person need her or his own? What are the advantages and disadvantages of various e-mail systems? How do costs compare to benefits of portable versus built-in data projectors? The IL technology manager should also be able to communicate this information to administrators, faculty/teachers, and other staff in a clear, convincing, and non-condescending manner.

Is there a way out of constant replacement and upgrading of both equipment and software? Equipment prices do seem to be coming down, so much so that purchasing hardware is now more feasible than leasing. Manual typewriters used to last a long time, much longer than electric typewriters. Yet even though electric typewriters had to be replaced every few years and needed quite a bit of maintenance, we preferred them because they improved productivity and made life easier for people who had to type. We take a lot for granted now in the way of equipment and software, but those who have been around for a while may well remember endless hours of phone tag, messy carbon copies, mimeographs, and even dittos, as well as typed "fan-fold" perforated strips of book order forms with as many as nine carbon copies. Making a single typographical mistake on any one of these forms was quite costly in terms of staff time and effort, not to mention the cost of the forms themselves. Today we can order materials online using forms that can be submitted electronically and pay for our purchases using secure sites. So, equipment and software upgrades that improve productivity are often well worth it, and in a wired world, they are just part of the cost of doing business.

*Planning Installation and Staff Training*

However, software and licensed database purchase or lease decisions involve more than just direct costs. They also involve the indirect costs of instruction in their effective use for both staff and users. IL technology managers need to plan for implementation or installation of new equipment and software in stages, to allow staff to learn their use before making them available to the public. The IL technology manager also needs to plan, develop, and deliver in-house staff training and accompanying materials, such as tutorials and paper point-of-use guides. Generally, two weeks of concentrated effort is enough time for IL technology managers to learn a new piece of software or equipment and prepare instructional materials for the staff, though this minimum preparation period may need to be increased depending on the complexity of the software and equipment. Ideally, staff should be allowed another two weeks to test our equipment and learn new software before making it available to the public, though again, staff may need more time if the technology is quite complex or if work-arounds need to be developed for new software. As staff go through this testing period, they can try out instructional materials and help revise them for public use. After all, the learning curve is called a *curve* for a reason. Learning generally is not instantaneous and does not proceed in a straight line simply because you wish it would.

"Digital learning objects" (DLOs) present a case in point. In 2003 and 2004, DLOs were the latest hot instructional technology topic to reach libraries. But what are DLOs? Definitions vary, even among researchers, techies, and instructional technologists (Metros 2004; Polsani 2003; Wiley 2000), so how do you help staff get a handle on what they really are and how they can be used for ILI? You could hold a "Learn about DLOs" session. Send out an attention-getting "learning invitation" (Masie 2004) listing a few benefits for staff: "Reuse your hard work! Extend your IL reach! Develop new DLOs or adapt what you already have! What are DLOs, anyway? Come to College Library on February 15th and find out. Want a hint? 'DLO' stands for 'Digital Learning Object.' "

Begin the workshop by displaying and having staff try out three DLOs of different granularity, for example:

- Center for Knee, Shoulder and Hip's "Orthopedic Animations" (2003), retrieved from the Bone and Joint Health Digital Learning Objects repository (2003)
- Virginia Kirsch's "Business Cards around the World," retrieved from the Wisconsin Online Resource Center (2004)
- "6 Billion Human Beings" (Pison and van Blyenburgh 2001), retrieved from the MERLOT repository (MERLOT n.d.)

After they have seen these three DLOs or a few others like them, explain that they are similar to coffee-cup sizes at Starbucks: "Small," "Tall," and "Grande." Save a very large DLO for last and call it "Vente." "Valley of the Shadow" is a very large historical Civil War site that includes both in-depth primary resources on two communities and provides links to means of making use of the site (Ayers 2004). Then ask participants to identify the general characteristics of DLOs and, together, prioritize them. If they do not include assessment, add it to the list. Then talk a bit about the uses of DLOs, particularly as self-service teaching/learning objects that faculty could insert into their curricula. End by giving some homework. Ask the participants to find three existing IL items that could be considered DLOs, label them as to size, list the characteristics of each, and e-mail the results to you. Compile the results in a table, grouping DLOs by size and listing characteristics of each. The next step could be a second in-person or Web conference session with the table mounted on a Web site. You can ask each participant to pick one of the items in the table that she or he did not submit, review it, break it down to its fundamental parts, and add notes about its elements. Another discussion could follow, in which the group discusses and tries to come to agreement on which of the most basic elements of existing DLOs are already available at your library, institution, organization, or corporation. After staff have become comfortable with analyzing existing DLOs and able to determine their characteristics and basic elements, you could turn to the next possible steps—creating your own DLO repository, with metadata standards, and then creating and describing your own new DLOs.

All of this takes time, time to plan, to introduce, to describe, and to digest. Whenever we introduce new software or equipment, new technological concepts or approaches, or even major upgrades, it is extremely important to allow staff the time to absorb, learn, and prepare for interaction with the public, no matter who the public may be—internal employees, students, teachers or faculty, members of the organization or corporation, or the general public.

*Technology-Related Policies*

Interaction with the public may also trigger other important concerns such as privacy, filtering, access, e-mailing, printing, and downloading. IL technology managers and other staff need to be prepared with policies and documentation regarding each of these critical issues, as well as technical policies and procedures regarding passwording, access, instructional statistics, and scheduling.

Make sure you understand your institution's policies regarding which instructional statistics need to be kept and how each category is defined. When does a reference interaction become an instructional interaction that needs to be recorded as such? Does it depend upon the number of people you work with in a group, in person, or remotely? Does it depend upon where the interaction takes place? Or does it depend upon how long and complex the interaction is? What constitutes an "orientation tour" as opposed to "group instruction"? Once you know which statistics need to be kept, if you have not done so already, you can use calendaring software or even a table created in Microsoft Word, to schedule room use. However, keeping track of detailed instructional statistics and information in a calendaring system may be problematic due to the technical constraints of the software.

Find out what policies are in place regarding scheduling rooms for instruction. Who can reserve a room? Does a group or individual need to be registered with, or affiliated with your institution in order to use your rooms for any purpose? How far in advance can rooms be reserved? Who is in charge of room reservations? How are room reservation and usage policies set? The more you think about it, the more it becomes clear that room scheduling can be a political issue in itself. IL librarians may need to compete with administrators and information systems staff within and outside the library for teaching/training/learning space, and some groups or individuals may not be permitted to use rooms in your institution, for a variety of political and other reasons.

These sorts of internal issues can be vexing, even for an experienced IL technology manager. Policies regarding public computers can be equally vexing but are also essential and should be posted publicly. Before you review or consider new policies regarding users, however, it is important to step back and review the history of public computer use in libraries in general and then in your library in particular.

*End-User Support*

Public workstations have been a fixture in many types of libraries since the early 1980s. People use them to get to the online library catalog (OPAC), as well as to stand-alone or networked licensed databases, both well-known databases such as "PsycInfo" (American Psychological Association 2004) and other less well known databases such as "Ethnic Newswatch" (n.d.) (complete text of articles from over 200 publications of underrepresented minority groups).

For a number of years, librarians have adapted instructional techniques, materials, and methodologies to accommodate creeping (or "leaping") technology, even to the extent of teaching two or more formats of the same information resource to the same clientele. For instance, the California Digital Library's "MELVYL Catalog" OPAC is available simultaneously in both telnet and Web versions (CDL 2004). Technology has also become an increasingly important instructional tool in itself. So, over the past fifteen to twenty years, libraries have come to utilize and now embrace technology, especially the Web, for users and staff alike. However, public computers with Internet connections present unique problems not previously encountered in libraries.

From a purely mechanical standpoint, use of the Internet, especially the Web, frequently requires typing skills, as well as use of a mouse to point, click, drag, and drop. For some users, it was bad enough when libraries replaced card catalogs with OPACs, as they often differed in look and feel from one library to another. Many older OPACs were text-based and required the use of a computer with a monitor and keyboard, but at least most people were familiar with typewriter keyboards, and novices could hunt-and-peck even if they could not touch-type. Even in the information age, some are still on what could be called the dark side of the digital divide. Now they have to surmount the mouse barrier, as they awkwardly learn the eye-hand coordination required to point, click, and drag.

In addition, these new Web users need to understand what Web browsers are and how they work. They need to know that some Web sites may open multiple browser windows in the same session. On a very basic level, they need to know how to scroll up and down or from side to side, click in boxes before typing, and click on graphic images, icons, or links in order to proceed. Graphic images and icons may also look confusingly different from one library to another or even from one Web page to another, even if they are accessed through the same library. Images and icons may be in different places on a screen, or a similar-looking icon may mean something different from one system or database to another. "Keyword" searching may mean "search all fields" in one database but "search all fields except author" in another. Most databases insert a Boolean "and" invisibly between search words. Infotrac (Expanded Academic ASAP) inserts a "within-1-word" proximity operator between words (Gale Group n.d.). What's a poor user to do? How is she or he supposed to know all of this? No wonder some people give up on libraries and just go to nice, simple Google, where there is just one search box. Type in your words and press enter, and voila, there are your results (admittedly often too many, though, and in many cases, only tangentially related to the intent of the search).

Essentially, users must now learn a broader set of skills than ever before, just to get access to information, and they are much more likely to feel embarrassed and frustrated. More people will need very basic help, and we need to provide that help for them in the most supportive manner possible. Items placed on the Web for free asynchronous use, such as interactive tutorials or exercises or library-specific databases like OPACs, open our doors to anyone with Internet access. Ideally, libraries of all kinds with freely available materials would help anyone who wants to learn how to use them, rather than considering ILI a scarce resource that must be rationed first to the institution's "primary" clientele. After all, if we are open to the public, then all of the public are our clientele and should at least receive the kind of basic help Philip Agre describes so simply and yet eloquently in "How to Help Someone Use a Computer" (1996).

Given this historical background, what sorts of policies do IL technology managers need to consider?

If you have too few computers to meet demand, you should consider authentication, time limits, and/or usage policies.

Do you need to restrict use of your public computers to your primary user population? If so, what sort of authentication system is available to allow you to set up automatic authentication? You can always use low-tech authentication, if need be, by posting signs stating that your primary users get sole or preferential computer use and requiring users to place their IDs in visible locations next to, or on top of, their computers. Consider, too, what sorts of policies and procedures you may need for visitors. Do you need to check your users' photo IDs for their age, for filtering purposes? If so, you may need to post signs to this effect.

Time limits for computer use tend to be easier to monitor than restrictions on types of usage. Time limits on usage also allow you to respect users' privacy and avoid unnecessary confrontations over intended and actual usage. Should children be allowed more, less, or the same amount of time on a computer than adults? If you tend to have a number of users who are new to computers or infrequent computer users, you may want to be as flexible as possible in terms of time limits to avoid increasing computer anxiety among newbies.

You may also need to consider policies regarding software, as well as hardware. If your institution or organization has public computers with just Internet browsers, you may want to consider adding other software in order to create an "information commons." Generally, this would mean adding word processing and other kinds of software and hardware, like scanners and printers, so that users can fill all of their computer needs in one location. Of course, adding hardware or software to their choices may mean that you will need to increase the time limits on usage. Another option is to turn electronic classrooms into computer labs when they are not scheduled for teaching.

Public computers, computer labs or information commons can be quite divorced from formal pedagogy, but informally, they support intentional or even accidental learning simply through exposure to various types of software. More formally, IL technology managers can work with other IL librarians to offer instruction in the use of various types of software and hardware available to their users. As we mentioned earlier in this chapter, you can use technology to support pedagogical goals in many different ways. You can use an electronic classroom for synchronous, face-to-face group instruction, or you can offer distance learning for synchronous or asynchronous instruction to groups or individuals. IL technology management for these types of instruction is similar in some ways and very dissimilar in others.

HOW DO YOU MANAGE ELECTRONIC CLASSROOMS?

Most in-person classrooms contain some form of technology, even if it is only chalk and a blackboard or a whiteboard and markers, a flip chart and easel, or an overhead projector and screen. By definition, electronic classrooms contain equipment of various kinds and provide instructor and, often, learner access to software used in instruction. Usually there are one or more network and Internet connections and often a data projector and screen. Whether or not the room has multiple computers, some IL librarians or others may use it for demos, while others may use it hands-on or in some combination of both. These classrooms may also be used for other purposes, including meetings and drop-in computer labs.

All of the equipment and software in an electronic classroom requires vigilant oversight, including troubleshooting, maintenance, and continual upgrading, as well as continual staff training in the use of new or upgraded equipment and software. Whoever is responsible for an electronic classroom should work closely with IL librarians in deciding on electronic classroom design and if and when to upgrade or replace software and equipment. Budget and timing are critical factors, of course, but establishing and maintaining an optimum learner-centered environment should be paramount. It will be easier to use a learner-centered approach if you can design or modify an electronic classroom to maximize learning. Hinchliffe wisely notes, though, that there is no one-size-fits-all design and that we must consider "what is the best design within given constraints (e.g., budget limitations, remodeling difficulties, and time limitations)" (1998), as well as whether or not you must work within the constraints of a given room. (See Grassian and Kaplowitz 2001, Chapter 17, for discussion of effective use of electronic classrooms in teaching, and Hinchliffe 2001.)

More recently, ILI librarians have debated the use of laptops in classrooms in place of desktops, as wireless connections are increasingly widespread these days (Hovis 2004; Michel 2004; Thomas 2004). If you use laptops instead of desktop computers, you may use your electronic classroom for a variety of purposes, including meetings and as a lab where students may bring their own laptops or borrow them for individual use. The drawbacks to using laptops include set-up and takedown time, fragility of laptops, limits on battery charge, decreased ability to share due to size and type of display, and problems using laptop hardware, like touch pads and small buttons in the middle of the keypad to move the cursor. Public library users, particularly senior citizens, may have problems with laptops, as many who attend public library computer classes are not familiar with computers, displays tend to be smaller, some key positions may vary, and you may need to attach mice to allow for those who have a hard time with touch pads and buttons in the middle of a keyboard to move the cursor (Walker 2004). Hinchliffe mentioned a number of these points as well, though since her book was published in 2001, manufacturers have been addressing many of these problems, especially battery life and fragility, with ever-improving results. Some wireless carts can hold up to thirty-two laptops and require only a single data port to connect all wireless laptops to the Internet. Current battery life for laptops used in this way is only about two hours, but while students use half the laptops, the other half can be charging (Ahn 2004).

Whether you use laptops or desktops, managing this constantly evolving electronic classroom technology requires much staff time, effort, and careful attention to detail. The same is true of technology management for remote IL instruction, whether "remote" refers to synchronous (simultaneous group) or asynchronous (individual, anytime, anyplace) use.

## HOW DO YOU MANAGE DISTANCE LEARNING TECHNOLOGY?

Costs, staffing, and other technology management issues for remote learning will vary greatly depending on the type of distance learning instructional mode you use. For example, if you want to create and mount static Web pages, your institution or organization may already have a Web designer on staff or may have a contract for Web site development. You may be able to work with these people to develop and mount static Web pages at little or no additional cost.

You may also be able to take a class, read some guides to creating Web pages, and practice creating some simple Web pages on your own. You could then work with others to enhance these pages by adding forms and other interactivity or graphics. Generally, though, the more complex the Web pages or other instructional modes, the more time, money, and effort it will cost to prepare, mount, and maintain them. The time you yourself or your IL team will need to invest to achieve your vision of effective distance learning materials and programs may be quite a bit more than you anticipate. You should consider carefully whether or not the complexity you envision is necessary to achieve expected learning outcomes and whether or not it would be worth your investment of time and that of others. The same is true for online courses.

As a number of publications indicate, teaching an online course is different from teaching a course in person. As the IL technology manager, you may want to develop an online course yourself, or you may be part of a team of IL librarians that wishes to do so. You will still need to start with a goal and expected learning outcomes, but if you want to turn an existing synchronous in-person course into a synchronous on-line course, some of the underlying foundation may already be there, but, you may need to use many different instructional formats in smaller chunks to get and hold learners' attention, help them achieve expected learning outcomes, and measure their success. Ko and Rossen offer general guidelines and examples (2001), while Levesque provides helpful guidance based on the mistakes she made in developing and offering an online IL course and the steps she took to improve it (2003). All would agree that the instructor or team of instructors of a success-ful online course must be very well organized and keep careful track of time. They would also agree that interactivity and visuals are impor-tant in engaging learners online and that group work can be conducted successfully online. In fact, Ko and Rossen devote nine pages of their book to online group activities (2001, pp. 111–120). Online courses can be extremely valuable to those who are unable to attend in-person instruction and to those who prefer to learn in this way. ACRL's Dis-tance Learning Section even offers useful "Guidelines for Distance Learning Library Services" for higher education (ALA. ACRL. Distance Learning Section 2004).

Laptops and wireless environments offer other possibilities as well, both for synchronous use in online courses, as described above, and for asynchronous use, even at the level of grades six through ten and up. St. Andrews Priory School in Honolulu, for instance, provides laptops and wireless connections for over 300 of its students. Librari-ans developed a Web page of many information resources and use it to teach introductory IL classes to the students. The students and teach-ers view these classes and the Web page as a taking-off point, and stu-dents, even at this age, rely heavily on their online resources, with the library at the center of intellectual engagement (Landgraf and Weaver 2003). You may wonder how many online resources a small school li-brary can afford. In Hawaii, a consortium of the university, public schools, and private institutions makes subscriptions much more af-fordable, even for very small schools. Technology management is im-portant in these small environments as well. In fact, librarians may have to manage much more technology than they do in large institu-tions, as they may be the only ones who know how to install and maintain servers, download upgraded software for printers and scan-ners, and keep up with mutating research tool interfaces, along with everyone else in large research institutions, public libraries, and spe-cial libraries.

Given all of this, you may wonder how to decide which sorts of technology to provide users and to use in teaching, whether or not to offer online courses or hybrid courses, or how much technology to include in in-person instruction. It may seem like an obvious point, but it is all too easy to get carried away with the possibilities offered by technology, especially if it seems that everywhere you turn, someone is using advanced technology for instruction. However, we must be realistic, consider the costs, and attempt to meet our goals with the technologies that will help us do so most effectively and for the least direct and indirect cost, including staff time. It is best, in fact, to write out all of your ideas about technology use in instruction and to link them to your written goals and objectives or expected learning outcomes. This exercise can be especially useful when you have to prepare a proposal for administrators or a grant proposal requesting funding to support your ideas. (See Chapter 6 for general proposal writing guidance and Hinchliffe 2001, Chapter 1, for guidance in justifying electronic classroom proposals.) Try to pull together a diverse planning team of librarians, faculty, and students, as Hinchliffe recommends (2001), or a team of community and business leaders, along with librarians. If you can get your team members to add value in some way, through direct or indirect funding (donating staff time, for instance), you may really get the attention of your administrators.

Of course, financial support can go only so far. In reality, few of us have enough staff, budget, and time to provide all sorts of instruction for anyone and everyone who wants it. What we can do, though, is provide at least *minimal* and simple help that most people who visit our Web sites can use. Or we can try to gear our materials to the average level of our primary audience. For instance, a high school library might gear its help to the level of the average high school student. This minimal basic help could take the form of online tutorials (passive or interactive) and paper point-of-use guides (Grassian and Kaplowitz 2001, Chapter 8) and should also include one-on-one reference help at the point and time of need. This approach would go a long way toward helping many users who have difficulty using computers and electronic materials. At the university level, you might want to create or link to Web sites like the "Research Paper Planner" (Grassian 2003) or the "Assignment Calculator" (University of Minnesota 2004). The former provides a linear list of steps to take in developing a research paper, with links to mostly free Web sites with detailed help and an indication of which steps to accomplish by which point in a term. The latter allows you to enter a start date and a due date and pick a general topic area. The program then returns a schedule for completing the various steps to developing a research paper and also provides suggestions for research resources for that discipline or subject area. As a bonus, the "Assignment Calculator" is open source software, which means that anyone interested may request the programming code and adapt it freely for use in his or her own library.

The "Research Paper Planner" and the "Assignment Calculator" are designed for college student use, but high school students may benefit from using them, along with the many help guides and basic IL tutorials now freely available on library Web sites, like "The Road to Research" (Grassian 2004b). So, think broadly about multiple purposes and audiences for your online materials. Consider, too, that we all had to start at the beginning with computers. It may be worthwhile investigating whether or not to offer a basic computer skills course for those who are just starting out, as many public libraries do. Yet, libraries of all kinds open to the public confront more than user problems with computers. As Stover points out, we need to remember that we have a relationship with, and a responsibility toward, our users, as well as a reasonable expectation of the rewards of helping them (Stover 1999). IL technology managers may also confront issues of filtering, censorship, privacy, security, and excessive demand for a scarce resource—time on Internet-connected workstations.

## HOW DO YOU DEVELOP PROPOSALS FOR UPGRADES?

Clearly, IL technology management is multifaceted and is essential even in the smallest environment, even if there is only one IL librarian. When a new IL technology management position is created, or when a new IL technology manager is appointed, an "instructional environmental scan" can be a good way to begin defining the scope of the task. Start by listing all of the institution's or organization's basic IL activities, their purpose, the means used to accomplish them, and who is responsible for each. Include development of instructional materials in all formats, as well as the instruction itself. Then take a second scan of equipment and software that are not currently being used and ask what sorts of equipment or software would help staff do a better job. Completed scans will reveal both heavy and light use and provide a basis for proposals to upgrade equipment and software. (See Hinchliffe's "Instructional Needs Assessment" worksheet 2001, Figure 3.1, and "Design Priorities Worksheet" 2001, Figure 3.5.) Hinchliffe lays out a wealth of useful detail about important factors you should consider as you plan to establish or upgrade an IL electronic classroom, including lighting, furniture, software, hardware, and the ever-knotty issue of layout (2001).

Generally, IL technology proposals should be developed in concert with those affected. In most cases, this means reference and instruction staff as well as administrators. Planning for electronic classrooms, in particular, should be a joint decision reached after discussion and consensus, which may mean making compromises. Decisions about whether or not to use classroom control software, presentation software, equipment and furniture selection, and classroom layout are all important pieces of the electronic classroom puzzle and may reflect the institution's IL mission and goals. In 1999, at the University of Washington, the UWired Collaboratory was set up with workstations on large circular tables to encourage collaborative learning, the IL program's primary goal (Tillman 2000). Other layouts, like a U-shape with instructor's workstation and large screen at the top of the U, may be designed to maximize the instructor's ability to view all of the learners' monitors at a glance and guide wayward learners. With still others, classroom control software may make this sort of arrangement unnecessary, though you may have to make an extra effort to avoid lecturing too much in rooms that are arranged like computer labs or like a traditional lecture hall, with all users facing the front of the room (Hinchliffe 1998; Hinchliffe 2001). At all costs, avoid having a forward-facing computer lab room arrangement where the instructor's workstation is behind some of the learners. With this arrangement, the learners sitting in front of you will have their backs to you. This means that you will have difficulty getting and maintaining eye contact with them, and you may have to walk around them to the front of the room to get their attention.

Do you have separate mouse platforms connected to keyboard trays? If so, make sure you have some left-handed ones or provide both right- and left-handed platforms for all of your computers. Check the chairs. Comfortable chairs with wheels are best, as they allow learners to move their chairs away from computers and into small groups, as necessary.

In all decisions regarding classroom layout, you should also take note of accessibility requirements and regulations. Make sure to allow enough room around doorway openings so people in wheelchairs can enter the room and get to computers. This may even mean reducing the number of computer stations in the room. The ABLEDATA site can be useful for technology-related products for the disabled (Hinchliffe n.d.).

How well does your room arrangement work? This is an important question. Check with librarians, with learners, and with instructors and use a variety of assessment methods (Hinchliffe 2001). You may find that opinions vary widely, almost as much as teaching and learning styles can vary. Some prefer to be as close to the learners as possible, while others may prefer to stand at the front of the room or to wander around the room, from front to back. How does all of this work in school, public, and special libraries? The answer is, very similarly, but with different populations of decision-makers and varying constraints. One important constraint may be the need to have multipurpose environments that can also be used for teaching and learning. (See Hinchliffe 2001, Appendix G, for school, public, and special library case studies.)

New or revised instruction programs can also provide a good reason for requesting additional software, hardware, and other equipment, as well as additional staff support. Curriculum revision or acquisition of new licensed databases or a new OPAC may all require new or upgraded equipment and software, for example. However, new equipment and software alone will not guarantee successful IL programs, especially if there is insufficient staff to make full use of them, or if staff are overworked and burdened with too many priority projects and other responsibilities. Sufficient staffing is crucial to success, even if it is only on a temporary basis, and it should be an important part of any IL technology proposal in support of new or revised IL programs.

## HOW DO YOU TRAIN STAFF?

Once a proposal has been developed and accepted, and equipment and software have been installed, the next step is to train staff in its use. Staff training can be easier than user training, because in many cases the IL technology manager (who may be the staff trainer as well) has a fairly good idea of the level of staff skills and their preferred learning styles, and there are almost always fewer staff to train than users. Staff trainers should be wary of making assumptions about staff knowledge and skills, however, and would do well to determine skill levels prior to instruction, just as with users. One quick and painless way to do so is to administer needs assessments as self-tests in the form of checklists, like "Basic Computer Literacy Skills" (University of Houston, Clear Lake n.d.) and "Sample Self-Training Checklist" (Barclay 2000, Figure 10-3), where learners identify areas in which they need instruction, and training is geared accordingly.

On the other hand, staff training can be more difficult than user training, as new software and equipment may require new ways of working, and some staff members may be reluctant to change old habits. If you are used to doing demos, and suddenly there are computers for learners as well as the instructor, you will have many more instructional options, particularly the use of active learning techniques. If you purchase classroom control software that allows you to turn learner's computers on and off, as well as display to the group what appears on an individual learner's machine, your options expand even further. When new IL tutorials appear, like "Bruin Success with Less Stress" (Swartz 2004), you may want to assign all or parts of it as a precursor to an in-person session on plagiarism, copyright, and documentation. Resistant learners, whether staff or users, can be a difficult audience, though it does help if you focus the learners' attention on the fact that the trainer is just the messenger and is merely trying to help staff by easing the pain of a new learning cycle. A buddy/mentor system that partners more experienced staff with less experienced staff may also be effective for staff training in new software and equipment.

Helping others can quickly demystify rooms full of scary new devices, as well, as mystification is quite common in wired environments (Stover 1999). To help build self-confidence, you might ask all staff to volunteer to serve as rovers at public workstations on a rotating basis or during group instruction in the electronic classroom. Offer some special training for them and introduce hardware, software, and other equipment in stages. Start with a basic training session for staff helpers and be sure to let them know frequently how much their help is appreciated. Make a checklist of all pieces of equipment and software that instructors *need* to use and another checklist of equipment and software they might *want* to use. Develop step-by-step instructions for turning on and off, logging on and off, and troubleshooting tips, along with phone numbers for help. Have each person, instructor and rover, go through all of the steps for using each piece of equipment. Some support staff may learn equipment use and troubleshooting well enough to help train or provide support for others, easing the direct burden on the IL technology manager.

Software training should be handled separately from hardware training, to the greatest degree possible. PowerPoint will probably require its own separate session, for example, as it is often overused and misused, as well as overwhelming to those who have never used it. Above all, remember that even with a small group, there may very well be someone who knows more about how to use a particular piece of equipment or software than the IL technology manager does. Call on the audience for their expertise, lean on them, get them to participate and teach their colleagues, or try to team up with a computer trainer. Stover suggests getting people to tell technology stories in order to relieve technostress (1999). At a 1994 LOEX Conference, Dan Ream gave an entertaining talk about technology glitches and then held a contest for the worst teaching experience involving technology at each of fifteen different tables of attendees. Just telling these "war stories" to each other made everyone feel better and helped illustrate common technological problems even at that time. You can find many of these stories along with excellent tips on avoiding technology glitches on one of his Web pages, "Scratch That Glitch" (Ream 2001).

Barclay suggests taking advantage of existing user training to develop staff training, as there will be overlap between the two (2000, p. 186). You might also consider turning this idea around, though. Once you have developed a draft user training session, ask staff to attend a rehearsal of it and give you feedback. The staff will learn whatever you were planning to teach users, and you will get useful suggestions for how to improve the user training. Then invite questions from the staff related to their own work and the software you are teaching. Plan to leverage whatever training you do by asking each trainee to go back to her or his environment after your session and train three others (Barclay 2000).

Of course, all of this effort is for naught if no one comes to your training session. Barclay offers a number of suggestions for attracting staff to training sessions, including using guest trainers, timing training appropriately, and using "bribes," like door prizes, an hour of compensatory time off, a poster, or an extra paid hour (2000, p. 188).

## WHAT ARE THE BENEFITS OF INSTRUCTIONAL PARTNERSHIPS?

It is important to realize that none of us can really know it all or do it all. Likewise, none of us can or should work in isolation any more. We are all enriched by the creative abilities and efforts of others working toward common goals. Working with other individuals like computer trainers can be a wonderful way to develop and provide varied and superior levels of instruction. In Chapter 3 we discussed how to form partnerships and encourage collaborative environments. These sorts of partnerships need to be nourished and appreciated. They may make a tremendous difference in future endeavors, especially as we turn our attention more and more to distance learning efforts.

A big question here is how well (or even whether) people can learn to learn how to identify, locate, evaluate, and make effective use of widely differing information tools and resources. The Los Angeles Public Library (LAPL), for instance, makes scores of licensed databases available remotely to any users with LAPL library cards (n.d.).

Is access enough, though? Are users able to figure out which of these databases will best suit their needs and how to use these multiple interfaces on their own? What sort of help do these libraries provide for asynchronous remote users? Can users easily find and utilize the help we provide? It is important to keep in mind that for the most part, just mounting a system or database on the Web does not automatically make it easy to use or understand. As ALA's "Principles for a Networked World" puts it, "Even the most well designed information systems are limited and require individuals to learn how to use them effectively" (ALA 2003c, p. 6).

Whether they are in the library or getting to library materials remotely, users may need clear and simple help in navigating systems and databases. Jakob Nielsen, the well-known Web usability guru, offers excellent advice on how to test whether or not your Web site is easy to use and inviting for your user population (Nielsen 1993, 2000, 2003, 2004). Although he addresses businesses primarily, his advice is so simple and commonsensical that it can be applied just as easily to almost any environment. He suggests that you test your pages with just a few of your typical users, one at time. Ask them to complete tasks using your Web site and ask them to talk about their thoughts as they are using your Web site. Take notes on where they click, where they stumble, what confuses them. After you have done this with a few people, make changes based on their comments and try it again with a few more people. Nielsen points out that major problems will pop up with the first few people, and as you make corrections and retest, problems should diminish, while your Web site becomes easier to use and more welcoming. You can test passive tutorials with naive users by asking them to sit with you and use your passive tutorial to learn whatever the tutorial is designed to teach. Again, ask them to verbalize their thoughts, take notes, and make corrections based on any problems they encountered. With online help in the form of interactive tutorials, you may be able to use another technique recommended by Nielsen and described quite fully by Snyder (Snyder 2003). With this approach, you prepare paper mock-ups of an interactive tutorial before you ever spend a dime or a minute preparing an online version. Again, Snyder recommends that you ask users, one by one, to complete tasks by using your tutorial, while someone acts as the "computer," changing pages when the user "clicks" on a mocked-up button, and while someone else takes notes. Of course, with any usability study, you may need to get IRB permission, or an IRB exemption, as you will be using human subjects to test something.

Once you have completed the testing and have mounted either passive or interactive forms of online help, you might want to consider adding counters or using other means of analyzing how many hits your help pages are getting. If you use forms for feedback, be sure they are prominent enough to get attention, yet not so prominent that they assault the reader with insistent blinking or repeated pop-up windows. You will need to find the most appropriate and useful level and type of help for your users. How will you know when you are there? Ask your users through usability testing and informally. They will tell you.

## DO LIBRARIANS TEACH TECHNOLOGY TO COMPENSATE FOR POORLY DESIGNED TECHNOLOGY?

It seems clear that we need to provide useful help for Web sites we create or interfaces we ourselves design. But why go to all of this trouble when vendors provide online help anyhow? As long as companies/vendors continue to create idiosyncratic interfaces for information tools and other resources, people will need help learning how to use them. Even as we develop instruction and teach existing technology, there is lots of room for improvement in user interfaces, and librarians on the front lines should provide input to database and interface designers on this important need. It is important for us to lobby technology producers to improve their products, to make them more user-friendly, and to provide help in the form of tutorials and context-sensitive help, including graphic examples.

The University of California's California Digital Library (CDL) System's MELVYL Catalog (n.d.) offers an excellent example of how a Web site vendor, sponsor, or content provider can be responsive and make good use of user comments to improve its product. A link on each page of the Web site leads to a feedback form that is easy to use. The CDL staff are quick to respond, and they take each comment seriously. Commercial vendors may require more direct lobbying to improve their products and to stop believing what Gaffney calls the "myth of the stupid user"—that is, that users are to blame if they cannot use a particular product, rather than the product developers. According to Gaffney, most people in the IT and Web development industry have this misconception about people who use their products, equating lack of technical experience or sophistication with stupidity (2000). Librarians who attend conferences and visit vendor exhibits need to take a more assertive, proactive stance and keep after vendors to make their products more user-friendly, both for our users and for ourselves.

Michael Gorman has taken a rather extreme view, suggesting that we would not need to teach people how to use technology if technological products were properly designed. Instead, according to Gorman, our goal should be getting technology producers to design technology properly. He even provides a sample, rather lengthy dialogue that he envisioned taking place between a user and the online catalog (Gorman 1991). Gorman's goal was quite admirable, to make the library easy to use from a user's point of view. Unfortunately, though, he did not take into account the diverse nature of humans, both in creating and in trying to utilize information resources. So, we have not yet attained Michael Gorman's "BI-less" (or "IL-less") library in any setting, and probably we never will, but there are some hopeful signs of standardization. Many Web sites now have site maps that can help users orient themselves and quickly locate specific information or pages. Navigation bars frequently appear at the tops and bottoms of Web pages. More often than not, too, each Web page on a site includes a link for Help and another for visitors to return to the top page.

However, though, we may never see in the Web the kind of standardization present in other fields or industries, such as the auto industry, where in the United States the steering wheel is always on the left, and speed and distance traveled are measured in miles. For better or worse, the Web is much more of a free-for-all enterprise. This means that designers can and will take very different approaches, some of which will be user-unfriendly, if not user-hostile, and thereby increase computerphobia among hesitant users. In fact, computerphobia is much more widespread than many people think, and this lack of user-friendliness is a powerful contributing factor (Grassian and Kaplowitz 2001, Chapter 5). User-hostile interfaces and just the sheer numbers of different programs and interfaces that IL librarians need to master in order to keep up can also lead to "technostress," "technoburnout," and incredibly creative means of avoiding learning new or upgraded technology.

## RECOGNIZE TECHNOSTRESS AND TECHNOADDICTION

The term "techno-stress" first appeared in the *Washington Post* in 1983 to describe a guide to exercises "designed to combat techno-stress" (*Oxford English Dictionary* 2004). Definitions of "technostress" include the phrase "modern disease" (*Eastern Airlines Review* 1984), "mental fatigue" (Brod 1984, p. 41), and "negative impact on . . . body physiology" (Weil and Rosen 1997, p. 5). As Weil's and Rosen's research indicates, technostress can occur due to information overload, as well as our inability to understand how technology of all kinds really works (1997, p. 33). In the early 1990s, in fact, their research in twenty-three countries indicated that a surprising percentage of those populations suffered from "technological discomfort," even in countries thought to have a computer-sophisticated populace, like Japan (1997, pp. 215–216).

In the United States it is still possible to get around and even work without the obvious aid of computer hardware and software, though unbeknownst to some, computer chips are hidden in our cars, our microwaves, our VCRs, and other household appliances. They are more obvious in automated teller machines (ATMs), which operate in a linear fashion, taking users through a series of menus in order to reach a goal—money. For IL librarians, however, technology occupies very large portions of the physical workplace and itself enables us to have virtual workplaces. Technostress in this environment often results from a too-much-too-fast syndrome and unexamined priorities. It can also result from an overload of information itself—"information fatigue syndrome." This syndrome has been reported in the United States, as well as a number of other countries around the world. It results from information overload and can lead to health problems and to social problems at work and at home (Weil and Rosen 1997, p. 188).

You can find both individual and group or organizational means for managing technostress related to IL (See Chapter 1 for more on stress and burnout, and Grassian and Kaplowitz 2001, Chapter 12, regarding the validity and reliability of assessment instruments.) For technostress in particular, it helps to have someone to call on who is more knowledgeable about technology, a techno-mentor who can empower others. Mini-sharing and brief training sessions during staff-meetings can also help. For example, you might ask each staff member to share one technology tip a week with other staff, vote on the best tip of the month, and then reward the person who provided the best tip. During IL staff meetings, you might ask each person to come up with one way she or he would like to use technology to support instructional goals or one thing that has been bothering her or him most about technology and instruction. If you bounce these problems and questions back to the entire group, you may be able to get IL staff to help one another.

Technostress is partially due to fear of technology—fear of breaking something or fear of looking dumb. "Knowledge is power!" we often tell learners, and the same is true for ourselves. The more empowered we feel about technology as a tool and the more attention we pay to prioritizing workloads, the less technostressed we are liable to feel. Of course, there is a flip side. Some people feel so empowered by, and attached to, computers that they feel compelled to use them more than necessary for more and more projects and activities or to enhance their own self-images. According to Weil's and Rosen's research, these people suffer from "Technosis," or "technological symbiosis." They form attachments to technology, which can take any or all of three forms: "'Can/Should' Paradox" (not knowing when they are really done using technology), "Technodependency" (expecting and wanting technology to be available at all times), and "Machine Machismo" (using technology to enhance or diminish identity) (1997, p. 63). Weil and Rosen note quite insightfully that we often take on too much these days because we cannot estimate accurately how much time each task will take. They recommend many different ways of overcoming all three types of technoaddictions, including the following:

1. Set time parameters for yourself by setting an alarm clock or timer.
2. Do some things the old-fashioned way, like writing a note to a friend.
3. Make a list of the qualities and skills that you're proud of; cross out anything to do with technology—reclaim your identity. (1997, pp. 67, 69)

Their basic message regarding technostress is that you can overcome it and make technology work for you. It is important for all of us to heed their advice, for as Cerise Oberman points out, IL librarians, too, can range from being technophobes to technojunkies. As she says so well, "BI [Bibliographic Instruction] librarians should view their instruction as a positive force in placing technology in its appropriate context by addressing its limitations while recognizing its strengths" (1995, p. 39). Not much seems to have changed since 1995 in terms of pressure, stress, and overwork, other than the increased pace of change and the fact that librarians may have become somewhat inured to it. Oberman's more balanced approach is still good advice, and it applies to our users, as well as ourselves, the learners who expect us to be ever ahead of the technological curve and to be able to answer their myriad technology-related questions. Even to begin to meet these expectations, IL librarians must run ever faster just in order to keep up.

KEEP UP WITH TECHNOLOGY, OR "TRIPPING THE LIGHT TECHNO-FANTASTIC!"

How can you keep up with new technology? This is the most difficult challenge facing librarians who teach technology, because keeping up with new technology really means staying ahead. Yet, how can IL librarians learn new technology or new versions of older technology in enough time and in enough depth to be able to develop quality technology-related instruction? It helps to have a method for keeping informed and a systematic plan for acquiring up-to-date technology, testing it out, developing goals and objectives, and then an instructional plan. It also helps to have a lively curiosity and an eagerness to try out new technology (Grassian and Kaplowitz 2001, Chapter 16). This is where the IL technology manager can take the lead.

As you may know quite well, listservs, newsgroups, journals, magazines, newspapers, user groups, blogs (weblogs), and savvy colleagues can provide invaluable information about new developments in technology, bugs, work-arounds, and other useful tips. If you have been more deeply involved with technology than with instruction, you may not know about ILI-L, the Information Literacy and Instruction Listserv (ILI-L n.d.). This listserv is an invaluable window into the current concerns and interests of instruction librarians. Elliott Masie's Techlearn Trends listserv provides a window into the broader e-Learning world with infrequent but, nevertheless, succinct, enthusiastic, and thought-provoking messages (Masie n.d.). The major drawback to listservs, of course, is that subscribers receive all listserv messages in their e-mail inboxes ("push" technology), whether or not these messages are useful to them. Many of the other types of resources listed above take extra effort on the part of the reader to remember to check them for articles or messages of interest ("pull" technology), though Really Simple Syndication (RSS) feeds via software like "intraV-news" can push blog messages to your e-mail inbox, sorted by topic (Fallows 2004). The San Diego State University's educational technology community runs EDTECH Beach, a useful blog on this topic (San Diego State University n.d.). (For more on blogging, see "Blogging 101," 2003; Feldman 2003; Gurak et al. 2004.)

Listservs and newsgroups can be wonderfully supportive communities, where members or visitors can ask questions and discuss topics of mutual interest and request help, but it is important to help your colleagues and users understand that you can get in trouble if you post messages without adhering to accepted protocols. The "Master the Basics: Netiquette" (Michael Lerner Productions 2004) and Rinaldi (1998) netiquette Web sites provide important guidelines for communicating in electronic forums. These guidelines, too, are a form of instruction for prospective users of these forms of communication. If your colleagues have never posted or responded to a message on a listserv before, you might suggest that they subscribe to ILI-L and read messages for a while ("lurk") and then read netiquette guidelines carefully before participating on the list. Most of all, encourage them to be courteous and to be succinct.

Journals, magazines, and newspapers, both print and online,

library-related or not, are also extremely valuable means for keeping up with new technology, both for yourself and for your colleagues and users. Good examples include *Wired*, *Syllabus*, *The Chronicle of Higher Education*'s Information Technology section (n.d.), the "Business" section of each Thursday's *New York Times*, and even the business or technology section of your local newspaper.

The MIT Media Lab's "Research" site gives you a peek into many possible futures (n.d.). There you will learn about new research endeavors like computers that are "affective learning companions." Cameras attached to these computers track and report your facial expressions. Pressure-sensitive mice can tell how hard you press a mouse button, and a sensor tells the computer how sweaty your palms are. Then an animated character reacts to what the sensors register and tries to help you (McDonagh 2004).

Organizations and partnerships both within and outside librarianship can be enormously helpful as well. Participation in any of the following organizations and partnership groups with computing center staff, instructional designers, and network administrators can mean timely exchange of information and still more support groups in the event of problems or questions about new technology. (For instance, see the UCLA "Scholarship in a New Media Society" Web site for examples of what a fruitful partnership effort can accomplish [UCLA. Office of Instructional Development 2004].)

- ALA Association of College & Research Libraries' Instruction Section (ALA. ACRL. Instruction Section 2004a)
- ALA Library Instruction Round Table (ALA. LIRT 2004)
- Southern California Instruction Librarians (ALA. ACRL. CARL. sCIL 2004)
- California Clearinghouse on Library Instruction, North (2004)
- American Association of Higher Education (AAHE 2003)
- ALA Reference & User Services Association's Machine Readable Services Section ( ALA. RUSA. MARS 2004).

Make it a habit to watch for announcements about when new technology or new versions of existing software will become available. Haunt excellent Web sites like Steven Bell's "Keeping Up Web Page" (Bell 2004a) and check his blog, "The Kept-Up Academic Librarian," for daily updates on higher education developments (Bell 2004b). Keep your technical support staff and administrators informed about new developments and the importance of keeping up-to-date with hardware and software and get copies of new and upgraded software to try out, including shareware and freeware. "SnapNDrag" is an excellent, easy to use, freeware screen capture software for the Macintosh (Yellow Mug Software 2004). If you are the only IL librarian, and you have little or no technical or peer support, daunting as it may seem, you can still learn new software on your own. Once the new or upgraded software has been installed, you might try an experimental trial-and-error approach, where you test out features that look interesting or useful to you. Look for free Web-based tutorials on software, created by others. For instance, WebEx offers very useful five-minute tutorials on many aspects of its complex software (WebEx Communications 2001).

On the other hand, you might feel more comfortable and in control if you use the following step-by-step approach to teach software to yourself.

1. Print out the online help or look through each section online.
2. Use it to test out each and every feature, making notes and starring features that seem essential.
3. Weigh the various features provided, listing those that should be covered in basic instruction, paper, online, group, or one-on-one.
4. Concentrate on developing means to help users learn how to take control of technology and how to think critically about it.
5. Write up all of the preceding in the form of goals and objectives in order to make development of an instructional plan a much simpler process.

Regardless of the approach you take, when you have succeeded even once, even in just small areas, you will feel much more confident and able to tackle more complex challenges as they arise.

PUTTING THE DOG'S ENDS IN PERSPECTIVE

Technology management is imperative, demanding, and yet highly satisfying to those who undertake it. Careful planning and outreach to other technology-based groups and individuals can result in powerful instructional partnerships that enrich all user groups and partners. Internal support is just as important as outreach. Staff generally view IL technology managers as powerful people who can fix almost any technological problem, because they always seem to know well in advance about new technological advances and enhancements and how they work. Whether or not they are truly powerful and all-knowing, if this is the perception, then IL technology managers must assist staff and the public in the most basic, noncondescending, and stress-reducing manner.

Equipment, software, and networks exist to help people and to help us realize our goals and objectives, rather than the other way around. In the end, why and how you use technology and its effectiveness in supporting your pedagogical goals and those of your colleagues may be more important than which technology you use (Castellan 1993; Koppi, Lublin, and Chaloupka 1997). As Cuban notes, the key to successful use of any sort of technology in instruction lies in its flexibility—the ability of the teacher to use the technology in a variety of ways, in order to fulfill pedagogical goals (Cuban 1986). In other words, the technological tail should not wag the pedagogical dog.

EXERCISES

1.  Create a table that includes the most important instructional technology factors for your environment. Then make a list of several different ways you can use this table to generate discussion about improved technological support for various program initiatives. Share your table with other computer-related groups or individuals outside the library to see whether you are duplicating other efforts or where efforts can be combined for best results.
2.  Subscribe to ILI-L and lurk for a week or two (read messages). Identify a thread (topic) of interest to you and compose a thoughtful message about it. Send the message to yourself first and read it the next day, then send it to a friend and ask for comments. When it passes the self- and friend-test, send it to ILI-L.
3.  Check the San Diego State University's "EDTECH Beach" blog and the MIT Media Lab's "Research" page. Identify three concepts or items that could be adapted or applied to ILI and write a brief paragraph about each. Continue to do this every month in order to build a file of new IL ideas and approaches.
4.  Study your immediate environment and then the larger environment. Identify two groups outside your immediate environment to contact regarding joining in a broad IL effort, or team-teaching online.

READ MORE ABOUT IT

ALA. ACRL. Distance Learning Section. 2004. "Guidelines for Distance Learning Library Services." http://www.ala.org/ala/acrl/acrlstandards/guidelinesdistancelearning.htm [9 September 2004].
Bell, Steven. 2004b. "The Kept-Up Academic Librarian." http://keptup.typepad.com/academic/ [2 September 2004].
Hinchliffe, Lisa Janicke. 2001. *Neal-Schuman Electronic Classroom Handbook*. New York: Neal-Schuman Publishers.

ILI-L. n.d. infolit@library.berkeley.edu.

Masie, Elliott. n.d. TechLearn Trends. techlearn-trends@lister.masie.com

Nielsen, Jakob. 1995– . "Alertbox." http://www.useit.com/alertbox/ [11 November 2004].

Oberman, Cerise. 1995. "Unmasking Technology: A Prelude to Teaching." *Research Strategies* 13(1): 34–39.

Ream, Dan. 2001. "Scratch That Glitch: The Fine Art of Glitch Management." http://www.people.vcu.edu/~dream/glitch.htm [16 May 2004].

San Diego State University. n.d. "EDTECH Beach." http://edweb.sdsu.edu/etbeach/ [29 May 2004].

Weil, Michelle M., and Larry D. Rosen. 1997. *Technostress: Coping with Technology @Work @Home @Play*. New York: John Wiley and Sons.

# Bibliography

AAHE. 2003. [Online]. Available: www.aahe.org/ [15 May 2004].

ABCNEWS.com. 2004. Cheaters Amok: A Crisis in America's Schools—How It's Done and Why It's Happening. [Online]. Available: www.softwaresecure.com/pdf/ABC onCHeating_050404_.pdf [18 July 2005].

ABLEDATA: Explore the World of Assistive Technology. n.d. [Online]. Available: www.abledata.com/[15 May 2004].

Absher, Linda. 2004. "The Lipstick Librarian." [Online]. Available: www.lipsticklibrar ian.com/[31 May 2004].

ACADEMICPR. n.d. ACADEMICPR@ALA.org.

Acker, Stephen R., Dennis K. Pearl, and Steven W. Rissing. 2003. "Is the Academy Ready for Learning Objects?" *Syllabus* 16(12): 28–31.

AFT (American Federation of Teachers). 1999. "First Accreditation Awarded to an Online University." *On Campus* 18(8): 8.

Agre, Phil. 1996. "How to Help Someone Use a Computer." [Online]. Available: http://polaris.gseis.ucla.edu/pagre/how-to-help.html [16 May 2004].

Ahn, Charles. 25 May 2004. "RE: Hub Question." Personal email.

ALA. 1996. *Library Bill of Rights*. [Online]. Available: www.ala.org/ala/oif/state mentspols/statementsif/librarybillrights.htm [8 September 2004].

———. 2001. "A Library Advocate's Guide to Building Information Literate Communities." [Online]. Available: www.ala.org/content/contentgroups/Advocacy/ informationliteracy.pdf [5 August 2003].

———. 2003a. *Download Logos*. [Online]. Available: www.ala.org/Content/Navigation_ Menu/Our_Association/Offices/Public_Information/Campaign_for_Americas_Li braries/ Download_Logos/Download_Logos.htm [1 January 2004].

———. 2003b. *National Library Week Grant*. [Online]. Available: http://staging.ala .org/ala/pressreleasesbucket/pressreleases2003aug/nationallibr.htm [31 December 2003].

———. 2003c. *Principles for the Networked World*. [Online]. Available: www.ala.org/ ala/washoff/washpubs/principles.pdf [2 September 2004].

——. 2003d. *PR Tools and Resources.* [Online]. Available: www.ala.org/ala/pio/campaign/prtools/prtoolsresources.htm [8 September 2004].

——. 2004a. NMRT [Online]. Available: www.ala.org/Template.cfm?Section-mrt [16 April 2004].

——. 2004b. *Spectrum Initiative—New Faces, New Era.* [Online]. Available: www.ala.org/ala/diversity/spectrum/spectruminitiative.htm [2 February 2004].

——. n.d. *Participation @ Your Library.* [Online]. Available: https://cs.ala.org/@yourlibrary/participatinglibraries/participating.cfm [1 January 2004].

——. AASL. 2003. *Toolkit for School Library Media Programs.* Chicago: American Library Association.

——. AASL . AECT. 1998. *Information Power: Building Partnerships for Learning.* Chicago: American Library Association.

——. ACRL. 2000. *Information Literacy Competency Standards for Higher Education.* [Online]. Available: www.ala.org/ala/acrl/acrlstandards/informationliteracycompetency.htm [17 April 2004].

——. ACRL. 2003. *Accreditation: Information Literacy and Accreditation Agencies.* [Online]. Available: www.ala.org/ala/acrl/acrlissues/acrlinfolit/infolitstandards/infolitaccred/accreditation.htm [17 April 2004].

——. ACRL. Distance Learning Section. 2004. "Guidelines for Distance Learning Library Services." [Online]. Available: www.ala.org/ala/acrl/acrlstandards/guidelinesdistancelearning.htm [9 September 2004].

——. ACRL. Instruction Section. 2004a. [Online]. Available: www.ala.org/ala/acrl/aboutacrl/acrlsections/instruction/hompage.htm [15 May 2004].

——. ACRL. Instruction Section. 2004b. "Awards." [Online]. Available: www.ala.org/ala/acrlbucket/is/isawards/awards.htm [28 August 2004].

——. ACRL. Instruction Section. 2004c. *PRIMO: Peer Reviewed Instructional Materials Online.* [Online]. Available: www.ala.org/ala/acrlbucket/is/iscommittees/webpages/emergingtech/primo/index.htm [2 September 2004].

——. ACRL. CARL. 1997. [Online]. Available: www.carl-acrl.org/Archives/Committees Archive/Task Force/TFinfolitappt.html [26 August 2004].

——. ACRL. CARL. n.d. "CARL Research Award: Application Process and Criteria." [Online]. Available: www.carl-acrl.org/Awards/Research/RAApplication.html [3 June 2004].

——. ACRL. CARL. sCIL. 2003. *Marketing/Teaching Information Literacy for Special Populations.* sCIL Open House 2003. Lynn Lampert, Presenter, Senior Assistant Librarian, Information Literacy Coordinator at California State University, Northridge. [Online]. Available: http://clics.ucsd.edu/scil/eventsandreports/winter2003openhouse/specialpopulations.html [29 February 2004].

——. ACRL. CARL. sCIL. 2004. [Online]. Available: http://clics.ucsd.edu/scil/ [15 May 2004].

——. LAMA. PRMS. n.d. "Swap & Shop's Best of Show Entry Form." [Online]. Available: www.ala.org/ala/lama/lamaawards/lamaprmsswap.htm [31 May 2004].

——. LIRT. 2004. "Library Instruction Round Table News." [Online]. Available: http://www3.baylor.edu/LIRT/lirtnews/ [19 May 2004].

——. LIRT. 2004. [Online]. Available: http://www3.baylor.edu/LIRT/ [28 August 2004].

——. LITA. 2004. *Top Technology Trends.* [Online]. Available: www.ala.org/ala/lita/litaresources/toptechtrends/toptechnology.htm [2 September 2004].

——. RUSA. MARS. 2004. [Online]. Available: www.ala.org/MARSTemplate.cfm?Section-MARS [15 May 2004].

Alire, Camila A. 2001. "The Color of Leadership." *Journal of Library Administration* 32(3/4): 95–109.

Amazon.com. 2004. [Online]. Available: http://a9.com/ [31 May 2004].

American Psychological Association. 2004. *PsycInfo.* [Online]. Available: www.apa .org/psycinfo/[8 September 2004].

Andersen, Bjorn, and Tom Fagerhaug. 2000. *Root Cause Analysis: Simplified Tools and Techniques.* Milwaukee: ASQ Quality Press.

Anderson, Terry D. 1997. *Transforming Leadership.* 2nd ed. Boca Raton: St. Lucie Press.

The Andrew W. Mellon Foundation. 2003. *Teaching and Technology.* [Online]. Available: www.mellon.org/programs/highered/teachingandtechnology/teachingandtechnology.htm [4 September 2004].

The Andrew W. Mellon Foundation. n.d. [Online]. Available: www.mellon.org/Mellon Programs.htm [4 September 2004].

Angelo, Thomas A., and K. Patricia Cross. 1993. *Classroom Assessment Techniques: A Handbook for College Teachers.* 2nd ed. Jossey-Bass Higher and Adult Education Series. San Francisco: Jossey-Bass Publishers.

*Annual Register of Grant Support: A Directory of Funding Sources.* 2004. Medford, NJ: Information Today.

Appleton, Elaine. "The Velcro Monkey." *Inside Technology Training* 3, no. 4. (1999).

ARL. 2003. *LibQual[TM]: Charting Library Service Quality.* [Online]. Available: www .libqual.org/[31 December 2003].1999)

Arnold, Judith M. 1998. "I Know It When I See It: Assessing Good Teaching." *Research Strategies* 16(1): 1–28.

Ask Jeeves—Ask.com. 2003. [Online]. Available: www.ask.com/ [11 November 2003].

Ayers, Edward L. 2004. *Valley of the Shadow.* [Online]. Available: http://valley.vcdh.vir ginia.edu/[2 September 2004].

Baker, Nicholson. 1994. "Discards." *New Yorker* 70(7): 64–85.

Barbour, Wendell, Christy Gavin, and Joan Canfield. 2004. "Integrating Information Literacy into the Academic Curriculum." *Educause Center for Applied Research Bulletin* (18). [Online]. Available: www.educause.edu/asp/doclib/abstract.asp?ID=ERB0418 [8 September 2004].

Barclay, Donald A. 2000. *Managing Public Access Computers: A How-to-Do-It Manual for Librarians.* New York: Neal-Schuman Publishers.

Barker, Andy, Clive Nancarrow, and Nigel Spackman. 2001. "Informed Eclecticism: A Research Paradigm for the Twenty-First Century." *International Journal of Market Research* 43(1): 3–27.

Barnes & Noble University. 2004. [Online]. Available: www.barnesandnobleuniversity.com/ index.asp?userid=2U4AE1C59V [1 October 2004].

Baron, David. 1999. *Moses on Management: 50 Leadership Lessons from the Greatest Manager of All Times.* New York: Pocket Books.

Barron, Daniel D. 1999. "Celebrating Our Past, Contemplating the Present, Looking to the Future." *School Library Media Activities Monthly* 15(5): 48–50.

Bartell, Carol A., Candace Kaye, and Joy Ann Morin. 1998. "Teaching Portfolios and Teacher Education." *Teacher Education Quarterly* 25(1): 5–8.

Bauer, David G. 2000. *Successful Grants Program Management.* San Francisco: Jossey-Bass.

Beasley, Augie E. 1996a. "Leadership 101: Becoming a Proactive Library Leader." *School Media Library Activities Monthly* 13(3): 20–22.

———. 1996b. "Leadership 101: Survival Skills for School Media Coordinators." *North Carolina Libraries* 54(3): 54–57.

Becker, Bill. November/December 2003. "Library Grant Money on the Web." *Searcher: The Magazine for Database Professionals* 11(10): 8–14.

Becker, Karen A. 1993. "The Characteristics of Bibliographic Instruction in Relation to the Causes and Symptoms of Burnout." *RQ* 43(3): 346–357.

Beckerman, Edwin. 1996. *Politics and the American Public Library: Creating Political Support for Library Goals.* Lanham, MD: Scarecrow Press.

Bell, Steven. 2004a. "Steven Bell's Keeping Up Web Site." [Online]. Available: http://staff.philau.edu/bells/keepup/ [2 September 2004].

———. 2004b. "The Kept-Up Academic Librarian." [Online]. Available: http://keptup.typepad.com/academic/ [2 September 2004].

Bennis, Warren. 1989. *On Becoming a Leader.* New York: Addison-Wesley.

———. 1994. *On Becoming a Leader.* New York: Addison-Wesley.

———. 1997. *Managing People Is Like Herding Cats.* Provo, UT: Executive Excellence Publishing.

———. 2000. *Managing the Dream.* Cambridge, MA: Perseus Publishing.

Bennis, Warren, and Burt Nanus. 1985. *Leaders.* New York: Harper and Row.

———. 1997. *Leaders.* New York: HarperCollins.

Bennis, Warren, Gretchen M. Spreitzer, and Thomas G. Cummings, eds. 2001. *The Future of Leadership.* San Francisco: Jossey-Bass.

Berger, Raymond M., and Michael A. Patchner. 1988a. *Implementing the Research Plan.* Newbury Park, CA: Sage.

———. 1988b. *Planning for Research.* Newbury Park, CA: Sage.

Bergmann, Horst, Kathleen Hurson, and Darlene Russ-Eft. 1999. *Everyone a Leader: A Grassroots Model for the New Workplace.* New York: John Wiley and Sons.

Berry, John N. 2004. "Library of the Year 2004: The San Jose Model." *Library Journal* 129(11): 34–37.

Bethel, Sheila Murry. 1995. "Servant-Leadership and Corporate Risk Taking: When Risk Taking Makes a Difference." In *Reflections on Leadership,* edited by Larry C. Spears. New York: John Wiley and Sons.

Biggs, Mary, and Glenna Kramer. 1994. "We Have Been There Too: Library Board Essentials for Effectiveness." *Wilson Library Bulletin* 68(9): 32–35.

BI-L BI-L@listserv.byu.edu. n.d.

Bill and Melinda Gates Foundation. 2003. *Libraries for the Future Wins Grant to Support National Transformation of Libraries into Centers for Information Literacy.* [Online]. Available: http://gatesfoundation.org/Libraries/Announcements/Announce-030618.htm [31 December 2003].

Blackett, Tom, and Graham Denton. 1987. "Developing New Brands." In *Branding: A Key Marketing Tool,* edited by John M. Murphy. New York: McGraw-Hill.

"Blogging 101." 2003. [Online]. Available: www.bu.edu/mfeldman/blog/blogging101.html [19 May 2004].

Boerner, Gerald L. 2002. "The Brave New World of Wireless Technology: A Primer for Educators." *Syllabus* 16(3): 19–22, 30–31.

Bollington, Rob, David Hopkins, and Mel West. 1990. *An Introduction to Teacher Appraisal: A Professional Development Approach.* London: Cassell.

Bone and Joint Digital Learning Objects. 2003. [Online]. Available: www.queryprojects.ca/pages/public/digital.htm [2 September 2004].

bookfinder.com. 2004. [Online]. Available: www.bookfinder.com/ [8 September 2004].

Bordons, Kenneth S., and Bruce B. Abbott. 1999. *Research Design and Methods: A Process Approach.* 4th ed. Mountain View, CA: Mayfield Publishing Company.

Botts, Carrol, and Mark Emmons. 2002. "Developing Teaching Competencies for Instructors in the Academic Library: A Case Study." *Public Services Quarterly* 1(3): 65–81.

Boyett, Joseph H., and Jimmie T. Boyett. 1998. *The Guru Guide: The Best Ideas of the Top Management Thinkers.* New York: John Wiley and Sons.

Braaksma, Betty. 26 April 2004. "Faculty/Librarian Relations." Personal e-mail to the author.

Braham, Brenda. 2004. "Workshops for Faculty—Summary" [electronic bulletin board].
    15 July 2004 [cited 20 July 2004]. Available from ILI-L@ala.org.
Brandon, Nathaniel. 1998. *Self Esteem at Work: How Confident People Make Powerful Compa-
    nies*. San Francisco: Jossey-Bass.
Bransford, John, Sean Brophy, and Susan Williams. 2000. "When Computer Technologies
    Meet the Learning Sciences: Issues and Opportunities." *Journal of Developmental Psy-
    chology* 21(1): 59–84.
Brasley, Stephanie. 2003. "Information Literacy Assignment Ideas." UCLA College Library.
    [Online]. Available: www.library.ucla.edu/libraries/college/instructors/strategies
    .htm [27 July 2004].
Bratton, Phyllis. 27 April 2004. "Faculty/Librarian Relations." Personal e-mail to the au-
    thor.
*The Bread Game*. 1973. San Francisco: Glide Publications.
Brewer, Ernest W., Charles M. Achilles, and Jay R. Fuhriman. 1998. *Finding Funding:
    Grantwriting from Start to Finish, Including Project Management and Internet Use*. 3rd
    ed. Thousand Oaks, CA: Corwin Press.
Brod, Craig. 1984. *Technostress*. Reading, MA: Addison-Wesley.
Budiansky, Stephen. 1996. "Local TV: Mayhem Central." *U.S. News & World Report* 120(9):
    63–65.
Burke, Mary Anne. 2002. *Simplified Grantwriting*. Thousand Oaks, CA: Corwin Press.
Burnam, Paul. 1993. "Fine-Tuning Classroom Technique: A Peer Coaching Experience."
    *Research Strategies* 11(1): 42–46.
California Association of Library Trustees and Commissioners. 1998. *Trustee Tool Kit for
    Library Leadership*. Sacramento, CA: California State Library.
California Clearinghouse on Library Instruction, North. 2004.
California Clearinghouse on Library Instruction, South. 2004. [Online]. Available:
    http://clics.ucsd.edu/scil/[26 August 2004].
California State University. 2004. "Call for Proposals: 2004; Information Competence Ini-
    tiative." [Online]. Available: www.calstate.edu/LS/call_for_proposals_2004.doc [4
    June 2004].
California State University. n.d. "CSU Information Competence Project." [Online]. Avail-
    able: www.lib.calpoly.edu/infocomp/ [26 August 2004].
California State University, Los Angeles. 2004. *Library Catalog*. [Online]. Available:
    www.calstatela.edu/library/opac/catalog.html [3 September 2004].
Campbell, Dorothy M., Beverly J. Mclenyzer, Diane Hood Nettles, and Richard M.
    Wyman Jr. 2000. *Portfolio and Performance Assessment in Teacher Education*. Boston: Al-
    lyn and Bacon.
Caplovitz, David. 1983. *The Stages of Social Research*. New York: John Wiley and Sons.
Caputo, Janette S. 1991. *Stress and Burnout in Library Service*. Phoenix, AZ: Oryx Press.
Caravello, Patti, et al. 2001. *Information Competence at UCLA: Report of a Survey Project*. Los
    Angeles: UCLA. [Online]. Available: http://repositories.cdlib.org/uclalib/il/01/ [8
    September 2004].
Carpenter, Beth. 1998. "Your Attention Please! Marketing Today's Libraries: We've Got
    to Tell Everyone That We Are Going Digital!" *Computers in Libraries* 18(8): 62–66.
    [Online]. Available: www.infotoday.com/cilmag/sep98/story2.htm [8 September
    2004].
Caspers, Jean, and Katy Lenn. 2000. "The Future of Collaboration between Librarians and
    Teaching Faculty." In *The Collaborative Imperative: Libraries and Faculty Working To-
    gether in the Information Universe*, edited by Dick Raspa and Dane Ward. Chicago:
    ALA, ACRL.

Castellan, N. John, Jr. 1993. "Evaluating Information Technology in Teaching and Learning." *Behavior Research Methods, Instruments, & Computers* 25(2): 233–237.

"Catalog of Federal Domestic Assistance." [Online]. Available: http://12.46.245.173/cfda/cfda.html [4 September 2004].

CDL. 2004. "MELVYL Catalog." [Online]. Available: http://melvyl.cdlib.org/[8 May 2004].

Center for Applications of Psychological Types. 2003. [Online]. Available: www.capt.org/ [31 May 2004].

Center for Knee, Shoulder and Hip. 2003. *Orthopedic Animations.* [Online]. Available: www.sportsknee.com/patient.htm [2 September 2004].

Chamberlain, Philip. 1995. "Team-Building and Servant-Leadership." In *Reflections on Leadership,* edited by Larry C. Spears. New York: John Wiley and Sons.

Chapman, Julie, and Michelle White. 2001. "Building Bridges with Faculty through Library Workshops." In *Library User Education: Powerful Learning, Powerful Partnerships,* edited by Barbara I. Dewey. Lanham, MD; London: Scarecrow Press.

Chappell, Tom. 1999. *Managing Upside Down: The Seven Intentions of Value-Centered Leadership.* New York: William Morrow and Co.

Charvet, Shelle Rose. 1997. *Words That Change Minds: Mastering the Language of Influence.* Dubuque, IA: Kendall Hunt.

Cherniss, Cary. 1995. *Beyond Burnout: Helping Teachers, Nurses, Therapists, and Lawyers Recover from Stress and Disillusionment.* New York: Routledge.

Chisom, Nancy Van Note, and Christine A. Stanley. 1999. *Peer Review of Teaching: A Sourcebook.* Bolton, MA: Anker Publishing Company.

Christiansen, Lars, Mindy Stombler and Lyn Thaxton. 2004. "A Report on Librarian-faculty Relations from a Sociological Perspective." *Journal of Academic Librarianship* 30(2): 116–121.

*The Chronicle of Higher Education.* n.d. "Information Technology." [column]. Washington, DC: Editorial Products for Education.

Clemente, Mark N. 1992. *The Marketing Glossary.* New York: AMACOM.

Cogdell, Edna. 2003. "School Library Media Management Skills." *Knowledge Quest* 32(2): 20–22.

Coley, Soraya M., and Cynthia A. Scheinberg. 1990. *Proposal Writing.* Newbury Park, CA: Sage.

Connor, Daryl R. Autumn 1993. "Managing Change: A Business Imperative." *Business Quarterly* 58: 88–91.

———. Autumn 1998. "How to Create a Nimble Organization." *National Productivity Review* 17: 31–36.

Corcoran, Mary, and Rebecca Jones. 1997. "Chief Knowledge Officers? Perceptions, Pitfalls and Potentials." *Information Outlook* 1(6): 30–31, 33, 35–36.

COS (Community of Science). 2005. [Online]. Available: www.cos.com/[12 April 2005].

Cosh, Jill. 1999. "Peer Observation: A Reflective Model." *ELT Journal* 53(1): 22–27.

Covey, Stephen R. 1966. "Line-of-Sight Leadership." *Executive Excellence* 13(4): 5–6.

———. 1990a. *Principle-Centered Leadership.* New York: Simon and Schuster.

———. 1990b. *Seven Habits of Highly Successful People: Powerful Lessons in Personal Change.* New York: Fireside.

———. 1991. *Principle-Centered Leadership.* New York: Summit.

———. 1996. "Three Roles of the Leader in the New Paradigm." In *The Leader of the Future,* edited by Frances Hesselbein, Marshall Goldsmith, and Richard Beckhard. San Francisco: Jossey-Bass.

Cuban, Larry. 1986. *Teachers and Machines: The Classroom Use of Technology since 1920.* New York: Teachers College Press, Columbia University.

Culligan, Matthew J., and Dolph Green. 1982. *Getting Back to the Basics of Public Relations & Publicity.* New York: Crown Publishers.

Davis, Mary Ellen. 2003. "American Library Association. Diversity Research Grants" [electronic bulletin board]. 24 April 2003 [cited 25 April 2003]. Available from ACR-LEADS@ala1.ala.org.

Dawson, Debbie. 2002. "Leadership Development in Libraries." *APLIS* 15(4): 155–159.

de Saez, Eileen Elliott. 2002. *Marketing Concepts for Libraries and Information Services.* 2nd ed. London: Facet Publishing.

Del Balso, Michael, and Alan D. Lewis. 1997. *First Steps: A Guide to Social Research.* Scarborough, Canada: Nelson.

Depree, Max. 1993. *Leadership Is an Art.* New York: Dell.

———. 1993. *Leadership Jazz.* New York: Dell.

Diaz, Joseph R., and Chestalene Pintozzi. 1999. "Helping Teams Work: Lessons Learned from the University of Arizona Library Reorganization." *Administration and Management* 13(1): 27–36.

Diffenbach, John. 1987. "The Corporate Identity as the Brand." In *Branding: A Key Marketing Tool,* edited by John M. Murphy. New York: McGraw-Hill.

Doctor, Ronald M., and Jason N. Doctor. 1994. "Stress." In *Encyclopedia of Human Behavior,* edited by Vilayanurf S. Ramachandran. San Diego: Academic Press.

Dodge, Bernie. 1995. "Some Thoughts about WebQuests." [Online]. Available: http://edweb.sdsu.edu/courses/edtec596/about_webquests. html [26 July 2004].

———. n.d. The "WebQuest Page at San Diego State University." [Online]. Available: http://webquest.sdsu.edu/ [26 July 2004].

Dowling, Grahame. 2001. *Creating Corporate Reputations: Identity, Image, and Performance.* Oxford: Oxford University Press.

Drawbaugh, Kevin. 2001. *Brands in the Balance: Meeting the Challenges to Commercial Identity.* London; New York: Person Education.

Drews, David R., W. Jeffrey Burroughs, and DeeAnn Nokovich. 1987. "Teacher Self-ratings as a Validity Criterion for Student Evaluations." *Teaching of Psychology* 14(1): 23–25.

Drucker, Peter F. 1996. "Not Enough Generals Were Killed." In *The Leader of the Future,* edited by Frances Hesselbein, Marshall Goldsmith, and Richard Beckhard. San Francisco: Jossey-Bass.

Dudley, Miriam. 1978. *Library Instruction Workbook.* Los Angeles: University of California Library.

———. 1983. "A Philosophy of Library Instruction." *Research Strategies* 1(2): 58–63.

Dupuis, Elizabeth A. 27 September 1999. "RE: Classes." Personal e-mail to author.

Durrance, Joan, and Karen Fisher-Pettigrew. 2000. *How Libraries and Librarians Help.* [Online]. Available: www.si.umich.edu/helpseek/ALACIS2000final1/sld001.htm [1 October 2004].

Dworkin, Kristine D. 2001. "Library Marketing: Eight Ways to Get Unconventionally Creative." *Online.* January/February 2001: 52–54.

Dwyer, Carol Anne. 1998. "Psychometrics of Praxis III: Classroom Performance Assessments." *Journal of Personnel Evaluation in Education* 12(2): 163–187.

Dylan, Bob. 1965. "Just Like Tom Thumb's Blues." *Highway 61 Revisited.* Columbia compact disk CK 9189.

*Eastern Airlines Review.* 1984. 27 September 1984: 2.

Edelstein, Wendy. 2004. "Improving Undergraduate Research Skills." *Berkeleyan* 32(1). [Online]. Available: www.berkeley.edu/news/berkeleyan/2004/01/21_mel lon.shtml [26 July 2004].

Educational Testing Service. 2002. *Digital Transformations.* [Online]. Available: www.ets.org/research/ictliteracy/index.html [17 April 2004].

Egan, Gerard. 1985. *Change Agent Skills*. Monterey, CA: Brooks Cole Publishing Company.

Ehrenberg, Andrew, et al. 2002. "Brand Advertising as Creative Publicity." *Journal of Advertising Research* 42(4): 7–19.

Ellis, Kristine. 2003. "Making Waves." *Training* 40(6): 16–21.

Erard, Michael. 22 May 2004. "Where to Get a Good Idea: Steal It Outside Your Group." *New York Times*, A17.

Ethnic Newswatch. n.d. [Online]. Available: http://uclibs.org/PID/4737 [19 May 2004].

Fallows, James. 16 May 2004. "Twilight of the Information Middlemen." *New York Times*. Section 3, column 1, p. 5.

Farber, Evan Ira. 1993. "Bibliographic Instruction at Earlham College." In *Bibliographic Instruction in Practice: A Tribute to the Legacy of Evan Ira Farber* edited by Larry Hardesty, J. Hasteiter, and D. Henderson. Ann Arbor, MI: Pierian Press.

Farren, Caela, and Beverly L. Kaye. 1996. "New Skills for New Leadership Roles." In *The Leader of the Future*, edited by Frances Hesselbein, Marshall Goldsmith, and Richard Beckhard. San Francisco: Jossey-Bass.

"FedGrants." [Online]. Available: www.fedgrants.gov/ [4 September 2004].

Feldman, Michael. 2003. "What Makes a Blog a Blog?" *Dowbrigade News*. [Online]. Available: http://blogs.law.harvard.edu/dowbrigade/2003/09/27 [19 May 2004].

Fiegen, Ann Manning. 2002. "Mentoring and Academic Librarians: Personally Designed for Results." *College and Undergraduate Libraries* 9(1): 23–32.

Fink, Arlene. 1998. *Conducting Research Literature Reviews: From Paper to Internet*. Thousand Oaks, CA: Sage.

Fister, Barbara. 27 April 2004. "Your ILI-L Question." Personal e-mail to the author.

Fitzgerald, Mary Ann. 2004. "Making the Leap from High School to College: Three New Studies about Information Literacy Skills of First-Year College Students." *Knowledge Quest* 32(4): 19–24.

Fitzwater, Diana. 2003. "Ideas for Library Research Assignments." College of DuPage. [Online]. Available: www.cod.edu/library/services/faculty/infolit/assignmentideas.htm [27 July 2004].

Flood, Robert Lewis. 1999. *Rethinking the Fifth Discipline*. London: Routledge.

Fogg, B. J. 2003. *Persuasive Technology: Using Computers to Change What We Think and Do*. San Francisco: Morgan Kaufmann Publishers.

The Foundation Center. 2004. Proposal Writing Short Course. [Online]. Available: http://fdncenter.org/learn/shortcourse/prop1.html [5 June 2004].

*The Foundation Directory*. 2005. 27th ed. New York: Foundation Center.

*The Foundation Directory Part 2*. 2004. New York: Foundation Center.

Frand, Jason, and Robert Bellanti. 2000. "Collaborative Convergence: Merging Computing and Library Services at the Anderson Graduate School of Management at UCLA." *Journal of Business & Finance Librarianship* 6(2).

Freudenberger, Herbert J., and Geraldine Richelson. 1980. *Burn-Out: The High Cost of High Achievement*. Garden City, NY: Anchor Press.

Fulmer, Robert M., and Marshall Goldsmith. 2000. *The Leadership Investment*. New York: AMACOM.

Gaffney, Gerry. Interview. 2000. "The Myth of the Stupid User (Revisited)." [Online]. Available: http://webword.com/interviews/gaffney2.html [19 May 2004].

Gale Group. n.d. "Expanded Academic ASAP." [Online]. Available: www.galegroup.com/ [16 May 2004].

Galloway, Ann-Christie. 2004. "Acquisitions." *College & Research Libraries News* 65(7): 395.

Gebb, Billie Ann. 2003. "Committees—Summary" [electronic bulletin board]. 19 December 2003 [cited 28 April 2004]. Available from ILI-L@ala.org.

Germain, C. A. February 2000. "99 Ways to Get Those Feet in the Door." *College and Research Libraries News* 61(2): 93–96.

Gilbert, Bruce. 2001. "What One Person Can Do: A Theory of Personal Involvement in Establishing Library–Faculty Partnerships." In *Library User Education: Powerful Learning, Powerful Partnerships*, edited by Barbara I. Dewey. Lanham, MD; London: Scarecrow Press.

Gitlin, Laura N., and Kevin J. Lyons. 1996. *Successful Grant Writing: Strategies for Health and Human Service Professionals*. New York: Springer Publishing Co.

Gladwell, Malcolm. 11 January 1999. "6 Degrees of Lois Weisberg." *New Yorker*, 52–63.

Glendenning, Barbara J., and James C. Gordon. 1997. "Professional Associations: Promoting Leadership in a Career." *Library Trends* 46(1): 258–277.

Gliner, Jeffrey A., and George A. Morgan. 2000. *Research Methods in Applied Settings: An Integrated Approach to Design and Analysis*. Mahwah, NJ: Lawrence Erlbaum.

Glitz, Beryl. 1998. *Focus Groups for Libraries and Librarians*. New York: Forbes.

Glosiene, Audrone. 2000. "Marketing or Public Relations: A Strategic Choice for Lithuanian Libraries." In *Adapting Marketing to Libraries in a Changing and World-Wide Environment*. Papers presented at the 63rd IFLA conference. Copenhagen, September 1997.

Goleman, Daniel. 1998. "What Makes a Leader?" *Harvard Business Review* 76(6): 92–102.

Goodson, Kymberly. 2003. "Coffee Shops in Libraries" [electronic bulletin board]. 7 August 2003 [cited 8 August 2003]. Available from ACADEMICPR@ala.org.

Google Answers. 2004. [Online]. Available: http://answers.google.com/answers/main [1 October 2004].

Gorman, Michael. 1991. "Send for a Child of Four! or Creating the BI-Less Academic Library." *Library Trends* 39(3): 354–362.

Graham, Clarke, and Mark Peroff. 1987. "The Legal Side of Branding." In *Branding: A Key Marketing Tool*, edited by John M. Murphy. New York: McGraw-Hill.

Grassian, Esther. 1993. "Setting Up and Managing a BI Program." In *Sourcebook for Bibliographic Instruction*, edited by Katherine Branch and Carolyn Dusenbury. Chicago: American Library Association.

———. 1993. "Setting Up and Managing a BI Program: Outline of Steps." In *Sourcebook for Bibliographic Instruction*, edited by Katherine Branch and Carolyn Dusenbury. Appendix A, p. 81. Chicago: ALA, ACRL, Bibliographic Instruction Section.

———. 2003. "Research Paper Planner." UCLA College Library. [Online]. Available: www.library.ucla.edu/libraries/college/classes/fsp-tsp/researchpaperCL2.html [8 May 2004].

———. 2004a. "Do They Really Do That? Librarians Teaching Outside the Classroom." *Change* 36(3): 22–28.

———. 2004b. "The Road to Research." UCLA College Library. [Online]. Available: www.sscnet.ucla.edu/library/ [3 June 2004].

———. 2004c. "Summary of Responses: Faculty/Librarian Relations" [electronic bulletin board]. 7 May 2004—[cited 18 July 2004]. Available from ILI-L@ala.org.

Grassian, Esther, and Susan E. Clark. 1999. "Internet Resources: Information Literacy Sites: Background and Ideas for Program Planning and Development." *College & Research Libraries News* 60(2): 78–81, 92. [Online]. Available: www.ala.org/ala/acrl/acrlpubs/crlnews/backissues1999/february4/informationliteracy.htm [26 August 2004].

Grassian, Esther, and Joan Kaplowitz. 2001. *Information Literacy Instruction: Theory and Practice*. New York: Neal-Schuman Publishers.

Graves, Rebecca S. 27 April 2004. "FW: Faculty/Librarian Relations." Personal e-mail to the author.

Greenleaf, Robert K. 1977. *Servant-Leadership*. New York: Paulist Press.

Grosser, Howard J. 1987. "Burnout among Librarians and Information Workers." *Library Automated Systems Information Exchange* 18(2): 32–41.

Guidestar. 2005. [Online]. Available: www.guidestar.org/ [12 April 2005].

Gurak, Laura, et al., eds. 2004. "Into the Blogosphere." [Online]. Available: http://blog.lib.umn.edu/blogosphere/ [9 September 2004].

Guyonneau, Christine H. 1996. "Re: Analogies" [electronic bulletin board]. 9 February 1996 [cited 10 February 1996]. Available from bi-l@listserv.byu.edu.

Hackett, Gail, and Susan Lonberg. 1993. "Models of Stress." In *Helping Students Manage Stress*, edited by Elizabeth M. Altmaier. San Francisco: Jossey-Bass.

Haig, Matt. 2003. *Brand Failures: The Truth about the 100 Biggest Branding Mistakes of all Time*. London, UK; Sterling, VA: Kogan Page.

Hardesty, Larry. 1995. "Faculty Culture and Bibliographic Instruction: An Exploratory Analysis." *Library Trends* 44(2): 339–367.

Hart, Keith. 1999. *Putting Marketing Ideas into Action*. London: Library Association.

Healy, Patrick. 1999. "Education Department Proposes Rules to Increase Flexibility in Accreditation." *Chronicle of Higher Education* 45(44): A34.

Heath, Marilyn. 2002. "Electronic Portfolios for Reflective Self-Assessment." *Teacher Librarian* 30(1): 19–23.

Heilig, Jean. 30 August 2004. "RE:RE Information Literacy Question." Personal e-mail to the author.

Helgesen, Sally. 1996. "Leading from the Grassroots." In *The Leader of the Future*, edited by Frances Hesselbein, Marshall Goldsmith, and Richard Beckhard. San Francisco: Jossey-Bass.

Henderson, Pamela W., and Joseph A. Cote. 1998. "Guidelines for Selecting or Modifying Logos." *Journal of Marketing* 62(2): 14–34.

Heron, Peter, Ronald R. Powell, and Arthur P. Young. 2001. "University Library Directors in the Association of Research Libraries: The Next Generation—Part One." *College and Research Libraries* 62(3): 16–145.

———. 2002. "University Library Directors in the Association of Research Libraries: The Next Generation—Part Two." *College and Research Libraries* 63(1): 73–90.

Heron, Peter, and Candy Schwartz. 1995. "Can Research Be Assimilated into the Soul of Library and Information Science?" *Library and Information Science Research* 17(2): 101.

Hersey, Paul, Kenneth H. Blanchard, and Dewey E. Johnson. 2001. *Management of Organizational Behavior: Leading Human Resources*. 8th ed. Upper Saddle River, NJ: Prentice-Hall.

Hiebert, Murray, and Bruce Klatt. 2001. *The Encyclopedia of Leadership*. New York: McGraw-Hill.

Hill, Linda A., John L. Gabarro, and John P. Kotter. 1998. *Leadership for New Managers*. Boston: Harvard Business School Publications.

Hinchliffe, Lisa Janicke. 1998. "Resources for Designing Library Electronic Classrooms." *MC Journal: The Journal of Academic Media Librarianship* 6(1). [Online]. Available: http://wings.buffalo.edu/publications/mcjrnl/v6n1/class.html [8 September 2004].

———. 2001. *Neal-Schuman Electronic Classroom Handbook*. New York: Neal-Schuman Publishers.

Hobfoll, S. E. 2001. "Social Support and Stress." In *International Encyclopedia of the Social and Behavioral Sciences*, edited by Neil. J. Smeleer and Paul Baltes. Amsterdam; New York: Elsevier.

Holland, Winford E. 2000. *Change Is the Rule: Practical Actions for Change.* Chicago: Dearborn.

Hollon, Tom. 2001. "NIH Budget Maintains Doubling Momentum." *The Scientist* 15(2): 1.

Holmes, John. 2000. "Re:_Weeks Notice?" [electronic bulletin board]. 25 April 2000 [cited 26 April 2000]. Available from bi-l@listserv.byu.edu.

Hosch, Harmon M., and Oliveri, Matthew W. 1998. "Indicators of Successful Submissions to the Law and Social Science Program of the National Science Foundation." *Law & Society Review* 32(2): 515–526.

Hovis, Janice. 2004. "RE: Planning a Laptop Classroom" [electronic bulletin board]. 5 February 2004 [cited 5 February 2004]. Available from ILI-L@ala.org.

Howe, Eleanor B. 2001. "Ten Tips for Leadership." *Knowledge Quest* 29(3): 16–10.

H. W. Wilson. 2004. "John Cotton Dana 2004 Award Winners on Display at ALA." [Online]. Available: www.hwwilson.com/news/news_2_4_04.htm [8 September 2004].

IFLA 3M INTERNATIONAL MARKETING AWARD. 2004. [Online]. Available: www.ifla.org/III/grants/3m-award.htm [22 January 2005].

ILI-L. n.d. ILI-L@ala.org.

Indiana University. 1999. "Indiana University Factbook." [Online]. Available: http://factbook.indiana.edu/fbook99/enroll99.html [26 August 2004].

Indiana University. School of Library and Information Science. 2004. "Distinguished Alumni Award." [Online]. Available: www.slis.indiana.edu/alumni/distinguished.html [28 August 2004].

IRIS (Illinois Researcher Information Service). 2005. [Online]. Available: www.library.uluc.edu/iris/about.html [12 April 2005].

Isabell, Dennis, and Lisa Kammerlocher. 1994. "A Formative, Collegial Approach to Evaluating Course-Integrated Instruction. *Research Strategies* 12(1): 24–32.

Jaeger, Richard M. 1997. "Survey Research in Education." In *Complementary Methods for Research in Education*, edited by Richard M. Jaeger. Washington, DC: American Educational Research Association.

Janov, Jill. 1994. *The Inventive Organization: Hope and Daring at Work.* San Francisco: Jossey-Bass.

Jarzobkowski, Paula, and Zelma Bone. 1998. "A 'How -To' Guide and Checklist for Peer Appraisal of Teaching." *Innovations in Education and Training International* 35(2): 177–182.

Jeffries, Shellie. 2000. "The Librarian as Networker: Setting the Standard for Higher Education." In *The Collaborative Imperative*, edited by Dick Raspa and Dane Ward. Chicago: ALA, ACRL.

Jones Pyddney, ed. *Great Library Promotion Ideas VI.* 1991. Chicago: ALA, Library Administration and Management Association.

Joseph, Miriam. 1992. "Term Paper Alternatives." University of California, Berkeley. [Online]. Available: http://lib.berkeley.edu/TeachingLib/PaperAlternatives.html [26 August 2004].

Kalas, John W. 1987. *The Grant System.* Albany: State University of New York Press.

Kamp, Di. 1999. *The 21st Century Manager.* London: Kogan Page.

Kaplan, Sherrie H., et al. 1996. Sex Differences in Academic Advancement—Results of a National Study of Pediatricians. *New England Journal of Medicine* 335(17): 1282–1290.

Kaplowitz, Joan. 1992. "Mentoring Library School Students: A Survey of Participants in the UCLA/GLIS Mentoring Program." *Special Libraries* 83(4): 219–233.

Kaplowitz, Joan, and Janice Contini. 1998. "Computer-Assisted Instruction: Is It an Option for Bibliographic Instruction in Large Undergraduate Survey Classes?" *College and Research Libraries* 59(1): 19–27.

Kaser, Joyce, Susan Mundry, Katherine E. Stiles, and Susan Loucks-Horsley. 2002. *Leading Every Day*. Thousand Oaks, CA: Corwin Press.

Kelley, Robert E. 1998. *How to Be a Star at Work*. New York: Times Business.

Kempcke, Ken. 2002. "The Art of War for Librarians: Academic Culture, Curriculum Reform, and Wisdom from Sun Tzu." Portal—*Libraries and the Academy* 2(4): 529–551.

Kendall, Sue. 15 September 2004. "Re: San Jose IL Questions." Personal e-mail to the author.

Kendrick, Jim. 1996a. Pricing and Winning Proposal Competitions. P2C2 Group. [Online]. Available: http://users.erols.com/p2c2/dec96.html [14 June 2004].

———. 1996b. Proposal Psychology. P2C2 Group. [Online]. Available: http://users.erols.com/p2c2/aug96.html [14 June 2004].

———. 1997. Powerful Executive Summaries. P2C2 Group. [Online]. Available: http://users.erols.com/p2c2/jan02nws2.html [14 June 2004].

———. 1997. Resume Writing for Competitive Proposals. P2C2 Group. [Online]. Available: http://users.erols.com/p2c2/jan97.html [14 June 2004].

———. 2001. Doing Good. P2C2 Group. [Online]. Available: http://users.erols.com/p2c2/jan01nws.html [14 June 2004].

———. 2004. Newsletters. P2C2 Group. [Online]. Available: www.p2c2group.com/s-news.html [14 June 2004].

Kets de Vries, Manfred F. R. 2001. *Struggling with the Demon*. Madison, CT: Psychosocial Press.

Kight, Dawn Ventress, and Emma Bradford Perry. 1999. "Grant Resources on the Web: Where to Look When You Need Funding." *College & Research Libraries News* 60(7): 543–545.

Kiritz, Norton J., and Jerry Mundel. 2002. "Program Planning and Proposal writing." In *Annual Register of Grant Support 2003*, 36th ed. Medford, NJ: Information Today.

Kline, Theresa J. B. 2003. *Teams That Lead: A Matter of Market Strategy, Leadership Skills, and Executive Strength*. Mahwah, NJ; London: Lawrence Erlbaum Associates, Publishers.

Ko, Susan, and Steve Rossen. 2001. *Teaching Online: A Practical Guide*. Boston: Houghton Mifflin Co.

Koppi, A. J., J. R. Lublin, and M. J. Chaloupka. 1997. "Effective Teaching and Learning In a High-Tech Environment." *Innovations in Education and Training International* 34(4): 245–251.

Kotter, John P. 1996. *Leading Change*. Boston: Harvard Business School Press.

Kouzes, James M., and Barry Z. Posner 1996. "Seven Lessons for Leading the Voyage to the Future." In *The Leader of the Future*, edited by Frances Hesselbein, Marshall Goldsmith, and Richard Beckhard. San Francisco: Jossey-Bass.

———. 2001. "Bringing Leadership Lessons from the Past into the Future." In *The Future of Leadership*, edited by W. Bennis, G. M. Spreitzer, and T. G. Cummings. San Francisco: Jossey-Bass.

Kreeger, Karen Young. 2000. "Winning, Managing, and Renewing Grants." *The Scientist* 14(21): 31–33.

Krug, Steve. 2000. *Don't Make Me Think: A Common Sense Approach to Web Usability*. Indianapolis: Macmillan.

Kupersmith, John. 1998. "Technostress in the Bionic Library." In *Recreating the Academic Library: Breaking Virtual Ground*, edited by Cheryl LaGuardia. New York: Neal-Schuman Publishers.

Kuyper-Rushing, Lois. 2001. "A Formal Mentoring Program in a University Library: Components of a Successful Experiment." *Journal of Academic Librarianship* 27(6): 440–446.

LaDuke, Bruce. 2004. "Knowledge Creation: The Quest for Questions." *The Futurist* 38(1): 68–69.

Landgraf, Tedd, and Ronald Weaver. 2003. "At the Center: The Library in the Wired School." *Library Journal* 128: S12–14.

Langer, Judith. 1997. "What Consumers Wish Brand Managers Knew." *Journal of Advertising Research* 37(6): 60–66.

Lary, Marilyn S. 1998. "Mentoring: A Gift for Professional Growth." *Southeastern Librarian* 47(4): 23–34.

LAUC. 2004a. *Research*. [Online]. Available: www.ucop.edu/lauc/committees/rpd/index.html [1 October 2004].

———. 2004b. *Research Resources for Librarians*. [Online]. Available: www.ucop.edu/lauc/committees/rpd/recipients/resources.doc [1 October 2004].

LAUC-B. 2004. "Distinguished Librarian Award." [Online]. Available: www.lib.berkeley.edu/LAUC/dla/ [28 August 2004].

LAUC-LA. 2004. "LAUC-LA Librarian of the Year Award." [Online]. Available: www.library.ucla.edu/committees/laucla/members/librarian/description.htm [28 August 2004].

Lauffer, Armand. 1984. *Grantsmanship and Fund Raising*. Beverly Hills, CA: Sage Publications.

Lawson, Mollie D. 2000. "Reaching the Masses: Marketing a Library Instruction Course to Incoming Freshmen." *Research Strategies* 17: 45–49.

"Learning Community Commons." n.d. [Online]. Available: http://learningcommons.evergreen.edu/03_start_entry.asp [29 July 2004].

Leckie, Gloria J. 1996. "Desperately Seeking Citations: Uncovering Faculty Assumptions about the Undergraduate Research Process." *Journal of Academic Librarianship* 22(3): 201–208.

Leithwood, Kenneth, Doris Jantzi, and Rosanne Steinbach. 1999. *Changing Leadership for Changing Times*. Philadelphia: Open University Press.

Leslie, Don. 2001. "Your Library of the Future." *Library Administration and Management* 15(3): 172–175.

Lester, June. 1988. "Roles of Schools of Library and Information Science." In *Leadership for Research Libraries*, edited by Anne Woodsworth and Barbara Von Wahlde. Metuchen, NJ: Scarecrow Press.

Leung, Wai-Ching. 2001. "How to Design a Questionnaire." *Student BMJ* 9 (June): 187–190.

Levene, Lee-Allison, and Polly Frank. 1992/1993. "Peer Coaching: Professional Growth and Development for Instruction Librarians." *Reference Services Review* 20/21(2): 35–42.

Levesque, Carla. 2003. "Taking Information Literacy Online." *Community & Junior College Libraries* 11(2): 7–11.

Lewis, Hedwig. 2000. *Body Language: A Guide for Professionals*. Thousand Oaks, CA: Sage.

"Librarians Index to the Internet." 2004. [Online]. Available: http://lii.org/ [28 August 2004].

Lipman-Blumen, Jean. 2001. "Why Do We Tolerate Bad Leaders?" In *The Future of Leadership*, edited by Warren Bennis, Gretchen M. Spreitzer, and Thomas G. Cummings. San Francisco: Jossey-Bass.

Litzinger, Mary Ellen. 1993. "Instructional Design." In *Sourcebook for Bibliographic Instruction*, edited by Katherine Branch, et al., pp. 17–27. Chicago: ALA, ACRL, BIS.

Locke, Lawrence F., Waneen Wyrick Spriduso, and Stephen J. Silverman. 1993. *Proposals That Work*. 3rd ed. Newbury Park, CA: Sage Publications.

LOEX. n.d. "Instruction Links." [Online]. Available: http://www.emich.edu/public/loex/islinks/islinks.htm [18 July 2004].

Long, Phillip D. 2002. "Blogs: A Disruptive Technology Coming of Age?" *Syllabus* 16(3): 8–10, 32.

———. 2003. "Learning Management Systems: Seeking Paradigms for Collaboration." *Syllabus* 16(6): 6–8, 35.

Long, Sarah. 2002. "Mentoring: A Personal Reflection." *New Library World* 103(1174): 94–97.

Lonsdale, Alan, N. Dennis, D. Openshaw, and G. Mullins. 1988. *Academic Staff Appraisal in Australian Higher Education. Part I: Principles and Guidelines.* Camberra, Australia: Department of Employment, Education and Training. Camberra, Australian Government Publishing Service.

Loomis, Abigail. 1995. "Building Coalitions for Information Literacy." In *Information for a New Age: Redefining the Librarian,* edited by LIRT Fifteenth Anniversary Task Force. Englewood, CO: Libraries Unlimited.

Lopez, Isabel O. 1995. "Becoming a Servant-leader: The Personal Development Path." In *Reflections on Leadership,* edited by Larry. C. Spears. New York: John Wiley and Sons.

Los Angeles Public Library. n.d. [Online]. Available: www.lapl.org/ [9 May 2004].

Lowman, Joseph. 1995. *Mastering the Techniques of Teaching.* 2nd ed., Jossey-Bass Higher and Adult Education Series. San Francisco: Jossey-Bass Publishers.

Macromedia, Inc. 2004. *Flash.* [Online]. Available: www.macromedia.com/software/flash/ [21 July 2004].

Manske, Fred A. 1987. *Secrets of Effective Leadership.* Memphis, TN: Leadership Education and Development.

Marchese, Ted. 1995. "Accreditation—the Next Phase." *Change* 27(6): 4.

Mark, Margaret, and Carol S. Pearson. 2001. *The Hero and the Outlaw: Building Extraordinary Brands through the Power of Archetypes.* New York: McGraw-Hill.

Martin, Graham A., and Jeremy M. Double. 1998. "Developing Higher Education Teaching Skills through Peer Observation and Collaborative Reflection." *Innovations in Education and Training International* 35(2): 161–170.

Martin, Rebecca R. 1997. "Recruiting a Library Leader for the 21st Century." *Journal of Library Administration* 24(3): 47–58.

Martorana, Janet, Sylvia Curtis, Sherry DeDecker, Sylvelin Edgerton, Carol Gibbens, and Lorna Lueck. 2001. "Bridging the Gap: Information Literacy Workshops for High School Teachers." *Research Strategies* 18(1): 113–120.

Masie, Elliott. 2004. "The Learning Invitation Process: Methods and Technology" [electronic bulletin board]. 2 March 2004 [cited 3 March 2004]. Available from techlearn-trends@lister.masie.com.

———. n.d. TechLearn Trends. techlearn-trends@lister.masie.com.

Maslach, Christina. 1982. *Burnout: The Cost of Caring.* Englewood Cliffs, NJ: Prentice-Hall.

Mayo, Renate Weidner. 1997. "Trends in Teacher Evaluation." *The Clearing House* 70(5): 269–270.

McDonagh, Sorcha. 2004. "Computers with Attitude." *Science News for Kids.* [Online]. Available: www.sciencenewsforkids.org/articles/20040303/Feature1.asp [15 May 2004].

McGowan, Judith. 2003. "Winning the Grant Game: Avoid the Pitfalls, Get the Federal Funding You Deserve." *School Library Journal* 49(3): 52–56.

McLean, Neil, and Clifford Lynch. 2004. "Interoperability between Library Information Services and Learning Environments—Bridging the Gaps: A Joint White Paper on Behalf of the IMS Global Learning Consortium and the Coalition for Networked Informa-

tion." [Online]. Available: www.imsglobal.org/digitalrepositories/CNIandIMS_2004
.pdf [29 May 2004].

Meany, Michael J. 2000. "Stress: Definition and Physiology." In *Encyclopedia of Psychology*, edited by Alan E. Kazdin. New York: Oxford University Press.

Mediavilla, Cindy. 2001. *Creating the Full-Service Homework Center in Your Library*. Chicago: American Library Association.

——. 2003. "Homework Helpers." *School Library Journal* 49(3): 56–61.

Memorial University of Newfoundland Libraries. 2000. "Ideas for Library/Information Assignments." [Online]. Available: www.library.mun.ca/qeii/instruction/assign ment_ideas.php [26 August 2004].

MERLOT (Multimedia Educational Resource for Learning and Online Teaching). n.d. [Online]. Available: www.merlot.org/Home.po [2 September 2004].

Metros, Susan E. 2004. "Learning Objects." *Encyclopedia of Distributed Learning*. Thousand Oaks, CA: Sage Publications.

Metz, Ruth E. 2001. *Coaching in the Library*. Chicago: American Library Association.

Michael Lerner Productions, Inc. 2004. "Master the Basics: Netiquette." [Online]. Available: www.learnthenet.com/english/html/09netiqt.htm [15 May 2004].

Michel, Stephanie. 2004. "RE; Practical Solutions for Laptop Instruction" [electronic bulletin board]. 23 February 2004—[cited 23 February 2004]. Available from ILI-L@ala.org.

Microsoft Corporation. 2004. Windows Sharepoint Services. [Online]. Available: www.mi crosoft.com/windowsserver2003/technologies/sharepoint/default.mspx    [5    May 2004].

Minkel, Walter. 1999. "Five Librarians, One 50-Foot Phone Cord, and a Whole Lot of Chutzpah." *School Library Journal* 45(3): 108–111.

MIT Media Lab. n.d. "Research." [Online]. Available: www.media.mit.edu/research/ index.html [15 May 2004].

MIT OpenCourseware. Health Sciences and Technology. 2003. *HST.502. Survival Skills for Researchers, Spring 2003*. [Online]. Available: http://ocw.mit.edu/OcwWeb/Health-Sciences-and-Technology/HST-502Survival-Skills-for-Researchers—The-Responsible-Conduct-of-ResearchSpring2003/LectureNotes/index.htm [1 October 2004].

Mizrachi, Diane, and Stephanie Brasley. 2004. "Sequential Steps to Information Literacy Nirvana." [Online]. Available: www.emich.edu/public/loex/loex2004/break out1.htm [25 July 2004].

Molfese, Victoria J., Karen S. Karp, and Linda A. Siegel. 2002. "Recommendations for Writing Successful Proposals from the Reviewer's Perspective (Shop Talk)." *Journal of Research Administration* 33(3): 21–25.

Mosbacher, Michael. 2002. *Marketing the Revolution: The New Anti-Capitalism and the Attack upon Corporate Brands*. London: Social Affairs Unit.

*The Mummy*. 1999. Universal Studios.

Muronaga, Karen, and Violet Harada. 1999. "The Art of Collaboration." *Teacher Librarian* 27(1): 9–14.

Murphy, John M. 1987. "What Is Branding?" In *Branding: A Key Marketing Tool*, edited by John M. Murphy. New York: McGraw-Hill.

Mycoted, Inc., 2003. "Creative Techniques." [Online]. Available: www.mycoted.com/ creativity/techniques/index.php [5 May 2004].

Nahl, Diane. 1999. "RE: Information Literacy—the Role of Librarians" [electronic bulletin board]. 11 May 1999 [cited 12 May 1999]. Available from bi-l@listserv.byu.edu.

Naisbitt, John, and Patricia Abardene. 1990. *Megatrends 2000: Ten New Directions for the 1990's*. New York: William Morrow and Co.

Nanus, Burt. 1989. *The Leader's Edge: The Seven Keys to Leadership in a Turbulent World*. New York: Contemporary Books.

National Commission for the Protection of Human Subjects of Biomedical and Behavioral Research. 1978. *The Belmont Report: Ethical Principles and Guidelines for the Protection of Human Subjects of Research*. Washington, DC: Government Printing Office.

National Council on Economic Education. n.d. "EconEdLink: The Mystery of Is It Mine or Ours?" [Online]. Available: www.econedlink.org/lessons/em462/popupActiv ity.htm [10 April 2004].

*National Endowment for the Humanities*. n.d. [Online]. Available: www.neh.gov/ [1 October 2004].

Neff, Jack. 15 July 2002. "Marketing Tactics—Ries' Thesis: Ads Don't Build Brands, PR Does: Controversial New Book Claims Publicity Is Now Tool of Choice." *Advertising Age* 73: 14–15.

New York Times. Community Affairs Department. 1 August 2004. "Announcing the Fourth Annual New York Times Librarian Awards for Public Librarians across the United States." *New York Times*, Style.

Nielsen, Jakob. 1993. *Usability Engineering*. Boston: AP Professional.

———. 2000. *Designing Web Usability*. Indianapolis: New Riders.

———. 2003. Why You Only Need to Test with 5 Users. [Online]. Available: www.useit.com/alertbox/2000319/html [5 August 2003].

———. 2004. "Alertbox." [Online]. Available: www.useit.com/alertbox/ [11 November 2004].

Nims, Julia K. 1999. "Marketing Library Instruction Services: Changes and Trends." *RSR: Reference Services Review* 27(3): 249–253.

Oakley, Karla. 1998. "The Performance Assessment System: A Portfolio Assessment Model for Evaluating Beginning Teachers." *Journal of Personnel Evaluation in Education* 11(4): 323–341.

Oberman, Cerise. 1995. "Unmasking Technology: A Prelude to Teaching." *Research Strategies* 13(1): 34–39.

Ogilvy, David. 1983. *Ogilvy on Advertising*. New York: Vintage Books.

Olsen, Florence. 1999. " 'Virtual' Institutions Challenge Accreditors to Devise New Ways of Measuring Quality." *Chronicle of Higher Education* 45(48): A29–30.

Orava, Hilkka. 2000. "Marketing Is an Attitude of Mind." In *Adapting Marketing to Libraries in a Changing and World-wide Environment*. Papers presented at the 63rd IFLA conference. Copenhagen, September 1997.

Orenstein, David. 1999. "Developing Quality Managers and Quality Management." *Library Administration and Management* 13(1): 44–51.

Orlans, Harold. 1995. "Shaking the House of Accreditation." *Change* 27(6): 8.

Orme, Bill. 22 October 1999. "The Information" Personal e-mail to the author.

O'Rourke, Thomas, and Diane O'Rourke. 2001. "The Ordering and Wording of Questionnaire Items: Part I." *American Journal of Health Studies* 17(3): 156–159.

———. 2002. "The Ordering and Wording of Questionnaire Items: Part II." *American Journal of Health Studies* 17(4): 208–212.

*Oxford English Dictionary*. 2nd ed. 2004. Oxford: Oxford University Press.

Palmer, Judith D. 1988. "For the Manager Who Must Build a Team." In *Team Building: Blueprints for Productivity and Satisfaction*, edited by W. Brendan Reddy and Kaleel Jamison. Alexandria, VA: NTL Institute for Applied Behavioral Sciences.

Papadopolou, Panagiota, et al. 2001. "Trust and Relationship Building in Electronic Commerce." *Internet Research: Electronic Networking Applications and Policy* 11(4): 322–332.

*Part-Time Public Relations with Full-Time Results: A PR Primer for Libraries.* 1995. Edited by Rashelle S. Karp for the Publications Committee of the Public Relations Section, Library Administration and Management Association. Chicago: ALA.

*Party Girl.* 1995. Columbia TriStar.

Patterson, Mimi, and Jana Edwards. 1999. "Should All Library Schools Offer Courses in Library Instruction? *LIRT News* 21(4). [Online]. Available: http://www3 .baylor.edu/LIRT/lirtnews/1999/jbi. html [21 July 2004].

Paulus, Paul B. 2000. "Groups, Teams and Creativity: The Creative Potential of Idea-generating Groups." *Applied Psychology: An International Review* 49(2): 237–262.

Peete, Gary, et al. 1983. *A Guide to Research and Funding for Librarians.* Santa Barbara, CA: LAUC-SB Research Sub-Committee of the Committee on Advancement and Promotion.

Peterson, Billie. 2004. "Tech Talk: Open URLs." *LIRT News* 26(3): 14–15.

Peterson, Susan. 2001. *The Grantwriter's Internet Companion: A Resource for Educators and Others Seeking Grants and Funding.* Thousand Oaks, CA: Corwin Press.

Pfohl, Dan, and Sherman Hayes. 2001. "Today's Systems Librarians Have a Lot to Juggle." *Computers in Libraries* 21(10): 30–33.

Pison, Gilles, and Ninian Hubert van Blyenburgh. 2001. *6 Billion Human Beings.* [Online]. Available: http://www-popexpo.ined.fr/english.html [2 September 2004].

Plas, Jeanne M., and Susan E. Lewis. 2001. *Person Centered Leadership for Nonprofit Organizations.* Thousand Oaks, CA: Sage.

Plenert, Gerhard, and Shozo Hibino. 1997. *Making Innovation Happen: Concept Management through Integration.* Boca Raton: St. Lucie Press.

Pollard, William C. 1996. "The Leader Who Serves." In *The Leader of the Future,* edited by Frances Hesselbein, Marshall Goldsmith, and Richard Beckhard. San Francisco: Jossey-Bass.

Polsani, Pithamber R. 2003. "Use and Abuse of Reusable Learning Objects." *Journal of Digital Information* 3(4): Article No. 164.

Porter, Andrew C. 1997. "Comparative Experiments in Educational Research." In *Complementary Methods for Research in Education,* edited by Richard M. Jaeger. Washington, DC: American Educational Research Association.

Powell, Ronald R. 1997. *Basic Research Methods for Librarians.* 3rd ed. Greenwich, CT: Ablex Publishing Corporation.

Prather, Charles L., and Lisa K. Gundry. 1995. *Blueprints for Innovation: How Creative Processes Can Make Your Company More Competitive.* New York: American Management Association.

Presti, Patricia. 2000. "Re:__Weeks Notice?" 25 April 2000 <bi-l@listserv.byu.edu> 26 April 2000.

Print, Murray, and John Hattie. 1997. Measuring Quality in Universities: An Approach to Weighting Research Productivity. *Higher Education* 33(4): 453–469.

Pusey, Sabrina. 2000. "Re:__Weeks Notice?" [electronic bulletin board]. 25 April 2000 [cited 26 April 2000]. Available from bi-l@ listserv.byu.edu.

puzzlemaker.com. 2003. [Online]. Available: www.puzzlemaker. com/ [18 April 2004].

Quick, James Campbell, Johnathan D. Quick, and Joanne H. Gavin. 2000. "Stress: Measurement." In *Encyclopedia of Psychology,* edited by Alan. E. Kazdin. New York: Oxford University Press.

Quinn, Robert E. 2004. *Building the Bridge as You Walk on It: A Guide for Leading Change.* San Francisco: Jossey-Bass.

Quint, Barbara. 2003. "OCLC project Opens WorldCat Records to Google." [Online]. Available: www.infotoday.com/newsbreaks/nb031027-2.shtml [27 July 2004].

Rader, Hannelore B. 2004. "Building Faculty–Librarian Partnerships to Prepare Students for Information Fluency: The Time for Sharing Information Expertise Is Now." *College & Research Libraries News* 65(2): 74–76,80.

Raspa, Dick, and Dane Ward. 2000. "Listening for Collaboration: Faculty and Librarians Working Together." In *The Collaborative Imperative: Librarians and Faculty Working Together in the Information Universe,* edited by Dick Raspa and Dane Ward. Chicago: ALA, ACRL.

Rawlinson, J. Geoffrey. 1981. *Creative Thinking and Brainstorming.* New York: John Wiley and Sons.

"Read, Write, Think." 2002–2004. [Online]. Available: www.readwritethink.org/index.asp [10 April 2004].

Ream, Dan. 2000. "Re:__Weeks Notice?" [electronic bulletin board]. 25 April 2000—[cited 26 April 2000]. Available from bi-l@listserv.byu. edu.

———. 2001. "Scratch That Glitch: The Fine Art of Glitch Management." [Online]. Available: www.people.vcu.edu/~dream/glitch.htm [16 May 2004].

Reave, Laura. 2002. Promoting Innovation in the Workplace: The Internal Proposal. *Business Communication Quarterly* 65(4): 8–21.

Reed, Sally Gardner. 1992. *Saving Your Library.* Jefferson, NC: McFarland and Co.

refdesk.com. 2004. [Online]. Available: www.refdesk.com/ [8 September 2004].

Regan, Jeanette. 2003. "Mentoring Schemes: Raising the Standards." *Library and Information Update* 2(4): 36–37.

Reichel, Mary, and Mary Ann Ramey, eds. 1987. *Conceptual Frameworks for Bibliographic Education.* Littleton, CO: Libraries Unlimited.

Renborg, Greta. 2000. "Marketing Library Service. How It All Began." In *Adapting Marketing to Libraries in a Changing and World-Wide Environment.* Papers presented at the 63rd IFLA conference. Copenhagen, September 1997, pp. 5–11.

Rice, Pranee Liamputtong, and Douglas Ezzy. 1999. *Qualitative Research Methods.* South Melbourne, Australia: Oxford University Press.

Richmond, Virginia P., James C. McCrosky, and Steven K. Payne. 1991. *Nonverbal Behavior.* 2nd ed. Englewood Cliffs, NJ: Prentice-Hall.

Ricigliano. Lori. 1999. "Ideas for Library Related Assignments." University of Puget Sound. [Online]. Available: http://library.ups.edu/instruct/assign.htm [27 July 2004].

Ries, Al. 1996. *Focus: The Future of Your Company Depends on It.* New York: HarperCollins.

———, and Laura Ries. 2000. *The 11 Immutable Laws of Internet Branding.* New York: HarperCollins.

———. 2002. *The Fall of Advertising and the Rise of PR.* New York: HarperCollins.

Ries, Al, and Jack Trout. 1986. *Marketing Warfare.* New York: McGraw-Hill.

———. 1989. *Bottom-Up Marketing.* New York: McGraw-Hill.

———. 1993. *The 22 Immutable Laws of Marketing: Violate Them at Your Own Risk!* New York: HarperCollins.

Riggs, Donald E. 1997. "What's in Store for Academic Libraries? Leadership and Management Issues." *Journal of Academic Librarianship* 23(1): 3–8.

Riley, Sabrina. 2003. "Re: First Year Orientation Activities" [electronic bulletin board]. 2 May 2003 [cited 27 September 2003]. Available from ILI-L@ala.org.

Rinaldi, Arlene H. 1998. "The Net: User Guidelines and Netiquette." [Online]. Available: www.fau.edu/netiquette/net/ [15 May 2004].

Ritchie, Ann, and Paul Genomi. 2002. "Group Mentoring and Professionalism: A Programme Evaluation. *Library Management* 23(1/2): 68–78.

Robson, Mike. 1993. *Problem Solving in Groups.* 2nd ed. Hants, England: Gower Publishing Co.

Rogers, Will. *The Illiterate Digest*. Stillwater, OK: Oklahoma State Univeristy Press, 1974.

Roitberg, Nurit. 2003. The Influence of the Electronic Library on Library Management: A Technological University Library Experience. [Online]. Available: www.IFLA .org/IV/ifla66/papers/050-132e.htm [5 August 2003].

Rooks, Dana C. 1988. *Motivating Today's Library Staff*. Phoenix, AZ: Oryz Press.

Rowley, Jennifer. 1997. "Managing Branding and Corporate Image for Library and Information Services." *Library Review* 46(4): 244–250.

Rubin, Hank. 1998. *Collaboration Skills for Educators and Nonprofit Leaders*. Chicago: Lyceum.

Ruskin, Karen B., and Charles M. Achilles. 1995. *Grantwriting, Fundraising and Partnerships: Strategies That Work!* Thousand Oaks, CA: Corwin Press.

Ryer, Mary Ann. 2002. "Designing Innovative Research Assignments: Innovative Assignments." Raritan Valley Community College. [Online]. Available: http://library.rari tanval.edu/ResearchAssignments/ResearchAssignments.html-innovations [27 July 2004].

San Diego State University. n.d. "EDTECH Beach." [Online]. Available: http://edweb .sdsu.edu/etbeach/ [29 May 2004].

San Jose Library. n.d. [Online]. Available: www.sjpl.lib.ca.us/ [4 May 2004].

San Jose Library. n.d. "Paths to Learning." [Online]. Available: www.sjpl.lib.ca.us/gate ways/index.htm [4 May 2004].

Sapolsky, Robert M. 1998. *Why Zebras Don't Get Ulcers: An Updated Guide to Stress, Stress-related Diseases, and Coping*. New York: W. H. Freeman and Co.

Sass, Rivkah K. 15 June 2002. "Marketing the Worth of Your Library." *Library Journal*, 37–38.

Schein, Edgar H. 1996. "Leadership and Organizational Culture." In *The Leader of the Future*, edited by Frances Hesselbein, Marshall Goldsmith, and Richard Beckhard. San Francisco: Jossey-Bass.

Schilling, Lynne S. 2003. "Ten Things I Learned While Writing My Last Research Grant." *Pediatric Nursing* 29(2): 150–151.

Schneider, William E. 1994. *The Reengineering Alternative*. Burt Ridge, IL: Irwin Professional Publishing.

Schoen, David. 2003. "Campus Wide Assessment Tools Needed" [electronic bulletin board]. 24 November 2003 [cited 25 November 2003]. Available from ili_modera tor@hotmail.com.

Schooler, Tonya Y., Angela Dougall, and Andrew Baum. 2000. "Stress: Impact on Health." In *Encyclopedia of Psychology*, edited by Halan E. Kazdin. New York: Oxford University Press.

Schreiber, Becky, and John Shannon. 2001. "Developing Library Leaders for the 21st Century." *Journal of Library Administration* 32(3/4): 35–57.

Schrock, Rockwell. 2000. "The Boolean Machine." [Online]. Available: http://kathy schrock.net/rbs3k/boolean/ [10 April 2004].

Schwartz, Mary. 2000. "Teaching PC Applications" [electronic bulletin board]. 17 May 2000—[cited 18 May 2000]. Available from bi-l@listserv.byu.edu.

Scriven, Michael. 1973. "The Methodology of Evaluation." In *Educational Evaluation: Theory and Practice*, edited by Blaine Worthen and James Sanders. Belmont, CA: Wadsworth.

Selye, Hans. 1936. "A Syndrome Produced by Diverse Nocuous Agents." *Nature* 138(1): 32.

Senge, Peter. 1990a. *The Fifth Discipline: The Art and Practice of the Learning Organization*. New York: Doubleday.

———. 1990b. "The Leader's New Work: Building Learning o\Organizations." *Sloan Management Review* 32(1): 7–19+.

———. 1996. "Leading Learning Organizations." In *The Leader of the Future*, edited by Frances Hesselbein, Marshall Goldsmith, and Richard Beckhard. San Francisco: Jossey-Bass.

Sevier, Robert. Winter 1989. "Conducting Focus Group Research." *Journal of College Admissions* 122: 4–9.

Shamel, Cynthia L. July/August 2002. "Building a Brand: Got Librarian?" *Searcher*, 60–71.

Sheldon, Brooke E. 1991. *Leaders in Libraries*. Chicago: American Library Association.

———. 1992. "Library Leaders: Attributes Compared to Corporate Leaders." *Library Trends* 40(3): 391–401.

Shoaf, Eric C. 2003. "Using a Professional Moderator in Library Focus Group Research." *College and Research Libraries* 64(2): 124–132.

Shonrock, Diana D., ed. 1996. *Evaluating Library Instruction: Sample Questions, Forms, and Strategies for Practical Use*. Chicago: American Library Association, Library Instruction Round Table.

Shonrock, Diana, and Craig Mulder. 1993. "Instruction Librarians: Acquiring the Proficiencies Critical to Their Work." *College & Research Libraries* 54(2): 137–149.

Sieber, Joan E. 1992. *Planning Ethically Responsible Research: A Guide for Students and Internal Review Boards*. Newbury Park, CA: Sage.

Siess, Judith A. 2003. *The Visible Librarian: Asserting Your Value with Marketing and Advocacy*. Chicago: American Library Association.

Simmons, Howard L. 1994. "The Concern for Information Literacy: A Major Challenge for Accreditation." *The Challenge and Practice of Academic Accreditation: A Sourcebook for Library Administrators*. Westport, CT: Greenwood Press.

Sladek, Frea E., and Eugene L. Stein. 1981. *Grant Budgeting and Finance: Getting the Most Out of Your Grant Dollar*. New York: Plenum Press.

Slattery, Charles, and Stephen Walker. 1999. "A Mentoring Program for New Academic Librarians." ERIC.: ED 438812.

Smalley, Topsey, and Stephen Pluto. 1982. "Teaching Library Researching in the Humanities and the Sciences: A Contextual Approach." In *Theories of Bibliographic Education: Designs for Teaching*, edited by Cerise Oberman and Katina Strauch. New York: R. R. Bowker.

Snyder, Carolyn. 2003. *Paper Prototyping: The Fast and Easy Way to Design and Refine User Interfaces*. San Francisco: Morgan Kaufmann, Elsevier.

Solomon, Gwen. 2001. "Deconstructing a Grant." *Technology & Learning* 21(11): 44–46.

Spears, Larry C. 1995. "Servant-Leadership and the Greenleaf Legacy." In *Reflections on Leadership*, edited by Larry C. Spears. New York: John Wiley and Sons.

Special Libraries Association. 2003. Competencies for Information Professionals of the 21st Century. Rev. ed. [Online]. Available: www.sla.org/content/learn/comp2003/index.cfm [1 October 2004].

SPIN (Sponsored Programs Information Network). n.d. [Online] Available: www.infoed.org/new_spin/spin.dsp [12 April 2005].

Stephenson, Elizabeth, and Cheryl Bartel. 28 September 2004. "FW: Please Send Citation . . ." ["UPDATA: Using Personal Digital Assistant Technology Applications—Health Sciences." Research grant funded by the Librarians Association of the University of California.] Personal e-mail to the author.

Stewart, Rodney D., and Ann L. Stewart. 1984. *Proposal Preparation*. New York: John Wiley and Sons.

Stover, Mark. 1999. *Leading the Wired Organization: The Information Professional's Guide to Managing Technological Change*. New York: Neal-Schuman Publishers.

Swartz, Pauline. 2004. "Bruin Success with Less Stress." [Online]. Available: www.li brary.ucla.edu/bruinsuccess/ [19 May 2004].

Sweeney, Richard. 1997. "Leadership Skills in the Reengineered Library." *Library Administration and Management* 11(1): 30–41.

———. 1995–2003. Creating Your Own Campaign/View Webcast. [Online]. Available: http://cms.3m.com/cms/US/en/2-115/czlRFFW/view.jhtml [8 September 2004].

TechSmith Corp. 2004. *Camtasia.* [Online]. Available: www.techsmith.com/products/stu dio/default.asp?lid=CamtasiaStudioHome [21 July 2004].

Tennant, Roy. August 1997. "Web Sites by Design: How to Avoid a 'Pile of Pages.'" *Syllabus* 49–50.

Thomas, William Joseph. 2004. "Summary of Responses: Laptop Instruction" [electronic bulletin board]. 25 February 2004 [cited 25 February 2004]. Available from ILI-L@ala.org.

Tillman, Mike. 2000. "The University of Washington: Collaboration through Instruction Technology," in Walter, Scott, "Case Studies in Collaboration," in *The Collaborative Imperative,* edited by Dick Raupa and Dane Ward. Chicago: ALA, ACRL, pp. 60–64.

Tocker Foundation. n.d. [Online]. Available: www.tocker.org/ [4 September 2004].

Todaro, Julie Beth. 2001. "The Effective Organization in the 21st Century." *Library Administration and Management* 15(3): 176–178.

Trout, Jack. 1996. *The New Positioning: The Latest on the World's #1 Business Strategy.* New York: McGraw-Hill.

Turock, Betty J. 2001. "Women and Leadership." *Journal of Library Administration* 32(3/4): 111–132.

UCLA College Library. 2005. "Information Literacy Teaching Modules." [Online]. Available: www.library.ucla.edu/libraries/college/instructors/modules.htm [18 July 2005].

UCLA. Office of Human Subjects Protection. 2004. [Online]. Available: http://training.arc .ucla.edu/ [30 May 2004].

UCLA. Office of Instructional Development. 2004. "Scholarship in a New Media Environment: Issues and Trends." [Online]. Available: www.oid.ucla.edu/sianme/[15 May 2004].

University of California, Berkeley. 2003. *Mellon Faculty Institute on Undergraduate Research.* 2004. [Online]. Available: www.lib.berkeley. edu/MellonInstitute/ [8 September 2004].

———. 2004. "Mellon Library/Faculty Fellows for Undergraduate Research." [Online]. Available: http://library.berkeley.edu/MellonInstitute/mellon_facts.pdf [26 July 2004].

University of Houston, Clear Lake. n.d. "Basic Computer Literacy Skills." [Online]. Available: http://pt3.cl.uh.edu/bs.cfm [9 May 2004].

University of Minnesota. 2004. "Assignment Calculator." [Online]. Available: www.lib.umn.edu/help/calculator/ [8 May 2004].

University of South Florida. 1998. "Designing and Implementing a Collaborative Assessment Process." http://web.usf.edu/~lc/assess/assessment_team.htm [1 October 2004].

U.S. Department of Education. 2004a. [Online]. Available: www.ed.gov/fund/land ing.jhtml [4 September 2004].

———. 2004b. *Research.* [Online]. Available: http://web99 .ed.gov/GTEP/Program2 .nsf/f2cabc788ab665d78525644400514f2f/e7be21fd424c8eb1852564110066d29a?Ope nDocument [4 September 2004].

U.S. GPO. 2004. *Federal Register.* [Online]. Available: www. gpoaccess.gov/fr/index.html [4 September 2004].

U.S. IMLS. 2003. *Keeping Librarians on Top of Their Game: Federal Grants for Continuing Education and Training of Library Staff.* [Online]. Available: www.imls.gov/whatsnew/03archive/071503-3.htm [1 October 2004].

U.S. IMLS. 2004. *IMLS Monthly Highlights.* [Online]. Available: www.imls.gov/closer/cls_hilt.htm [7 September 2004].

U.S. IMLS. n.d. *Institute of Museum and Library Services.* [Online]. Available: www.imls.gov/ [24 January 2005].

U.S. National Endowment for the Humanities. n.d. *Implementation Grants for Humanities Projects in Libraries and Archives.* [Online]. Available: www.neh.gov/grants/guidelines/implement-libraries.html [1 October 2004].

U.S. National Institute for Literacy. 1999. "EFF Standards for Adult Literacy and Lifelong Learning." [Online]. Available: www.loyno.edu/~enaabls/EFFwheel.html [26 August 2004].

U.S. National Research Council. 1999. *Being Fluent with Information Technology.* [Online]. Available: www.nap.edu/books/030906399X/html/ [17 April 2004].

U.S. NEH. 2004. *Summer Stipends.* [Online]. Available: www.neh.gov/grants/guidelines/stipends.html [4 September 2004].

———. "21st Century Community Learning Centers." [Online]. Available: www.ed.gov/programs/21stcck/index.html [18 July 2005].

VanGundy, Arthur B. 1992. *Idea Power: Techniques & Resources to Unleash the Creativity in Your Organization.* New York: American Management Association.

Ver Steeg, Jennie. 2000. "Earlham College: Collaboration through Course-Integrated Instruction." In Walter, Scott, "Case Studies in Collaboration," in *The Collaborative Imperative,* edited by Dick Raspa and Dane Ward. Chicago: ALA, ACRL.

"Volcanoes Online." n.d. [Online]. Available: http://library.thinkquest.org/17457/english.html?tqskip1=1 [1 October 2004].

Wagner, Pat. 2003. "Marketing as If Your Library Depended on It." Dynix Online Workshop, 24 September 2003. [Presenter's e-mail: Pattern Research: www.pattern.com].

Walker, Darcy. 2004. "RE: Planning a Laptop Classroom" [electronic bulletin board]. 3 February 2004—[cited 3 February 2004]. Available from ILI-L@ala.org.

Wankat, Phillip, and Frank Oreovicz. 2000. "How Much Preparation Time Is Enough? Too Much Class Preparation May Not Pay Off." *Prism Online: Exploring the Future of Engineering Education.* [Online]. Available: www.asee.org/prism/sept00/html/teaching.cfm [4 May 2004].

"We Value Your Feedback—It Helps Us to Addle Our Brains." 6 November 2003. *Marketing Week,* p. 78.

Weaver, Angela E. 2001. "What Is the Matrix? Constructing a Virtual Presence for the Library Instruction Program." In *Library User Education: Powerful Learning, Powerful Partnerships,* edited by Barbara I. Dewey. Lanham, MD; London: Scarecrow Press.

Web Surveyor. 2004. [Online]. Available: www.websurveyor.com/home.asp? [1 October 2004].

Weber, Steven. 2004. *The Success of Open Source.* Cambridge, MA: Harvard University Press.

WebEx Communications, Inc. 2001. "WebExpress Learning modules." [Online]. Available: http://webexpress.webex.com/webexpresslearning/randp.asp [16 May 2004].

Weiss, Allen. 2002. What Is Marketing? [Online]. Available: www.marketingprofs.com/2/whatismarketing.asp [1 October 2004].

Wells, Melanie. 16 April 2001. "Cult Brands." *Forbes,* 198.

Wentz, Deleyne. 27 April 2004. "FW: Re: Faculty/Librarian Relations." Personal e-mail to the author.

Welcome to About.com. 2004. [Online]. Available: www.about.com/ [1 October 2004].

Westbrook, Lynn. 1997. "Qualitative Research." In *Basic Research Methods for Librarians*, edited by Ronald R. Powell. Greenwich, CT: Ablex Publishing Group.

Westmeyer, Paul. 1994. *A Guide for Use in Planning, Conducting and Reporting Research Projects.* 2nd ed. Springfield, IL: Thomas.

Whatis.com. 2002. "Web Year." [Online]. Available: http://searchwebservices.techtarget.com/sDefinition/0,,sid26_gci853845,00. html [6 May 2004].

Wheatley, Margaret J. 1999. *Leadership and the New Science.* 2nd ed. San Francisco: Berrett-Koehler Publishers.

White, Herbert S. 1990. "Librarian Burnout." *Library Journal* 115(5): 64–65.

Wickman, Floyd, and Terri Sjodin. 1997. *Mentoring: The Most Obvious Yet Overlooked Key to Achieving More in Life Than You Dreamed Possible.* Chicago: Irwin Professional Publishing.

Wiley, David A., II. 2000. "Connecting Learning Objects to Instructional Design Theory: A Definition, a Metaphor, and a Taxonomy." In *The Instructional Use of Learning Objects.* [Online]. Available: www.reusability.org/read/ [31 March 2004].

Wilkinson, Leland, and Task Force on Statistical Inference. 1999. "Statistical Methods in Psychology Journals. *American Psychologist* 54(8): 594–604.

Williams, Delmus F. 2001. "Developing Libraries and Nimble Organizations." *Technical Services Quarterly* 18(4): 35–46.

Williams, James F. 2001. "Leadership Evaluation and Assessment." *Journal of Library Administration* 32(3/4): 145–167.

Wilson, Leslie. 1996. *People Skills for Library Managers.* Englewood, CO: Libraries Unlimited.

Wilson, Lizabeth. 2000. "The Lone Ranger Is Dead: Success Today Demands Collaboration." *College & Research Libraries News* 61(8): 698–701.

Wilson, Robin. 2 May 2003. "Professors Question 'Bonuses' Based on Grants." *Chronicle of Higher Education*, 20.

Winkler, Agnieszka. 1999. *Warp-Speed Branding.* New York: Wiley & Sons.

Winner, Marian C. 1998. "Librarians as Partners in the Classroom: An Increasing Imperative." *RSR: Reference Services Review* 26(1): 25–30.

Wisconsin Online Resource Center. 2004. [Online]. Available: www.wisc-online.com/index.htm [2 September 2004].

Wolf, Kenneth, and Mary Dietz. 1998. "Teaching Portfolios: Purposes and Possibilities." *Teacher Education Quarterly* 25(1): 9–22.

Woodard, Beth S., and Lisa Janicke Hinchliffe. 2002. "Technology and Innovation in Library Instruction Management." In *Information Literacy Programs: Success and Challenges*, edited by Patricia Durisin, pp. 39–55. New York: Haworth Press.

Woodward, James, and David Goodstein. 1996. "Conduct, Misconduct and Structure of Science." *American Scientist* 84(5): 479–490.

Wurtzel, Barbara. 27 April 2004. "Re: Faculty and Librarians." Personal e-mail to the author.

Wyoming Community Foundation. Carol McMurry Library Endowment. n.d. [Online]. Available: http://www-wsl.state.wy.us/mcmurry/ [5 June 2004].

Yellow Mug Software. 2004. "SnapNDrag." [Online]. Available: www.yellowmug.com/snapndrag/ [15 May 2004].

Young, Rosemary M., and Stephena Harmony. 1999. *Working with Faculty to Design Undergraduate Information Literacy Programs.* New York: Neal-Schuman Publishers.

Young, Virginia G. 1992. "The Trustee of a Small Public Library." *Small Libraries Publications—No. 1.* 2nd ed. Chicago: American Library Association, Library Administration and Management Association.

————. 1995. *The Library Trustee: A Practical Guidebook*. Chicago: American Library Association.

Youngblood, Mark D. 1997. "Leadership at the Edge of Chaos: From Control to Creativity." *The Forum* 25(5): 8–14.

Yuanking, Du. 2000. "Marketing of Libraries and Information Centers in China: A Case Study." In *Adapting Marketing to Libraries in a Changing and World-wide Environment*. Papers presented at the 63rd IFLA conference. Copenhagen, September 1997, pp. 74–83.

Yukl, Gary A. 1998. *Leadership in Organizations*. Upper Saddle River, NJ: Prentice-Hall.

Zemke, Ron. 1993. "Train Wreck: Off the Track." *Training* 40(6): 12.

Zemon, Mickey. 1996. "Designing a Camel: A How to Approach to Managing Meetings." *College and Undergraduate Libraries* 3(2): 1–10.

Zick, Laura. 2000. "The Work of Information Mediators: A Comparison of Librarians and Intelligent Software Agents." *First Monday* 5(5), May 2000. [Online]. Available: http://firstmonday.org/issues/issue5_5/zick/index.html [26 August 2004].

Zoomerang. 2004. [Online]. Available: http://info.zoomerang.com/ [1 October 2004].

# Index

one-person libraries, 79
online courses. *See* distance
    learning
Open Source movement, 72–73
operational definitions, 156
organizational culture, 22–25. *See
    also* collaboration culture;
    competence culture;
    control culture;
    cultivation culture
organizations, grants by,
    192–193
orientations and marketing, 244
"Orthopedic Animations," 256
Outrageous Idea, 80
oversight, 38, 44

P

parallel techniques in creative
    problem-solving, 78
participatory management, 8–9
Partnership for 21st Century
    Skills, xi
partnerships. *See* collaboration
passion, 11–12
PDAs, 181
peer appraisal. *See under*
    appraisal
Pepsi, marketing of, 237
Performing. *See* teams: process
perpetual learners, 21–22
Personal Digital Assistants
    (PDAs), 181
personal space, 48
personality issues. *See under*
    attitudes
persuasive communication, 15
Peterson, Billie, 251, 253
PI, 181
pilot projects and proposals. *See
    under* grants
planning instruction, manager's
    role in, 60

political groups
    and accreditation, 105–107
    advisory boards/trustees,
        96–98, 110–111
    businesses, 98–99
    cities, 99
    computer-center staff, 107–110
    faculty/teachers, 83–96
    and instructional statistics,
        102–103
    universities, 99
    and faculty status for
        librarians, 100–102
politics and political pressures
    on individuals, 76–77
    in your environment, 69
    *See also* administrators;
        colleagues
population selection. *See under*
    research
positive deviants, 7
posture. *See* nonverbal
    communication
pre- and post-tests, 156, 161–162
predictions. *See under* research
Principal Investigator, 181
"Principles for a Networked
    World" (ALA), 270
problem solving, 73–74, 76–78,
    83. *See also* creative
    problem-solving
problem-based research
    proposals, 181
product analysis. *See under*
    research
professional development. *See*
    training
professional jealousy, 75
professional organizations
    and creative problem-solving,
        79
program assessment
    and funding requests, 72

proposals, 168–170
quasi-experimental, 160–161
questionnaires, 162–164
    question design, 229–231
reliability, 156–157
statistics in, 170
    qualitative methods, 160
    quantitative methods, 160
validity, 157
    *See also* grants
research journals, 158
"Research Paper Planner,"
    264–265
research paper publication,
    171–172
dissemination of grant results,
    183, 215
"Research Resources for
    Librarians," 193
rewards, 38–39
Riggs, Donald E., xi
risk-taking, 18–19
root causes, 74. *See also* burnout;
    creative problem-solving
roving leaders. *See* grassroots
    leadership; seed carriers

S

sampling, 151–159
    criterion, 158
    frame, 157
    homogenous group, 158
    random, 158
    snowball or chain, 158–159
    techniques, 158–159
    *See also* research
San Jose Public Library, 99–100,
    241
San Jose State University, 99–100,
    241
scheduling ILI, 62–63
School Library Media Specialists.
    *See under* K–12 schools

screen capture software, 70
seed carriers, 8. *See also* grassroots
    leadership
senior citizens, 99
service learning and IL, xi
Sharepoint, 72
shareware, 70
situational leadership, 5–7, 36
"6 Billion Human Beings," 256
SLA, librarian competencies, 232
slogans, mistranslation, 237
small groups
    and creative problem-solving,
        80
social support systems, 139. *See
    also* burnout;
Socrates, 68
special libraries, 98
    and ALA marketing efforts,
        232
    and librarian competencies,
        232
Special Libraries Association,
    librarian competencies,
        232
SPIN (grants database), 197, 198
Sponsored Programs Information
    Network (SPIN) (grants
    database), 197, 198
staff
    development. *See* training
    inexperienced, 83
    new, 77
Stakeholders, 31, 50. *See also*
    collaboration
statistics in research, 170
status of librarians. *See* faculty
    status for librarians;
    image
Stephenson, Elizabeth, 181
Storming. *See* teams: process
Stover, Mark, 252
stress. *See* burnout

student
feedback surveys, 124–125
interviews, 125–126
*See also* appraisal
summative teacher appraisal,
123–124. *See also*
appraisal
surveys. *See* research:
questionnaires
syllabus, IL-enhanced, 94
*Syllabus Magazine,* 252
synergy, team, 55

T
teacher appraisal, 122–130. *See
also* appraisal
teachers. *See* faculty
teaching portfolios, 129–130
teaching style, 77
teambuilding, 79
teams, 37, 45, 52–58
norms. *See* ground rules
process, 52–54, 57–58
proposal development by,
181–182
"Tech Talk," 253
technoaddiction, 272–274
technological change, 68, 274–277
technological symbiosis, 274
technology, 69
budget, 254–255
change, 68, 274–277
computer-center staff, 107–110,
269
computer trainers, 107–110,
269
computerphobia, 85, 272
distance learning, 262–265
audiences, 264
guidelines, 263
electronic classrooms, x,
260–262

layout, 266–267
wireless, 261–262
expertise, 69
grants for, 264
installation, 255
and "instructional
environmental scan," 265
instructional technology
specialist, 71
laptops, 261, 263
LINUX system, 73
LITA "Top Technology
Trends," 253
managers, technostress and
burnout of, 252–253
new, 69, 71, 255–257
Open Source movement, 72–73
Peterson, Billie, 251, 253
policies, 257–260
poorly designed, 271
"Principles for a Networked
World" (ALA), 270
programmers, 73 (*see also*
collaboration)
remote use of, 262–265, 269
skills, 69
staff training in use of,
255–257, 267–269
symbiosis, 274
teaching, to novices, 258–259
technoaddiction, 272–274
technostress, 272–274
of IL librarians, 272
of technology managers,
252–253
training for, 255–257, 267–269
upgrades, 265–267
and usage time limits, 260
and "web year," 254
*See also* Educational Testing
Service; electronic
classrooms; Peterson,

# About the Authors

**Esther S. Grassian** earned a Master's in Library Science from UCLA in 1969. Since that time, she has served in a variety of reference- and instruction-related positions in the UCLA College Library. Her working titles have ranged from "Reference Librarian," to "Electronic Services Coordinator," to her current title, "Information Literacy Outreach Coordinator" (2003–present).

She has also held various elected and appointed positions in information-literacy-related and other organizations, including chairing the California Clearinghouse on Library Instruction, south, the ACRL Instruction Section, and the Librarians Association of the University of California, both the Los Angeles Division and statewide. Her publications include the coauthored (with Joan Kaplowitz) *Information Literacy Instruction: Theory and Practice*, honored with an ACRL Instruction Sections 2004 Publication Award. Her more recent publications include "Do They Really Do That? Librarians Teaching Outside the Traditional Classroom" (*Change Magazine*, April/May 2004), and "Information Literacy: Building on Bibliographic Instruction" (*American Libraries*, October 2004), as well as "Information Literacy: Wilder Makes (Some Right, But) Many Wrong Assumptions" http://www.ucop.edu/lauc/opinions/literacy.html. She has also led workshops and spoken at programs at the local, regional, state, and national level on a variety of topics, including outreach to faculty for information literacy, syllabus reviews, and how to teach the Internet and critical thinking.

She taught an undergraduate and a graduate information literacy course in the UCLA Information Studies Department a number of times since the mid-1980s. She collaborated with UCLA faculty to develop, and she has taught, one-unit information literacy courses for undergraduates in the UCLA English Composition Department and in the UCLA Honors Program. She designed a one-unit information literacy FIAT LUX course in the latter, specifically to support information research needs of freshmen taking a three-quarter-long multidisciplinary UCLA General Education course, Frontiers in Human Aging. She currently chairs a UCLA Library Information Literacy Program Task Force investigating "blended instruction" courses, those that combine elements of online and in-person instruction. She has also recently completed work on a basic online information literacy tutorial in collaboration with Mike Franks at the UCLA Social Sciences Computing Center, and Sue Phares, Instructional Technologist at the UCLA Office of Instructional Development. The tutorial, "Road to Research," is freely available for all to use: http://www.sscnet.ucla.edu/library/. She received a UCLA Office of Instructional Development grant and UCLA Library support to develop and complete the tutorial.

**Joan R. Kaplowitz** has a Doctorate in Psychology as well as a Master's in Library Science. She has been at UCLA since graduating from UCLA's Library and Information Science program in 1984. Dr. Kaplowitz began her UCLA career as a reference/instruction librarian and later Educational Services Coordinator and Head of Public Services at the Education and Psychology Library. She is currently the head of the Research, Instruction, and Collections Services (RICS) division at the Louise M. Darling Biomedical Library. She also serves on both the Life Sciences and Medicine liaisons teams and acts as the Psychology selector and specialist for the library.

Dr. Kaplowitz has been heavily involved in library instruction at the local, state, and national levels for her entire career. During her early years at UCLA she taught several sections of UCLA's undergraduate course Library and Information Resources. In 1989 she collaborated with UCLA's Esther Grassian to propose and develop the UCLA graduate library program's course User Education/Bibliographic Instruction: Theory and Technique (currently known as Information Literacy Instruction: Theory and Technique). She and Ms. Grassian have alternated presenting the course since 1990. Dr. Kaplowitz was also part of the faculty development team for ACRL's Institute for Information Literacy's Immersion Program and has taught in six Immersion Programs between 1999 and 2004.

Dr. Kaplowitz has published and made numerous presentations on various topics such as the psychology of learning and cognitive styles, evaluating information literacy, the pros and cons of computer-assisted instruction, student-centered learning, and mentoring within the profession. She has been awarded several Librarian's Association of the University of California research grants to support her research and publication endeavors. Dr. Kaplowitz has held several offices in ALA's New Members Round Table and the California Clearinghouse on Library Instruction (now know as SCIL or the Southern California Instruction Librarians). Her most recent professional commitments involve working with ALA's Committee on Accreditation.

From 2001 to 2003, Dr. Kaplowitz and Ms. Grassian served on the UCLA Library's Information Literacy Initiative steering committee. They are both currently part of the UCLA Library's Information Literacy Plan's coordinating group. In 2004 Dr. Kaplowitz and Ms. Grassian received the ACRL Instruction Section's Publication of the Year Award for their book *Information Literacy Instruction: Theory and Practice*, also published by Neal-Schuman.